Ho

Throu... ...will find Japanese honorifics left intact in the translations. ...se not familiar with how the Japanese use honorifics and, more important, how they differ from American honorifics, we present this brief overview.

Politeness has always been a critical facet of Japanese culture. Ever since the feudal era, when Japan was a highly stratified society, use of honorifics—which can be defined as polite speech that indicates relationship or status—has played an essential role in the Japanese language. When addressing someone in Japanese, an honorific usually takes the form of a suffix attached to one's name (example: "Asuna-san"), is used as a title at the end of one's name, or appears in place of the name itself (example: "Negi-sensei," or simply "Sensei!").

Honorifics can be expressions of respect or endearment. In the context of manga and anime, honorifics give insight into the nature of the relationship between characters. Many English translations leave out these important honorifics and therefore distort the feel of the original Japanese. Because Japanese honorifics contain nuances that English honorifics lack, it is our policy at Del Rey not to translate them. Here, instead, is a guide to some of the honorifics you may encounter in Del Rey Manga.

-san: This is the most common honorific and is equivalent to Mr., Miss, Ms., or Mrs. It is the all-purpose honorific and can be used in any situation where politeness is required.

-sama: This is one level higher than "-san" and is used to confer great respect.

-dono: This comes from the word "tono," which means "lord." It is an even higher level than "-sama" and confers utmost respect.

-kun: This suffix is used at the end of boys' names to express familiarity or endearment. It is also sometimes used by men among friends, or when addressing someone younger or of a lower station.

-chan: This is used to express endearment, mostly toward girls. It is also used for little boys, pets, and even among lovers. It gives a sense of childish cuteness.

Bozu: This is an informal way to refer to a boy, similar to the English terms "kid" and "squirt."

Sempai/
Senpai: This title suggests that the addressee is one's senior in a group or organization. It is most often used in a school setting, where underclassmen refer to their upperclassmen as "sempai." It can also be used in the workplace, such as when a newer employee addresses an employee who has seniority in the company.

Kohai: This is the opposite of "sempai" and is used toward underclassmen in school or newcomers in the workplace. It connotes that the addressee is of a lower station.

Sensei: Literally meaning "one who has come before," this title is used for teachers, doctors, or masters of any profession or art.

-[blank]: This is usually forgotten in these lists, but it is perhaps the most significant difference between Japanese and English. The lack of honorific means that the speaker has permission to address the person in a very intimate way. Usually, only family, spouses, or very close friends have this kind of permission. Known as *yobisute*, it can be gratifying when someone who has earned the intimacy starts to call one by one's name without an honorific. But when that intimacy hasn't been earned, it can be very insulting.

Yozakura Quartet

2

Suzuhito Yasuda

Translated by Satsuki Yamashita
Adapted by Nunzio DeFilippis and Christina Weir
Lettered by North Market Street Graphics

Ballantine Books · New York

Yozakura Quartet volume 2 is a work of fiction. Names, characters, places, and incidents are the products of the author's imagination or are used fictitiously. Any resemblance to actual events, locales, or persons, living or dead, is entirely coincidental.

A Del Rey Manga/Kodansha Trade Paperback Original

Published in the United States by Del Rey Books, an imprint of The Random House Publishing Group, a division of Random House, Inc., New York.

Publication rights arranged through Kodansha Ltd.

First published in Japan in 2007 by Kodansha Ltd., Tokyo.

ISBN 978-0-345-50410-4

Printed in the United States of America

www.delreymanga.com

9 8 7 6 5 4 3 2

Translator: Satsuki Yamashita
Adapters: Nunzio DeFilippis and Christina Weir
Lettering and retouch: North Market Street Graphics

Contents

A Note from the Author

It seems that time has flown
since the first volume, but six months
have passed. Even if life is long, six months
is still a big chunk of it. I hope that I'm
better than I was six months ago.

Suzuhito Yasuda

Yozakura
Quartet 2

Suzuhito Yasuda

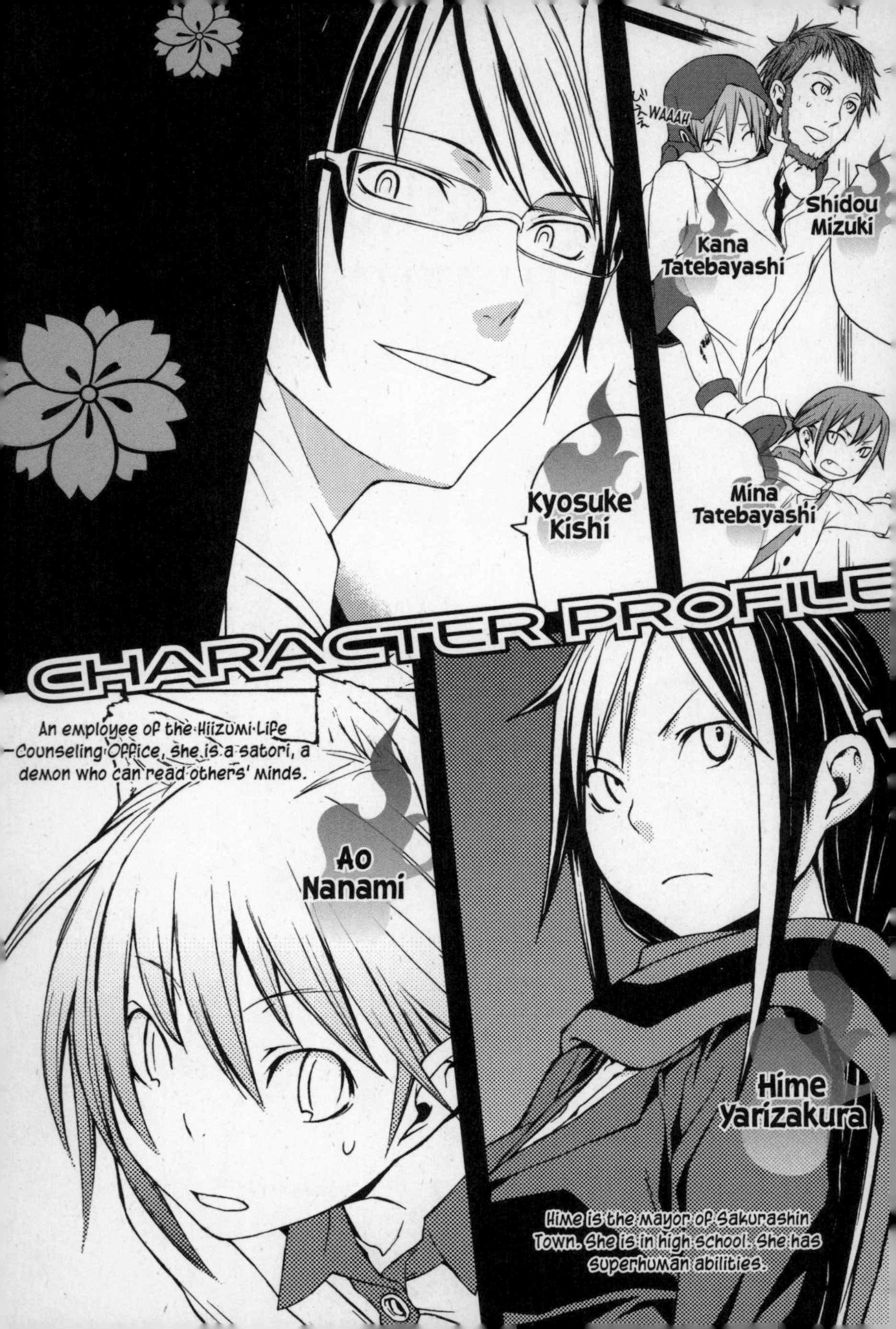
WAAAH
Shidou Mizuki
Kana Tatebayashi
Mina Tatebayashi
Kyosuke Kishi
CHARACTER PROFILE
Hime Yarizakura
Hime is the mayor of Sakurashin Town. She is in high school. She has superhuman abilities.
Ao Nanami
An employee of the Hiizumi Life Counseling Office, she is a satori, a demon who can read others' minds.

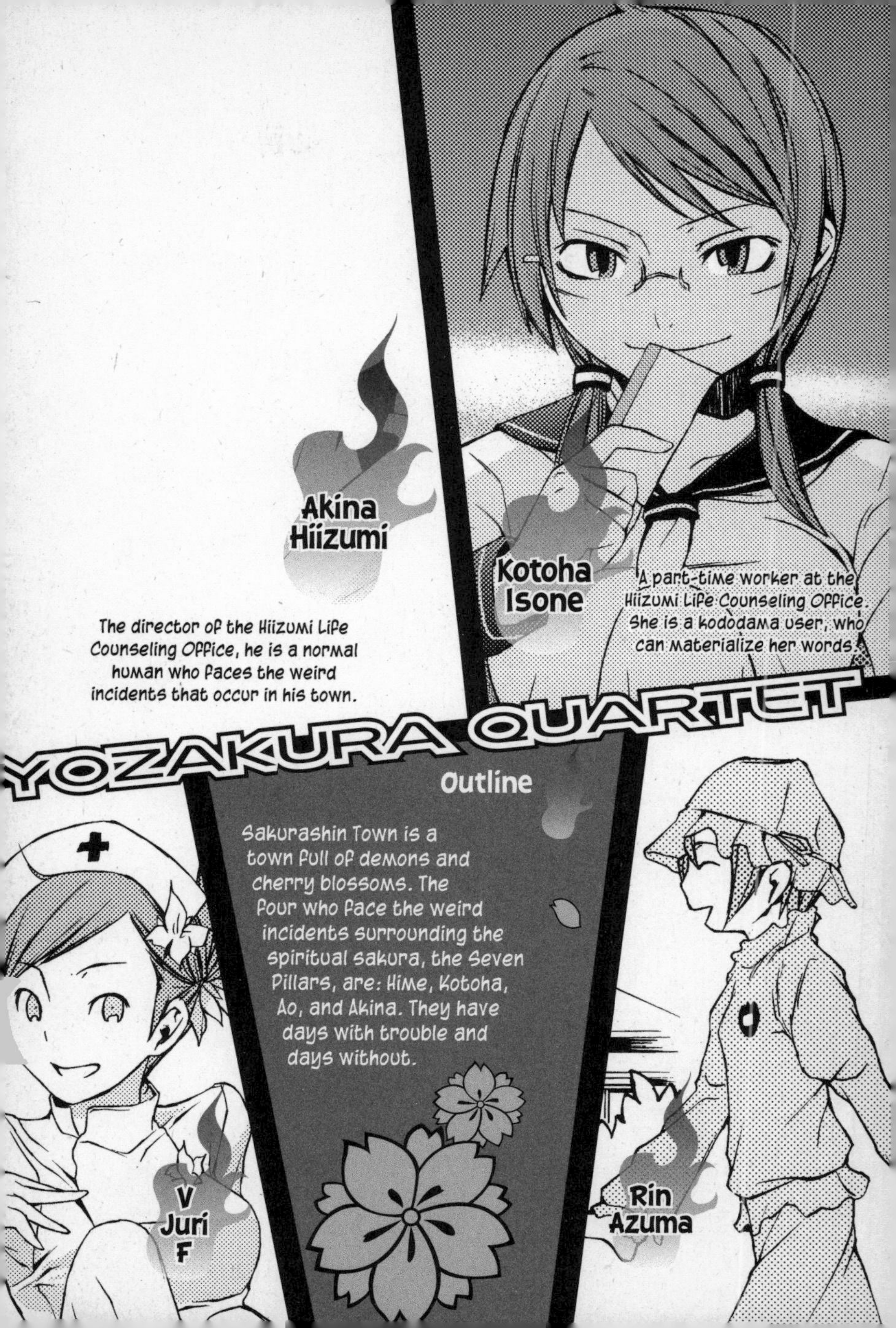
Kotoha Isone
A part-time worker at the Hiizumi Life Counseling Office. She is a kododama user, who can materialize her words.
Akina Hiizumi
The director of the Hiizumi Life Counseling Office, he is a normal human who faces the weird incidents that occur in his town.
YOZAKURA QUARTET
Rin Azuma
Outline
Sakurashin Town is a town full of demons and cherry blossoms. The four who face the weird incidents surrounding the spiritual sakura, the Seven Pillars, are: Hime, Kotoha, Ao, and Akina. They have days with trouble and days without.
V Juri F

Yozakura Quartet Contents

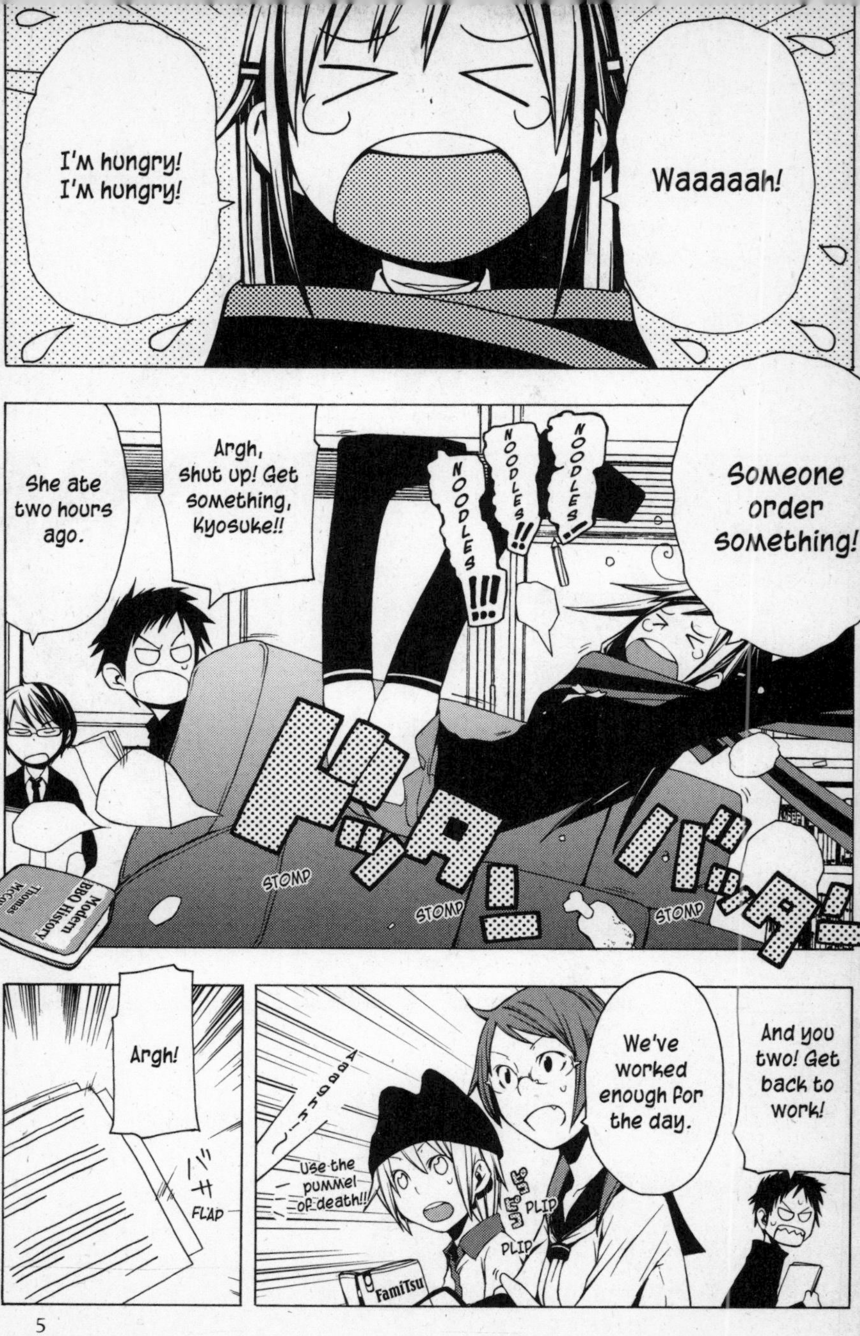
Waaaaah!
I'm hungry! I'm hungry!
Someone order something!
NOODLES!!!
NOODLES!!
NOODLES!
Argh, shut up! Get something, Kyosuke!!
She ate two hours ago.
STOMP
STOMP
STOMP
Modern BBQ History Thomas McCoy
And you two! Get back to work!
We've worked enough for the day.
PLIP
PLIP
Use the pummel of death!!
FamiTsu
Argh!
FLAP

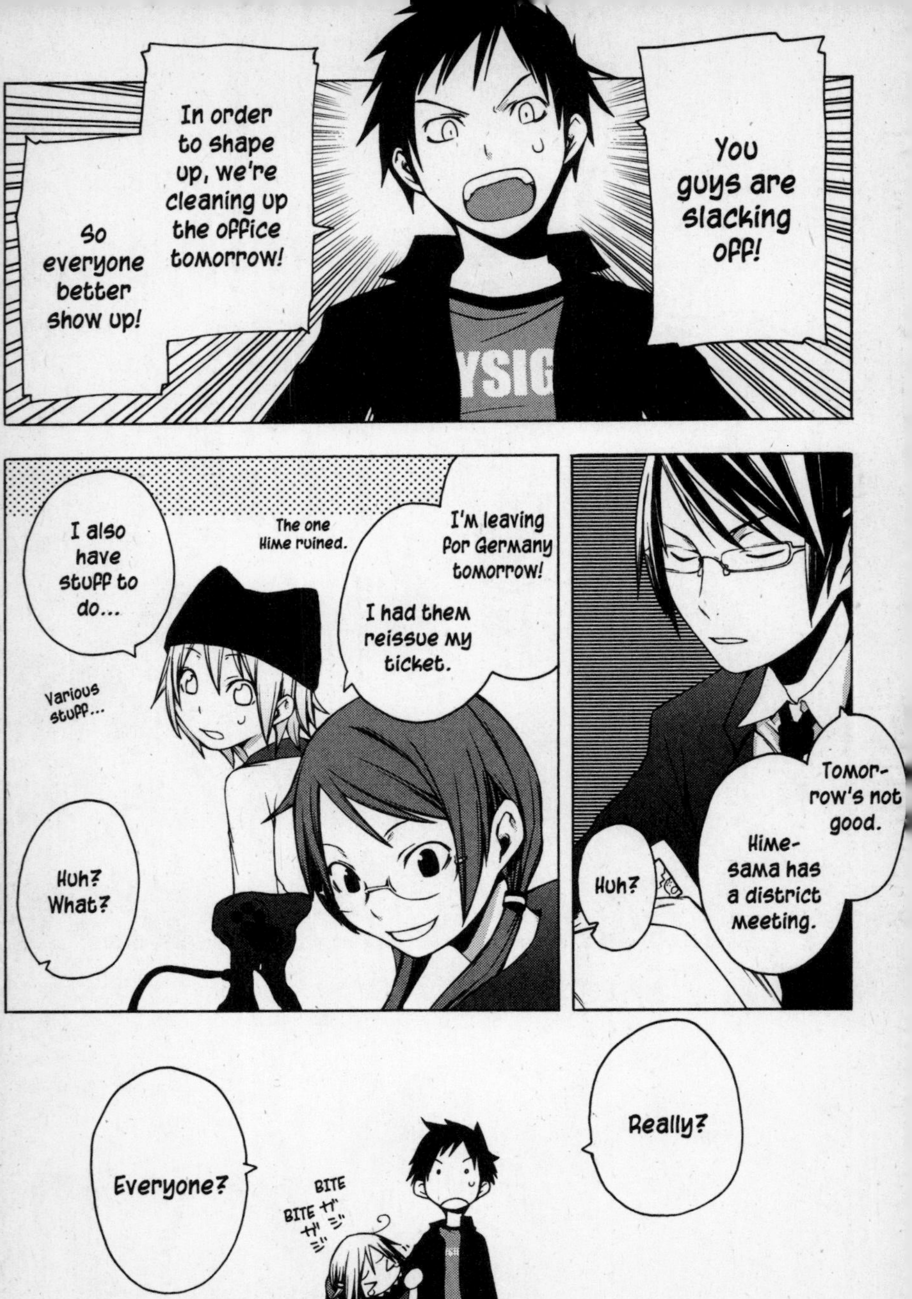
You guys are slacking off!
In order to shape up, we're cleaning up the office tomorrow!
So everyone better show up!
Tomorrow's not good.
Hime-sama has a district meeting.
Huh?
I'm leaving for Germany tomorrow!
I had them reissue my ticket.
The one Hime ruined.
I also have stuff to do...
Various stuff...
Huh? What?
Really?
BITE
BITE
Everyone?

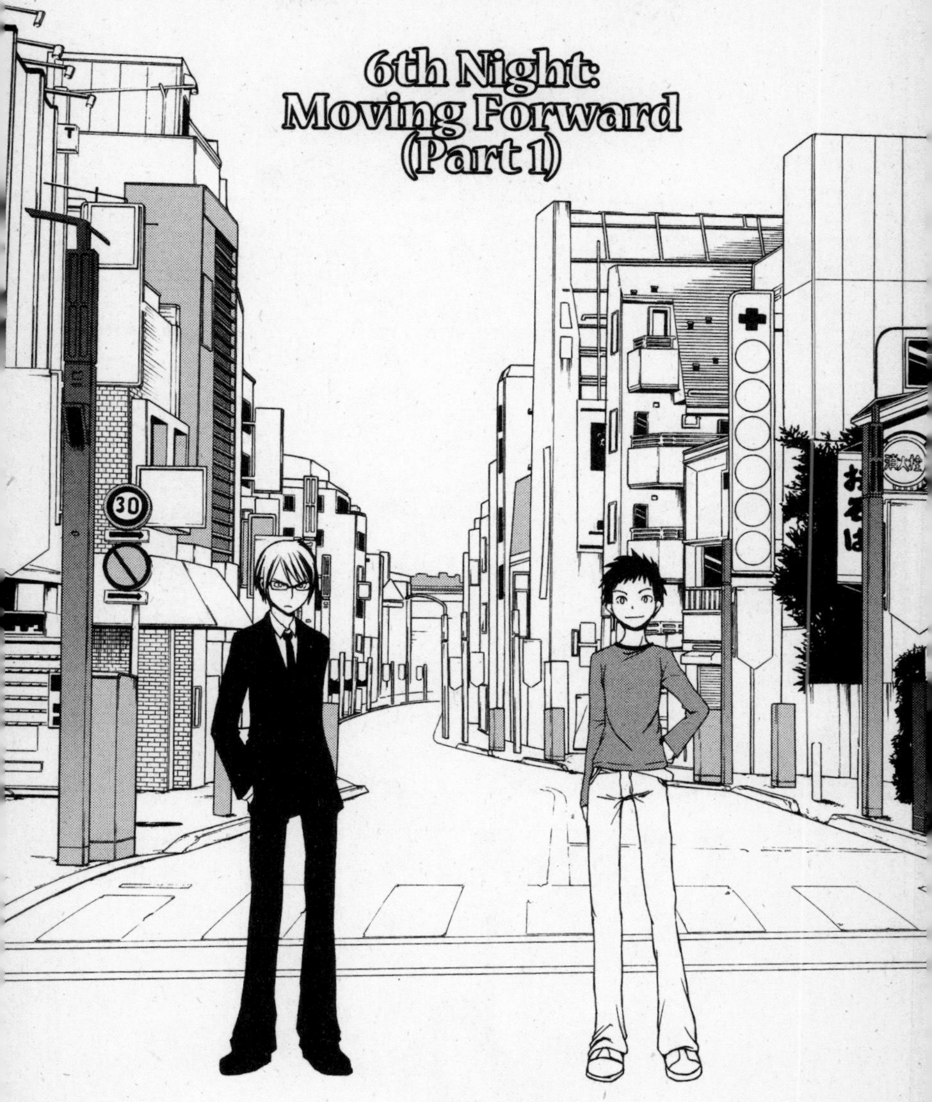
6th Night:
Moving Forward
(Part 1)
30

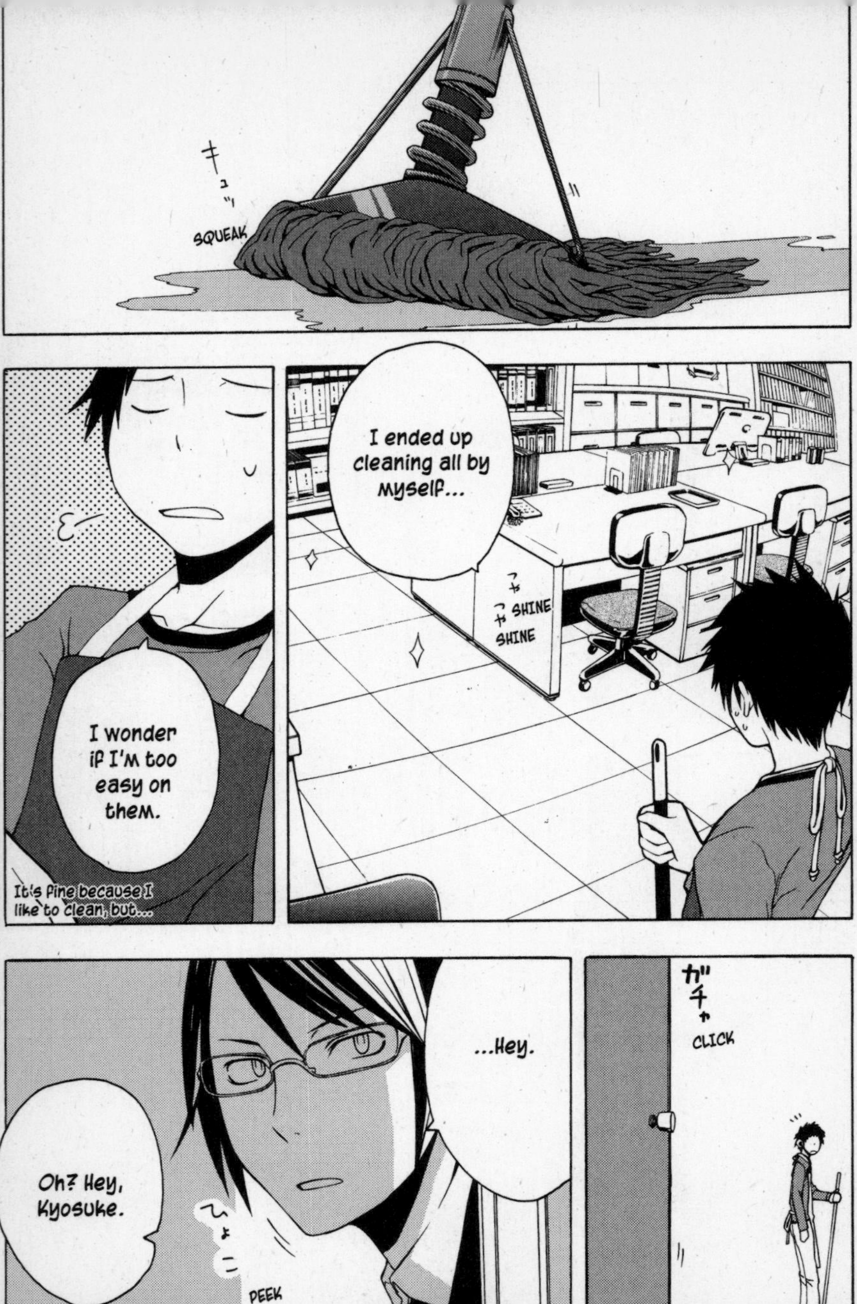
キュッ
SQUEAK
I ended up cleaning all by myself...
SHINE
SHINE
I wonder if I'm too easy on them.
It's fine because I like to clean, but...
ガチャ
CLICK
...Hey.
Oh? Hey, Kyosuke.
ひょこ
PEEK

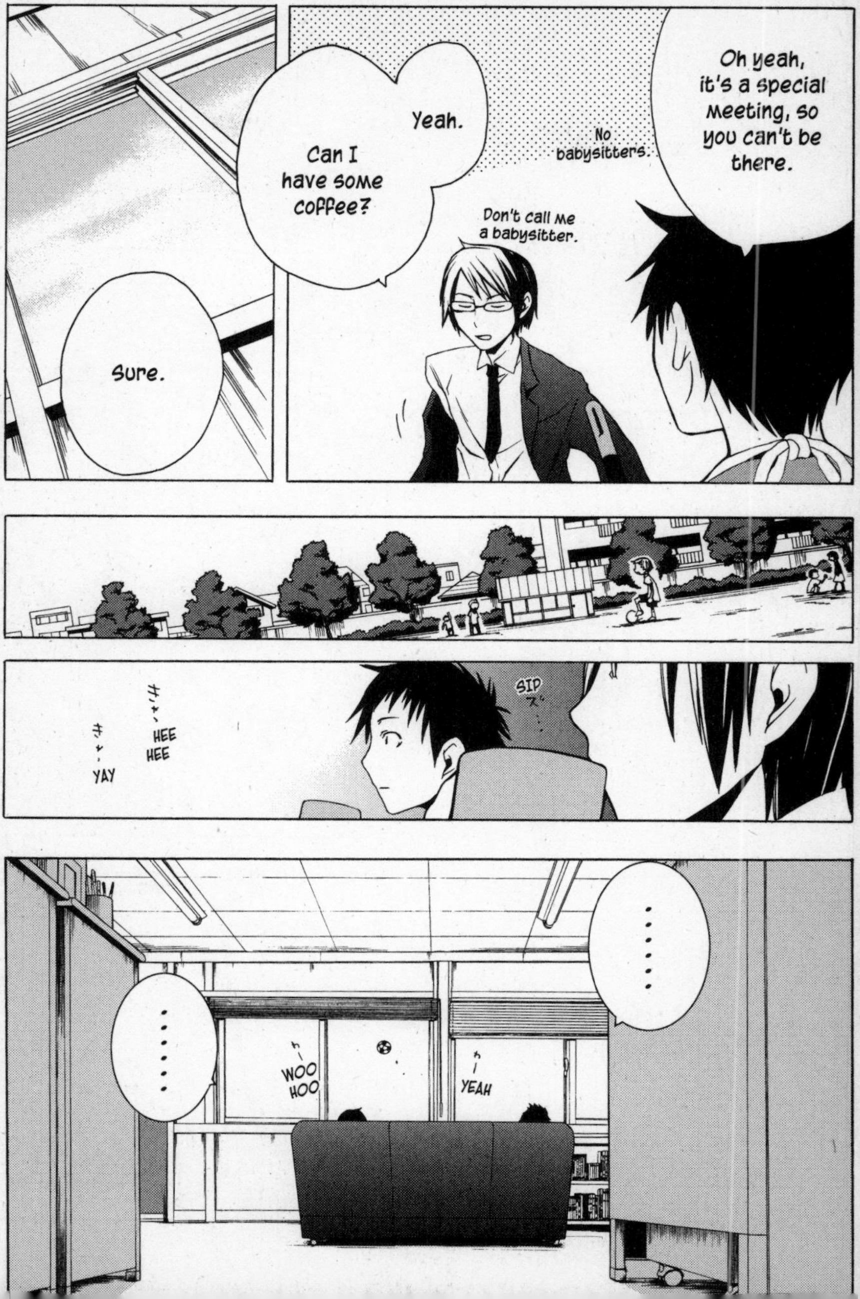
Oh yeah, it's a special meeting, so you can't be there.
No babysitters.
Don't call me a babysitter.
Yeah.
Can I have some coffee?
Sure.
SIP
HEE HEE
YAY
......
......
YEAH
WOO HOO

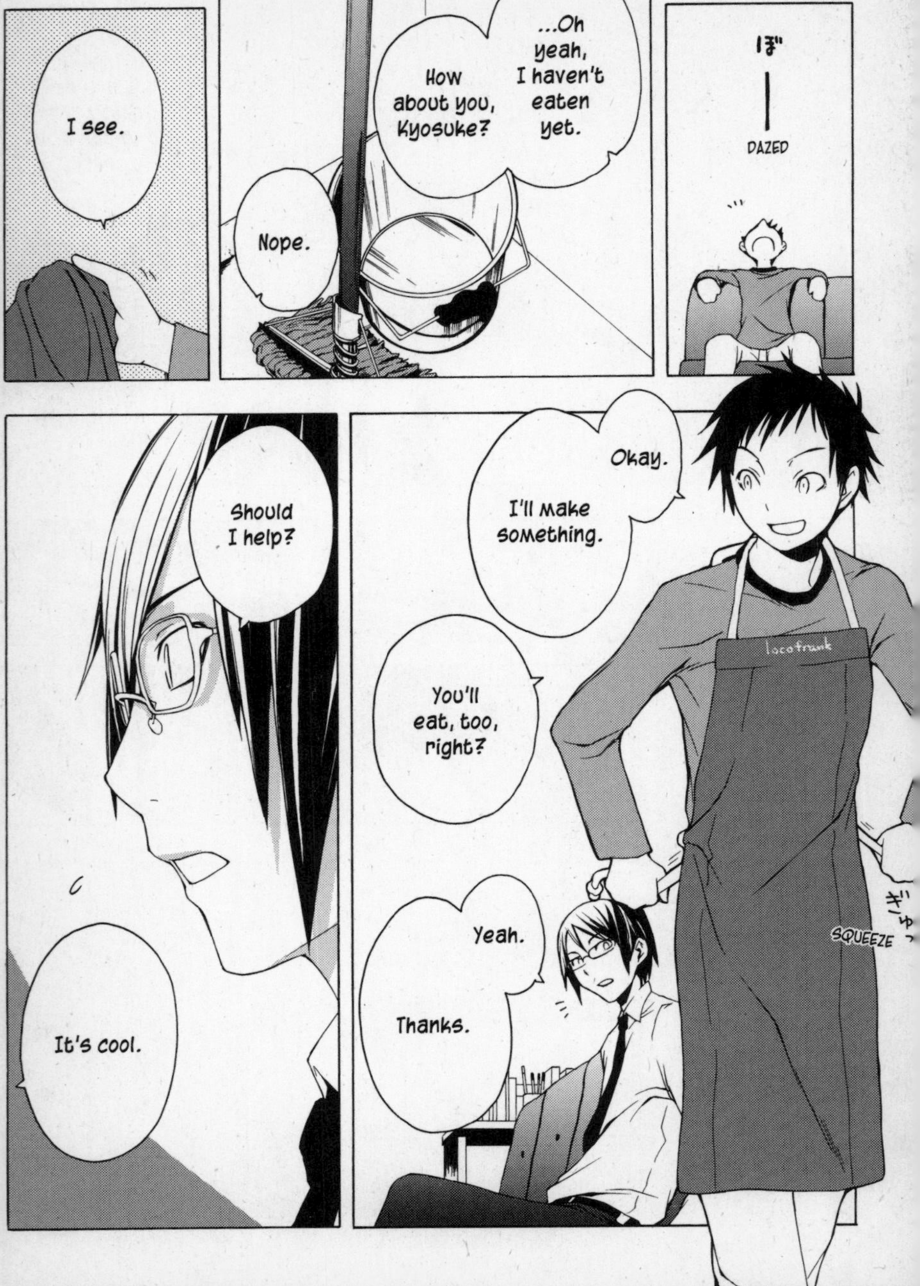
ぼ
DAZED
...Oh yeah, I haven't eaten yet.
How about you, Kyosuke?
Nope.
I see.
Okay.
I'll make something.
You'll eat, too, right?
Yeah.
Thanks.
ぎゅっ
SQUEEZE
Should I help?
It's cool.

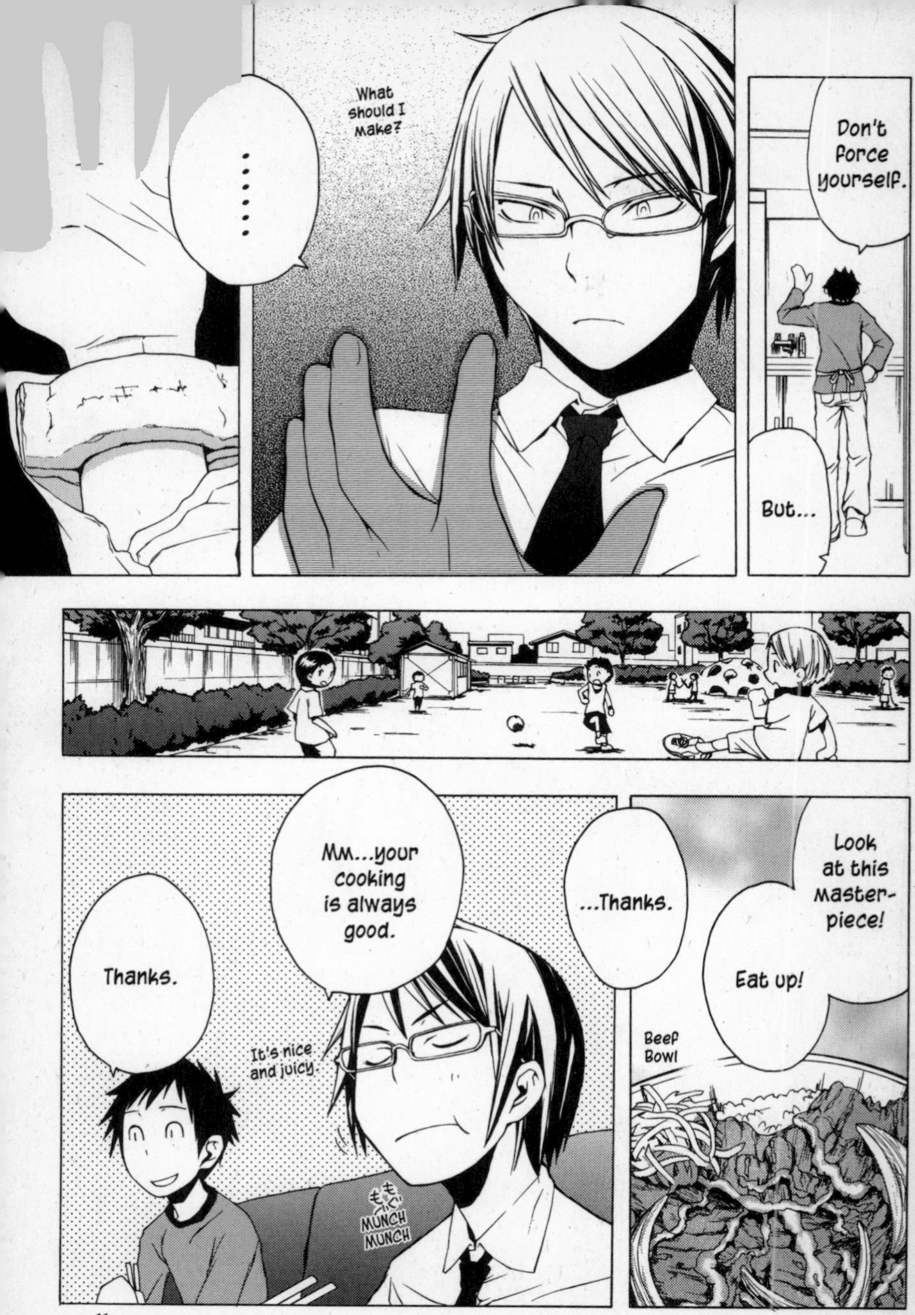
Don't force yourself.
But...
What should I make?
......
Look at this master-piece!
Eat up!
Beef Bowl
...Thanks.
Mm...your cooking is always good.
Thanks.
It's nice and juicy.
MUNCH MUNCH

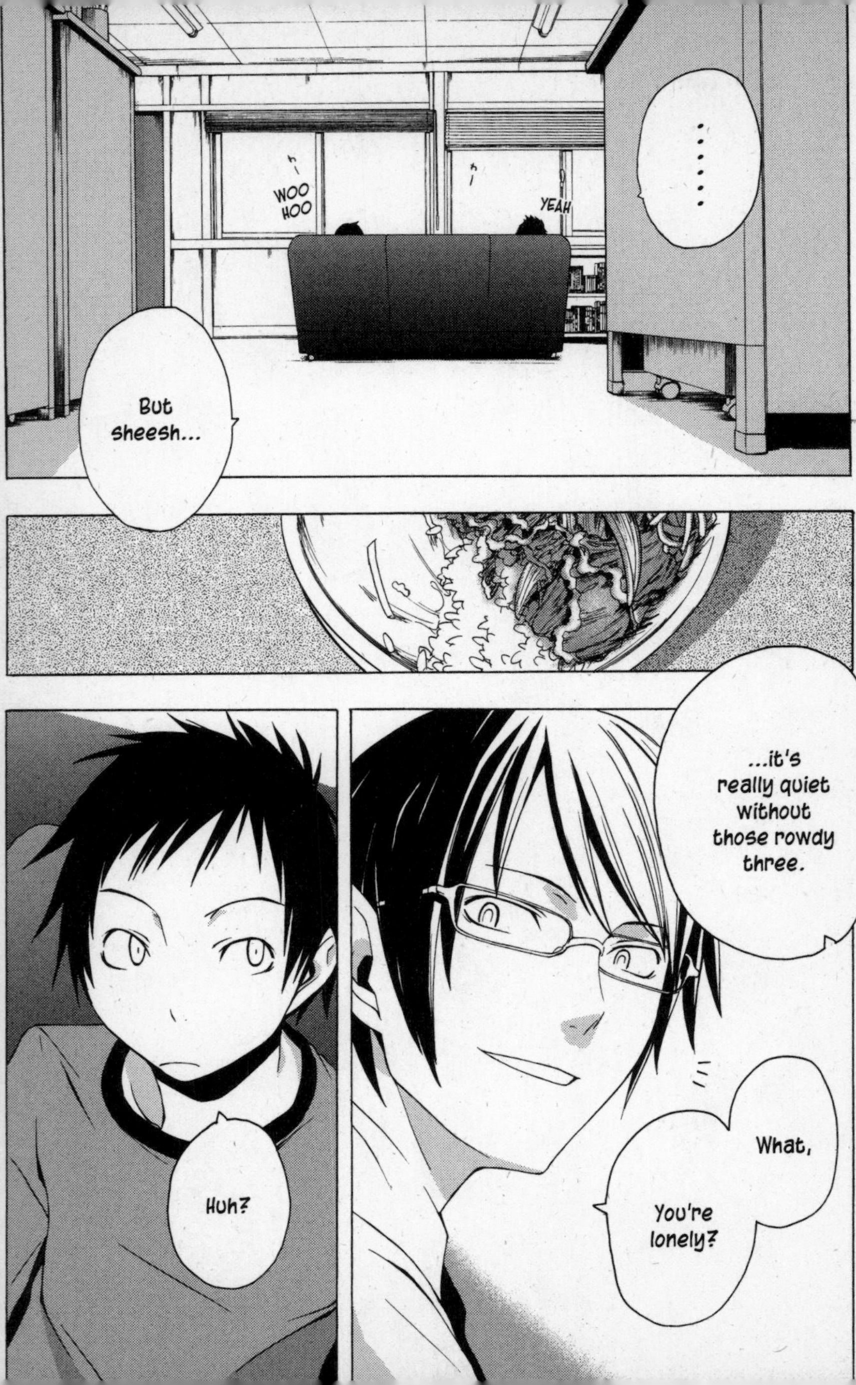
......
YEAH
WOO HOO
But sheesh...
...it's really quiet without those rowdy three.
What,
You're lonely?
Huh?

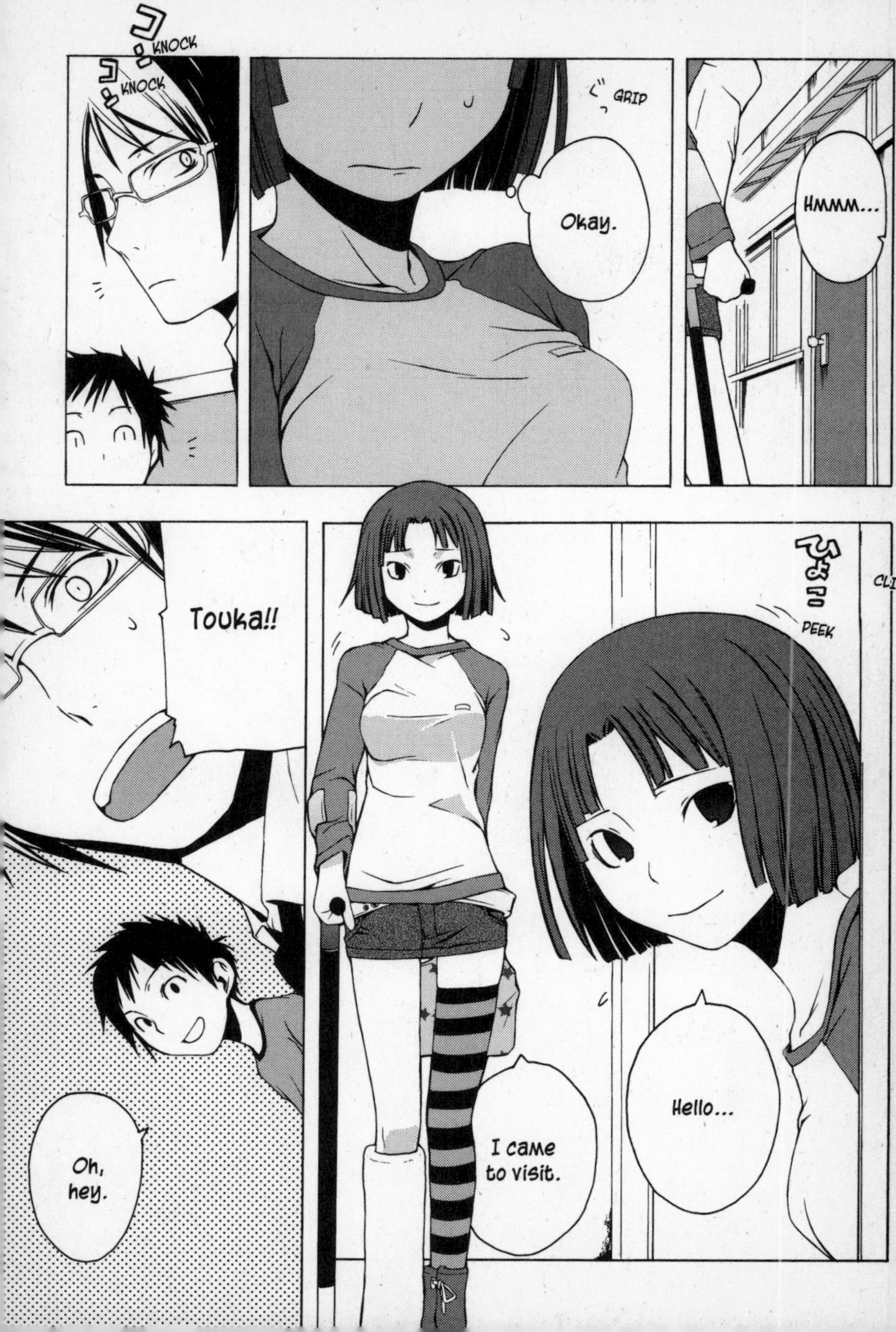
HMMM...
GRIP
Okay.
KNOCK
KNOCK
CLIC
PEEK
Hello...
I came to visit.
Touka!!
Oh, hey.

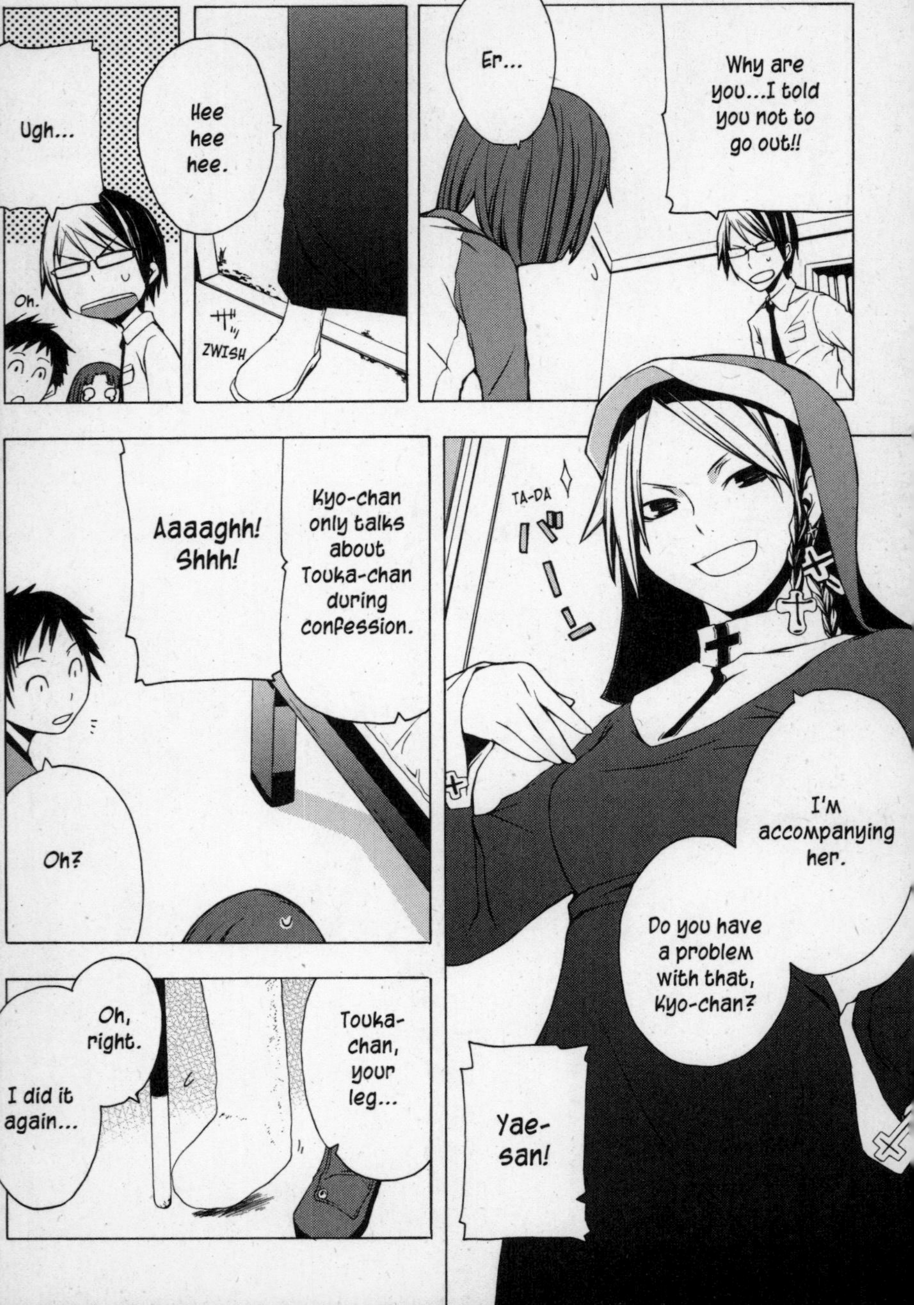
Why are you...I told you not to go out!!
Er...
Hee hee hee.
ZWISH
Ugh...
Oh.
TA-DA
I'm accompanying her.
Do you have a problem with that, Kyo-chan?
Yae-san!
Kyo-chan only talks about Touka-chan during confession.
Aaaaghh! Shhh!
Oh?
Touka-chan, your leg...
Oh, right.
I did it again...

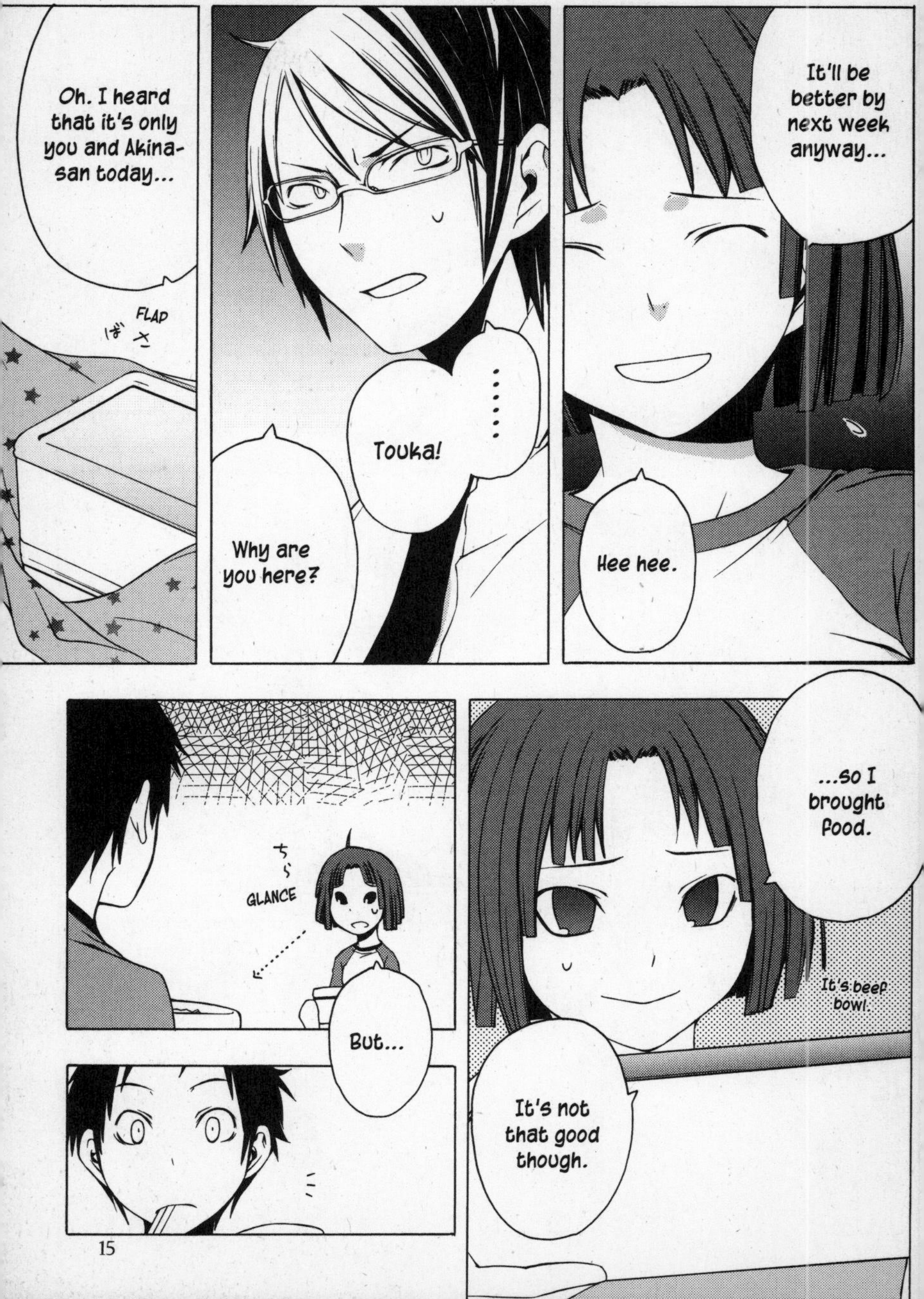

It'll be better by next week anyway...
Hee hee.
......
Touka!
Why are you here?
Oh. I heard that it's only you and Akina-san today...
ばさ
FLAP
...so I brought food.
It's beef bowl.
It's not that good though.
ちら
GLANCE
But...

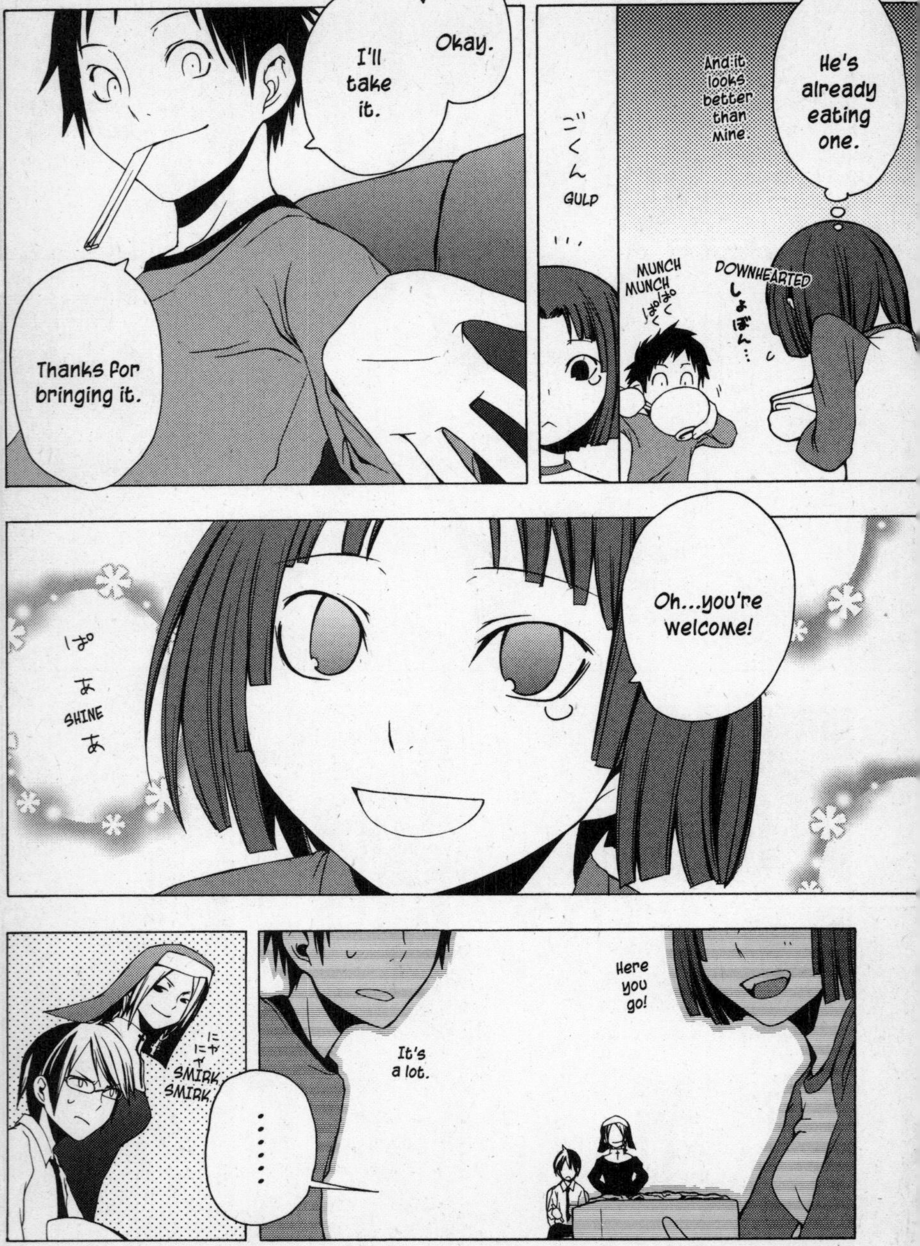
He's already eating one.
And it looks better than mine
ごくん
GULP
DOWNHEARTED
しょぼん…
MUNCH MUNCH
ぱくぱく
Okay.
I'll take it.
Thanks for bringing it.
Oh...you're welcome!
ぱああ
SHINE
Here you go!
It's a lot.
にやにや
SMIRK SMIRK
......

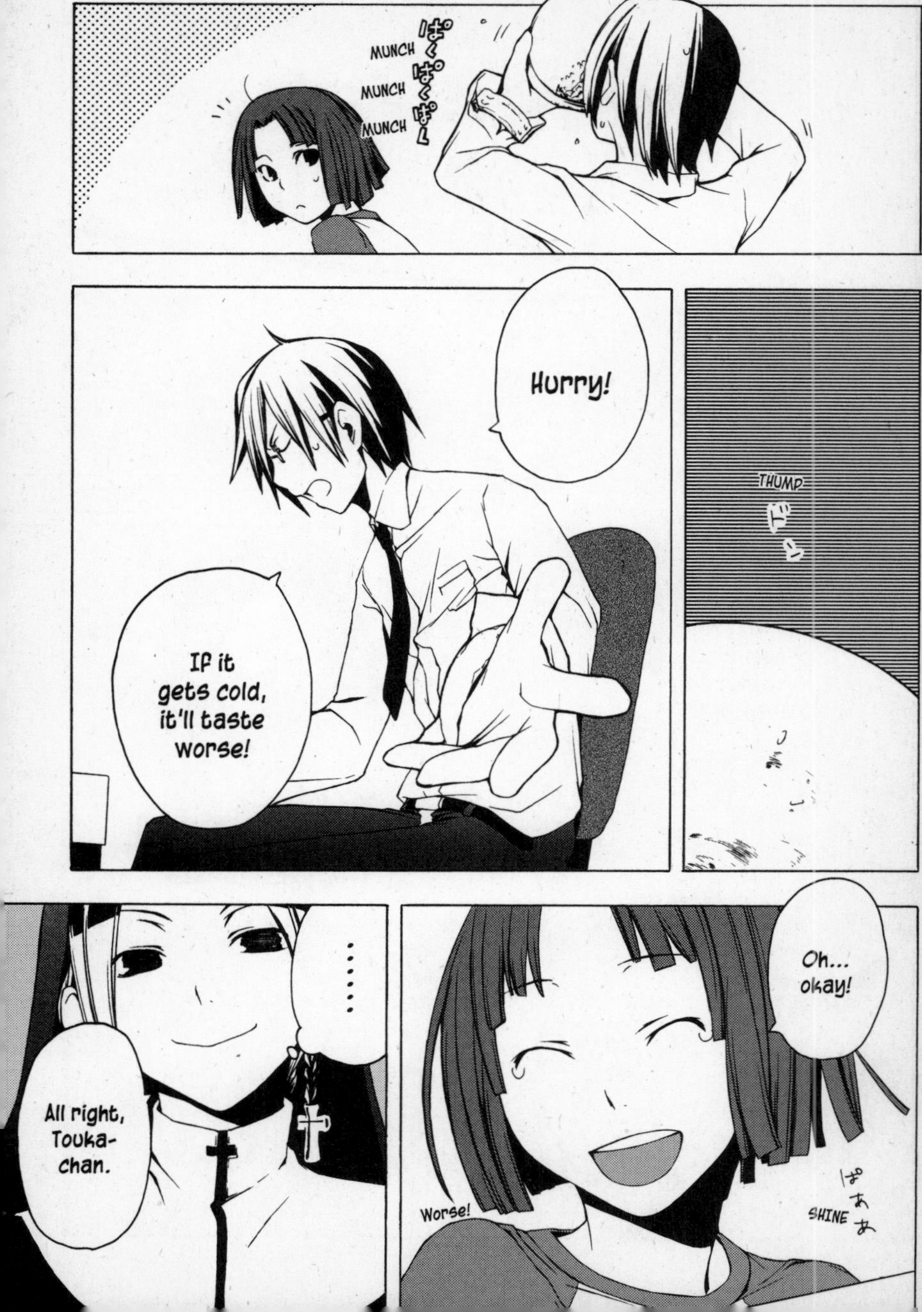
MUNCH
MUNCH
MUNCH
ぱくぱくぱく
THUMP
ドン
Hurry!
If it gets cold, it'll taste worse!
Oh... okay!
Worse!
SHINE
ぱああ
......
All right, Touka-chan.

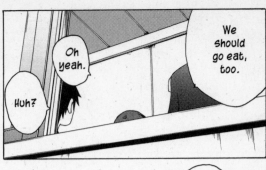

We should go eat, too.
Oh yeah.
Huh?
You guys didn't eat yet?
Um, no.
Oh. You should've told me.
Thank you for the food.
I'll make something then.
You came all the way here, so take your time.
Really?
You're going to make us food!?
Akina-san's food...
Touka-chan, you're drooling.

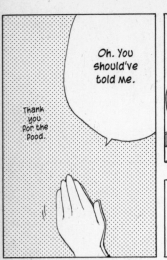

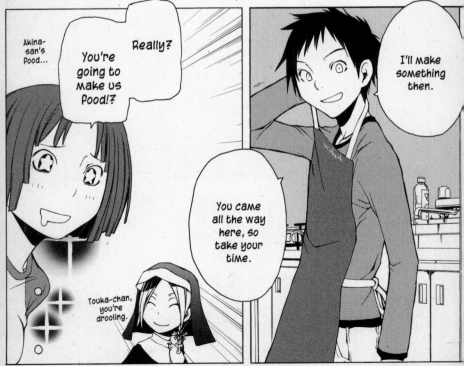

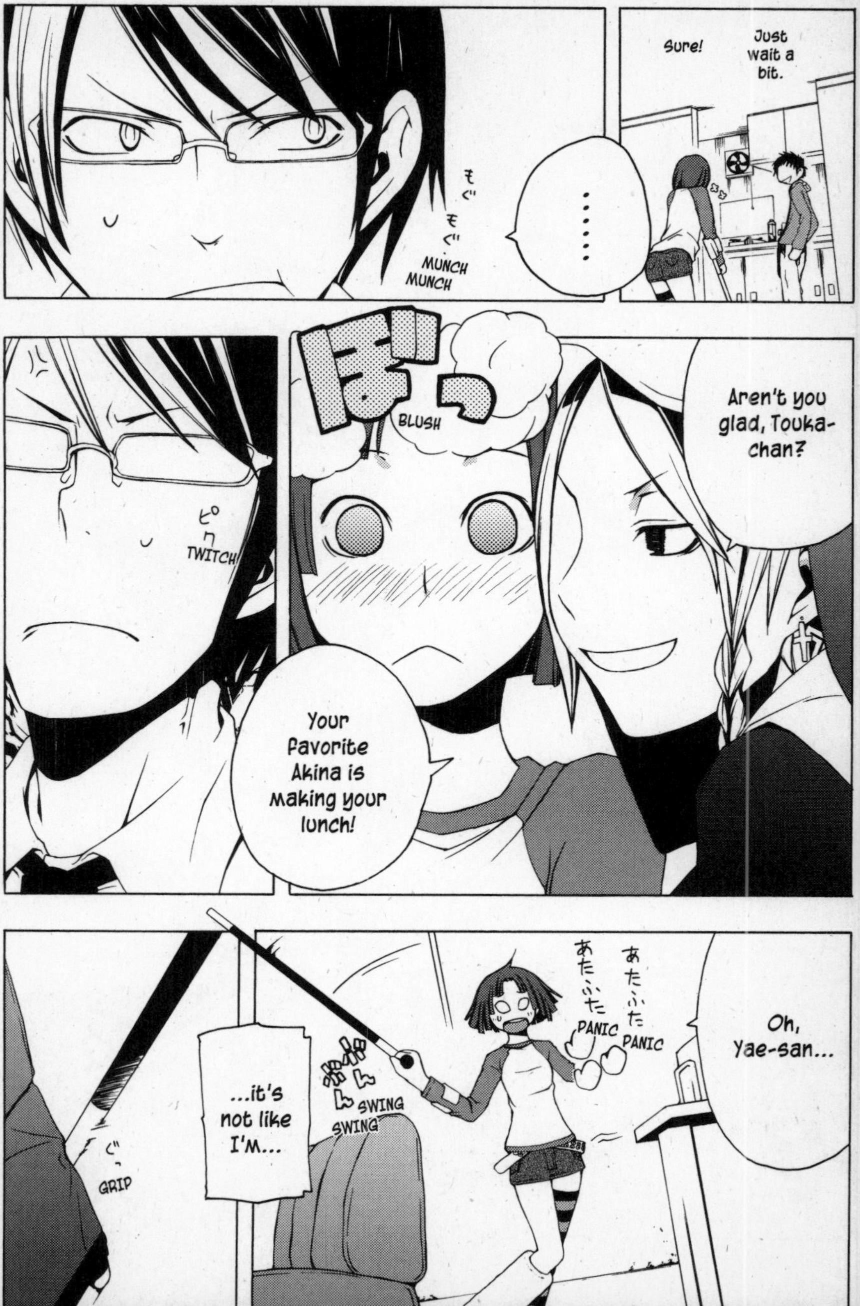
Just wait a bit.
Sure!
......
もぐもぐ
MUNCH MUNCH
Aren't you glad, Touka-chan?
ぼっ
BLUSH
Your favorite Akina is making your lunch!
ピク
TWITCH
Oh, Yae-san...
あたふた
PANIC
あたふた
PANIC
SWING SWING
...it's not like I'M...
ぐっ
GRIP

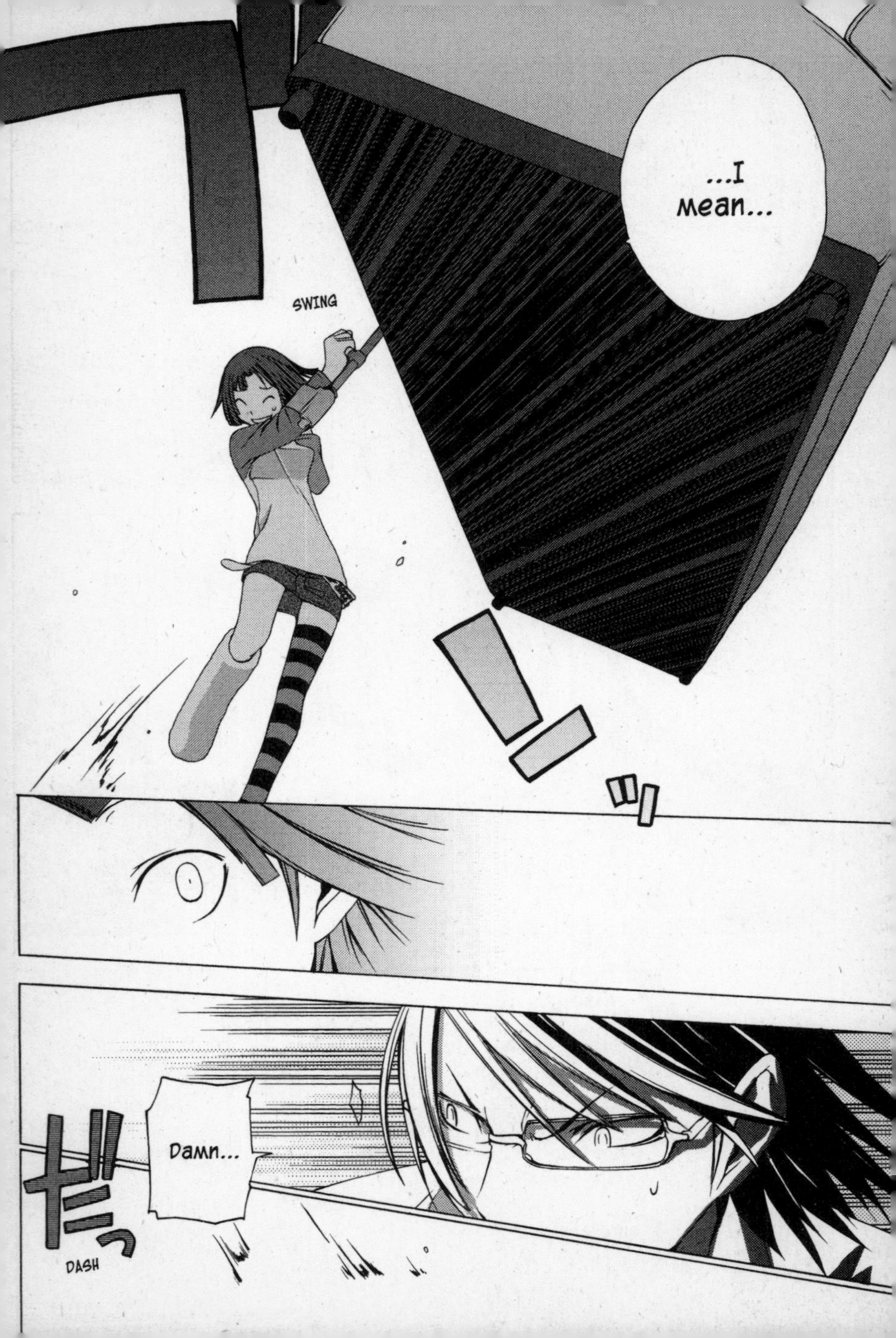
...I mean...
SWING
Damn...
DASH

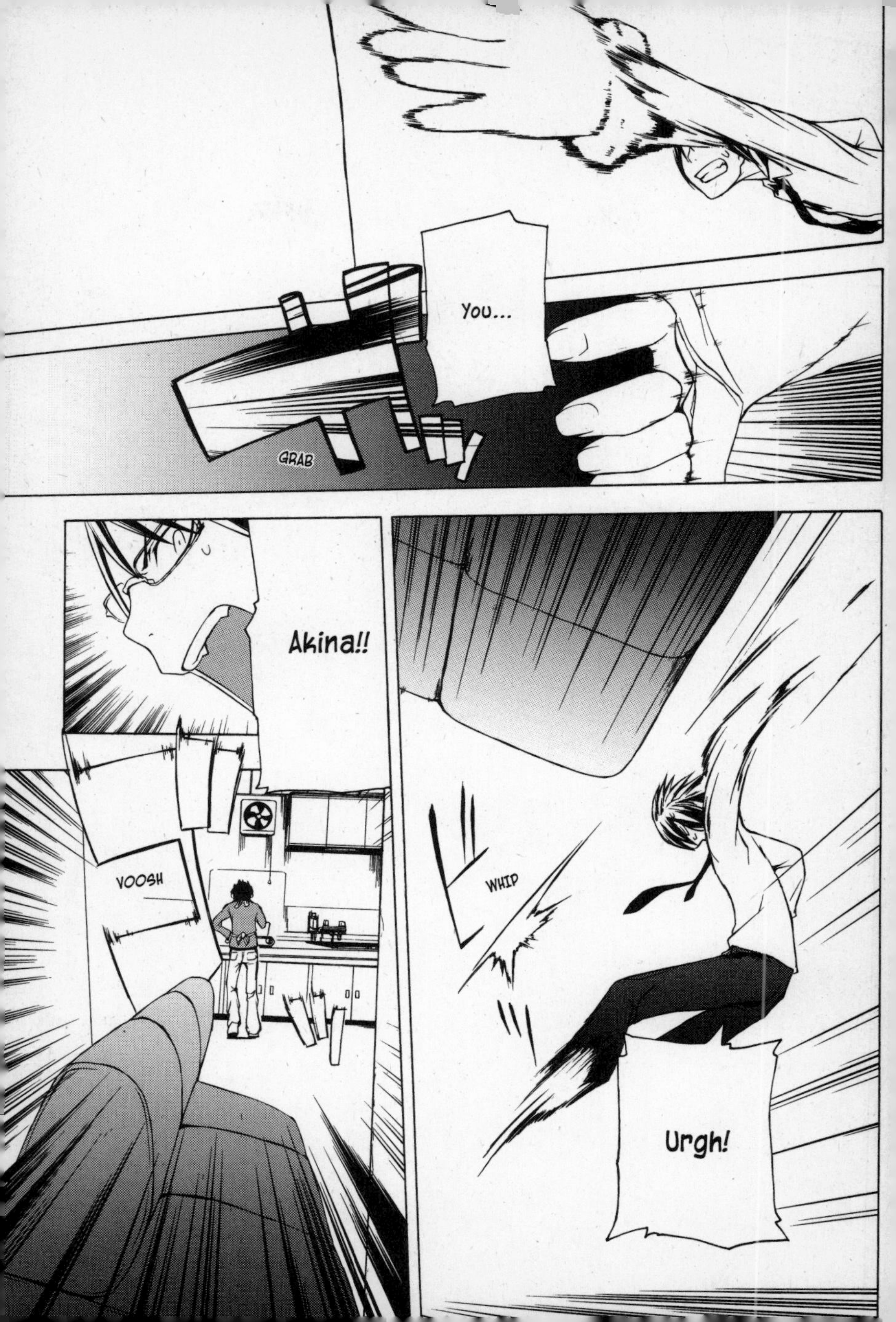
YOU...
GRAB
WHIP
Urgh!
Akina!!
VOOSH

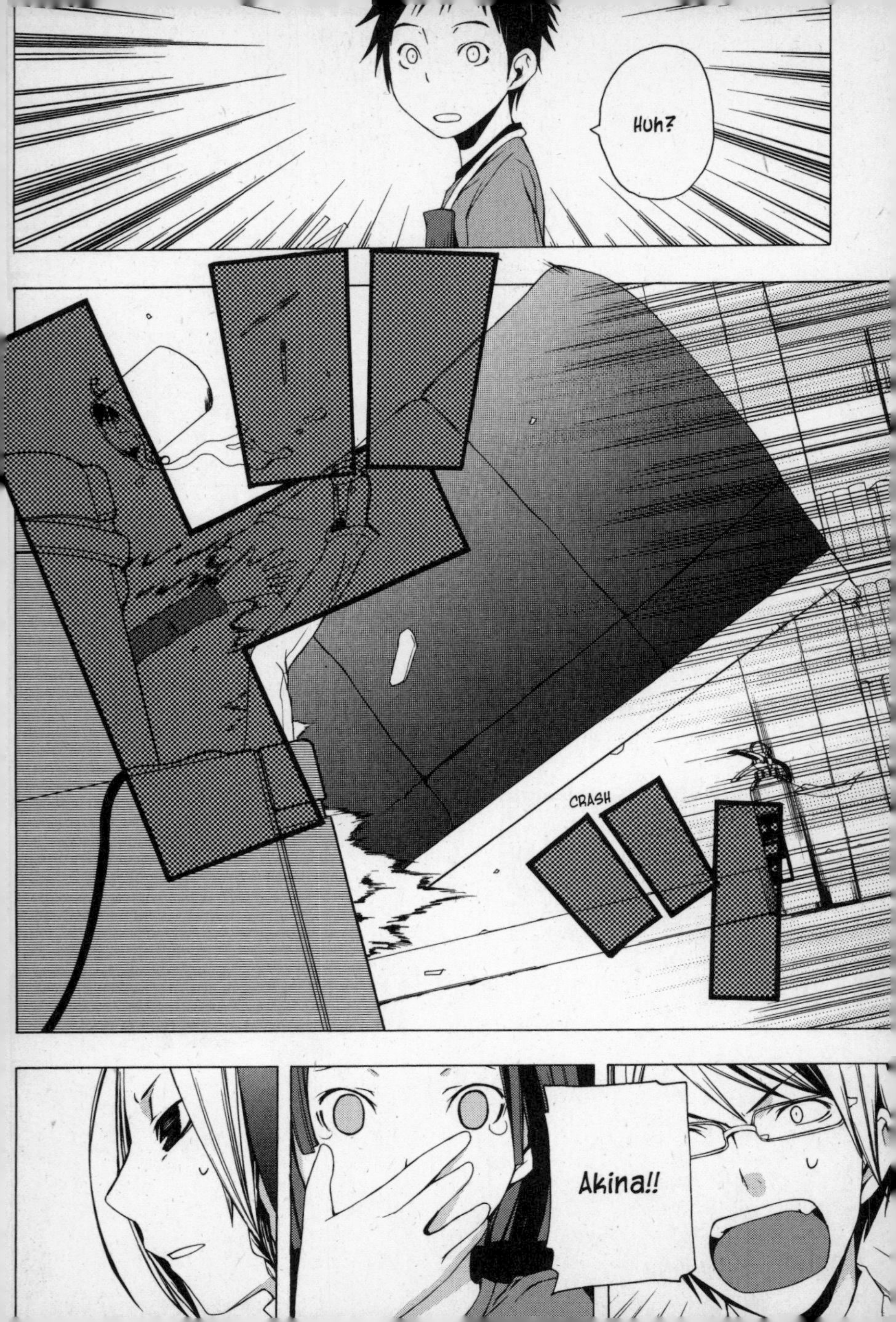
Huh?
CRASH
Akina!!

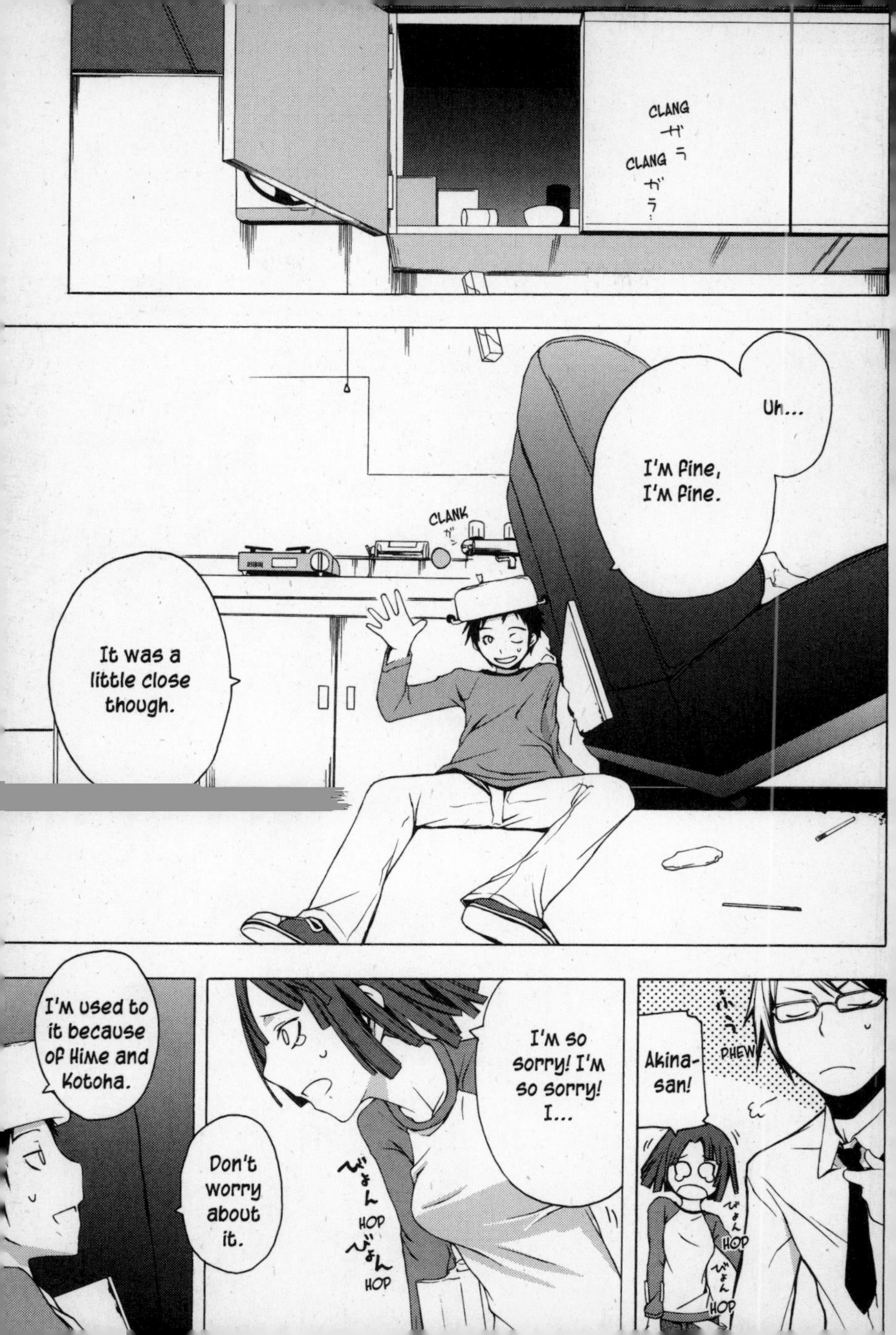
CLANG
ガラ
CLANG
ガラ
Uh...
I'm fine, I'm fine.
CLANK
It was a little close though.
ふぅ
PHEW
Akina-san!
ぴょん
HOP
ぴょん
HOP
I'm so sorry! I'm so sorry! I...
ぴょん
HOP
ぴょん
HOP
I'm used to it because of Hime and Kotoha.
Don't worry about it.

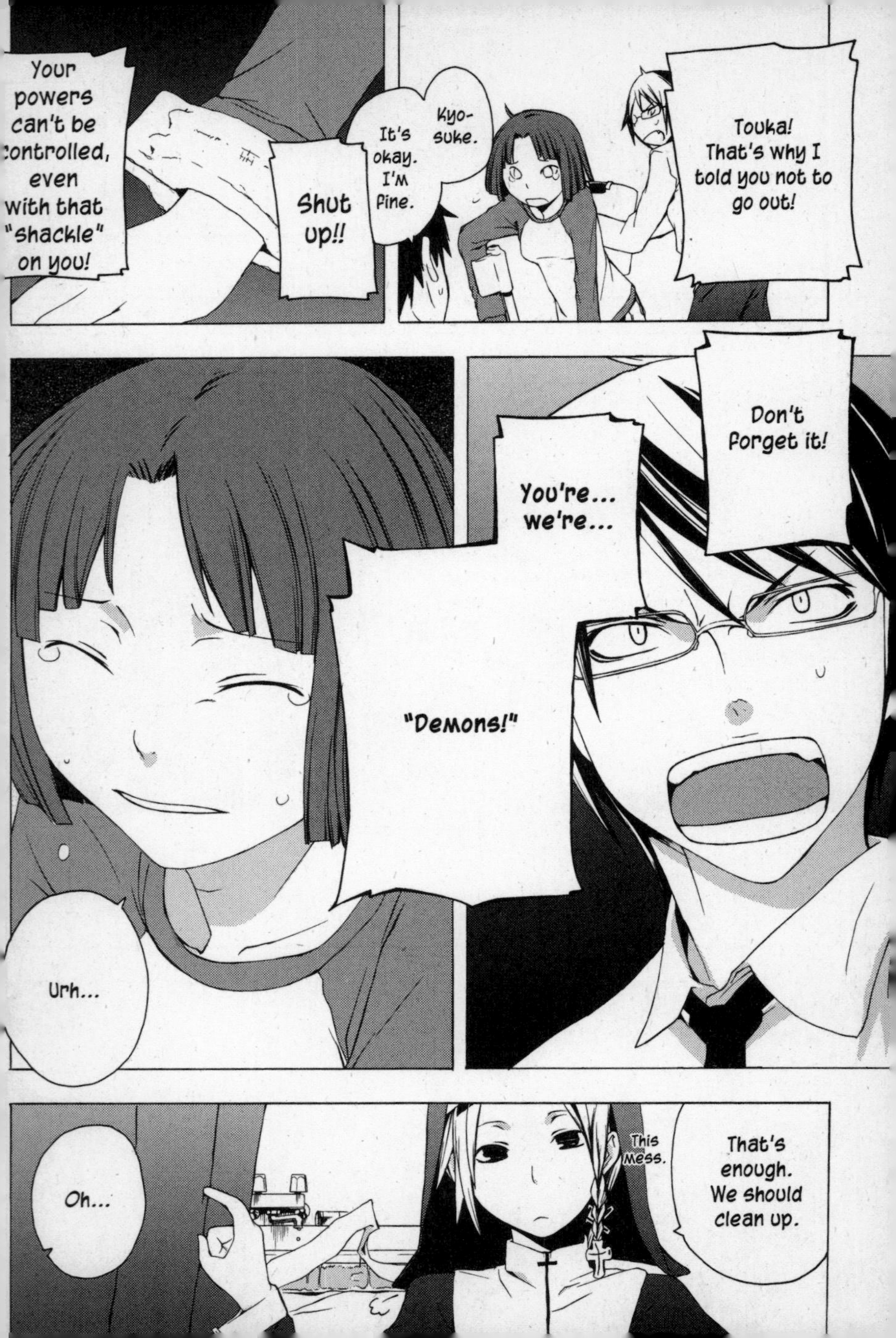
Touka! That's why I told you not to go out!
Kyo-suke.
It's okay. I'm fine.
Shut up!!
Your powers can't be controlled, even with that "shackle" on you!
Don't forget it!
You're... we're...
"Demons!"
Urh...
That's enough. We should clean up.
This mess.
Oh...

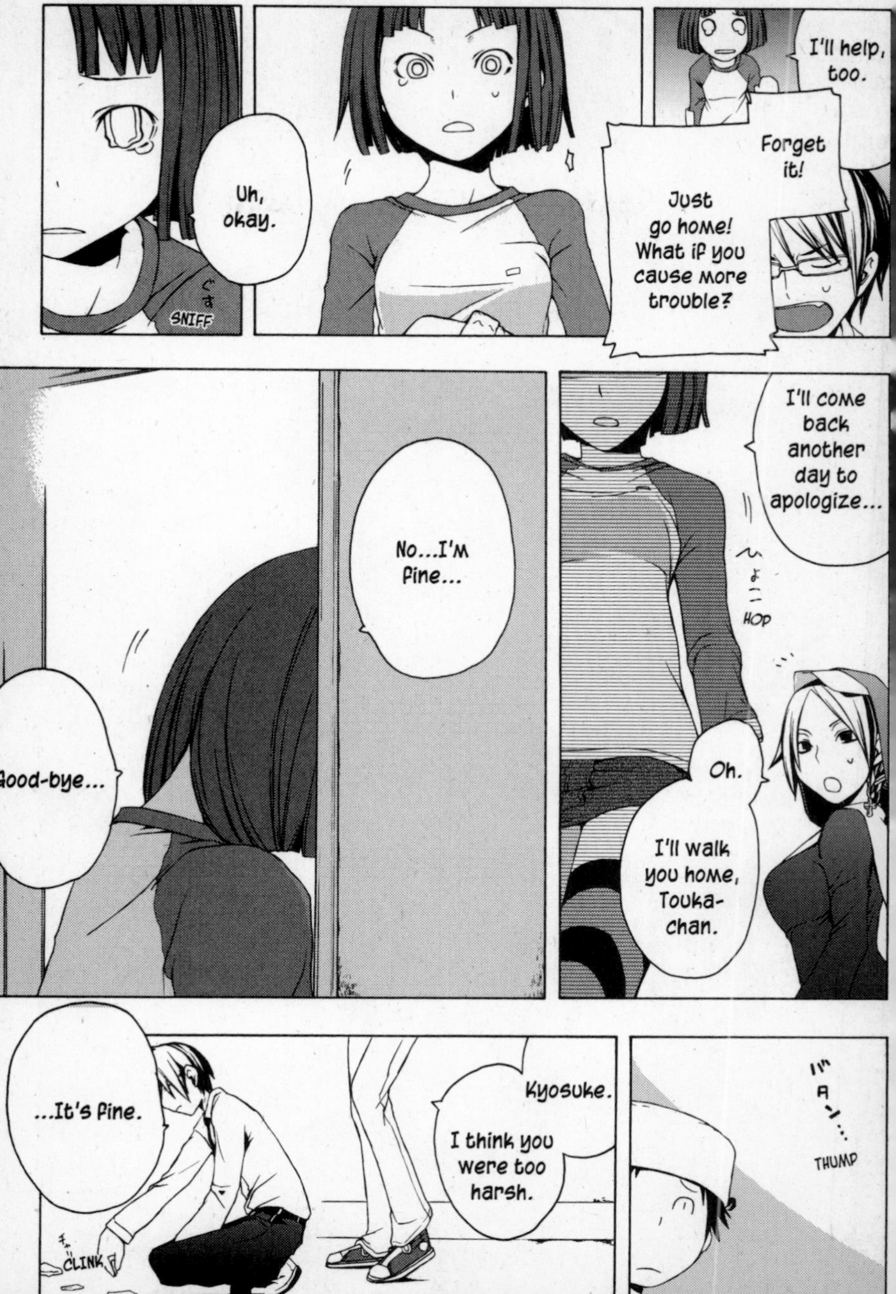
I'll help, too.
Forget it!
Just go home! What if you cause more trouble?
Uh, okay.
ぐす
SNIFF
I'll come back another day to apologize...
HOP
Oh.
I'll walk you home, Touka-chan.
No...I'm fine...
Good-bye...
THUMP
Kyosuke.
I think you were too harsh.
...It's fine.
CLINK

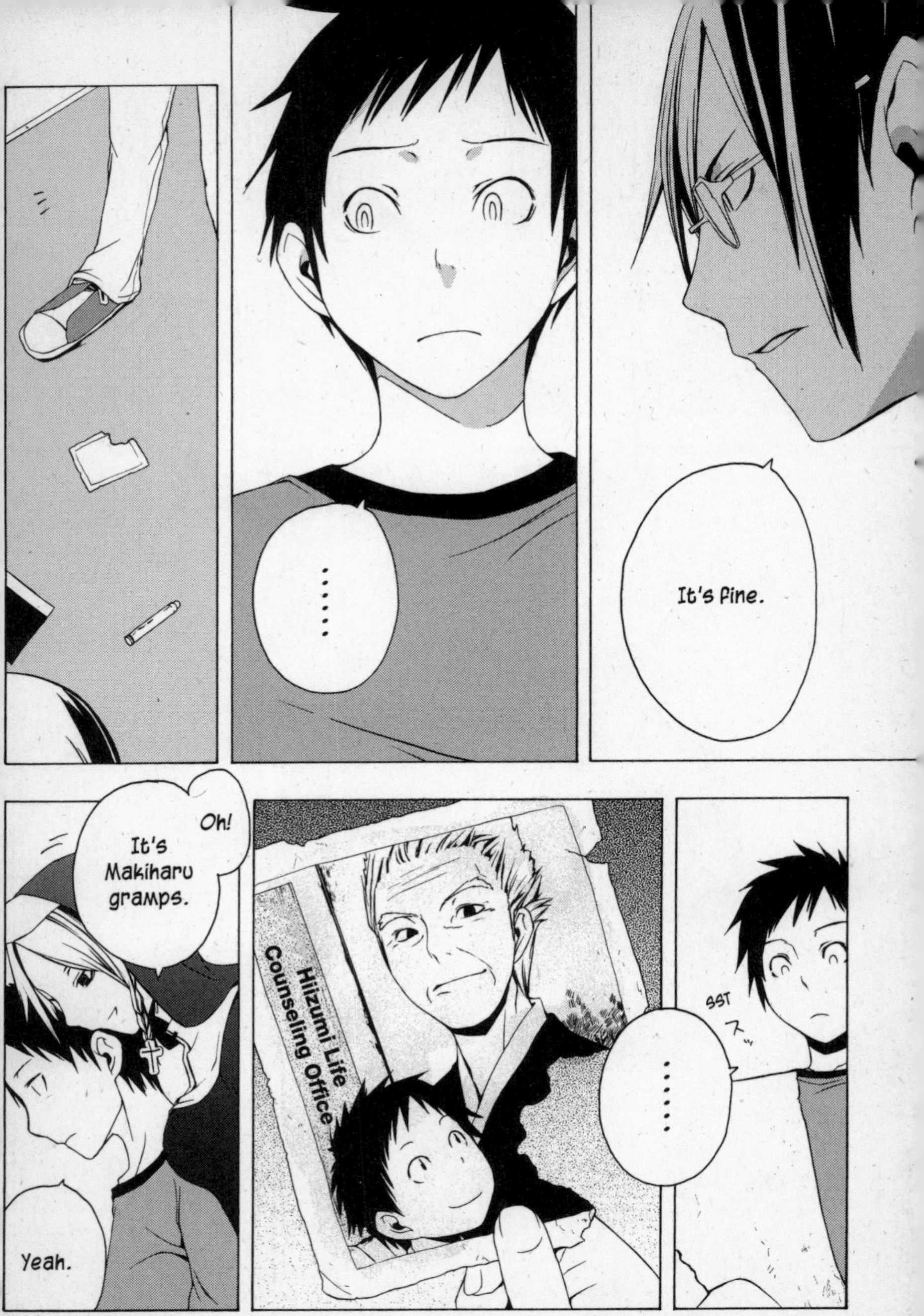
It's fine.
......
SST
ス
......
Hiizumi Life Counseling Office
Oh!
It's Makiharu gramps.
Yeah.

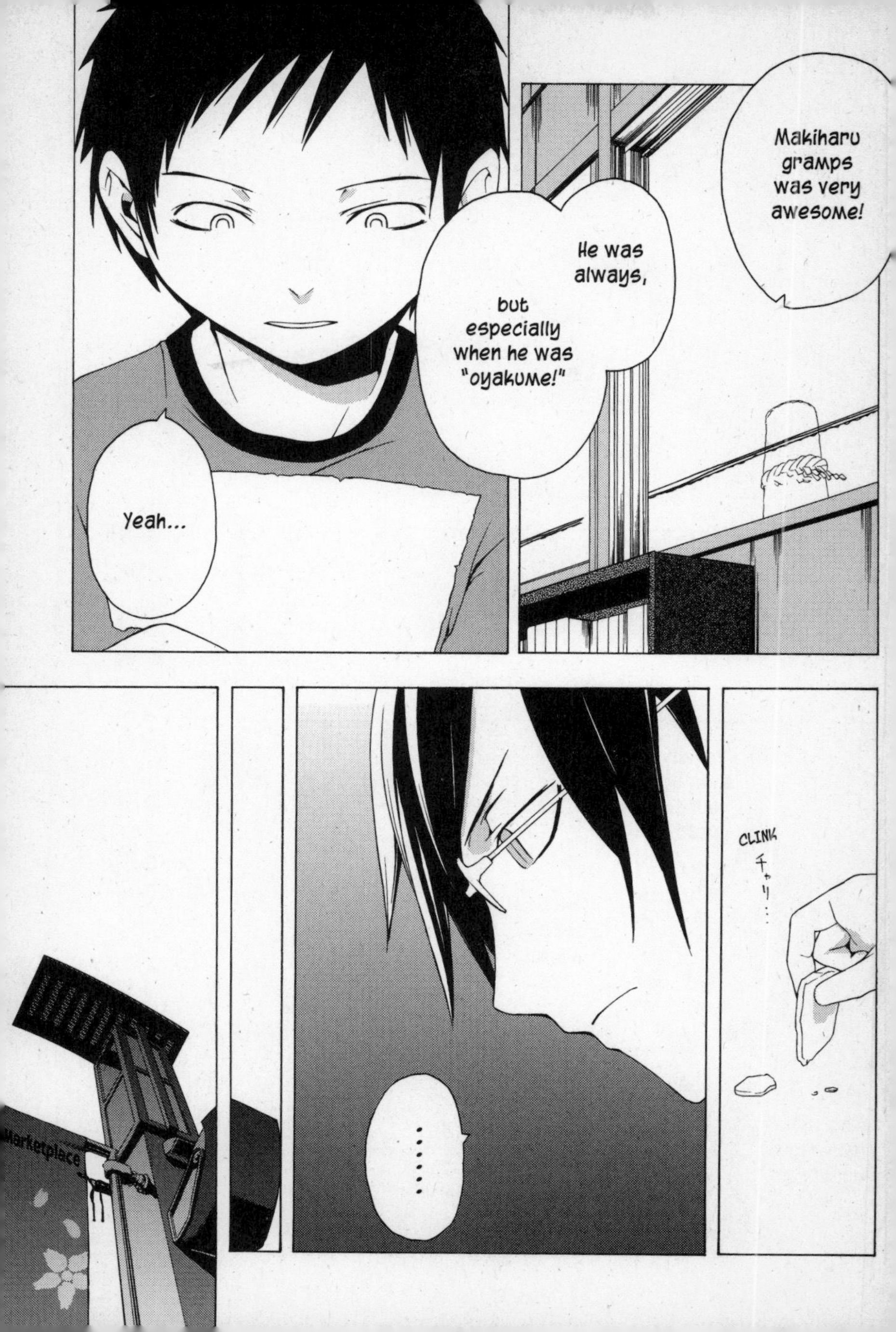
Makiharu gramps was very awesome!
He was always,
but especially when he was "oyakume!"
Yeah...
CLINK
チャリ…
……
Marketplace

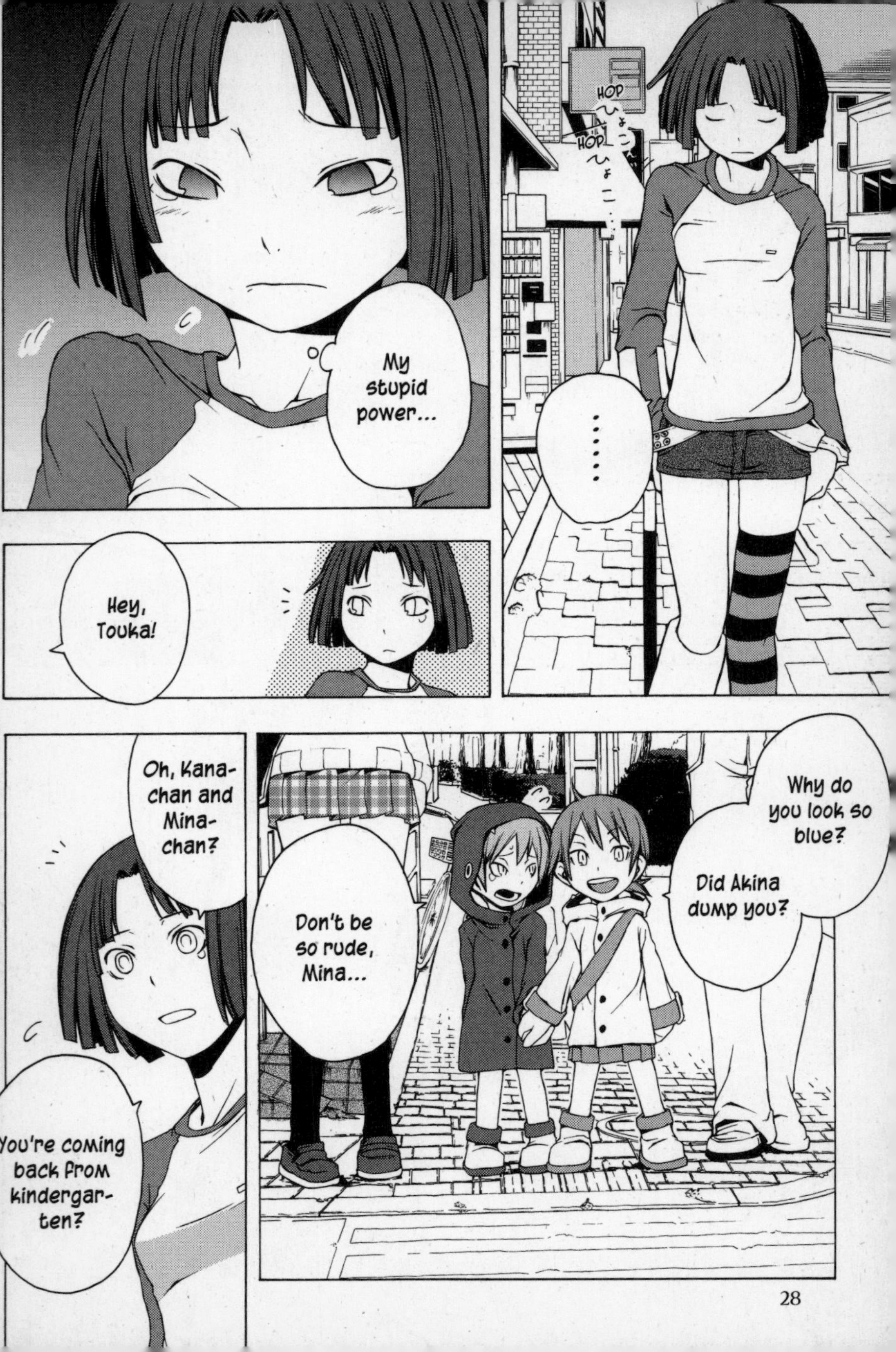
HOP
ひょこ
HOP
ひょこ…
......
My stupid power...
Hey, Touka!
Why do you look so blue?
Did Akina dump you?
Don't be so rude, Mina...
Oh, Kana-chan and Mina-chan?
You're coming back from kindergar-ten?

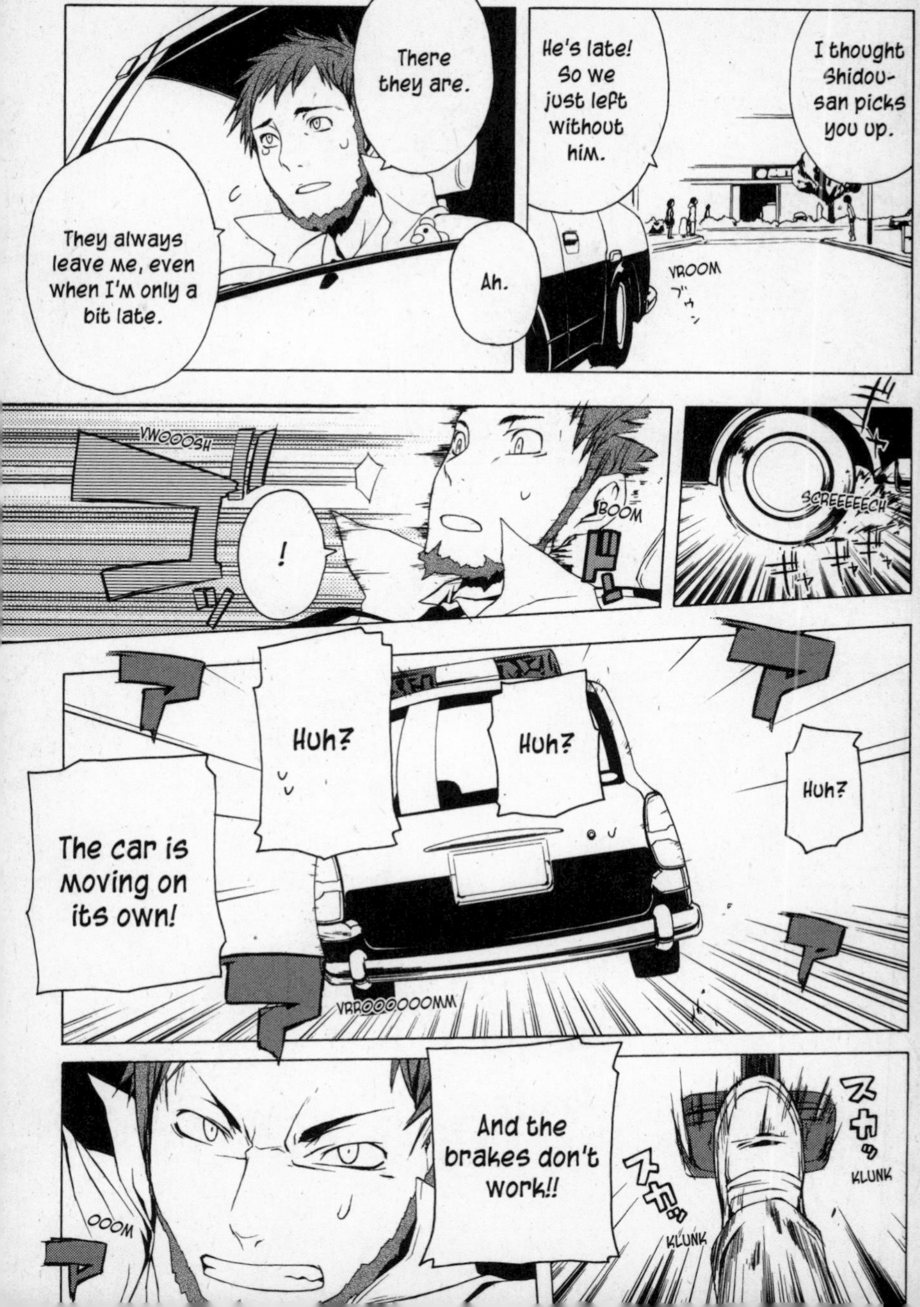
I thought Shidou-san picks you up.
He's late! So we just left without him.
VROOM
ブゥン
There they are.
Ah.
They always leave me, even when I'm only a bit late.
SCREEEEECH
BOOM
!
VWOOOSH
Huh?
Huh?
Huh?
The car is moving on its own!
VRROOOOOOMM
KLUNK
KLUNK
And the brakes don't work!!
OOOM

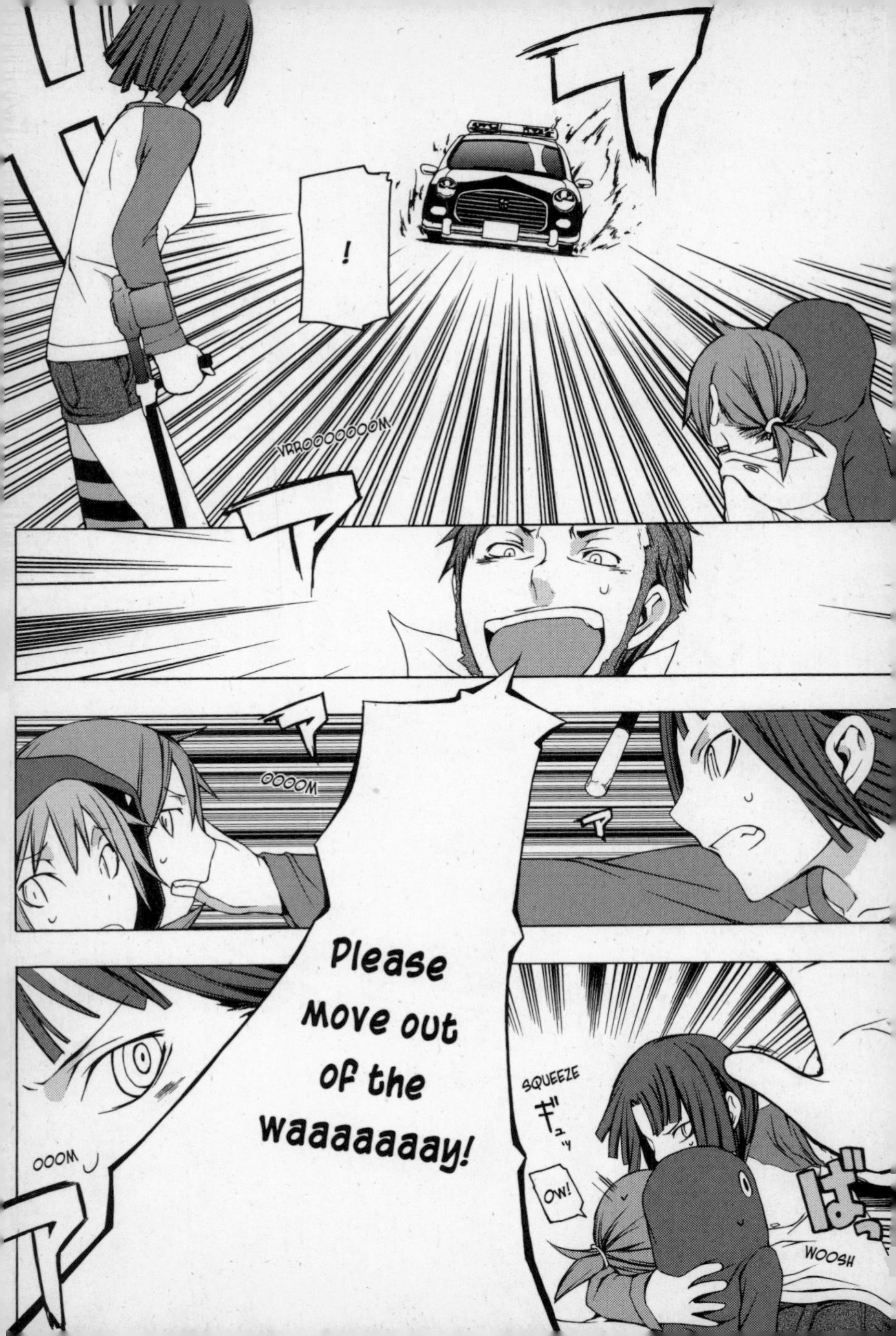
!
VRROOOOOOOOM
Please move out of the waaaaaaaay!
OOOOM
SQUEEZE
ギュッ
OW!
ばっ
WOOSH
OOOM

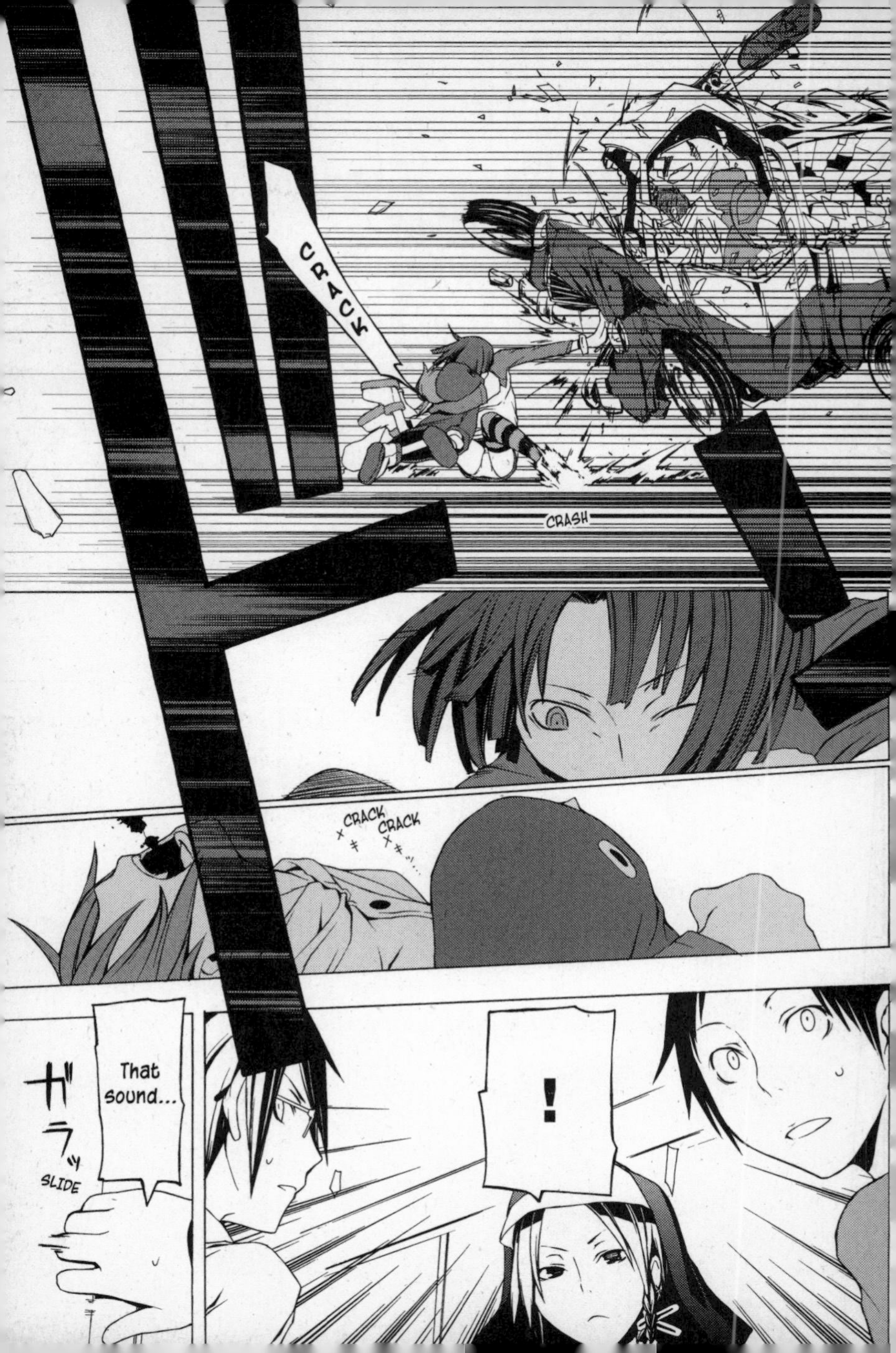
CRACK
CRASH
CRACK CRACK
!
That sound...
ガラッ
SLIDE

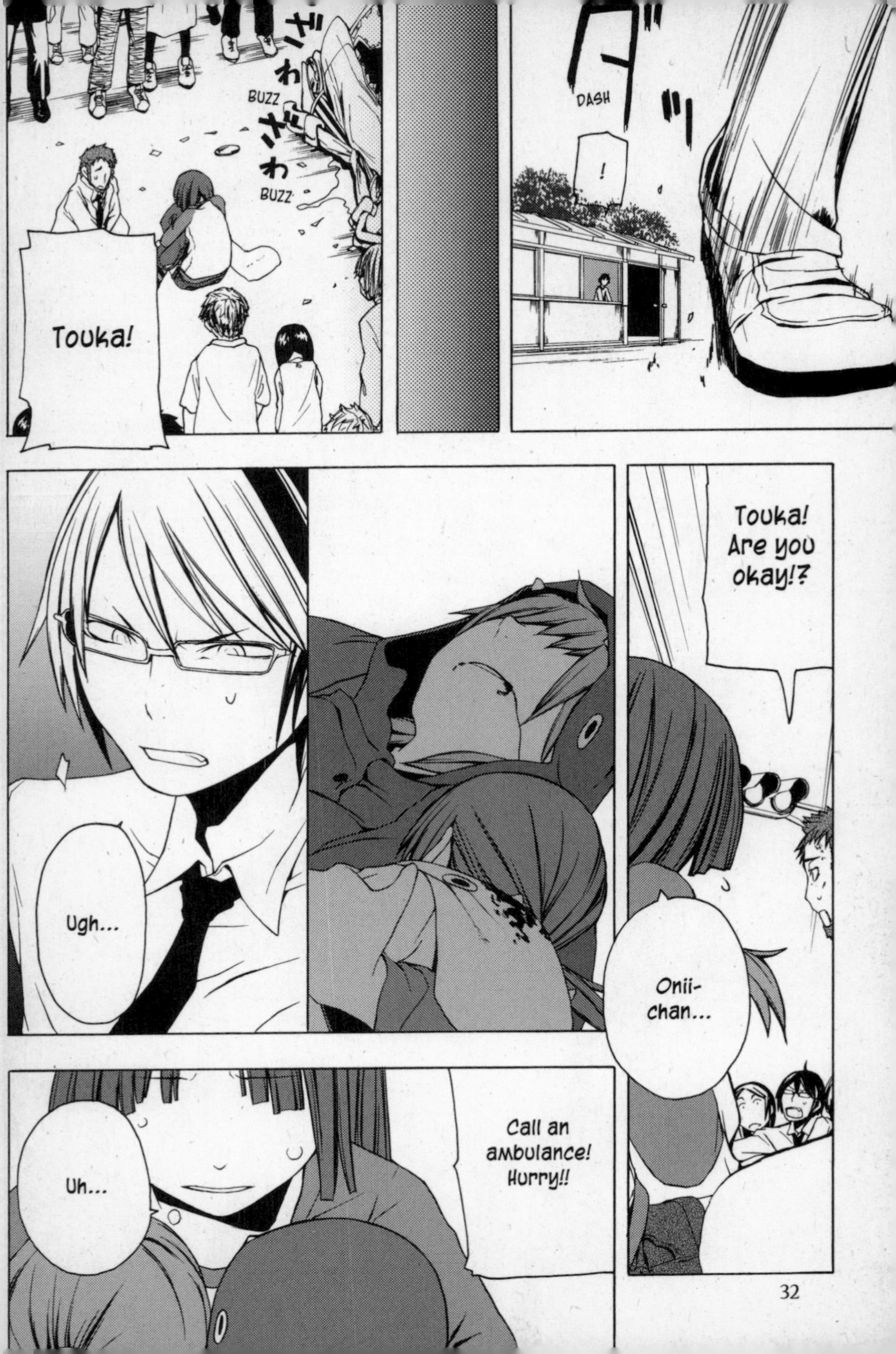
ダッ
DASH
!
ざわ
BUZZ
ざわ
BUZZ
Touka!
Touka! Are you okay!?
Ugh...
Onii-chan...
Call an ambulance! Hurry!!
Uh...

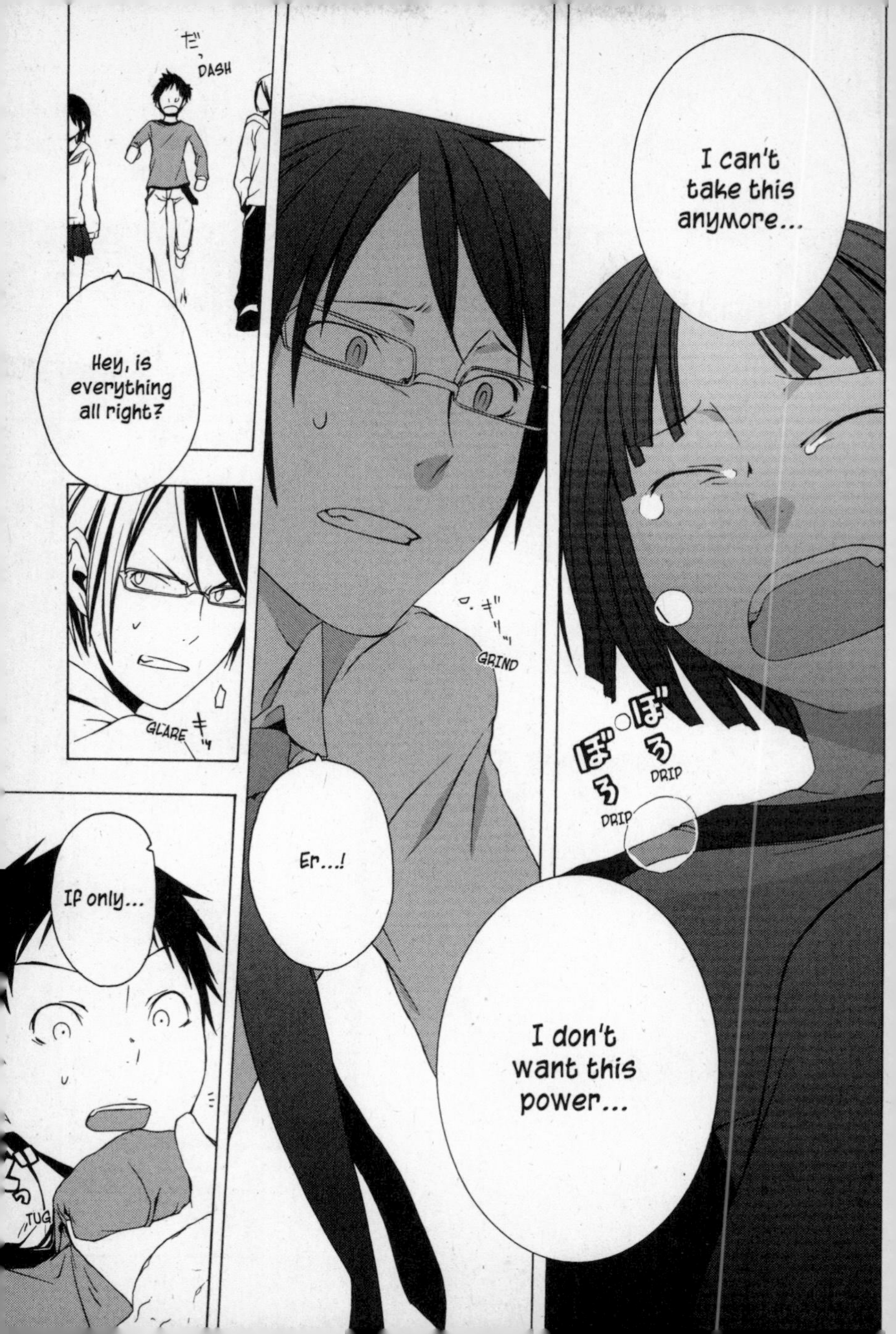

I can't take this anymore...
ぼろ ぼろ
DRIP DRIP
I don't want this power...
GRIND
Er...!
DASH
Hey, is everything all right?
GLARE
If only...
TUG

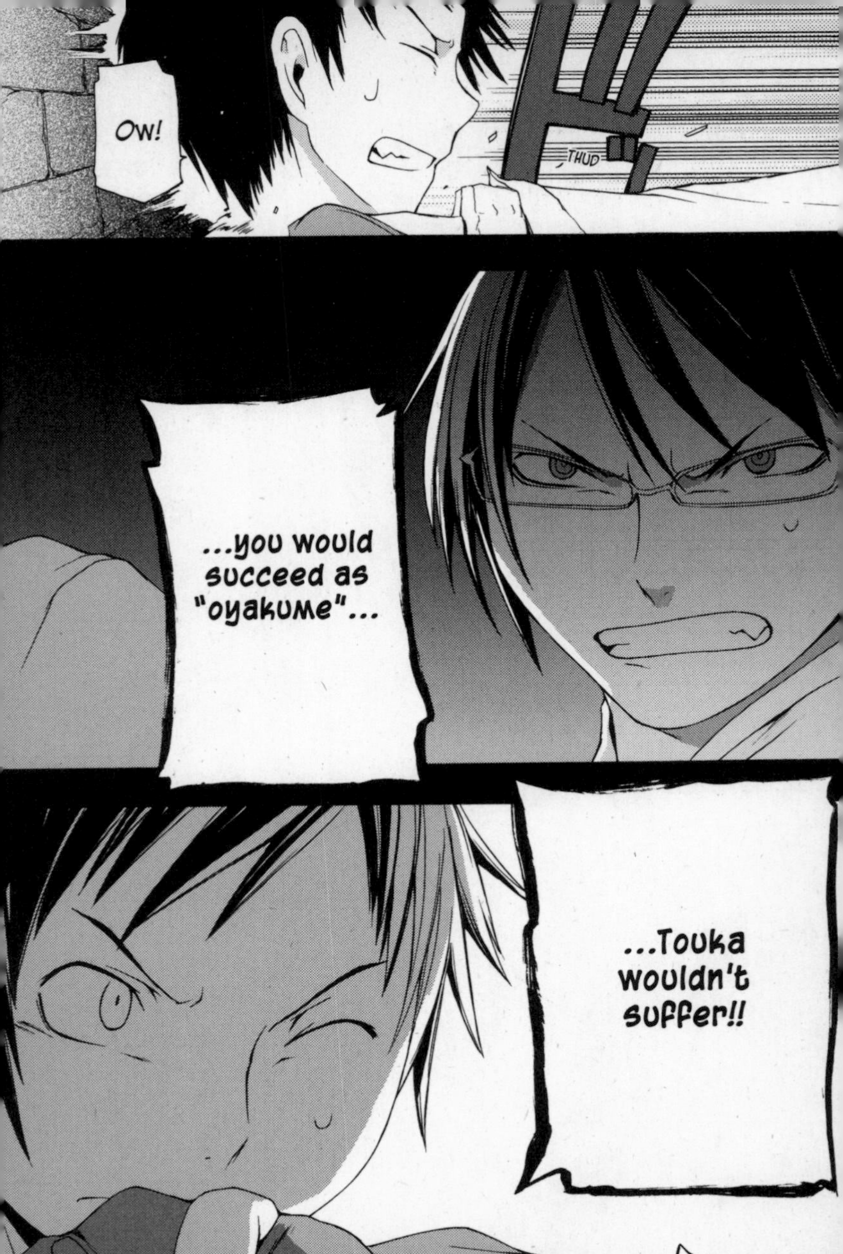
THUD
OW!
...you would succeed as "oyakume"...
...Touka wouldn't suffer!!

Yozakura Quartet 2

Primary Stages of Yozakura Quartet 2

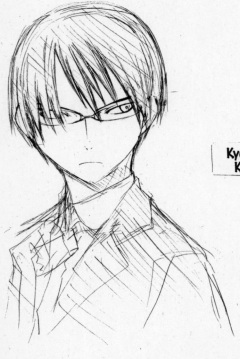

Kyosuke Kishi

Age: 18

Hobbies:
reading

Favorites

Food:
beef bowl

Music Group:
Eldar Djangirov

Comedian:
Chidori

Uchi-P Member:
Fukawa

Little-Known Fact:
He is from Okayama.

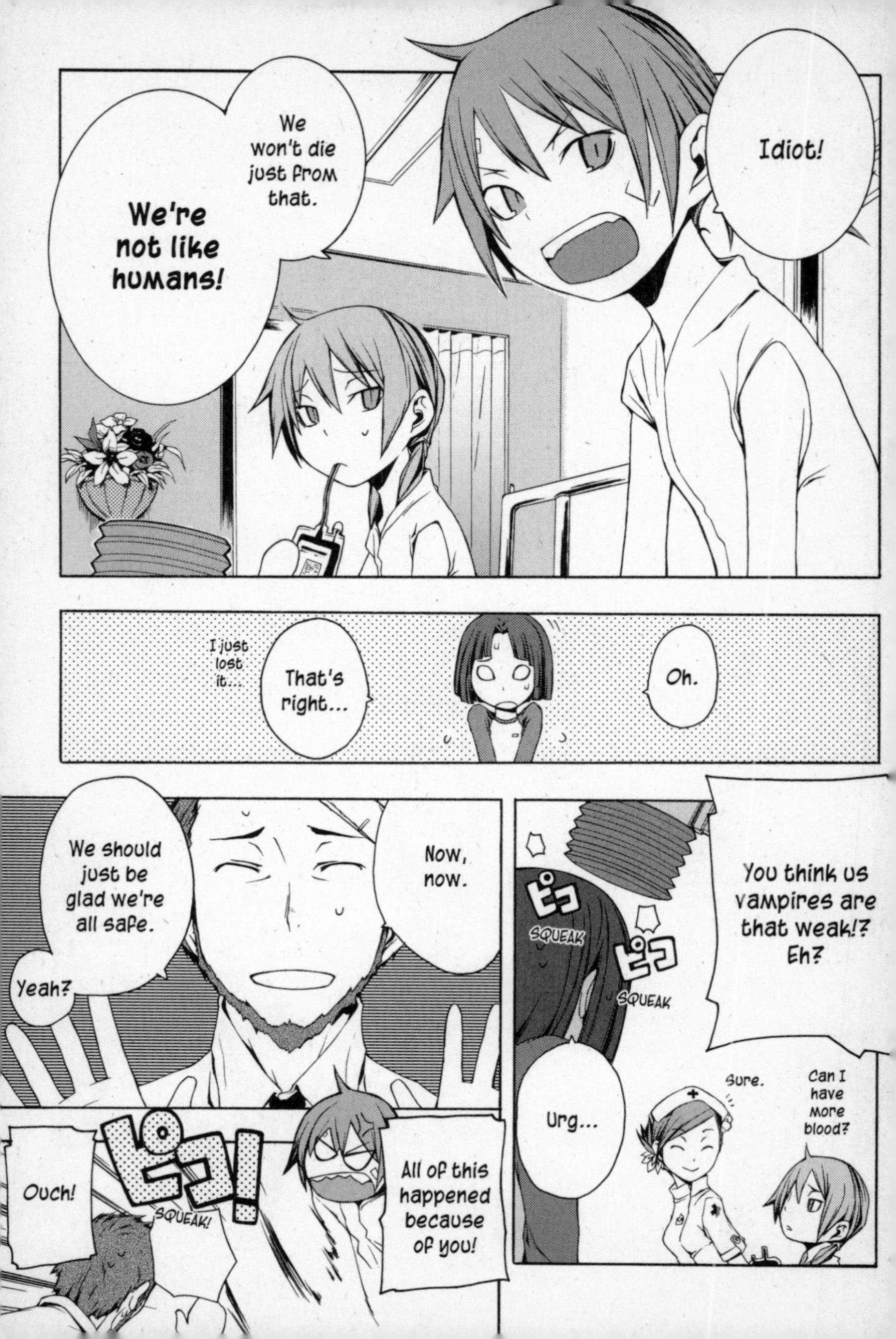
Idiot!
We won't die just from that.
We're not like humans!
Oh.
That's right...
I just lost it...
You think us vampires are that weak!? Eh?
SQUEAK
SQUEAK
Urg...
Can I have more blood?
Sure.
Now, now.
We should just be glad we're all safe.
Yeah?
All of this happened because of you!
SQUEAK!
Ouch!

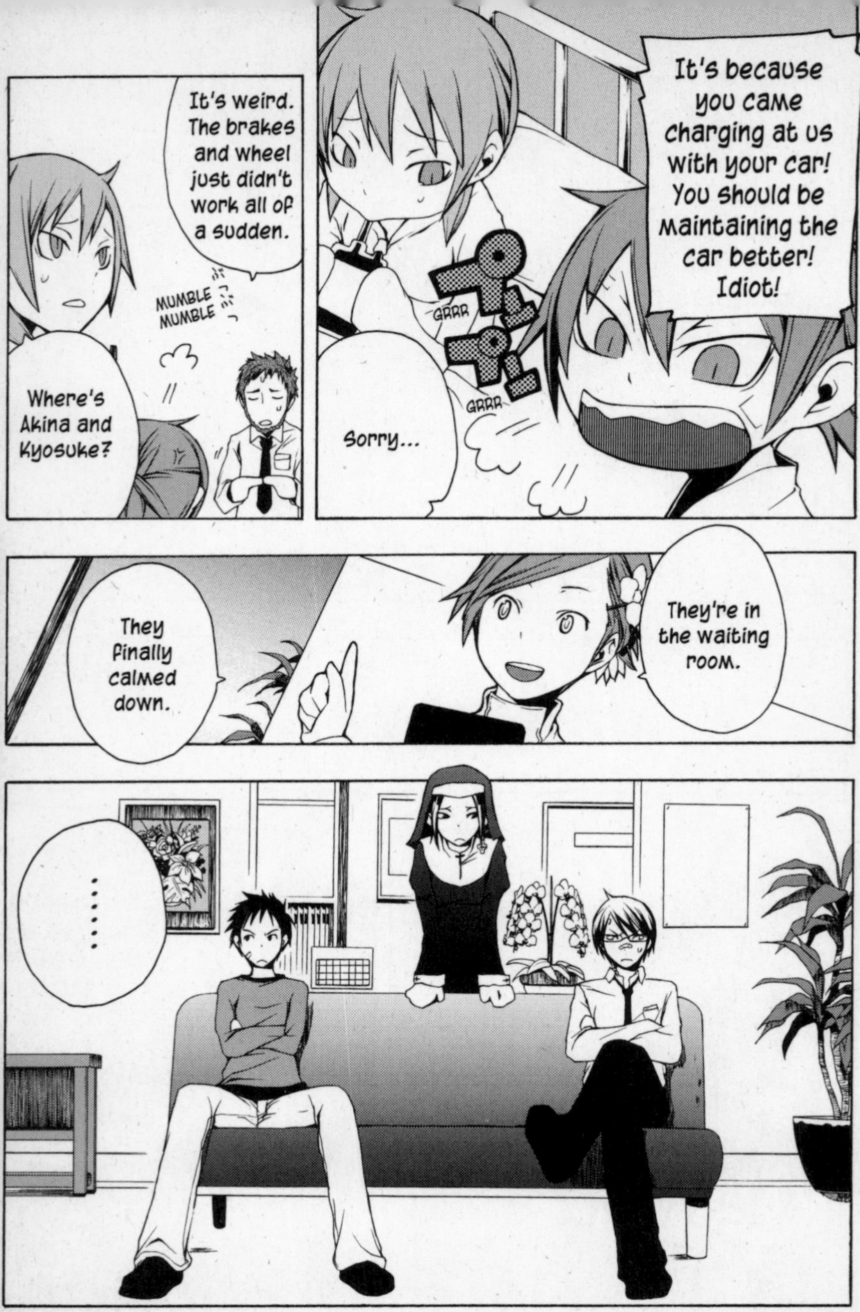
It's because you came charging at us with your car! You should be maintaining the car better! Idiot!
GRRR
GRRR
Sorry...
It's weird. The brakes and wheel just didn't work all of a sudden.
MUMBLE MUMBLE
Where's Akina and Kyosuke?
They're in the waiting room.
They finally calmed down.
......

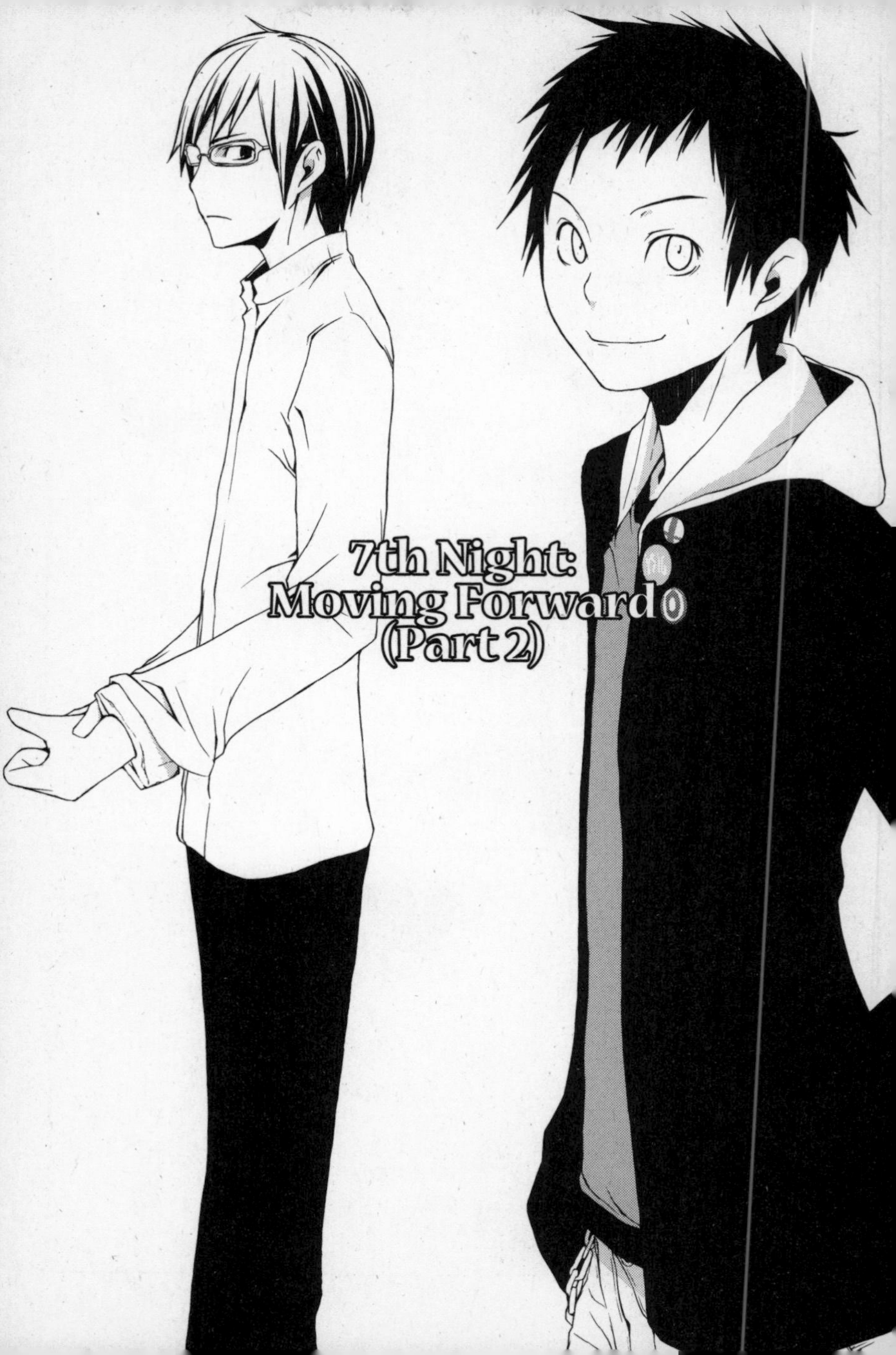
7th Night:
Moving Forward
(Part 2)

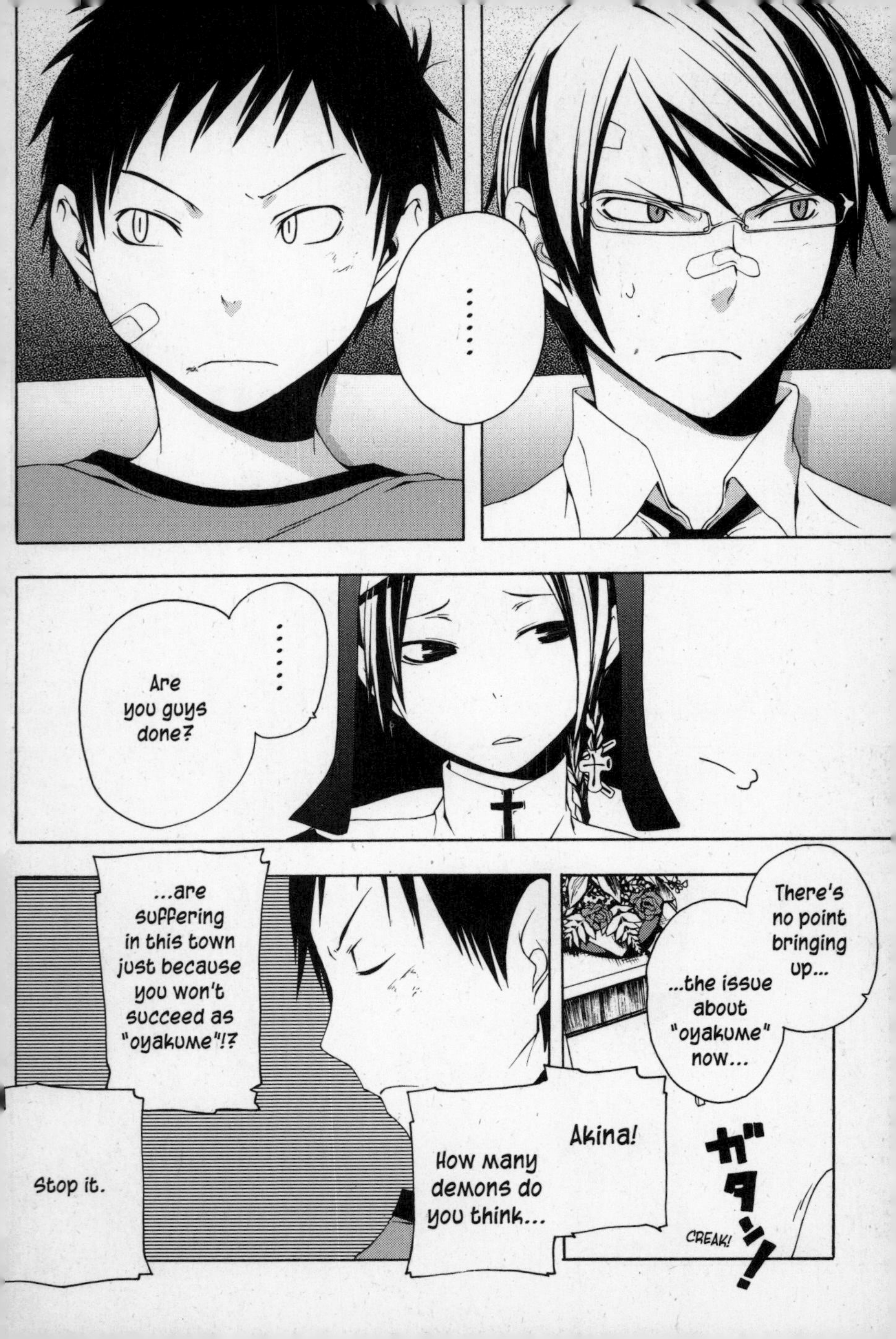
......
......
Are you guys done?
There's no point bringing up...
...the issue about "oyakume" now...
ガタン
CREAK!
Akina!
How many demons do you think...
...are suffering in this town just because you won't succeed as "oyakume"!?
Stop it.

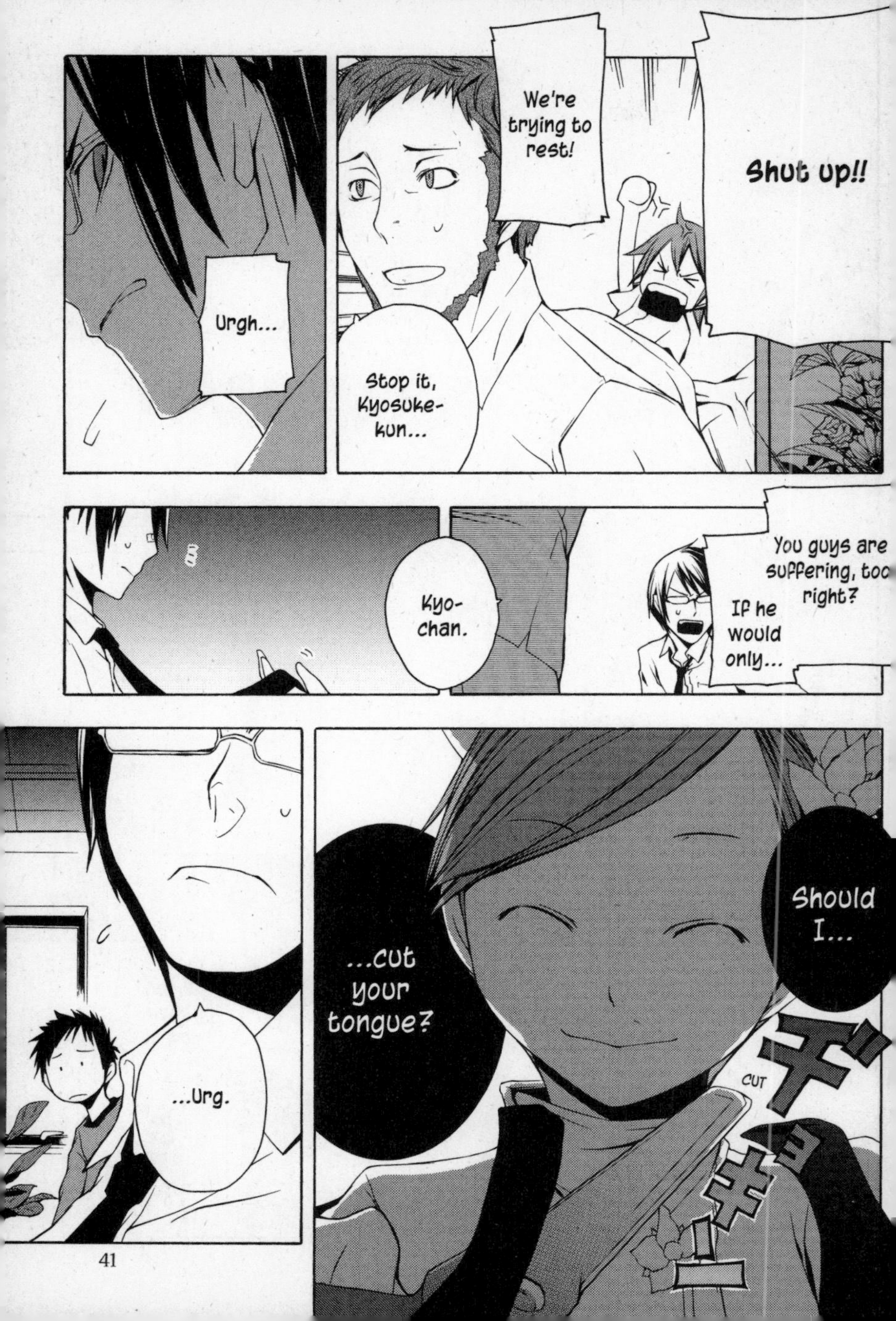
Shut up!!
We're trying to rest!
Stop it, Kyosuke-kun...
Urgh...
You guys are suffering, too right?
If he would only...
Kyo-chan.
Should I...
...cut your tongue?
CUT
...Urg.

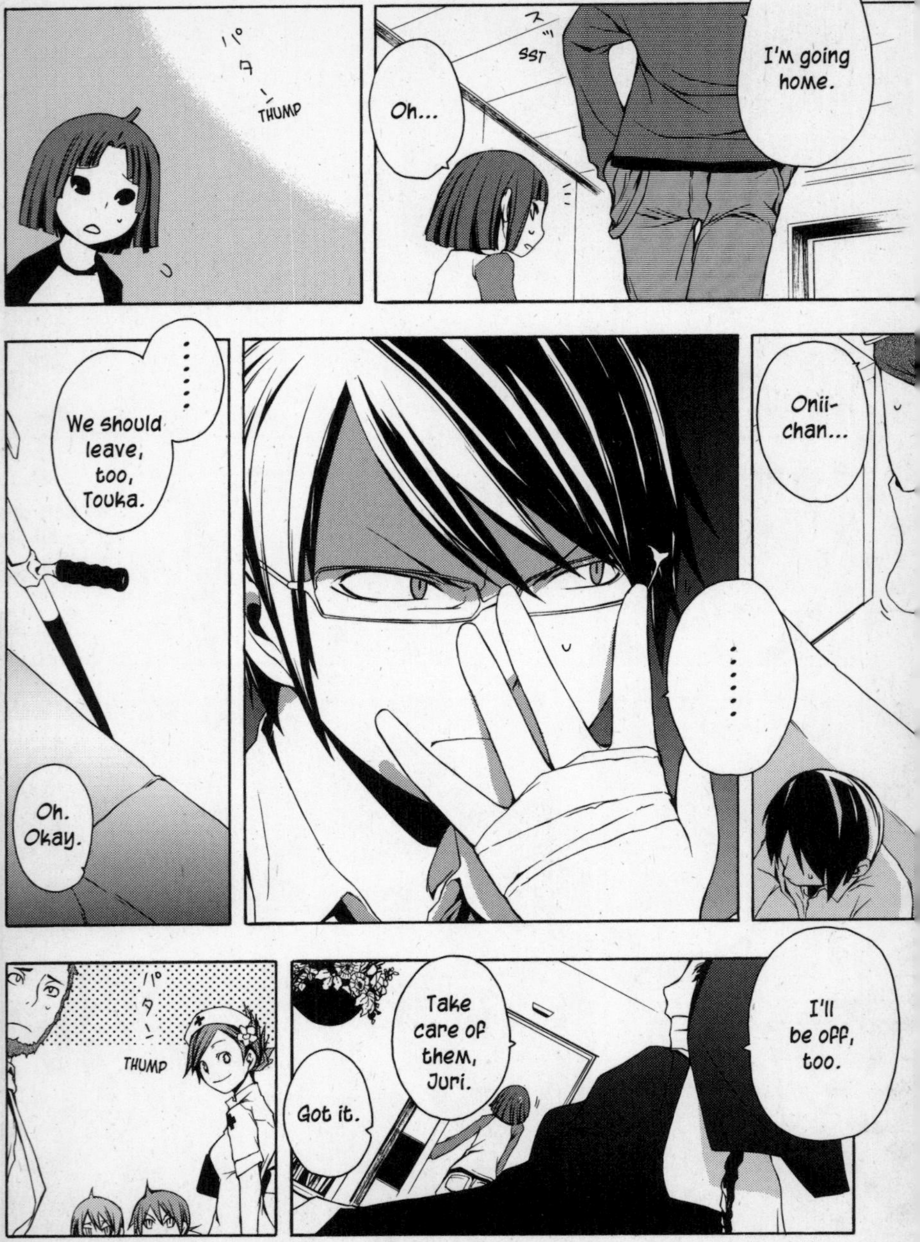

I'm going home.
SST
Oh...
THUMP
Onii-chan...
......
...... We should leave, too, Touka.
Oh. Okay.
I'll be off, too.
Take care of them, Juri.
Got it.
THUMP

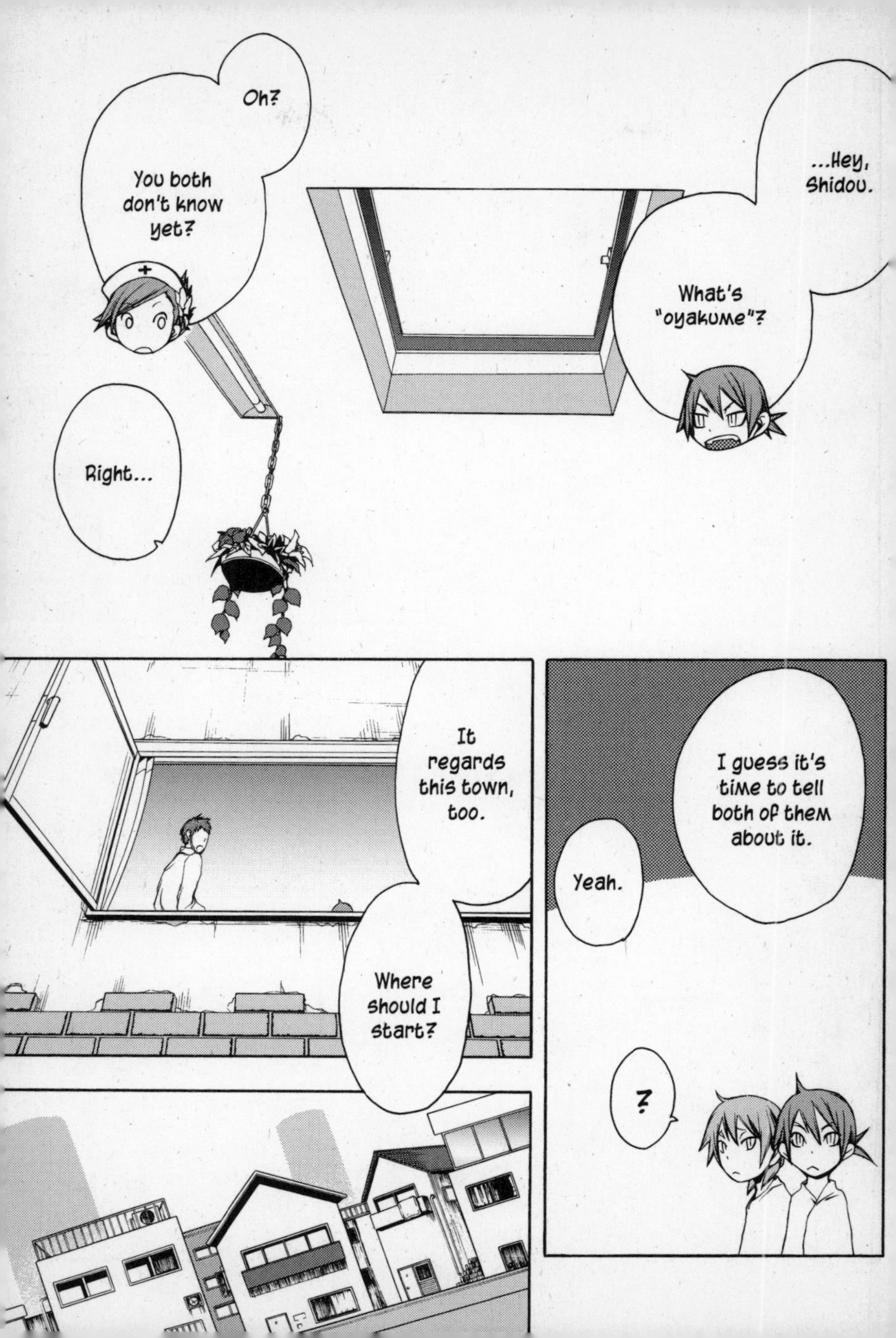
...Hey, Shidou.
What's "oyakume"?
Oh?
You both don't know yet?
Right...
I guess it's time to tell both of them about it.
Yeah.
?
It regards this town, too.
Where should I start?

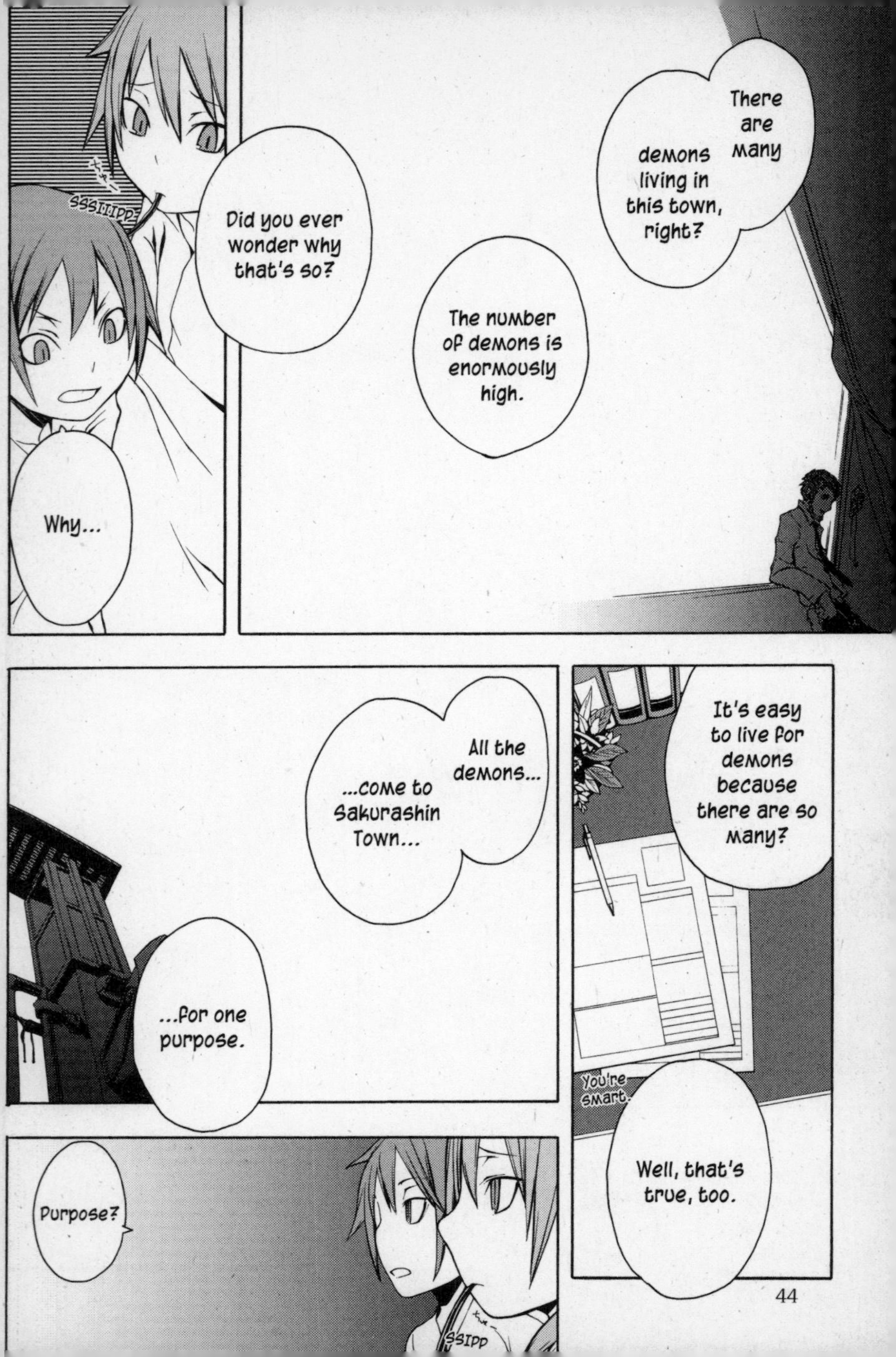
There are many demons living in this town, right?
The number of demons is enormously high.
Did you ever wonder why that's so?
SSSIIIPP
Why...
It's easy to live for demons because there are so many?
You're smart.
Well, that's true, too.
All the demons...
...come to Sakurashin Town...
...for one purpose.
Purpose?
SSIPP

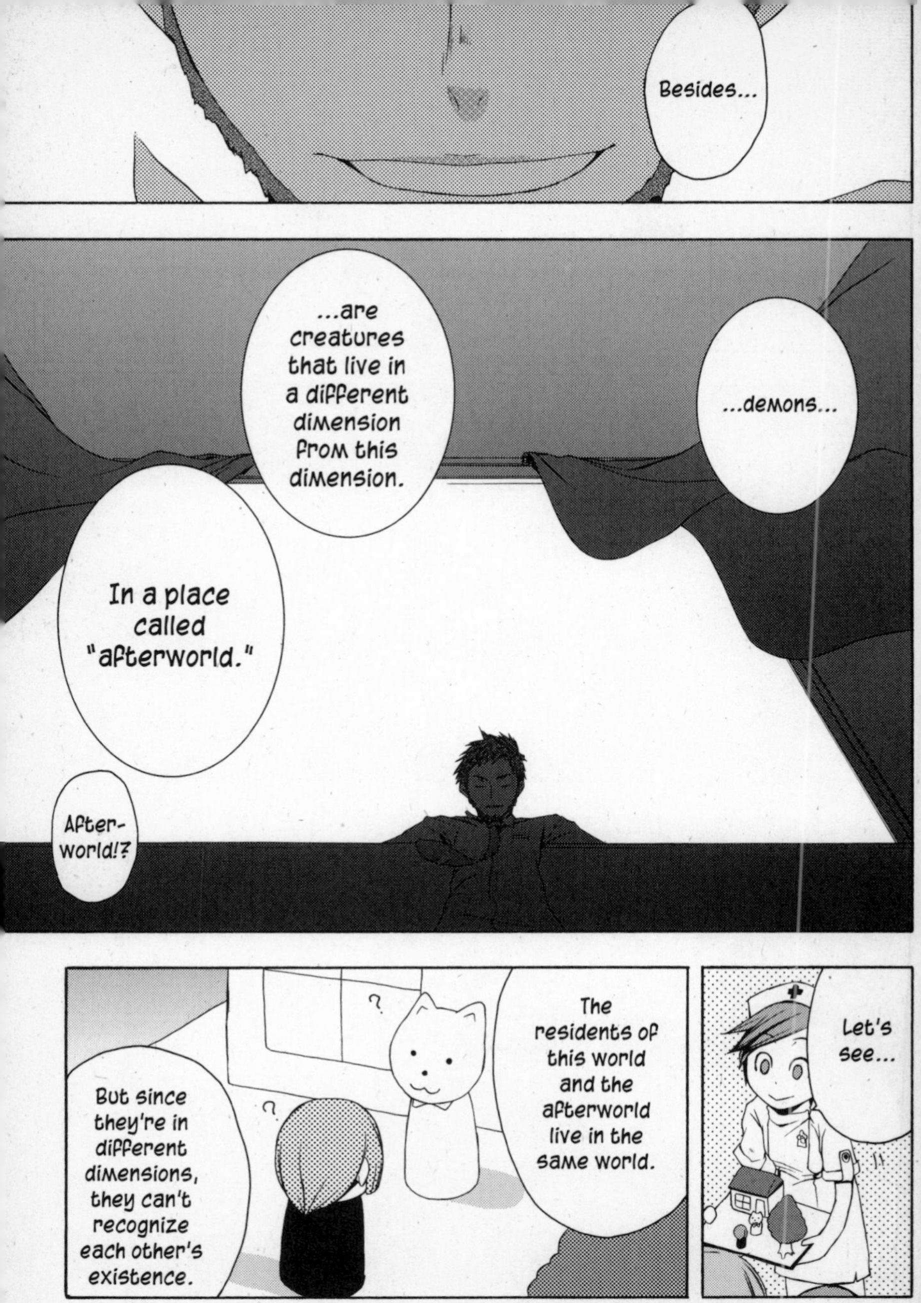
Besides...
...demons...
...are creatures that live in a different dimension from this dimension.
In a place called "afterworld."
After-world!?
Let's see...
The residents of this world and the afterworld live in the same world.
But since they're in different dimensions, they can't recognize each other's existence.

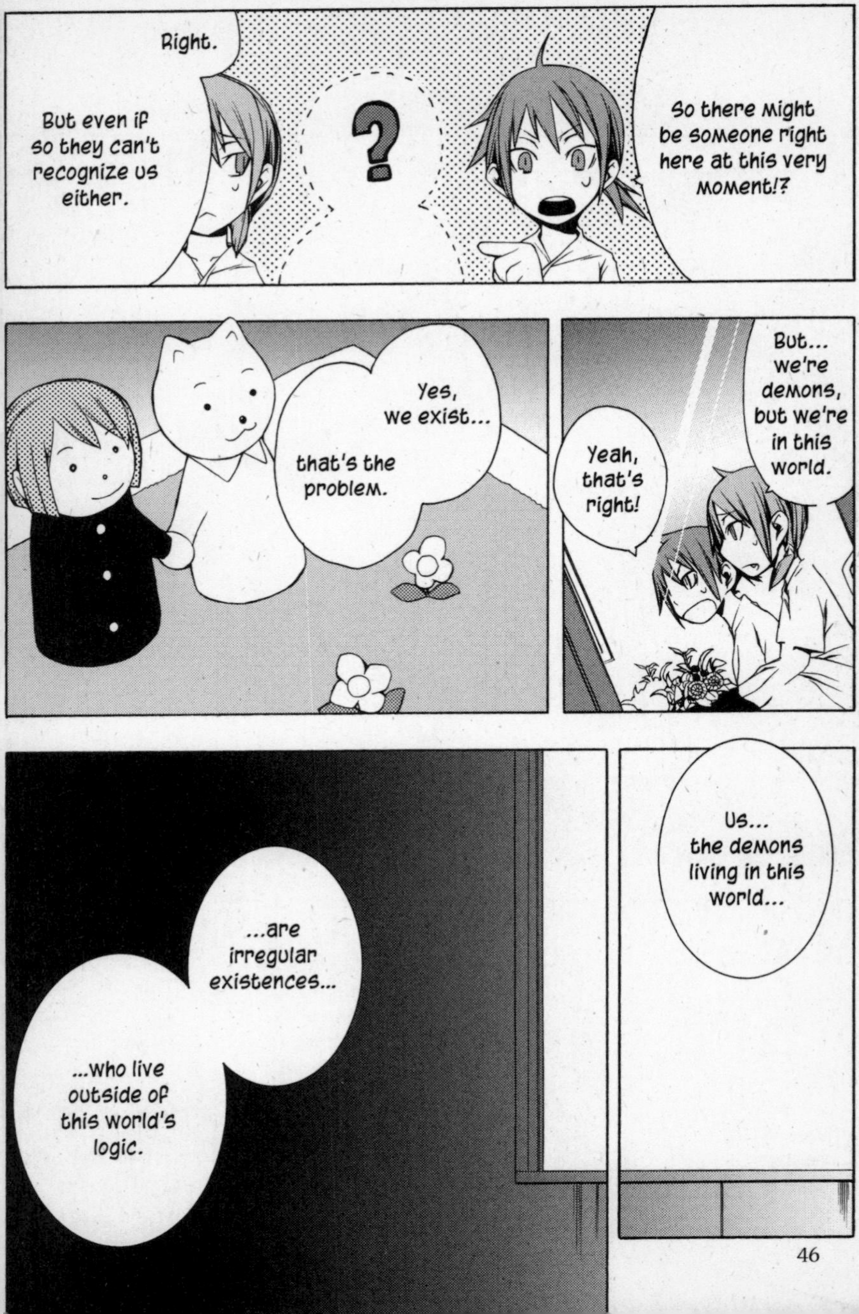
So there might be someone right here at this very moment!?
?
Right.
But even if so they can't recognize us either.
But... we're demons, but we're in this world.
Yeah, that's right!
Yes, we exist...
that's the problem.
Us... the demons living in this world...
...are irregular existences...
...who live outside of this world's logic.

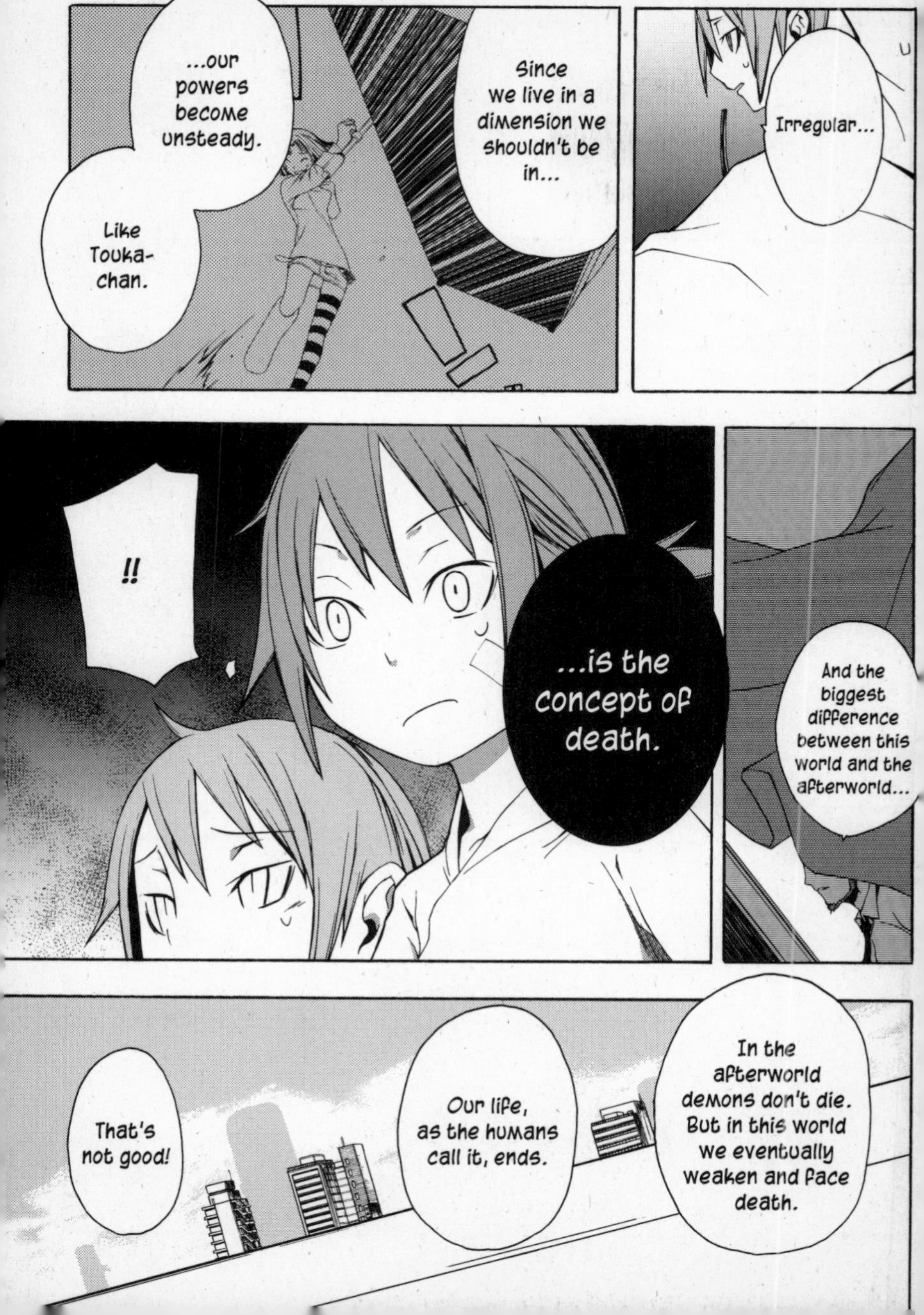
Irregular...
Since we live in a dimension we shouldn't be in...
...our powers become unsteady.
Like Touka-chan.
And the biggest difference between this world and the afterworld...
...is the concept of death.
!!
In the afterworld demons don't die. But in this world we eventually weaken and face death.
Our life, as the humans call it, ends.
That's not good!

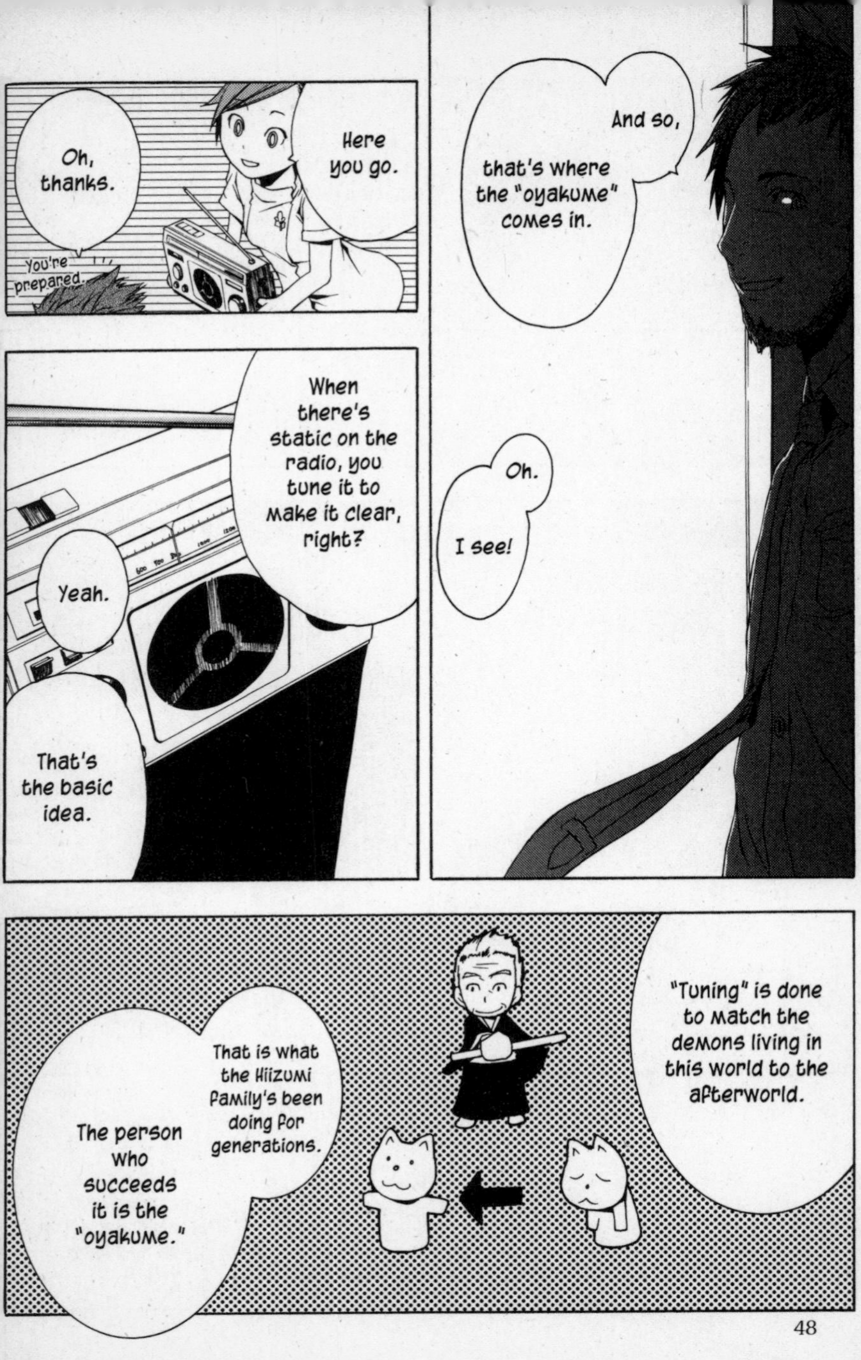
And so,
that's where the "oyakume" comes in.
Oh.
I see!
Here you go.
Oh, thanks.
You're prepared.
When there's static on the radio, you tune it to make it clear, right?
Yeah.
That's the basic idea.
"Tuning" is done to match the demons living in this world to the afterworld.
That is what the Hiizumi family's been doing for generations.
The person who succeeds it is the "oyakume."

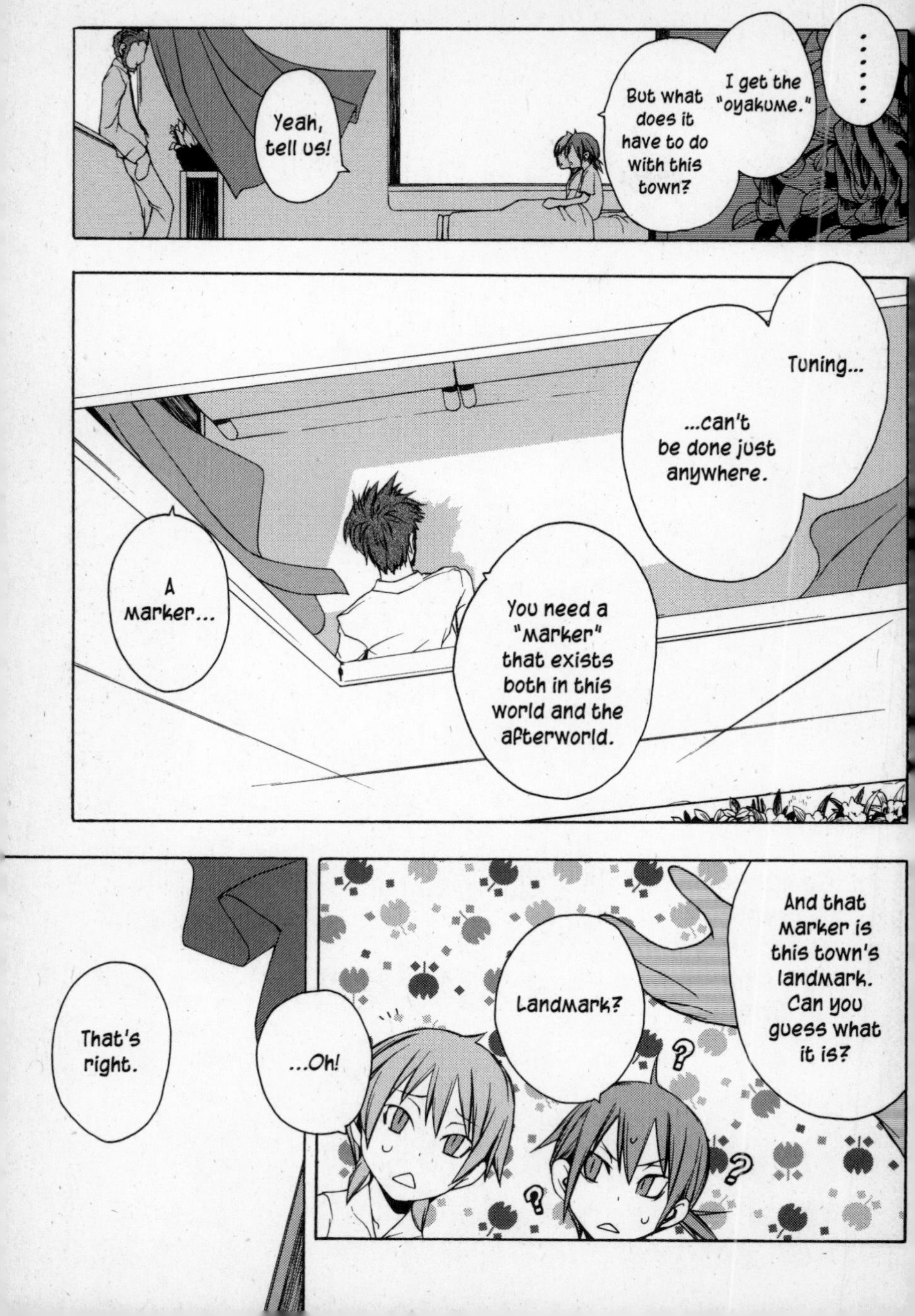
......
I get the "oyakume."
But what does it have to do with this town?
Yeah, tell us!
Tuning...
...can't be done just anywhere.
You need a "marker" that exists both in this world and the afterworld.
A marker...
And that marker is this town's landmark. Can you guess what it is?
Landmark?
...Oh!
That's right.

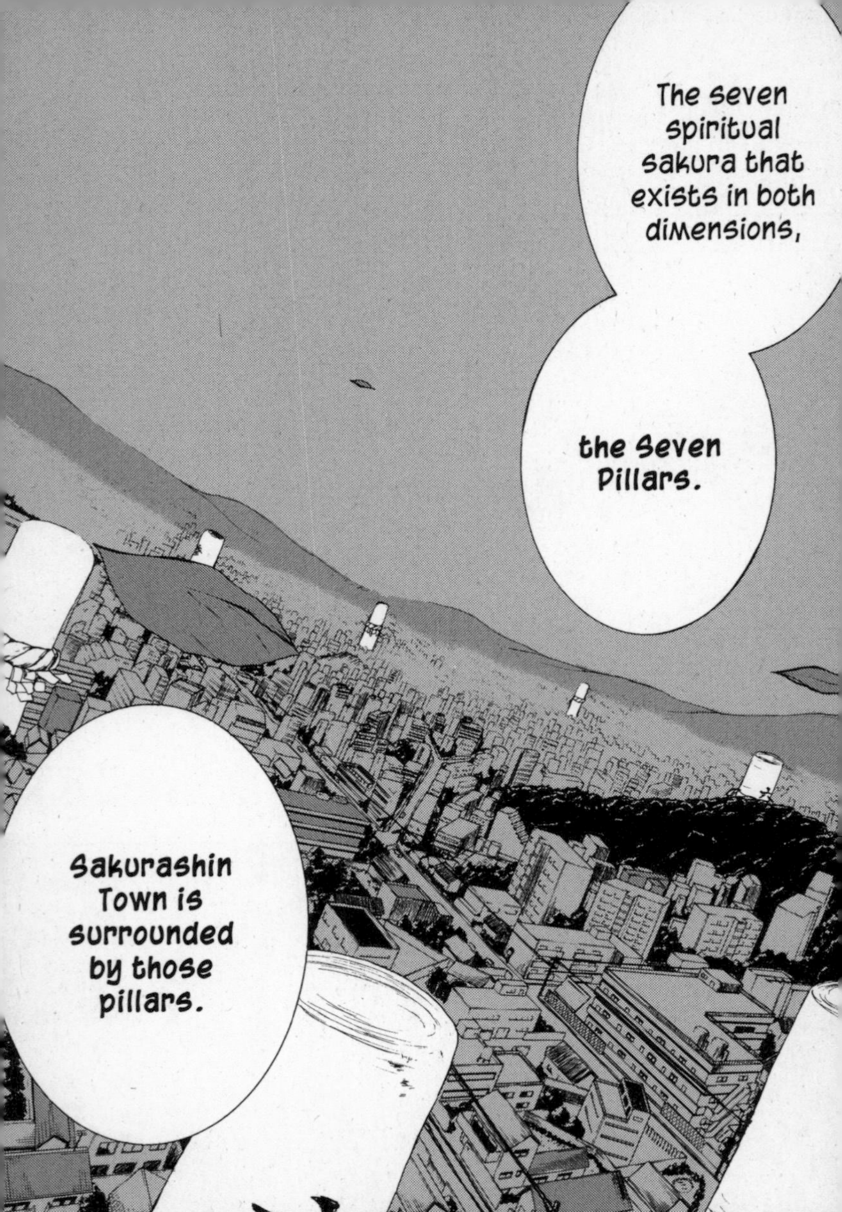
The seven spiritual sakura that exists in both dimensions,
the Seven Pillars.
Sakurashin Town is surrounded by those pillars.

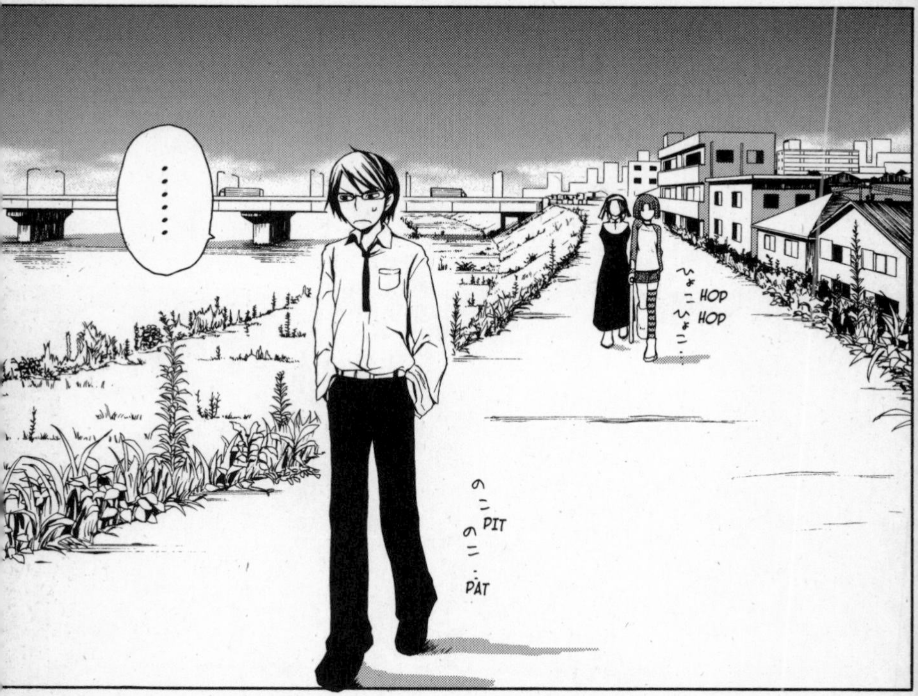
......
ひょこ ひょこ…
HOP HOP
のこ のこ…
PIT PAT

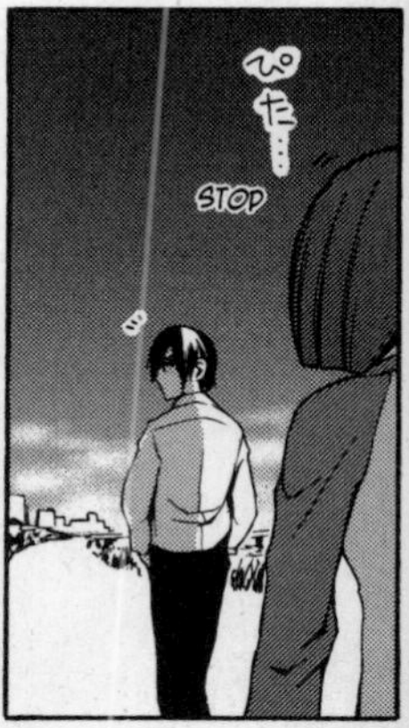
ぴた…
STOP

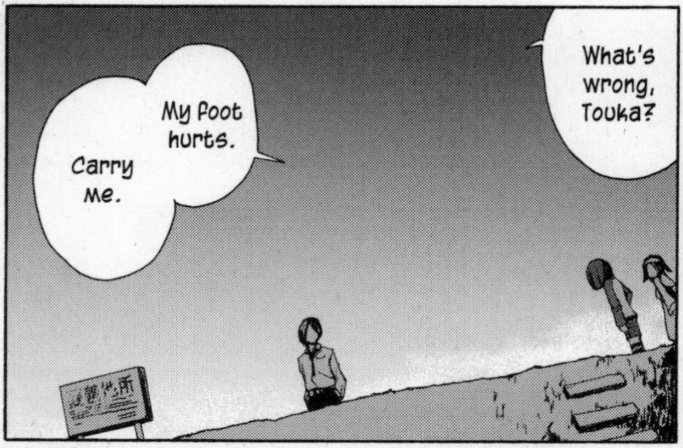
What's wrong, Touka?
My foot hurts.
Carry me.

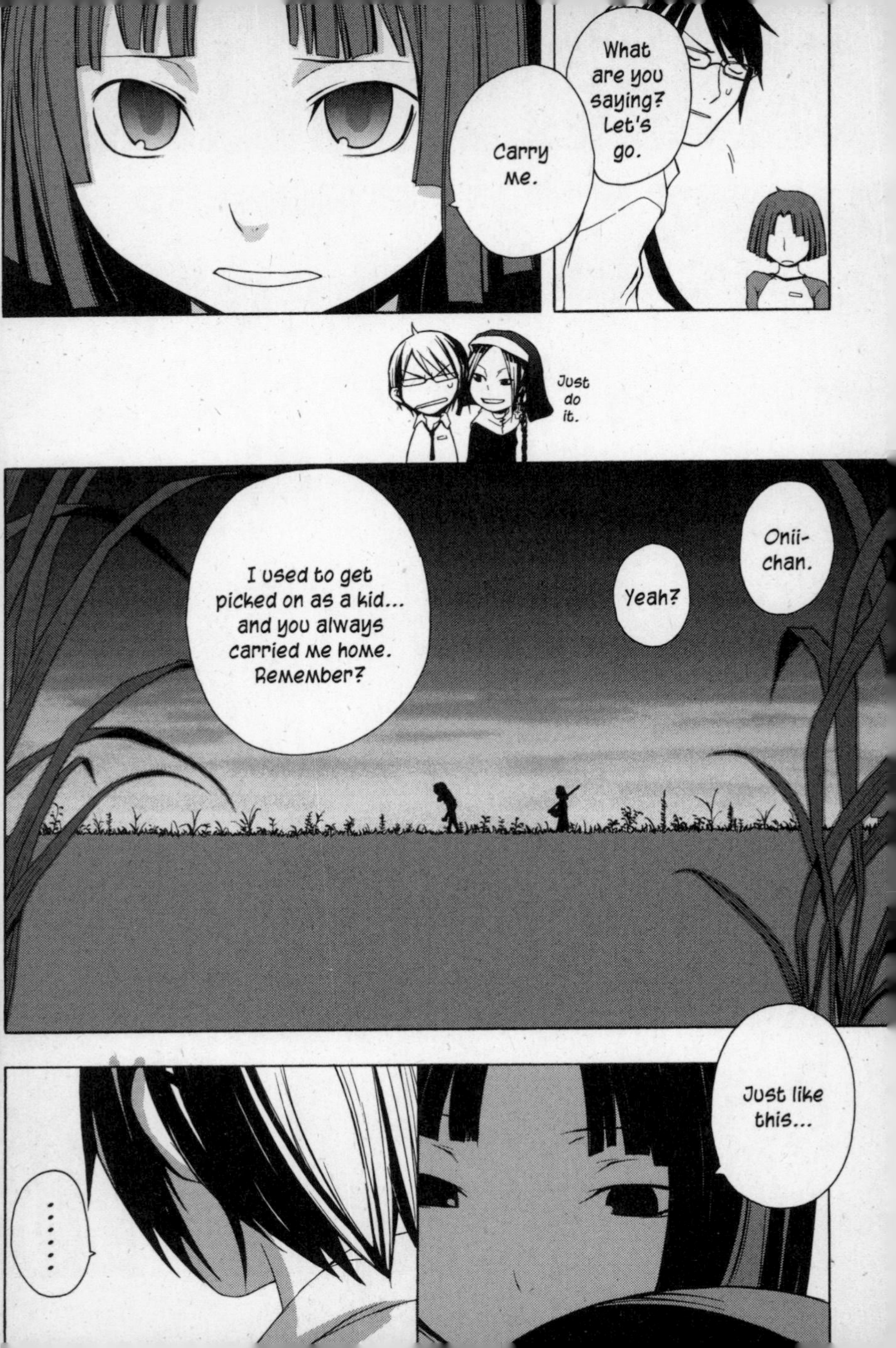
What are you saying? Let's go.
Carry me.
Just do it.
Onii-chan.
Yeah?
I used to get picked on as a kid... and you always carried me home. Remember?
Just like this...
......

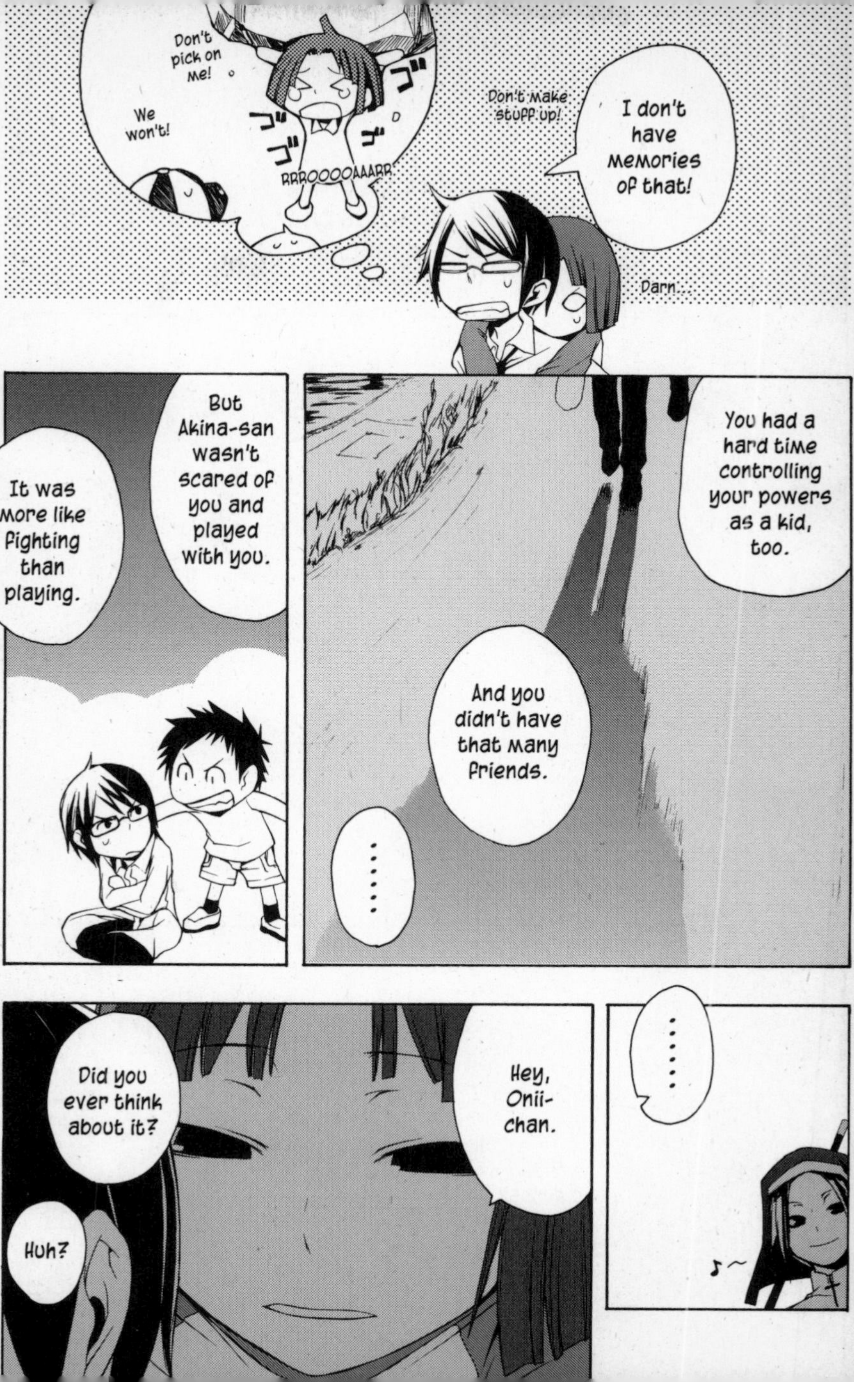
I don't have memories of that!
Don't make stuff up!
Darn...
Don't pick on me!
We won't!
ゴゴゴ
RRROOOOAAARR
You had a hard time controlling your powers as a kid, too.
And you didn't have that many friends.
......
But Akina-san wasn't scared of you and played with you.
It was more like fighting than playing.
......
♪~
Hey, Onii-chan.
Did you ever think about it?
Huh?

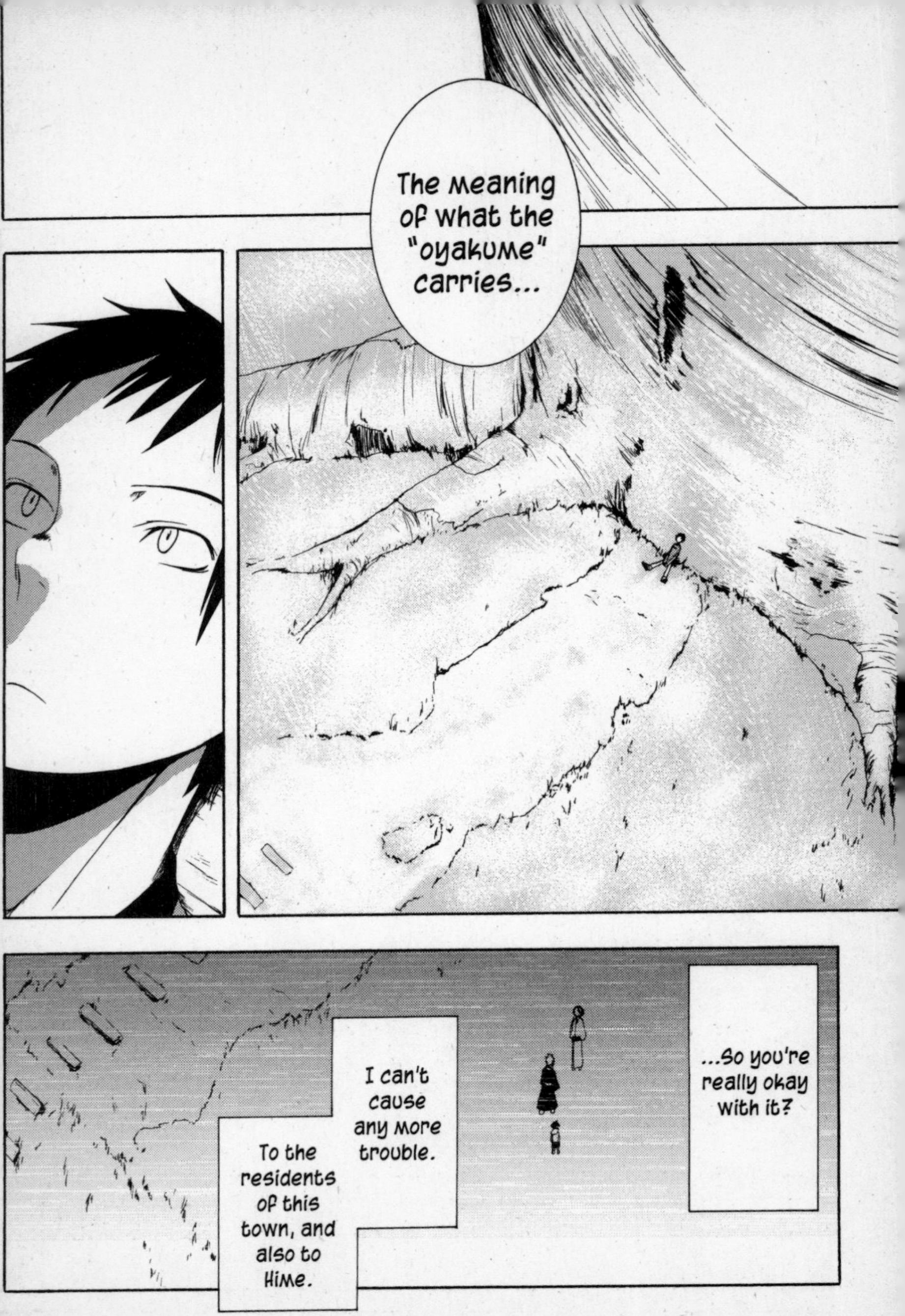
The Meaning of what the "oyakume" carries...
...So you're really okay with it?
I can't cause any more trouble.
To the residents of this town, and also to Hime.

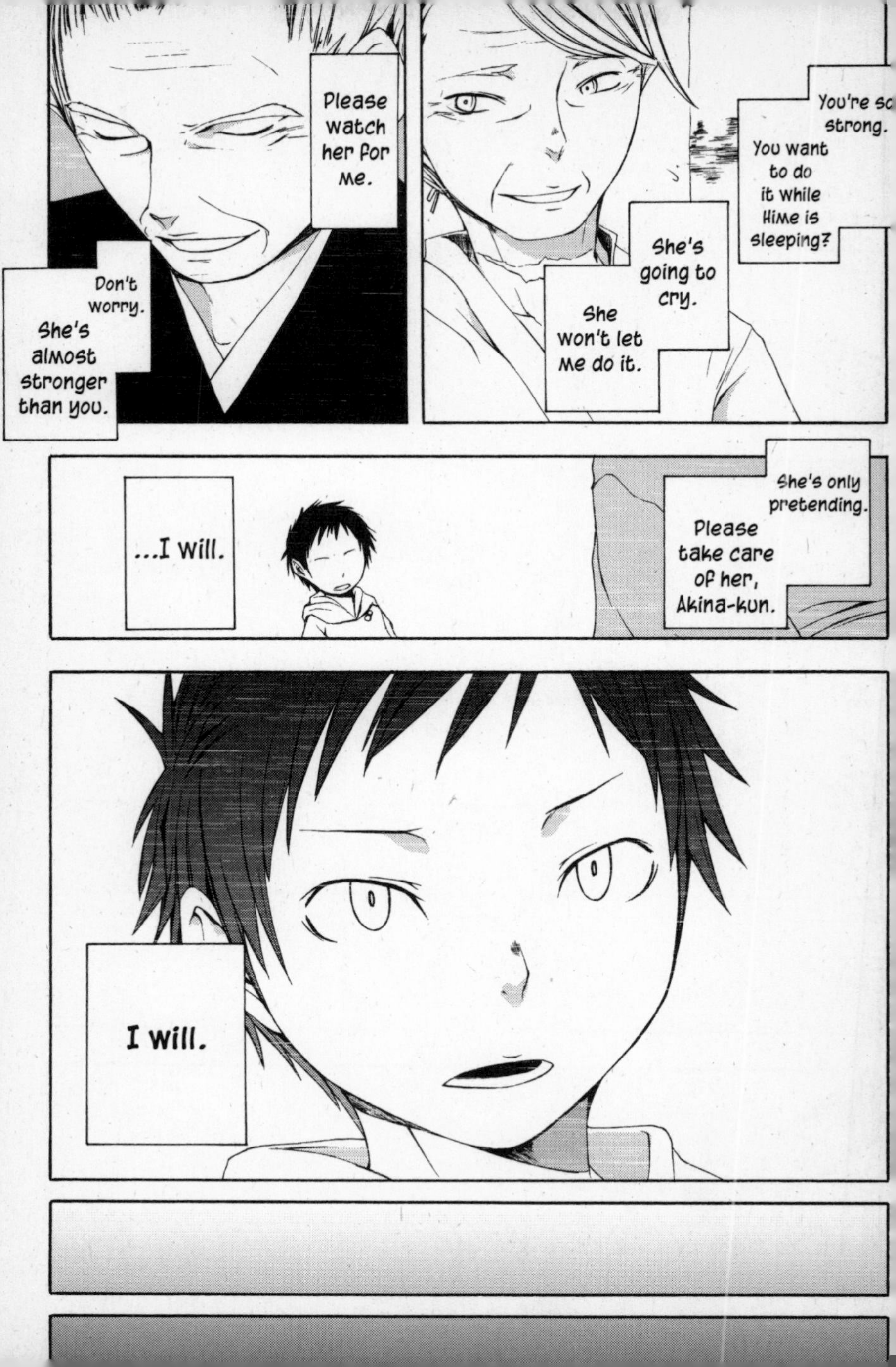
You're so strong.
You want to do it while Hime is sleeping?
She's going to cry.
She won't let me do it.
Please watch her for me.
Don't worry.
She's almost stronger than you.
She's only pretending.
Please take care of her, Akina-kun.
...I will.
I will.

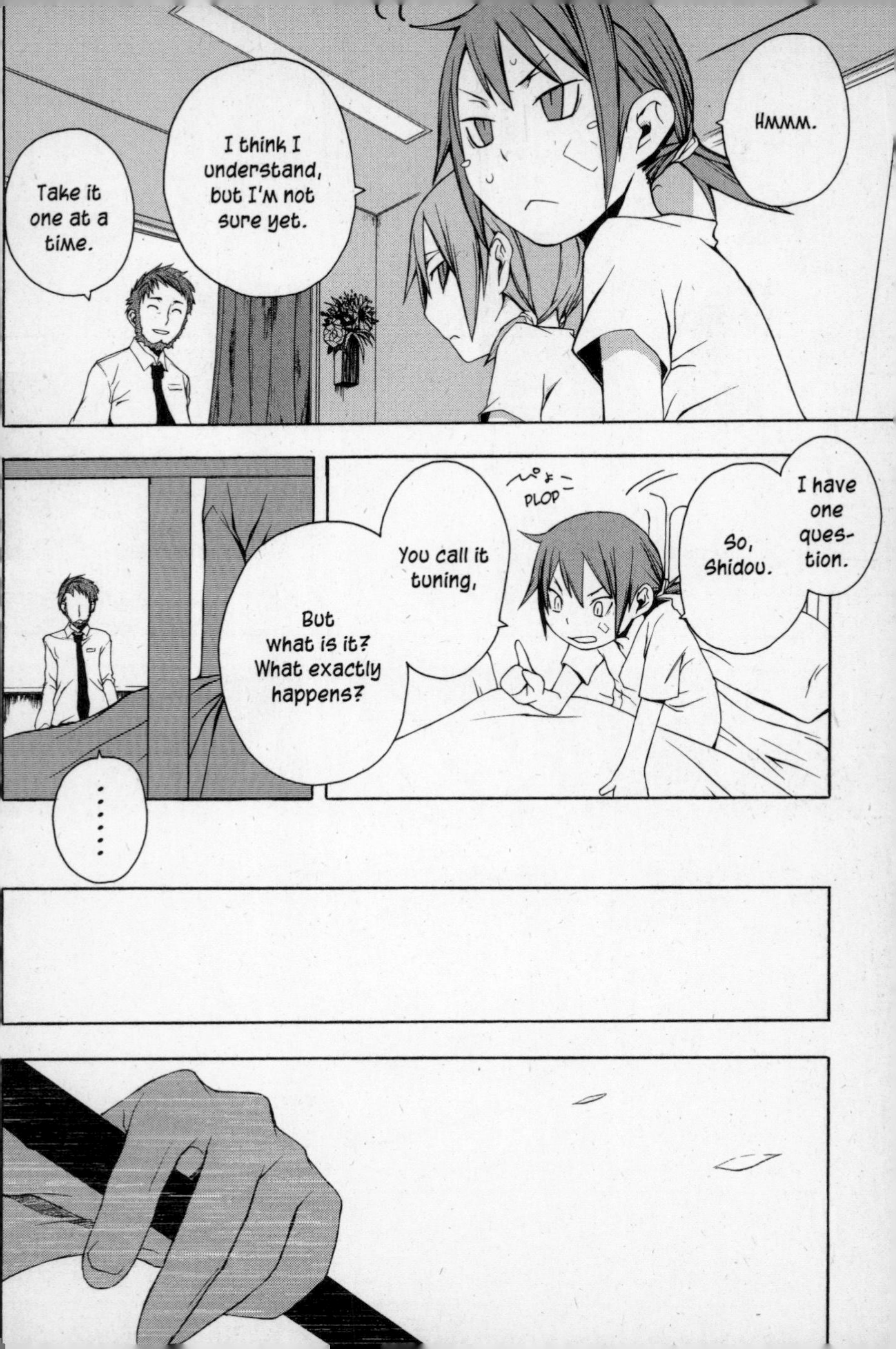
HMMM.
I think I understand, but I'm not sure yet.
Take it one at a time.
I have one ques-tion.
So, Shidou.
PLOP
You call it tuning,
But what is it? What exactly happens?
......

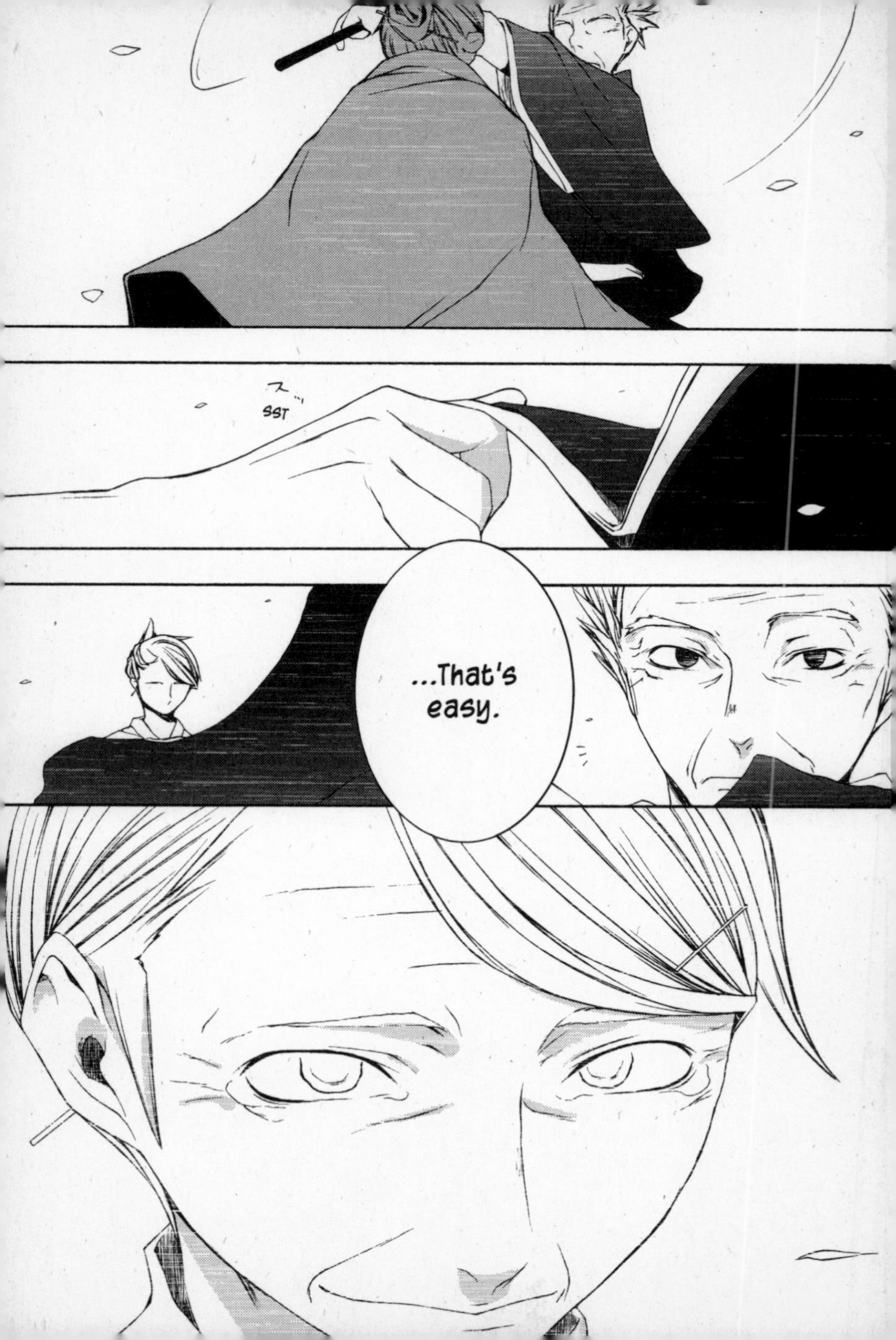

ス…
SST
...That's easy.

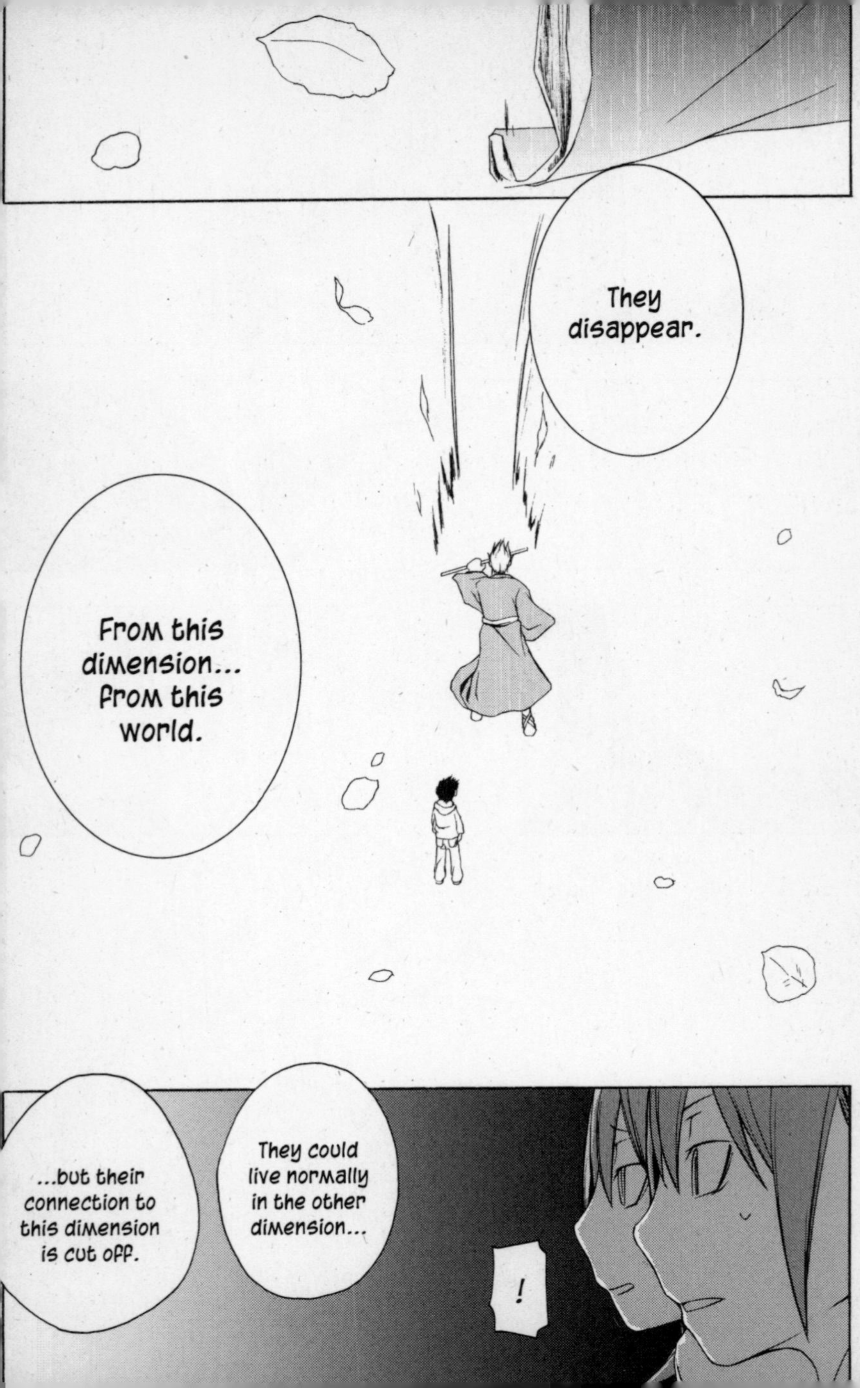
They disappear.
From this dimension... from this world.
They could live normally in the other dimension...
...but their connection to this dimension is cut off.
!

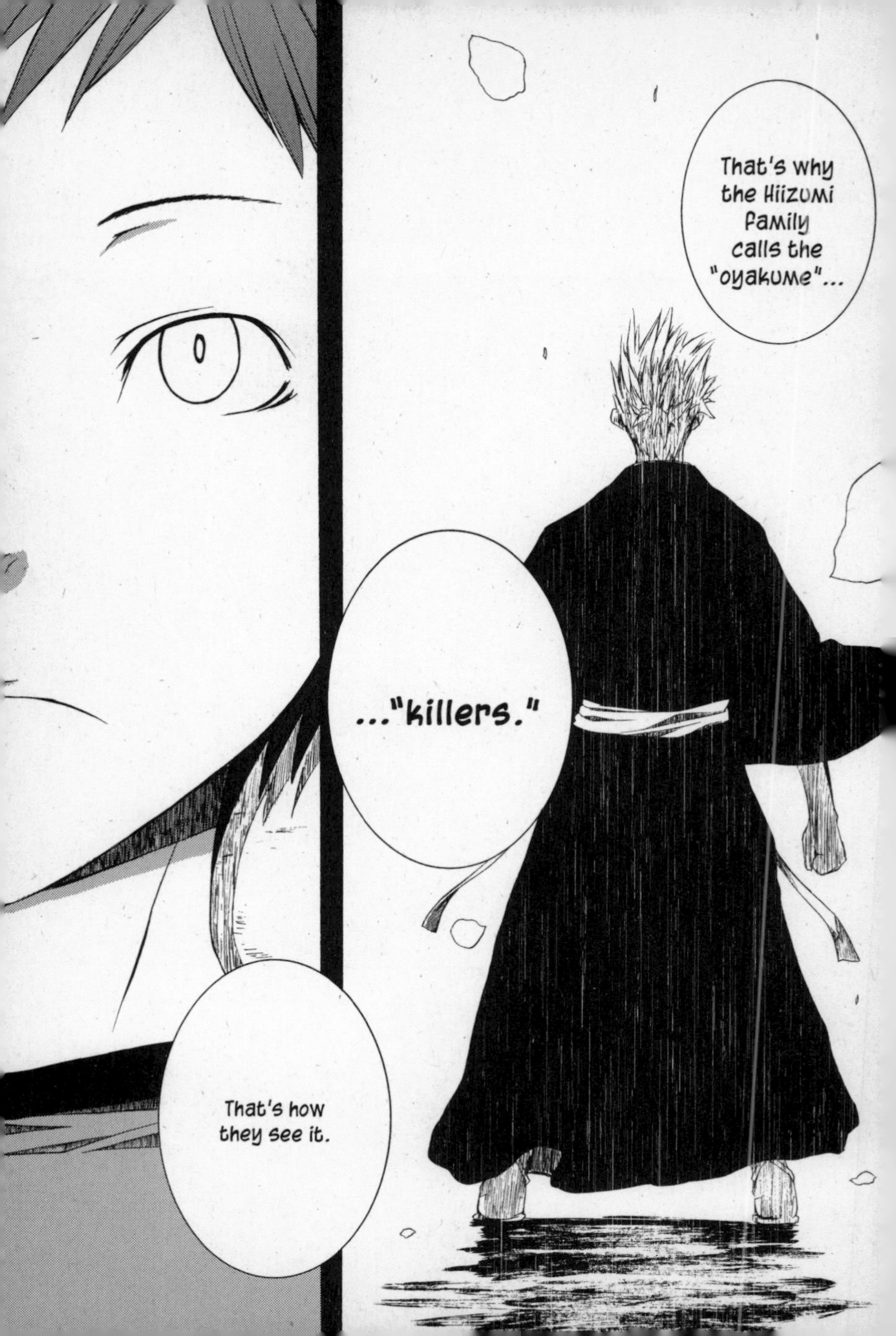
That's why the Hiizumi family calls the "oyakume"...
..."killers."
That's how they see it.

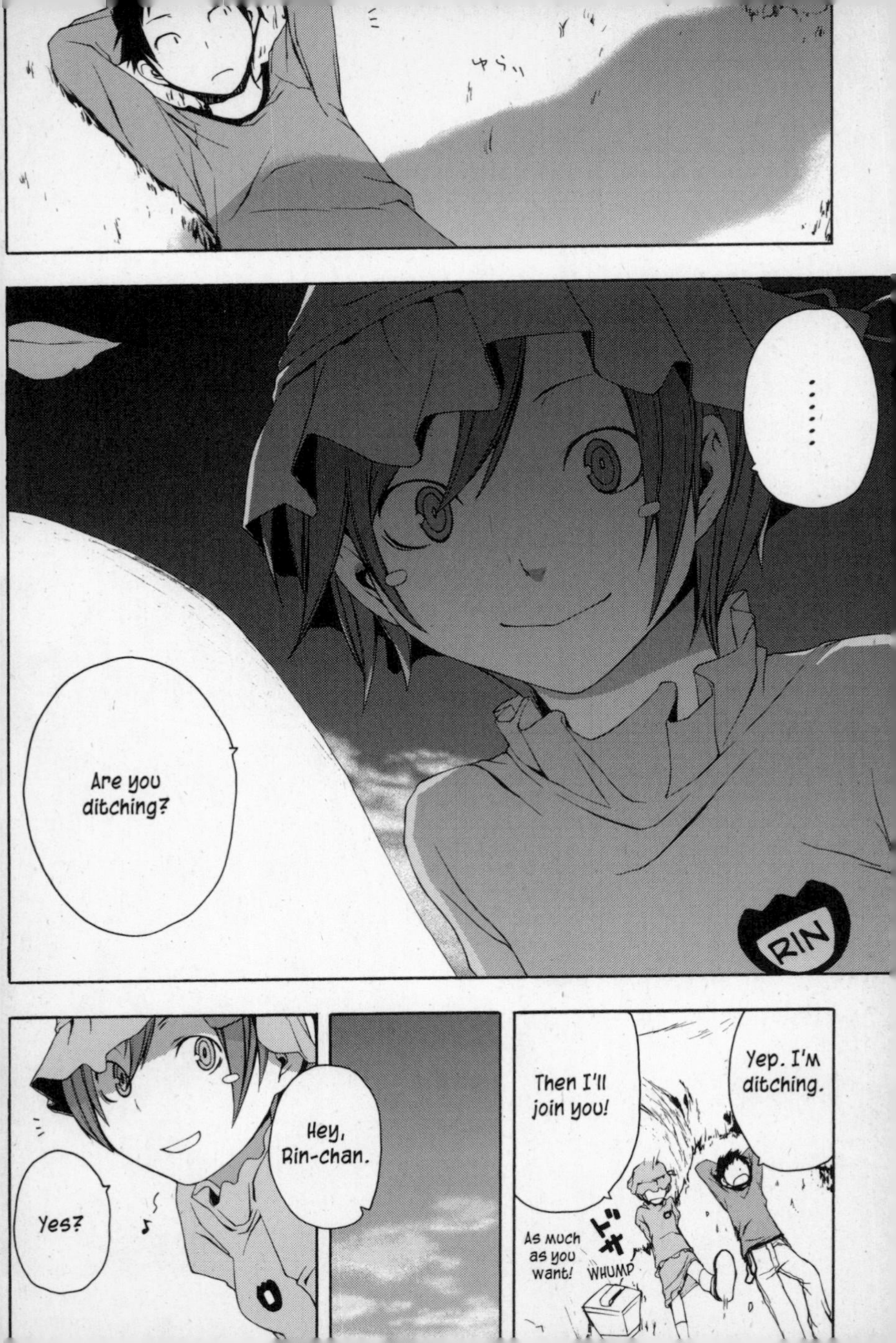
......
Are you ditching?
Yep. I'm ditching.
Then I'll join you!
ドサ
WHUMP
As much as you want!
Hey, Rin-chan.
Yes?

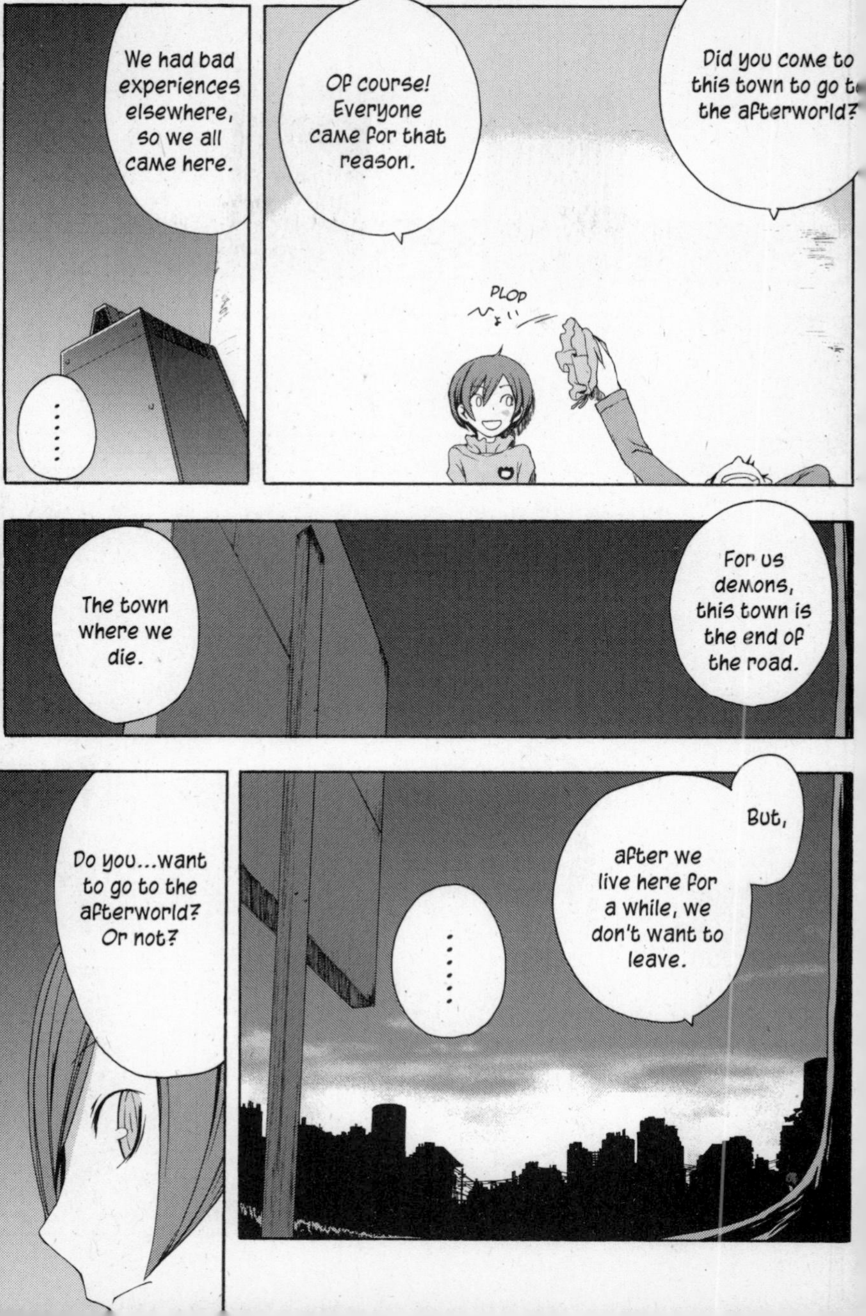
Did you come to this town to go t the afterworld?
Of course! Everyone came for that reason.
PLOP
We had bad experiences elsewhere, so we all came here.
......
For us demons, this town is the end of the road.
The town where we die.
But,
after we live here for a while, we don't want to leave.
......
Do you...want to go to the afterworld? Or not?

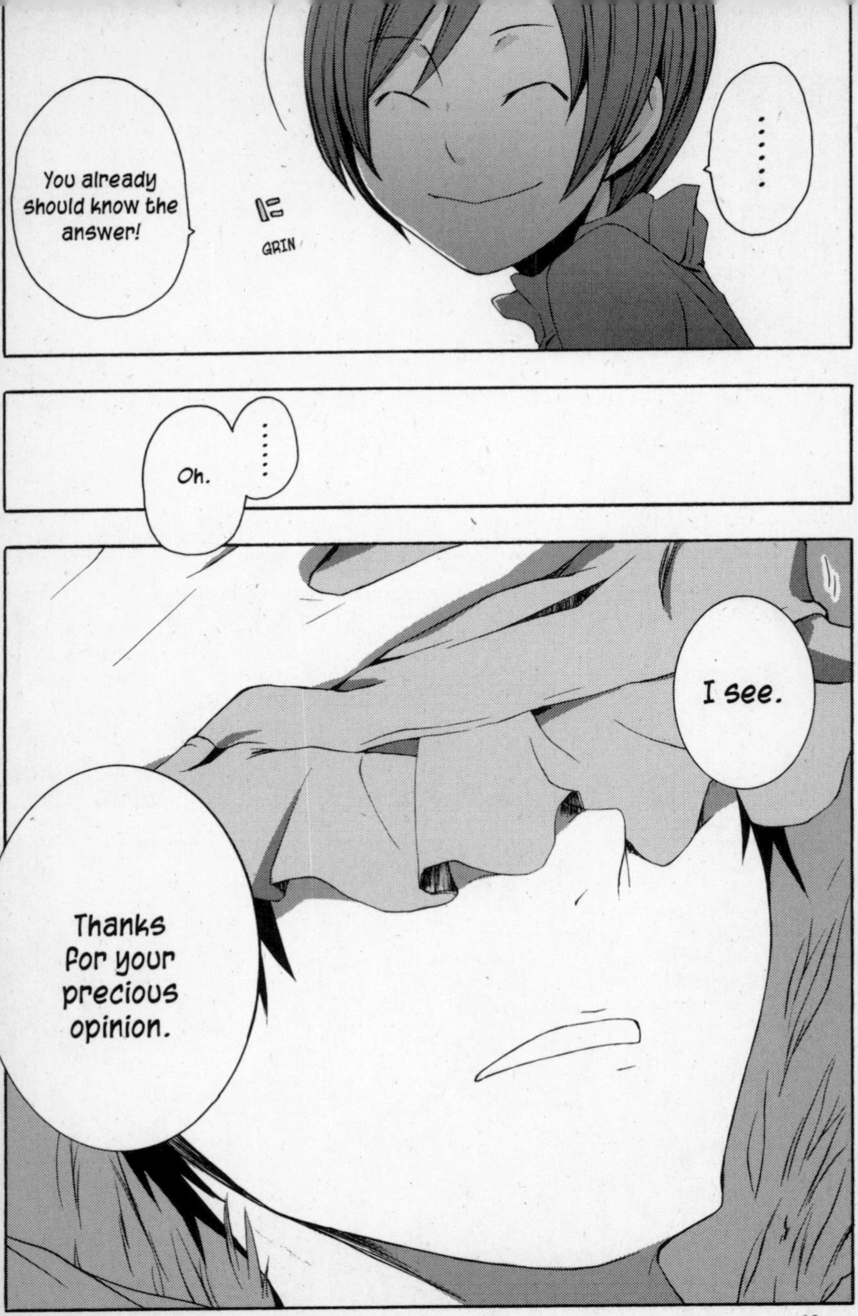
……
You already should know the answer!
GRIN
Oh. ……
I see.
Thanks for your precious opinion.

7th Night: Moving Forward (Part 2) END

Yozakura Quartet 2

Primary Stages of Yozakura Quartet

Age: 16

Hobbies:
archery, listening to music

Favorites

Food:
beef bowl

Music Group:
ROCO

Comedian:
Chidori

Uchi-P Member:
Golgo

Little-Known Fact:
She is from Okayama.

Touka Kishi

She's the one who changed the most from the primary stages.

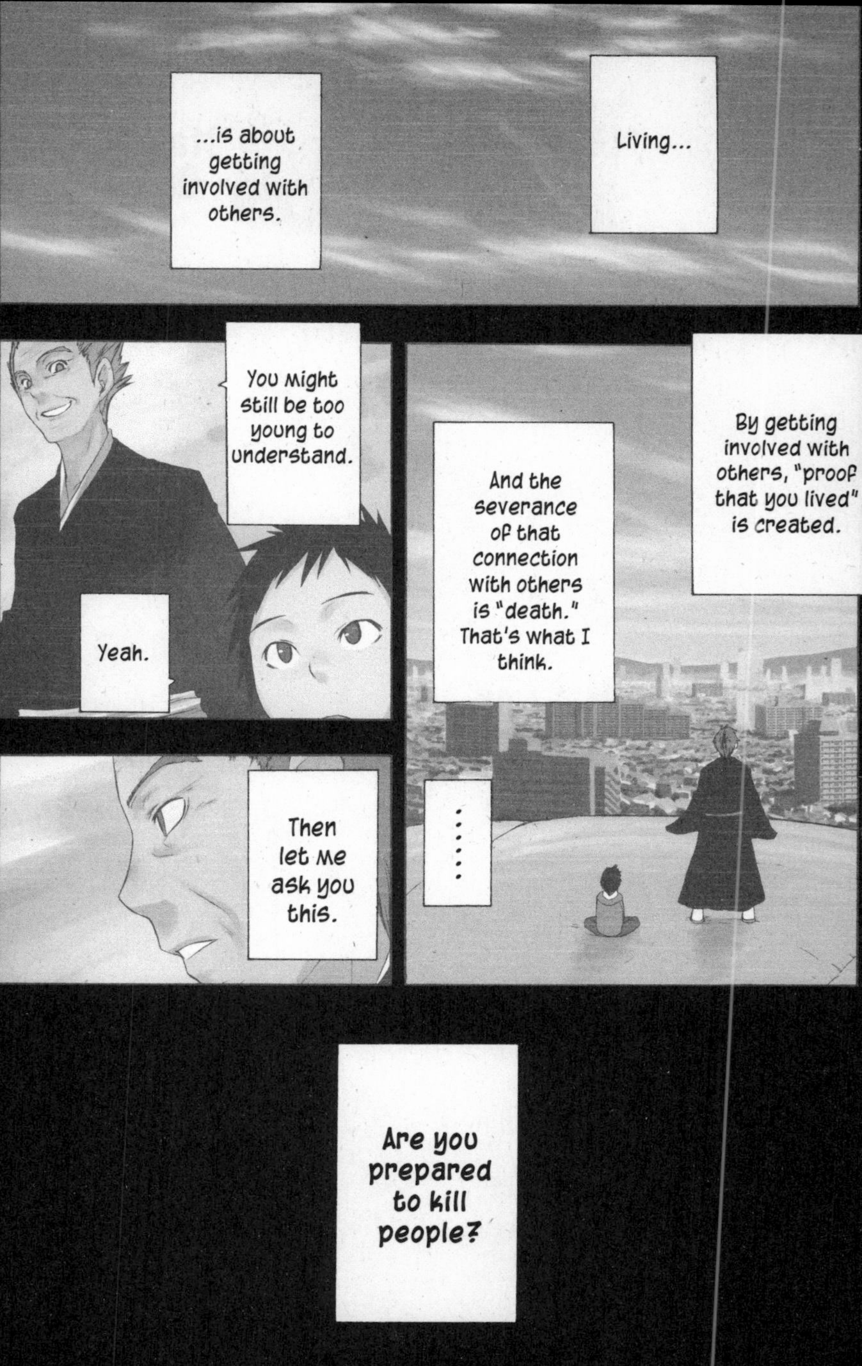
Living...
...is about getting involved with others.
By getting involved with others, "proof that you lived" is created.
And the severance of that connection with others is "death." That's what I think.
......
You might still be too young to understand.
Yeah.
Then let me ask you this.
Are you prepared to kill people?

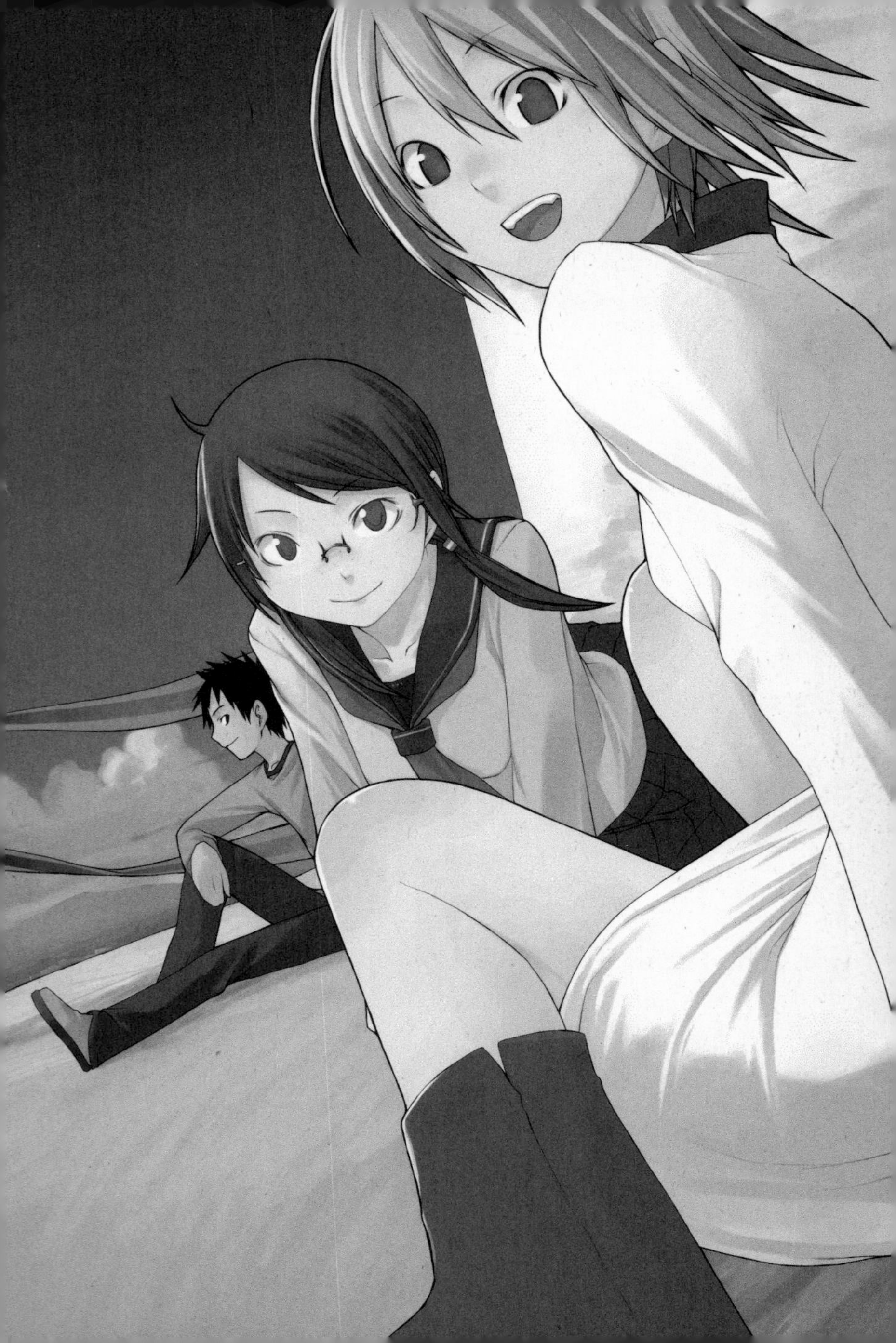

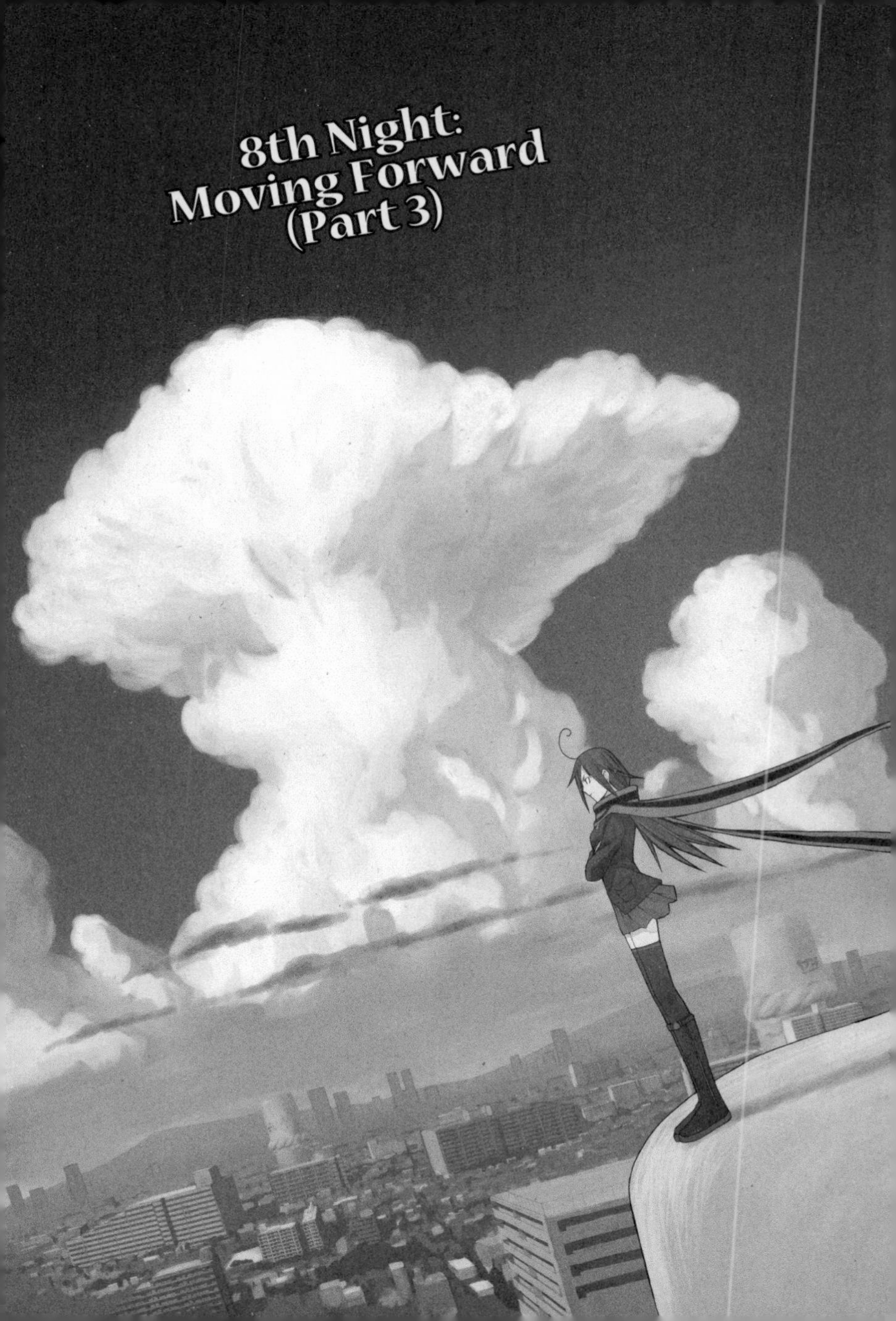
8th Night:
Moving Forward
(Part 3)

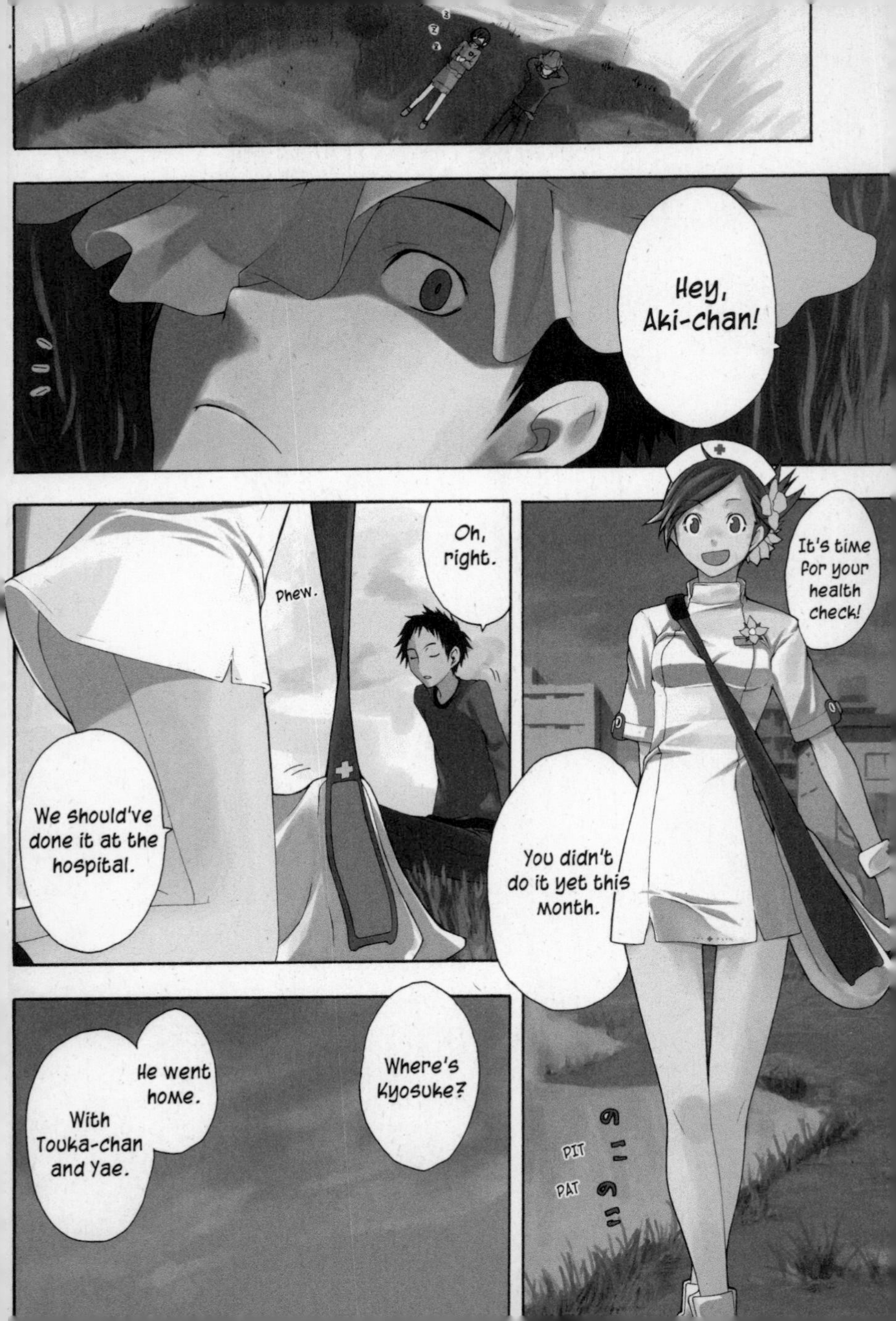
Hey, Aki-chan!
It's time for your health check!
You didn't do it yet this month.
PIT
PAT
Oh, right.
Phew.
We should've done it at the hospital.
Where's Kyosuke?
He went home.
With Touka-chan and Yae.

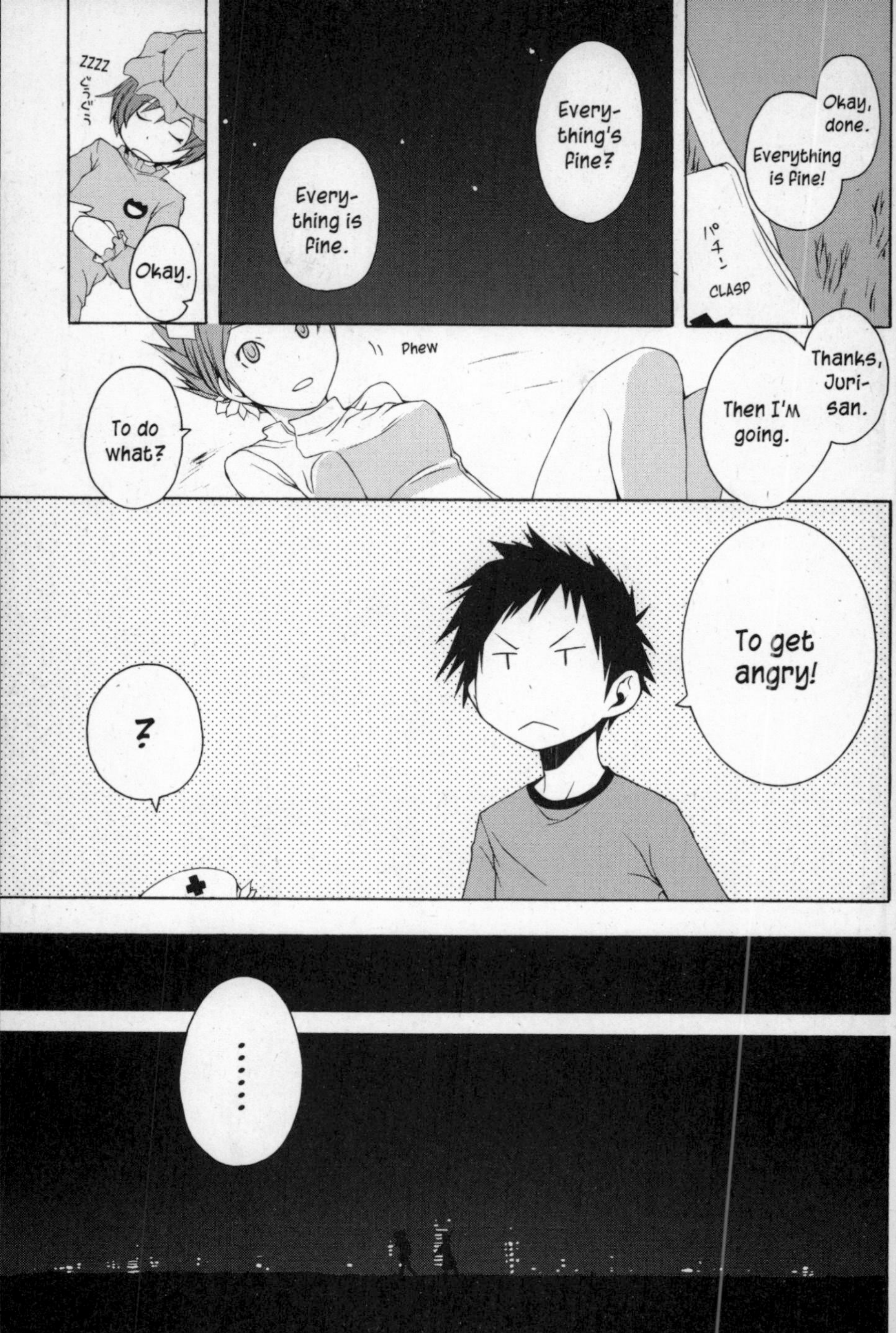

Okay, done.
Everything is fine!
パチン
CLASP
Every-thing's fine?
Every-thing is fine.
ZZZZ
Okay.
Thanks, Juri-san.
Then I'm going.
Phew
To do what?
To get angry!
?
......

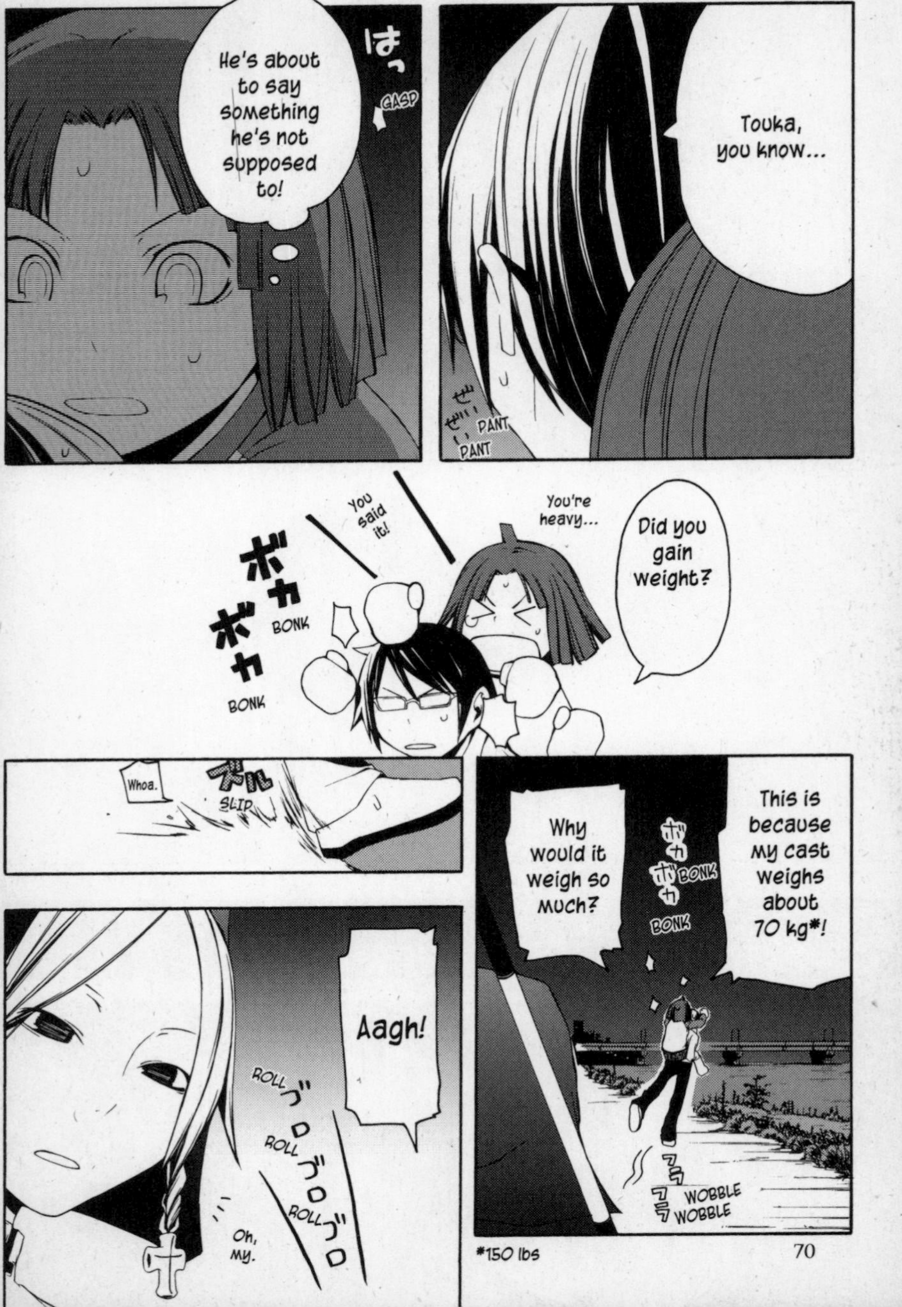
Touka, you know...
PANT
PANT
はっ
GASP
He's about to say something he's not supposed to!
Did you gain weight?
You're heavy...
You said it!
BONK
BONK
This is because my cast weighs about 70 kg*!
BONK
BONK
Why would it weigh so much?
WOBBLE
WOBBLE
Whoa.
SLIP
Aagh!
ROLL
ROLL
ROLL
Oh, my.

*150 lbs

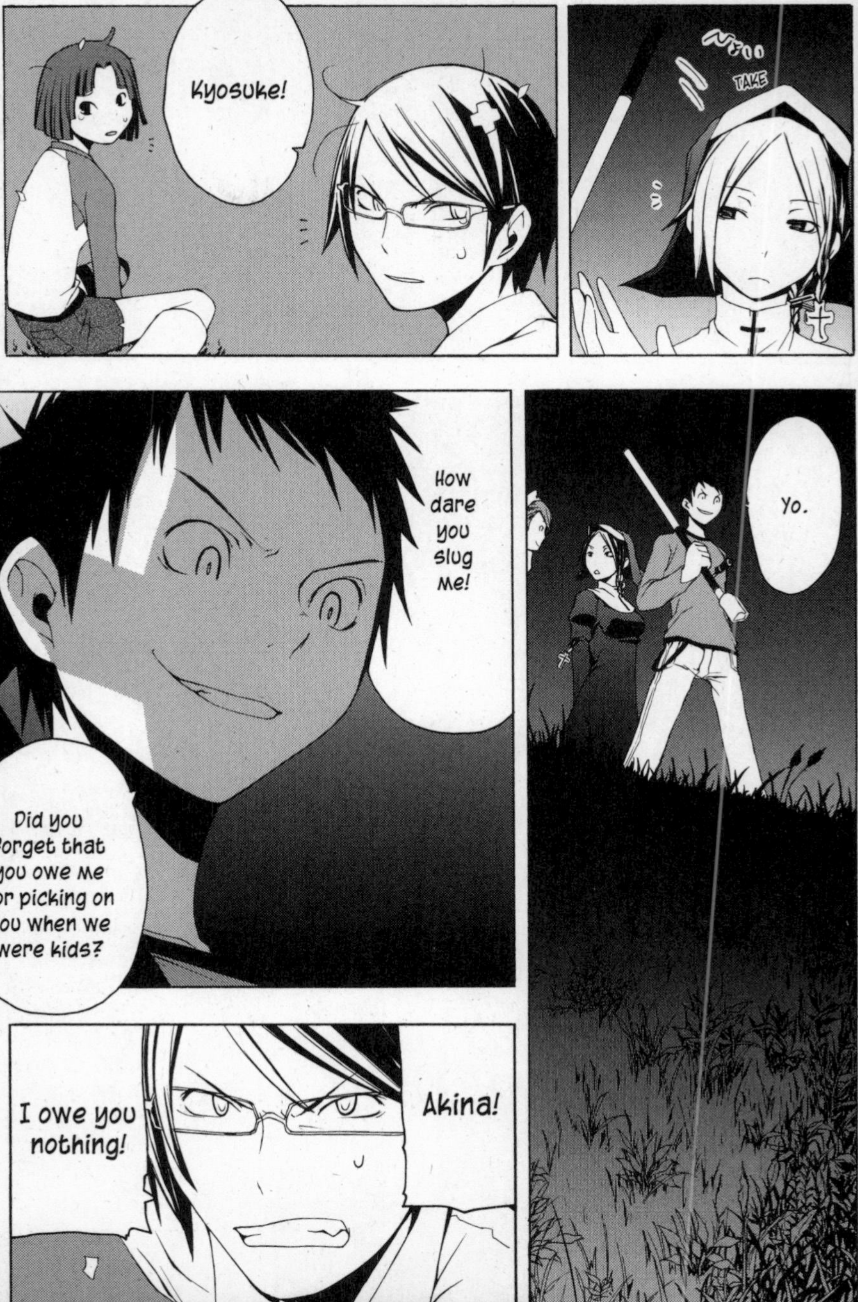
TAKE
Kyosuke!
Yo.
How dare you slug me!
Did you forget that you owe me for picking on you when we were kids?
Akina!
I owe you nothing!

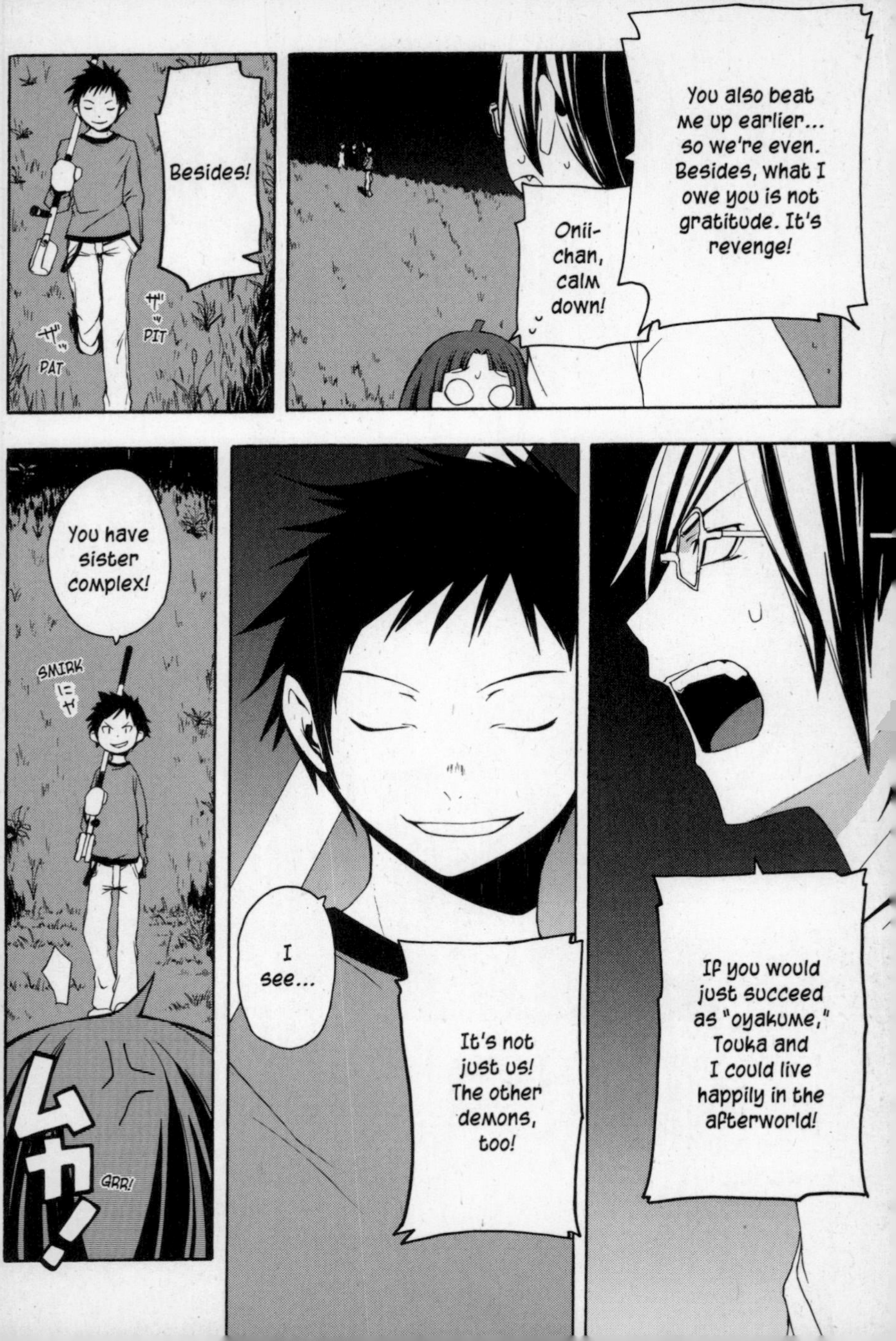

You also beat me up earlier... so we're even. Besides, what I owe you is not gratitude. It's revenge!
Onii-chan, calm down!
Besides!
ザッ
PIT
ザッ
PAT
If you would just succeed as "oyakume," Touka and I could live happily in the afterworld!
It's not just us! The other demons, too!
I see...
You have sister complex!
SMIRK
ニヤ
ムカッ!
GRR!

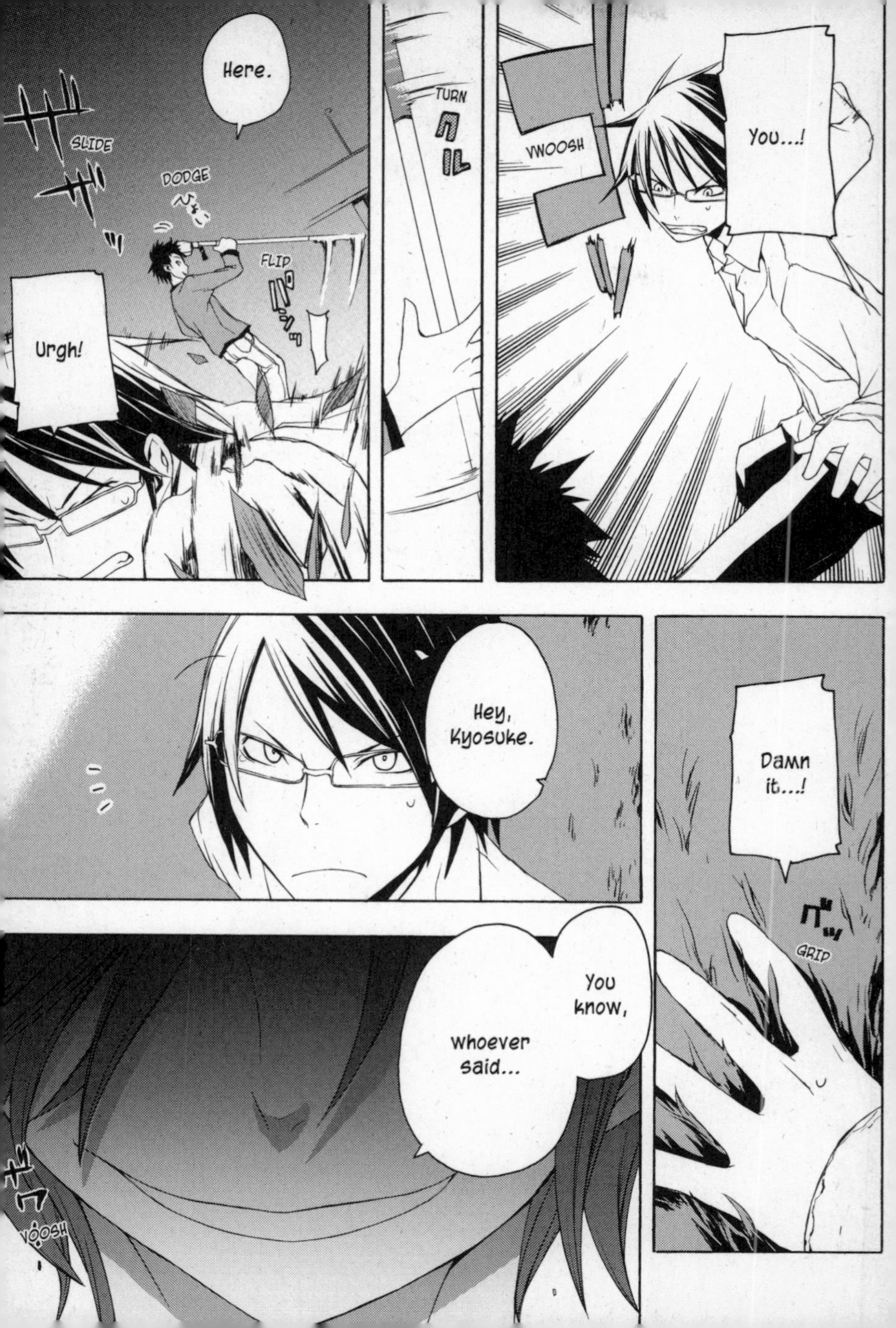
VWOOSH
You...!
TURN
Here.
SLIDE
DODGE
FLIP
Urgh!
Damn it...!
GRIP
Hey, Kyosuke.
You know, whoever said...
VOOSH

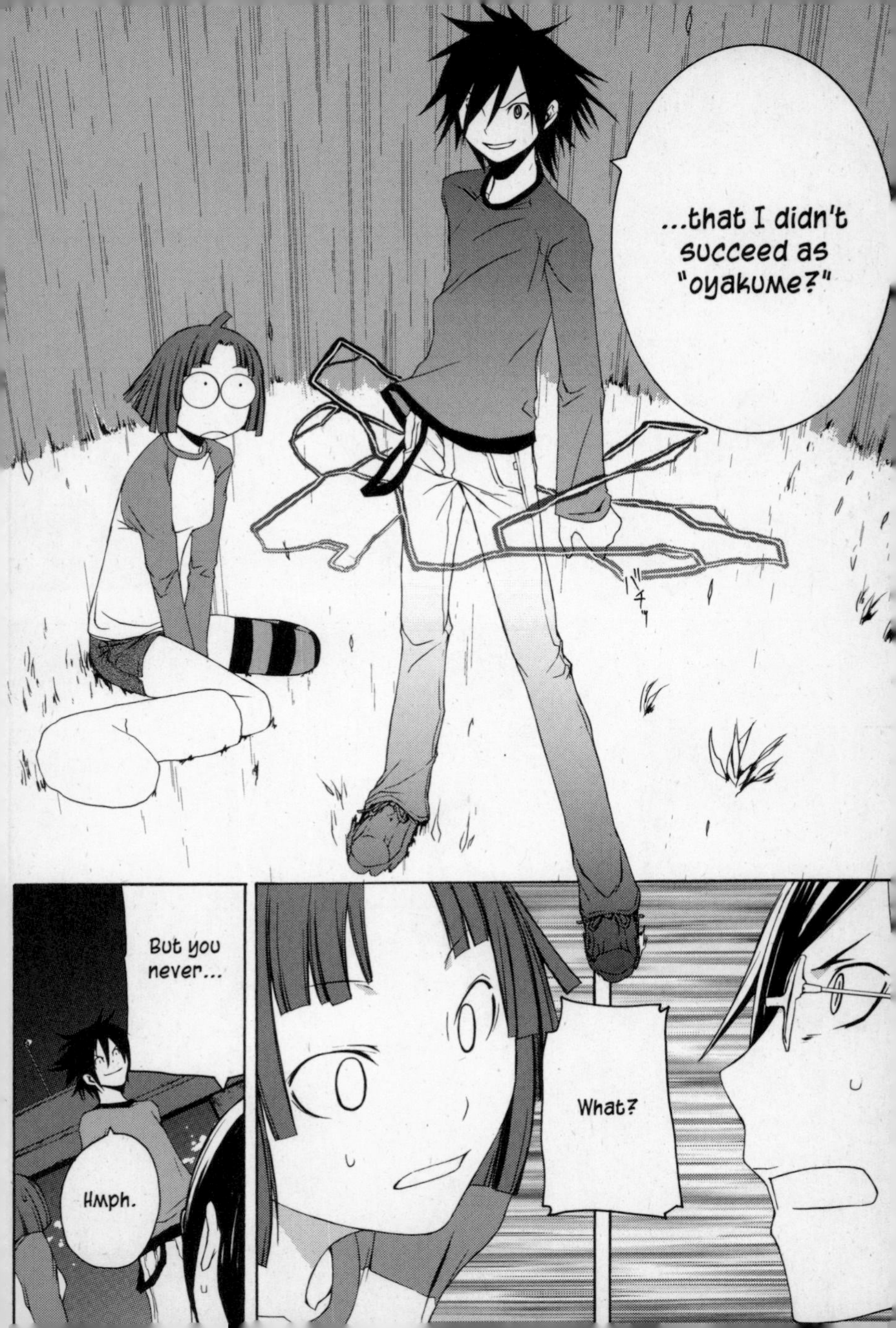
...that I didn't succeed as "oyakume?"
バチッ
What?
But you never...
Hmph.

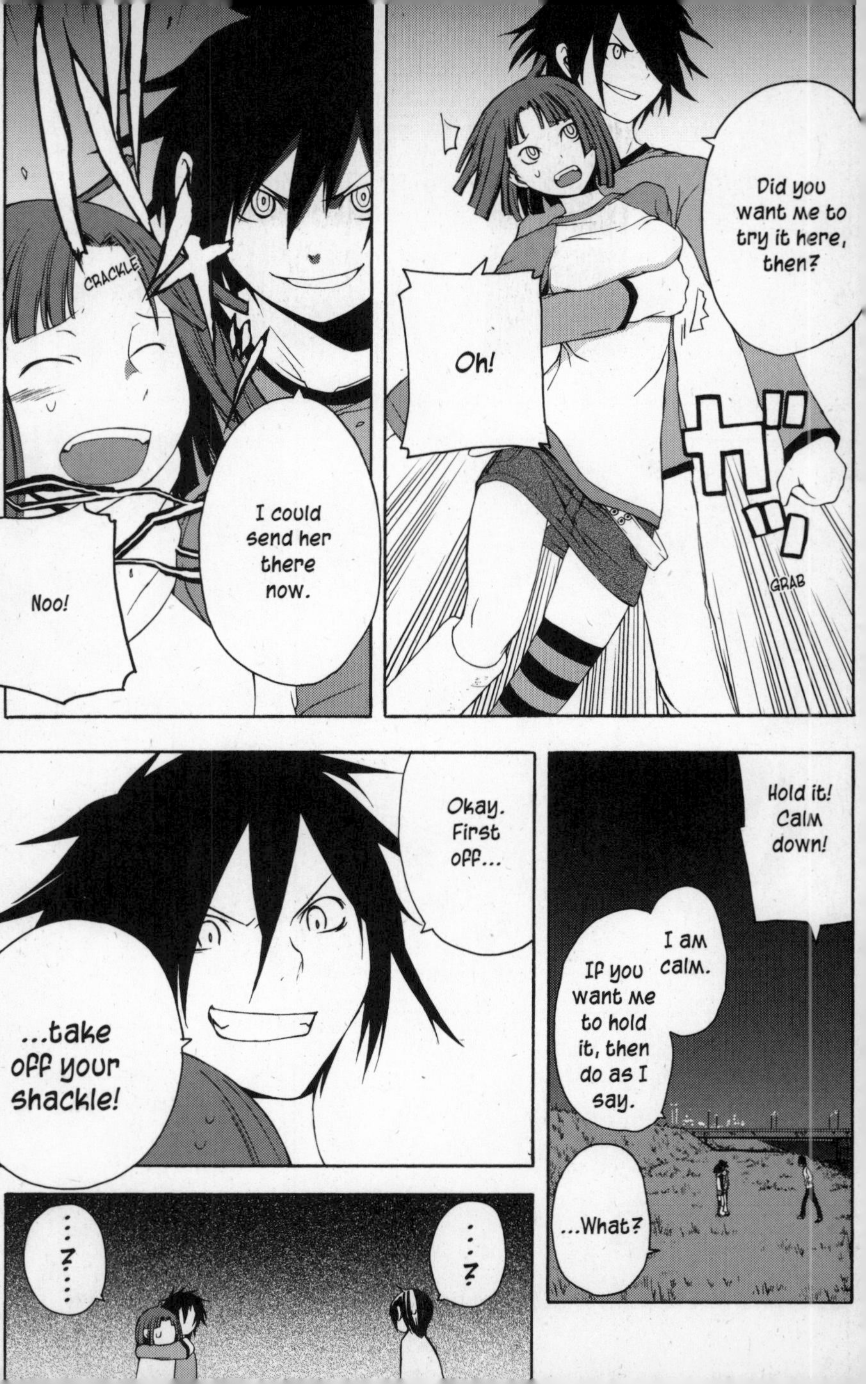
Did you want me to try it here, then?
Oh!
ガッ
GRAB
I could send her there now.
CRACKLE
Noo!
Hold it! Calm down!
I am calm.
If you want me to hold it, then do as I say.
...What?
Okay. First off...
...take off your shackle!
...?
...?...

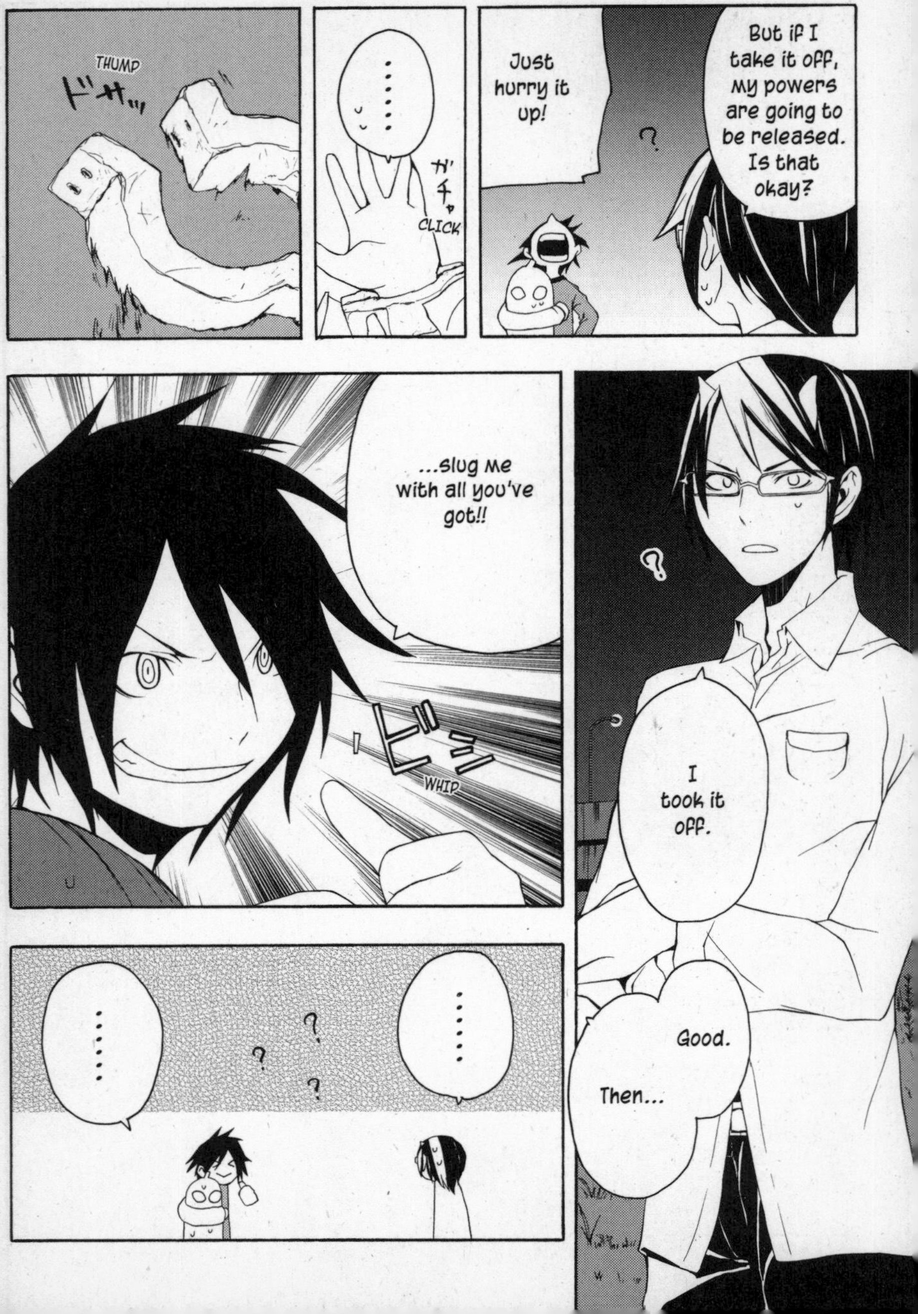
But if I take it off, my powers are going to be released. Is that okay?
Just hurry it up!
?
......
ガチャ
CLICK
THUMP
ドサッ
?
I took it off.
Good.
Then...
...slug me with all you've got!!
WHIP
......
......
?
?
?

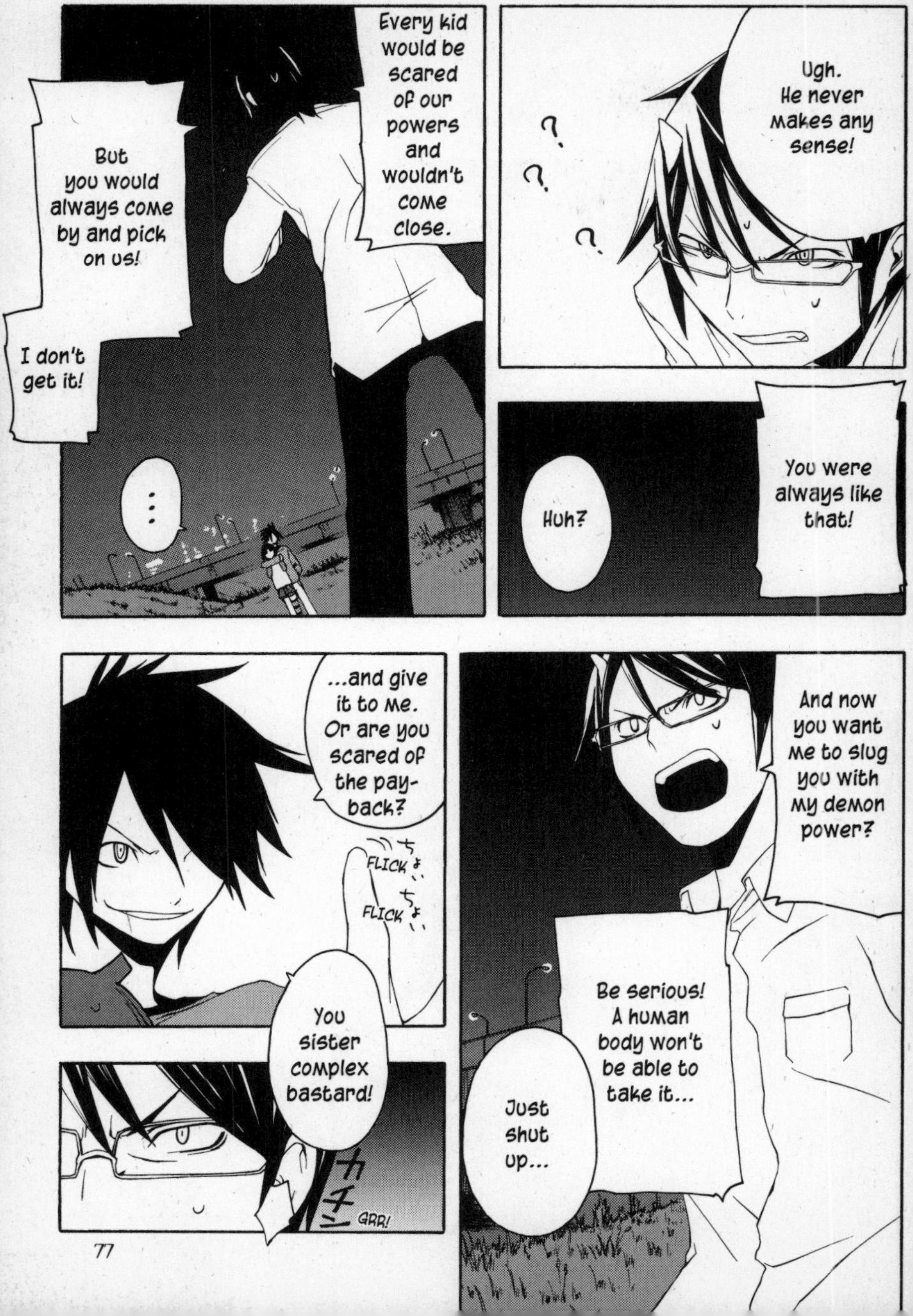
Ugh. He never makes any sense!
?
?
?
You were always like that!
Huh?
Every kid would be scared of our powers and wouldn't come close.
But you would always come by and pick on us!
I don't get it!
...
And now you want me to slug you with my demon power?
Be serious! A human body won't be able to take it...
Just shut up...
...and give it to me. Or are you scared of the pay-back?
FLICK
FLICK
You sister complex bastard!
GRR!

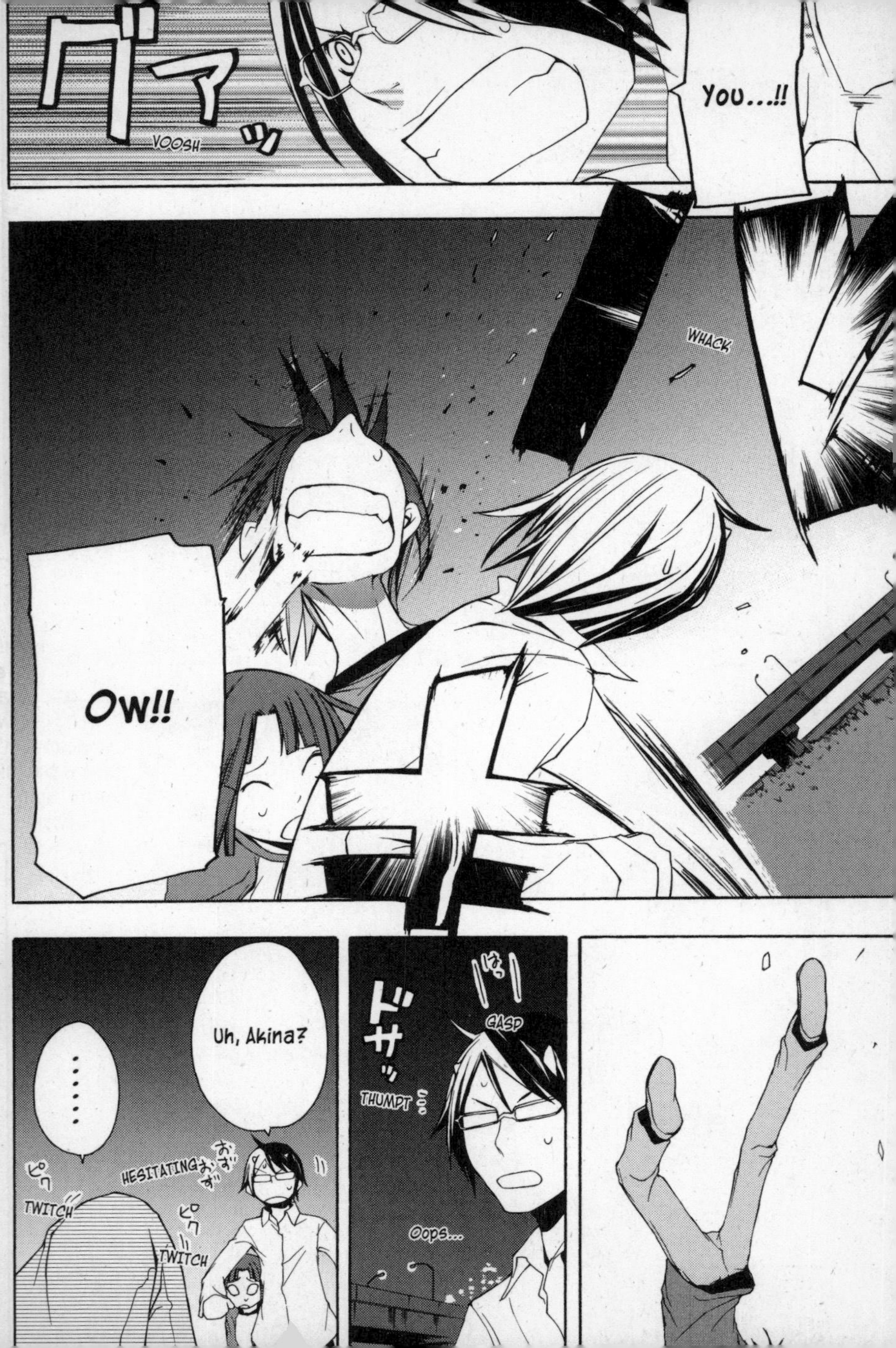
YOU...!!
ヴァッ
VOOSH
WHACK
OW!!
はっ
GASP
ドサッ
THUMPT
Oops...
Uh, Akina?
......
おずおず
HESITATING
ピク
TWITCH
ピク
TWITCH

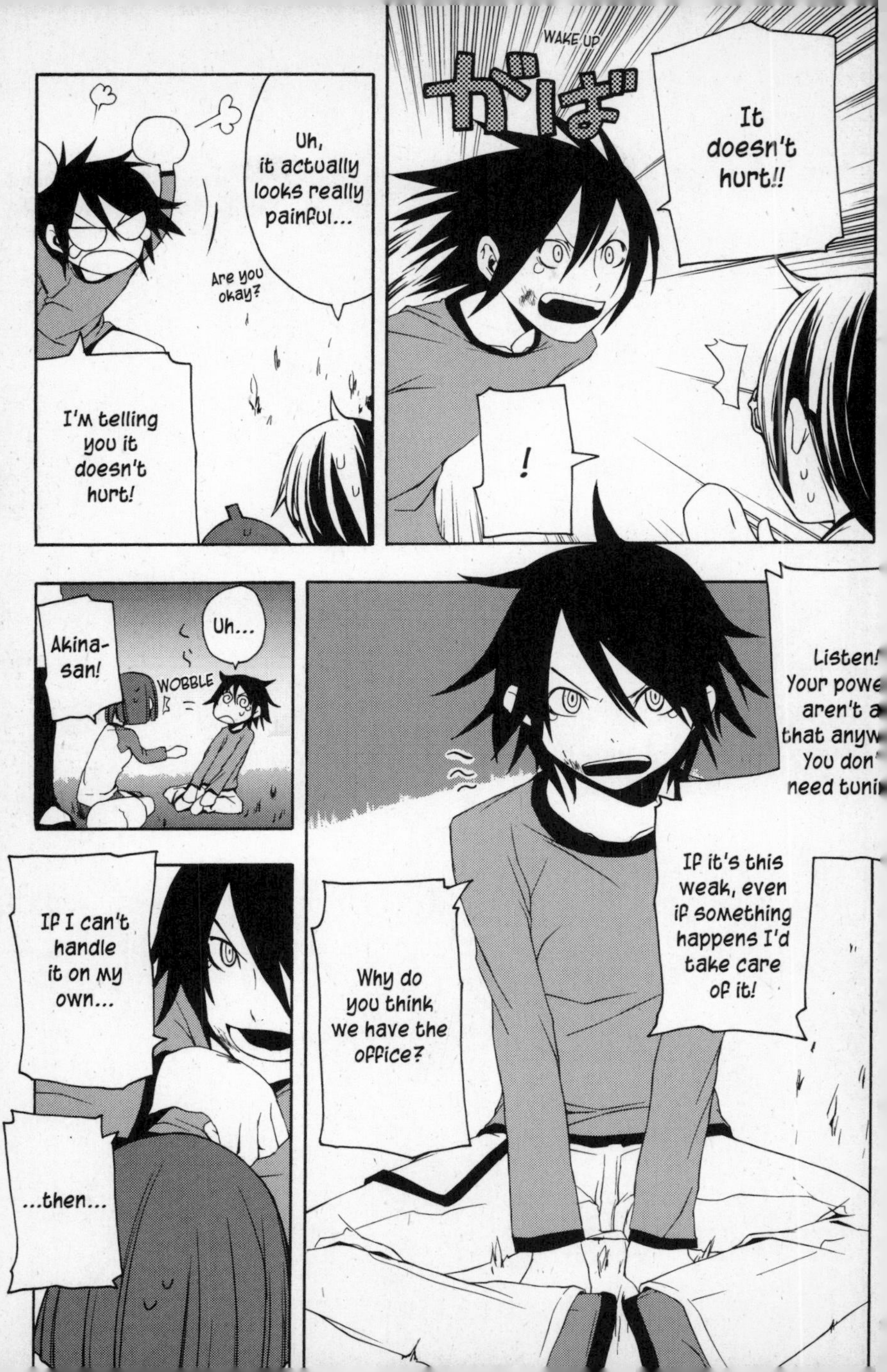
WAKE UP
がば
It doesn't hurt!!
!
Uh, it actually looks really painful...
Are you okay?
I'm telling you it doesn't hurt!
Listen! Your powe aren't a that anyw You don' need tuni
If it's this weak, even if something happens I'd take care of it!
Why do you think we have the office?
Akina-san!
Uh...
WOBBLE
If I can't handle it on my own...
...then...

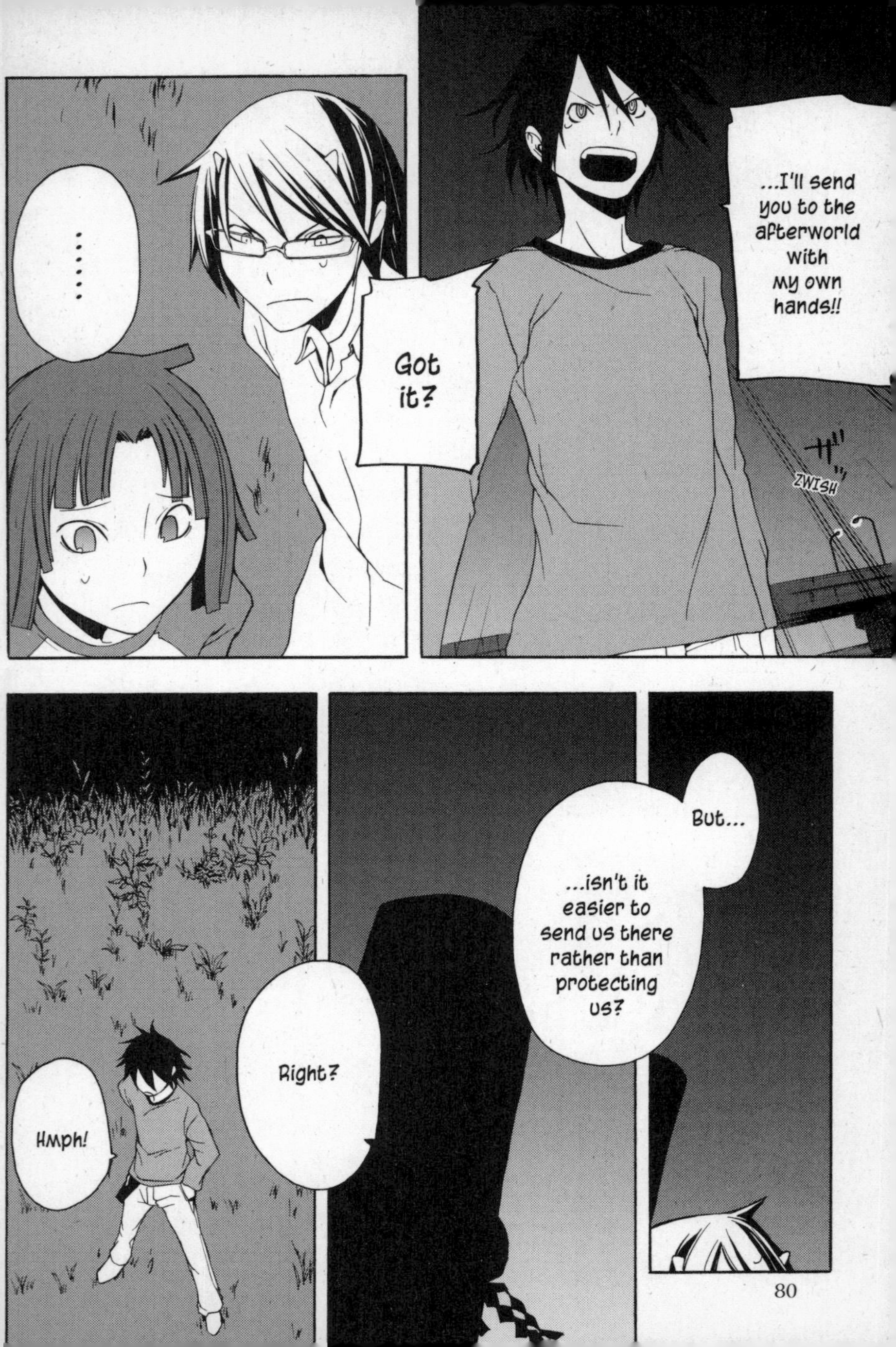
...I'll send you to the afterworld with my own hands!!
ZWISH
Got it?
......
But...
...isn't it easier to send us there rather than protecting us?
Right?
Hmph!

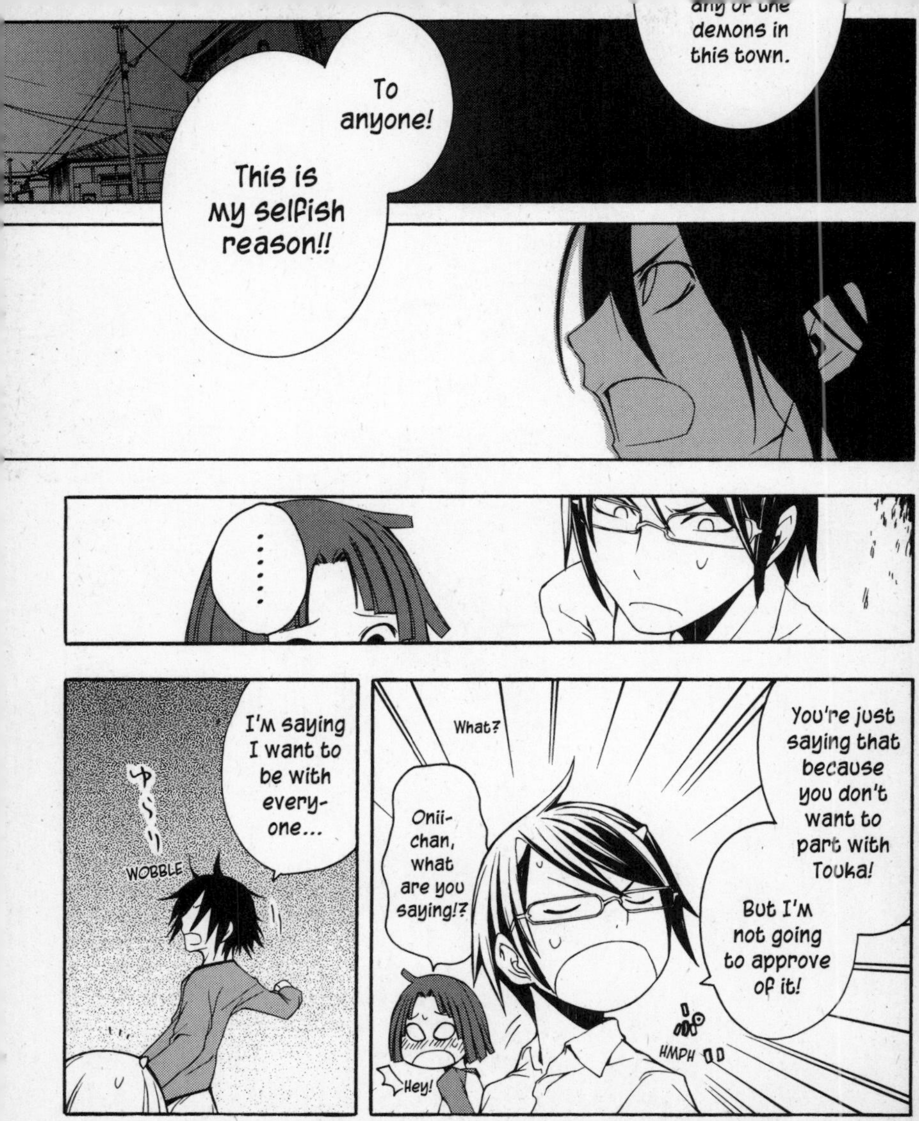
any of the demons in this town.
To anyone!
This is my selfish reason!!
......
You're just saying that because you don't want to part with Touka!
But I'm not going to approve of it!
What?
Onii-chan, what are you saying!?
HMPH
Hey!
I'm saying I want to be with every-one...
WOBBLE

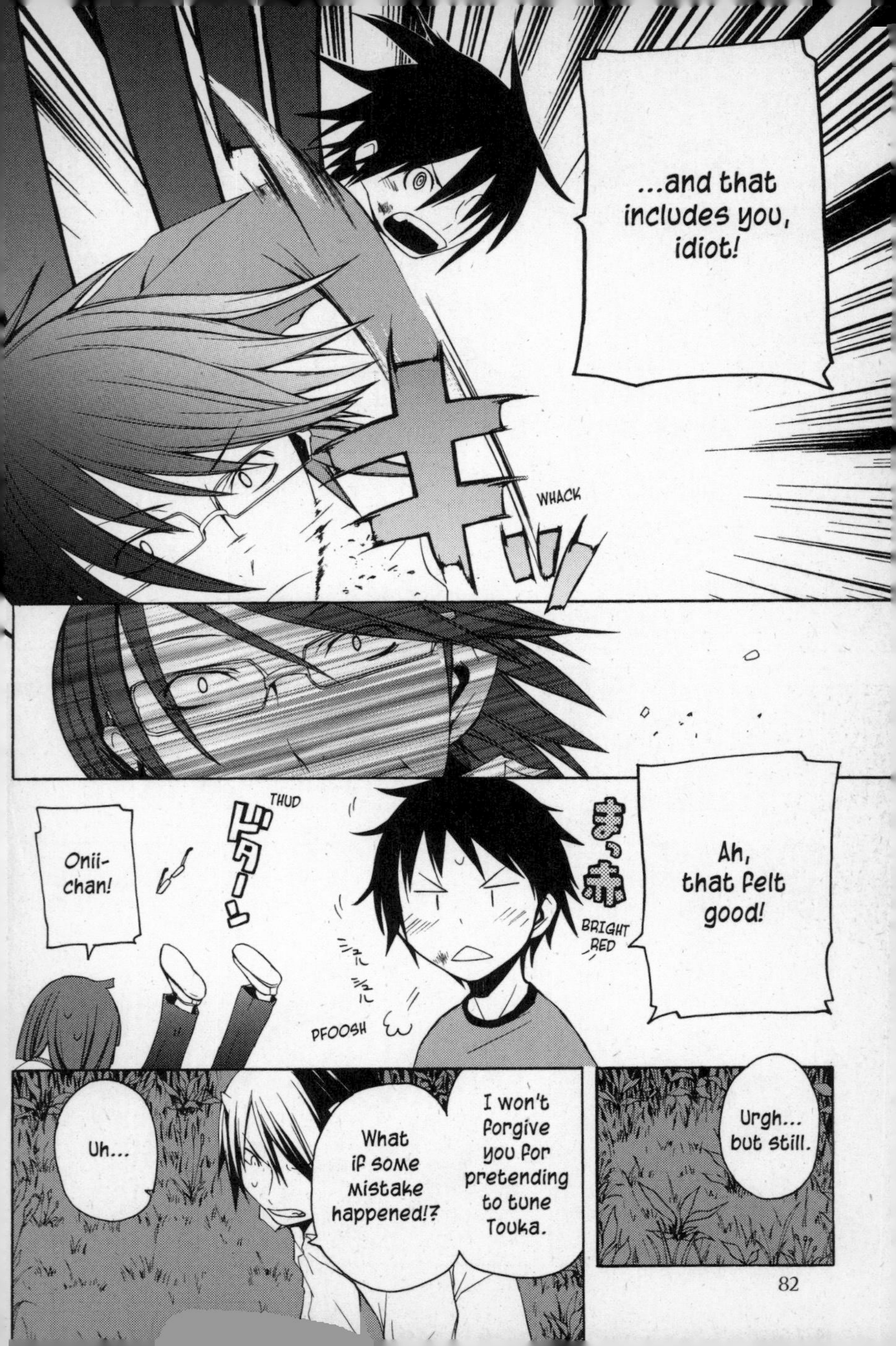
...and that includes you, idiot!
WHACK
Ah, that felt good!
まっ赤
BRIGHT RED
ドターッ
THUD
Onii-chan!
PFOOSH
Urgh... but still.
I won't forgive you for pretending to tune Touka.
What if some mistake happened!?
Uh...

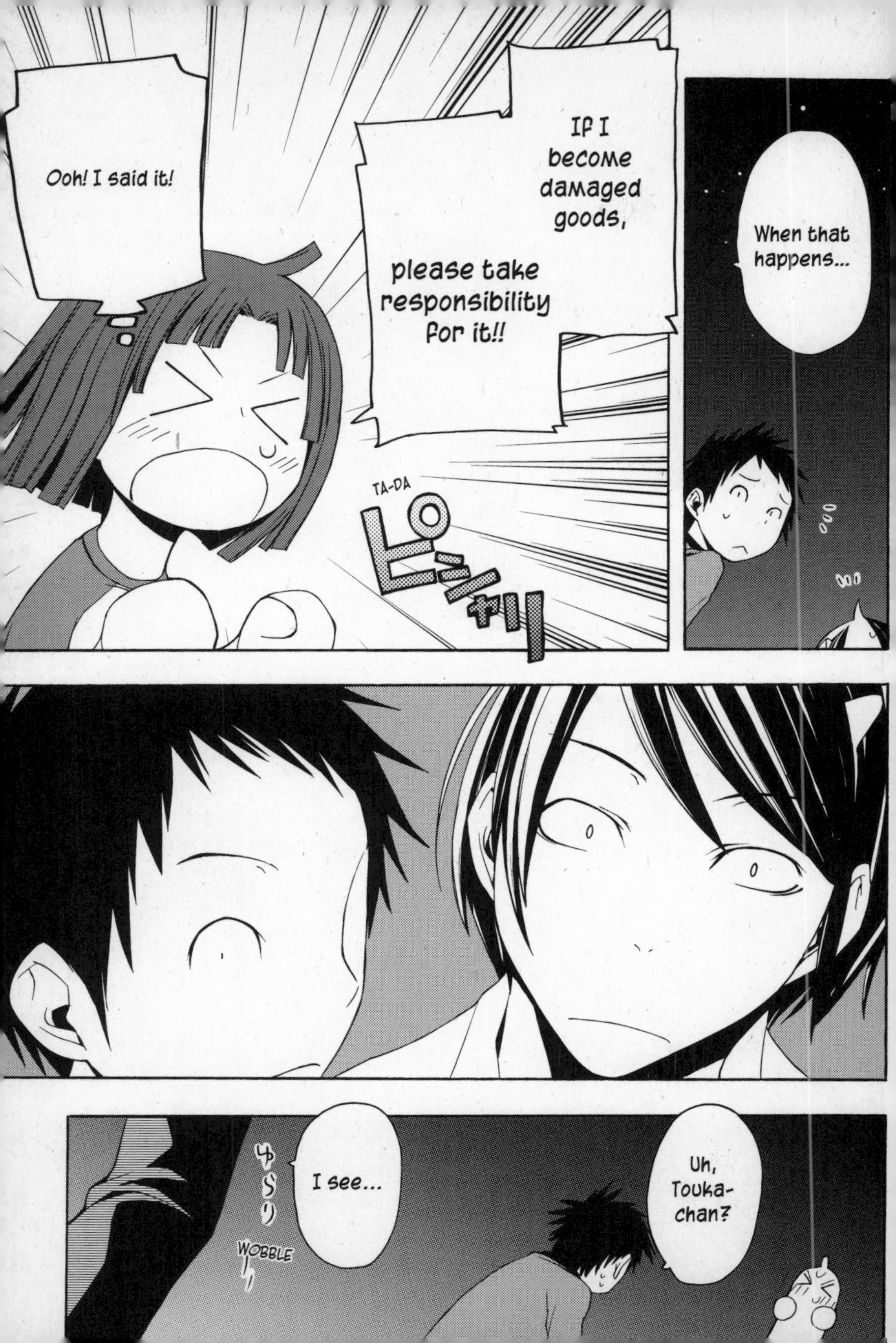
When that happens...
If I become damaged goods,
please take responsibility for it!!
Ooh! I said it!
TA-DA
ピシャリ
Uh, Touka-chan?
I see...
ゆらり
WOBBLE

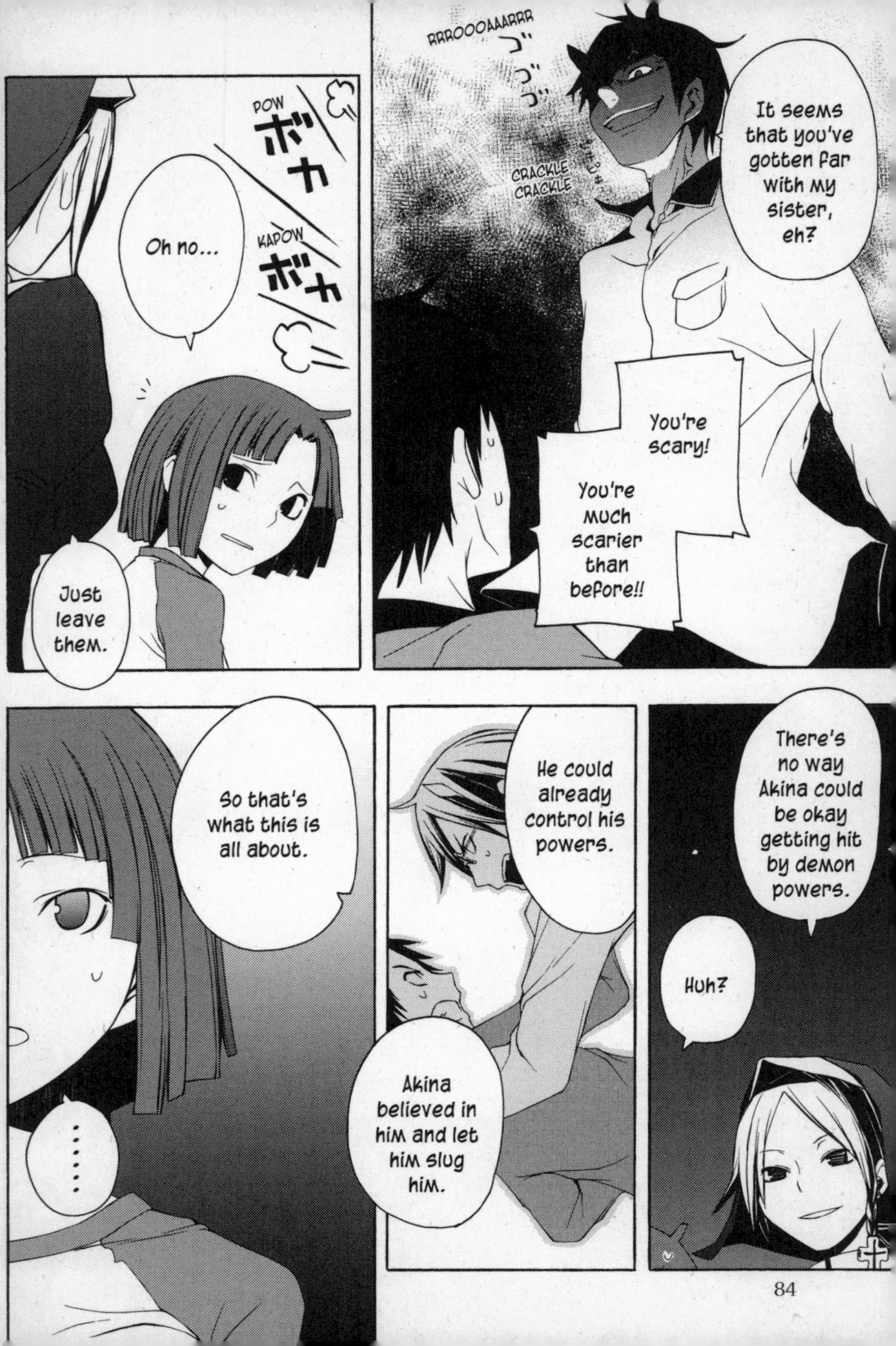
RRROOOAAARRR
ゴゴゴ
CRACKLE CRACKLE
It seems that you've gotten far with my sister, eh?
You're scary!
You're much scarier than before!!
POW
ボカ
Oh no...
KAPOW
ボカ
Just leave them.
There's no way Akina could be okay getting hit by demon powers.
Huh?
He could already control his powers.
Akina believed in him and let him slug him.
So that's what this is all about.
......

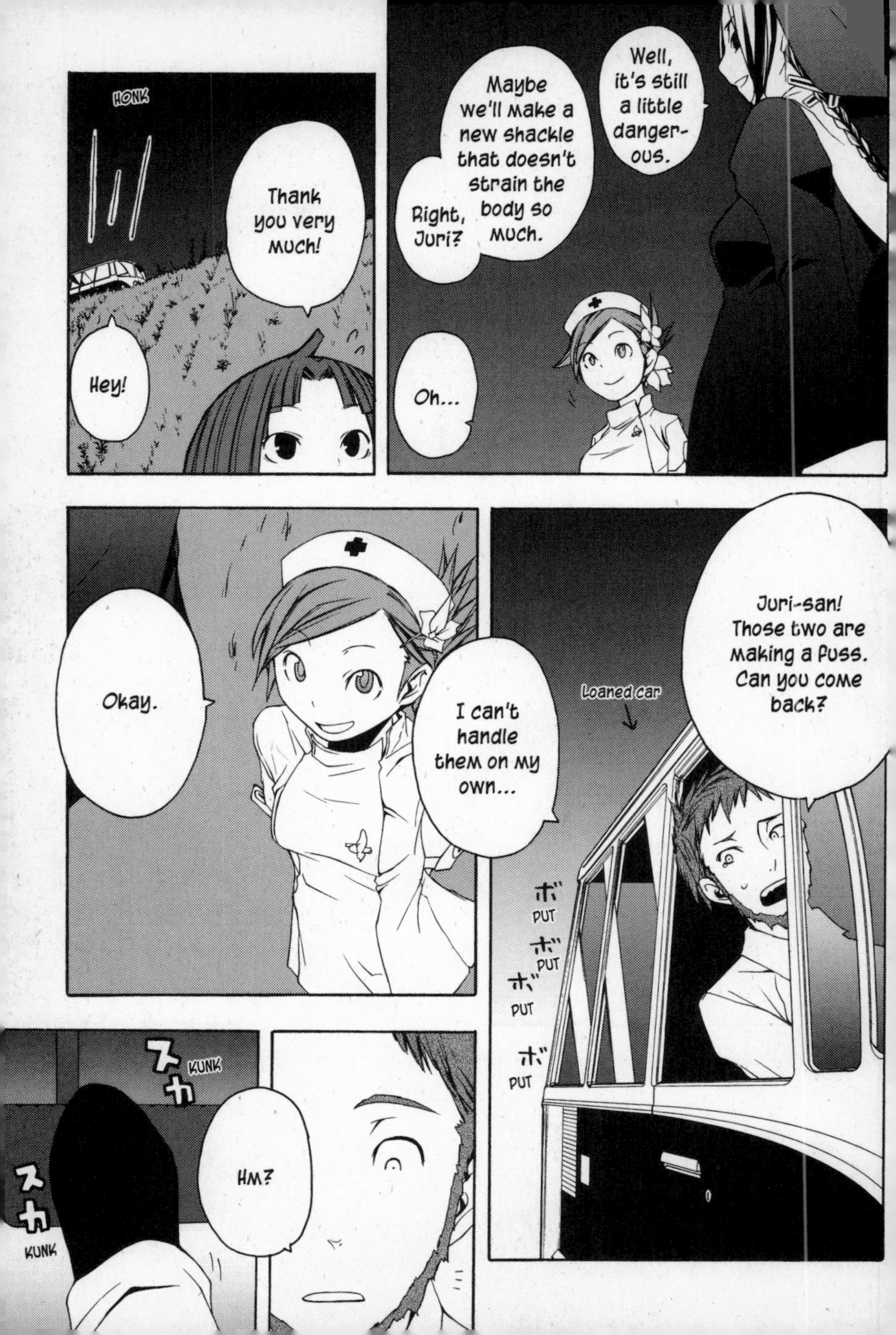

Well, it's still a little danger-ous.
Maybe we'll make a new shackle that doesn't strain the body so much.
Right, Juri?
Oh...
HONK
Thank you very much!
Hey!
Juri-san! Those two are making a fuss. Can you come back?
Loaned car
ボ PUT
ボ PUT
ボ PUT
ボ PUT
I can't handle them on my own...
Okay.
Hm?
スカ KUNK
スカ KUNK

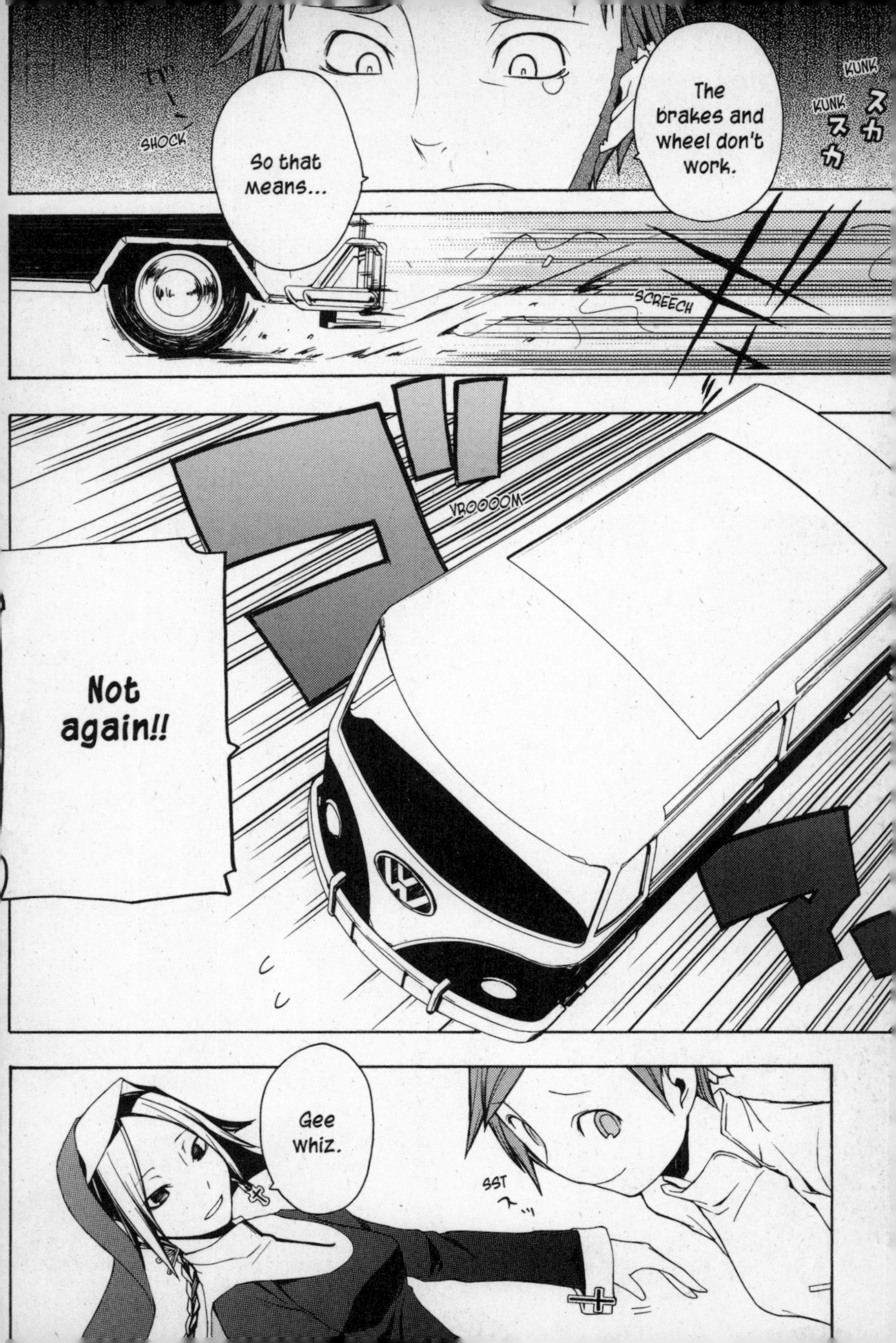
KUNK
KUNK
スカスカ
The brakes and wheel don't work.
So that means...
SHOCK
SCREECH
VROOOOM
Not again!!
Gee whiz.
SST

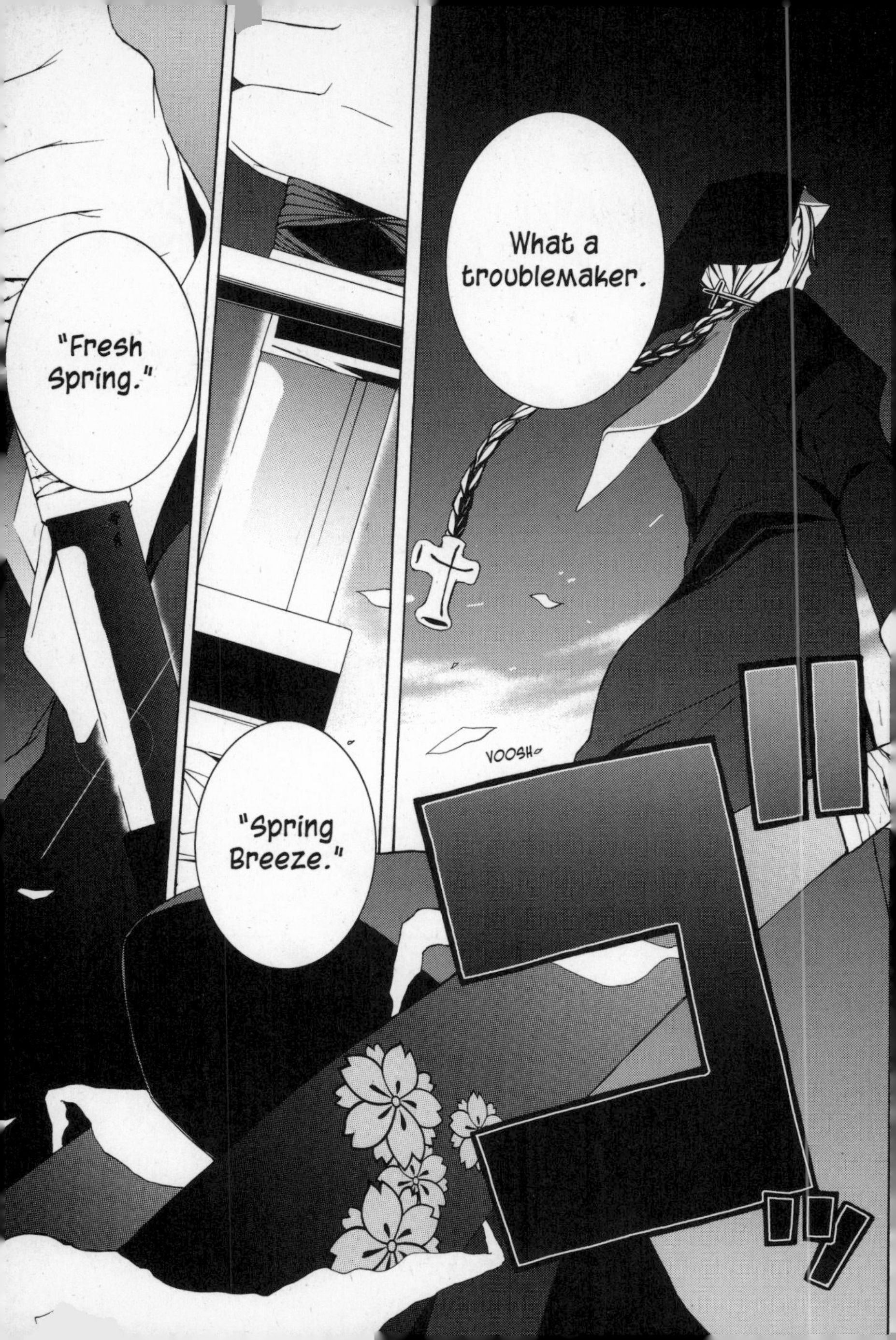
What a troublemaker.
VOOSH
"Spring Breeze."
"Fresh Spring."

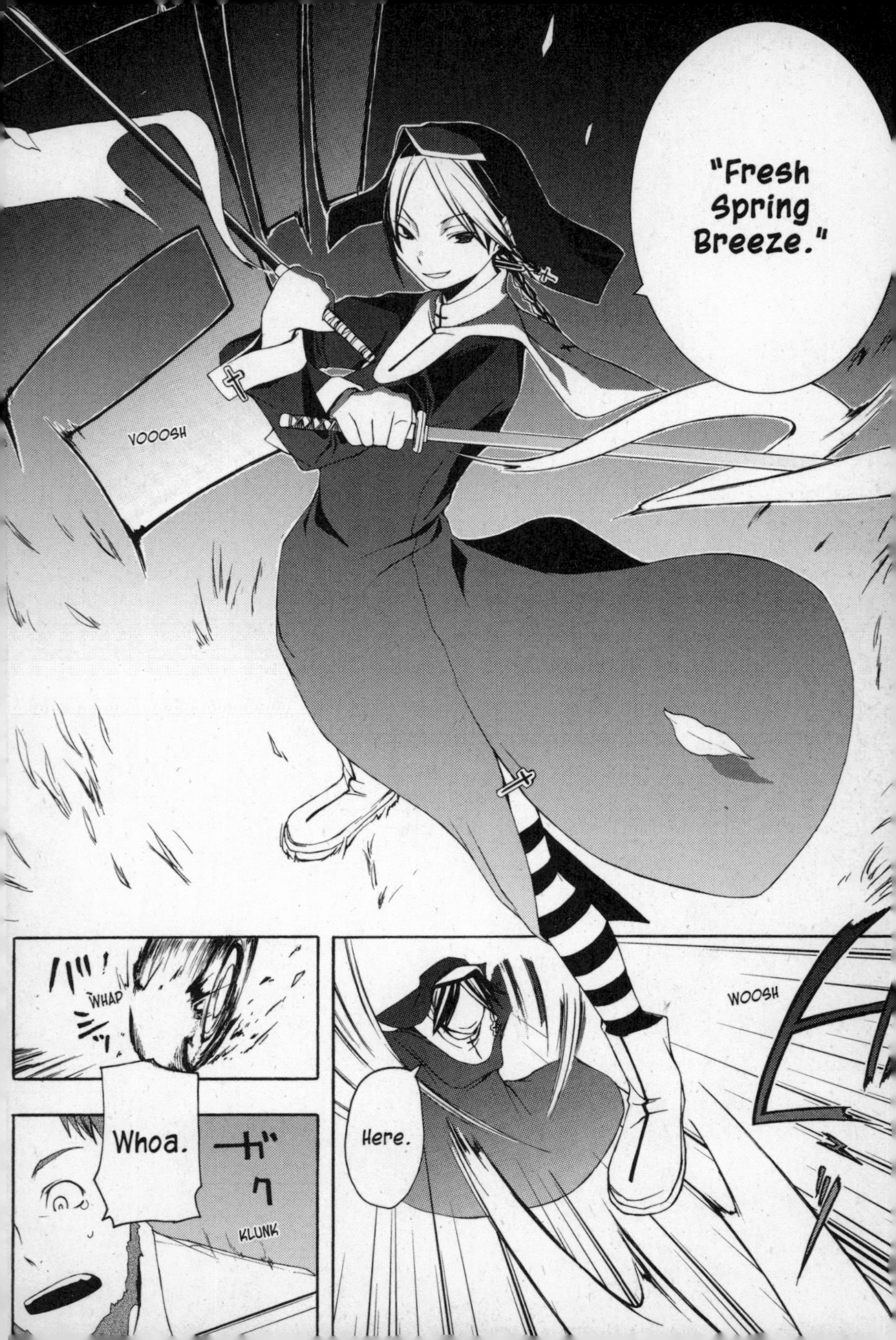
"Fresh Spring Breeze."
VOOOSH
WOOSH
Here.
WHAP
Whoa.
KLUNK

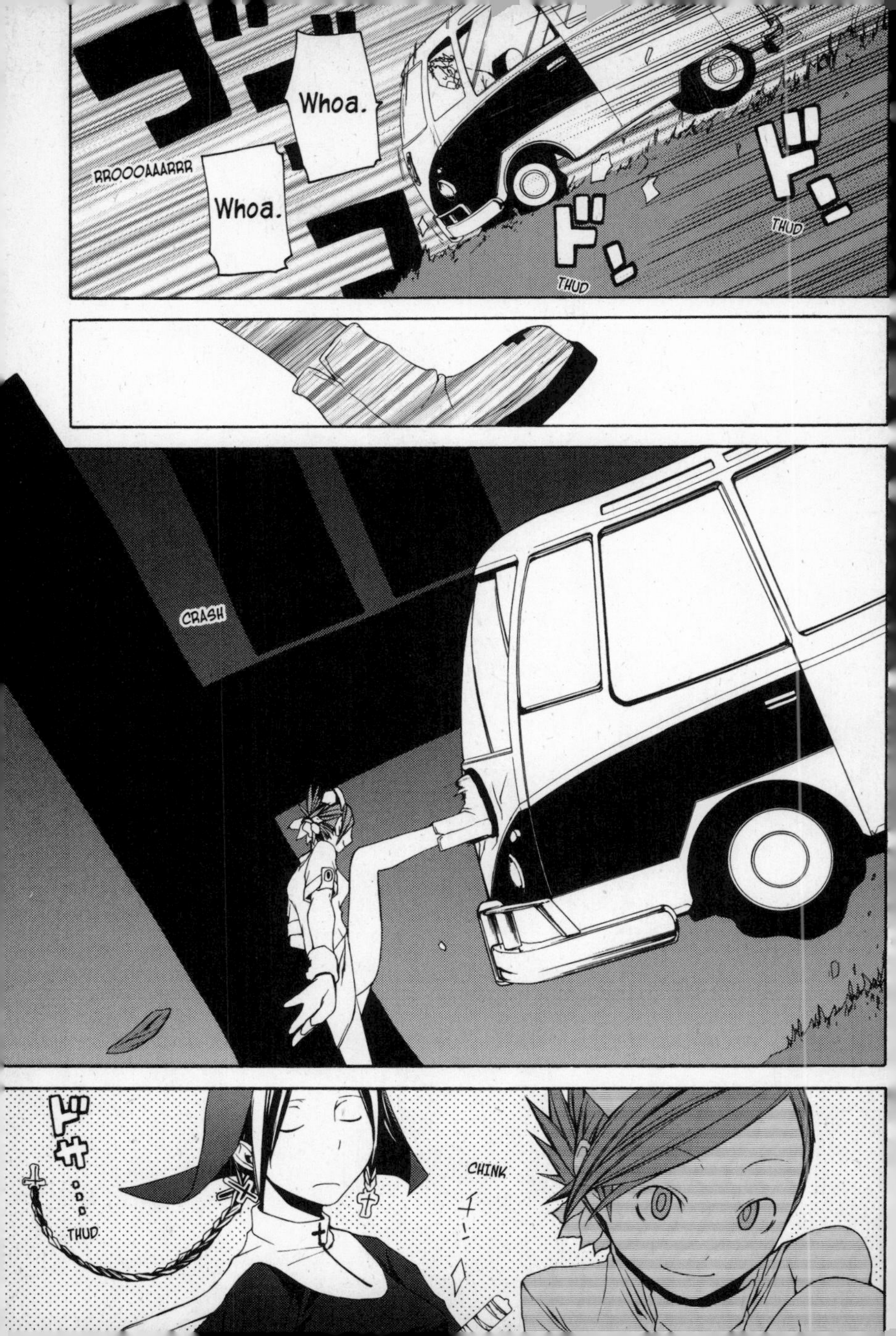

THUD
THUD
Whoa.
Whoa.
BROOOAAARRR
CRASH
CHINK
THUD

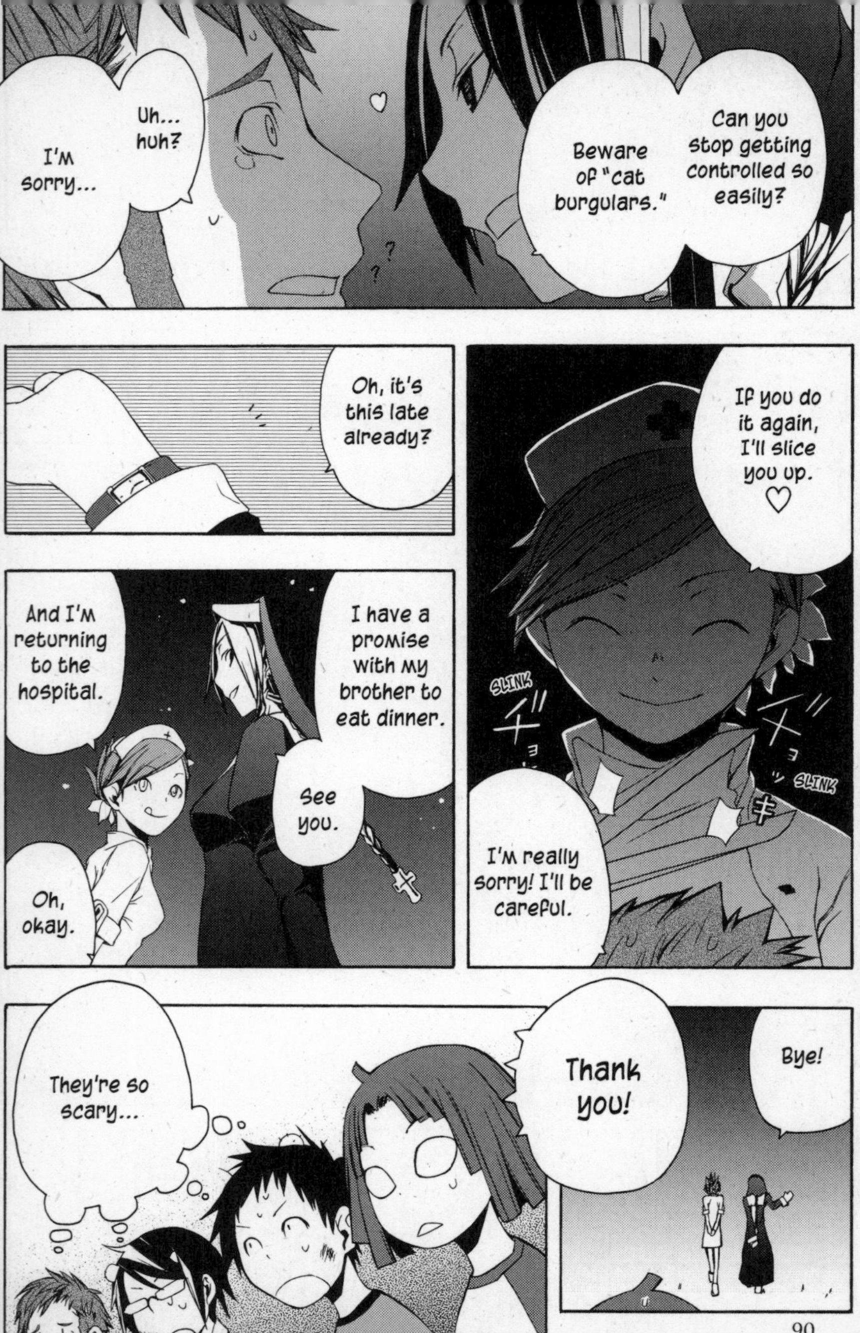
Can you stop getting controlled so easily?
Beware of "cat burgulars."
Uh... huh?
I'm sorry...
If you do it again, I'll slice you up. ♡
SLINK
SLINK
I'm really sorry! I'll be careful.
Oh, it's this late already?
I have a promise with my brother to eat dinner.
And I'm returning to the hospital.
See you.
Oh, okay.
Bye!
Thank you!
They're so scary...

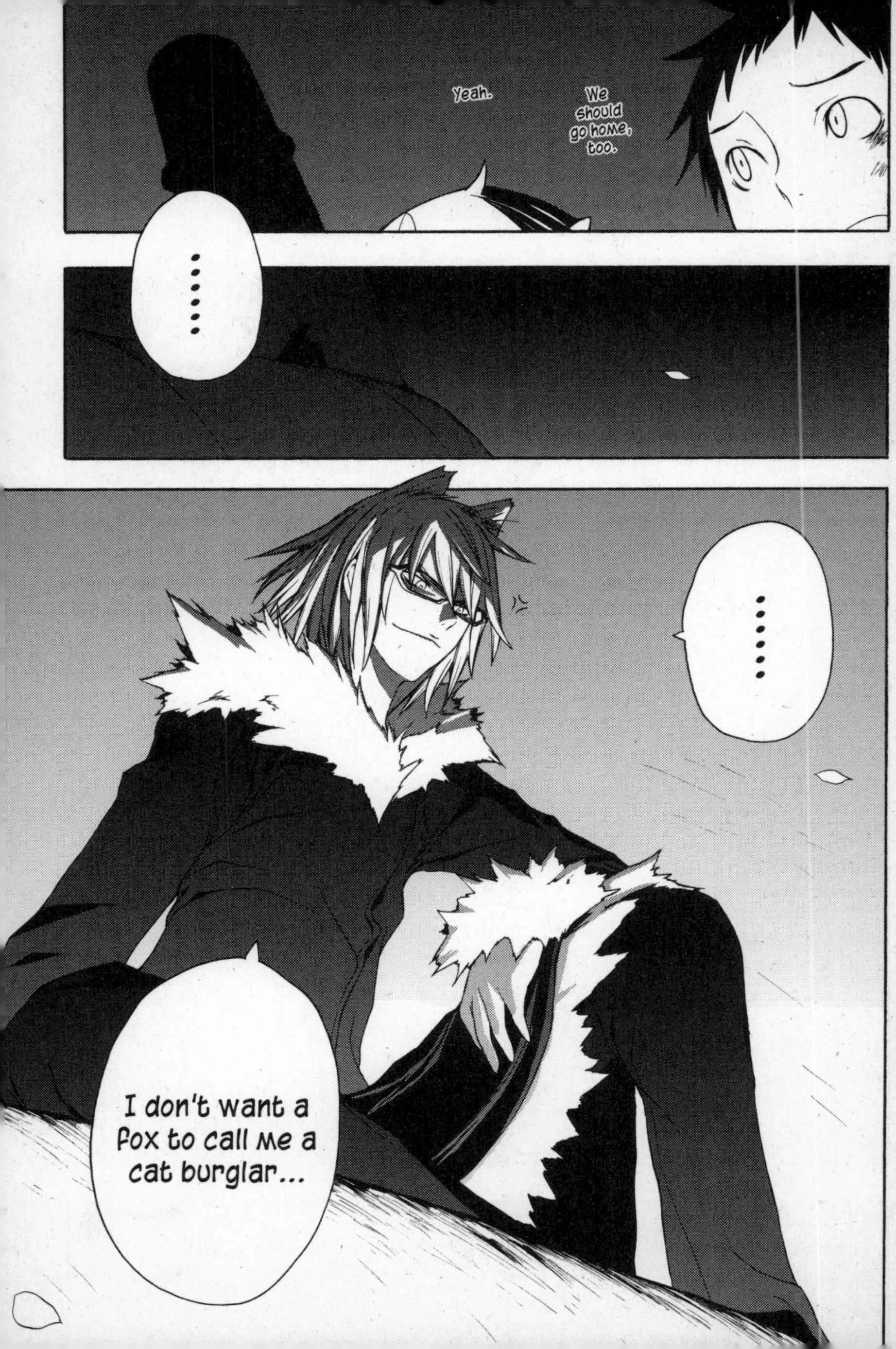
We should go home, too.
Yeah.
......
......
I don't want a fox to call me a cat burglar...

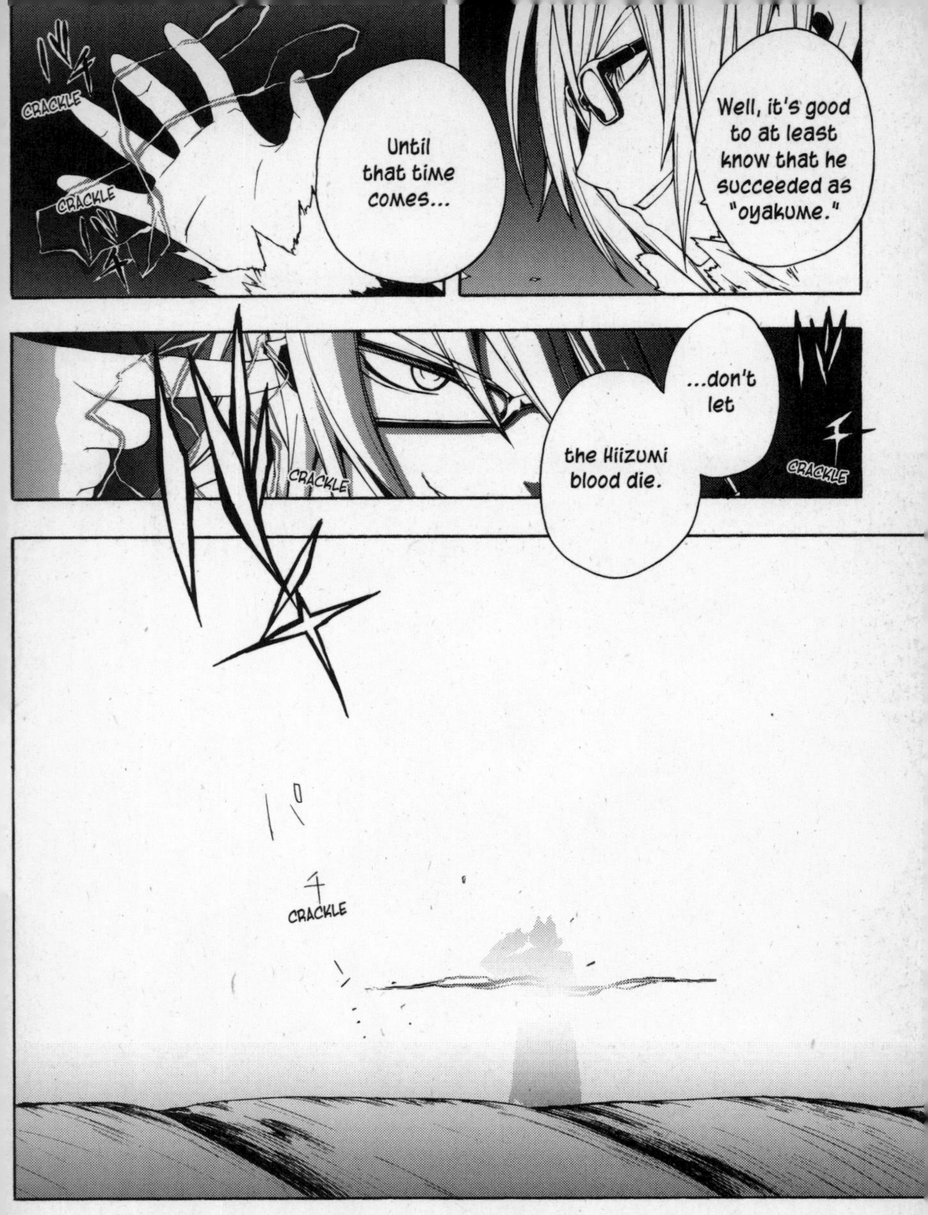
Well, it's good to at least know that he succeeded as "oyakume."
Until that time comes...
CRACKLE
CRACKLE
...don't let
the Hiizumi blood die.
CRACKLE
CRACKLE
CRACKLE

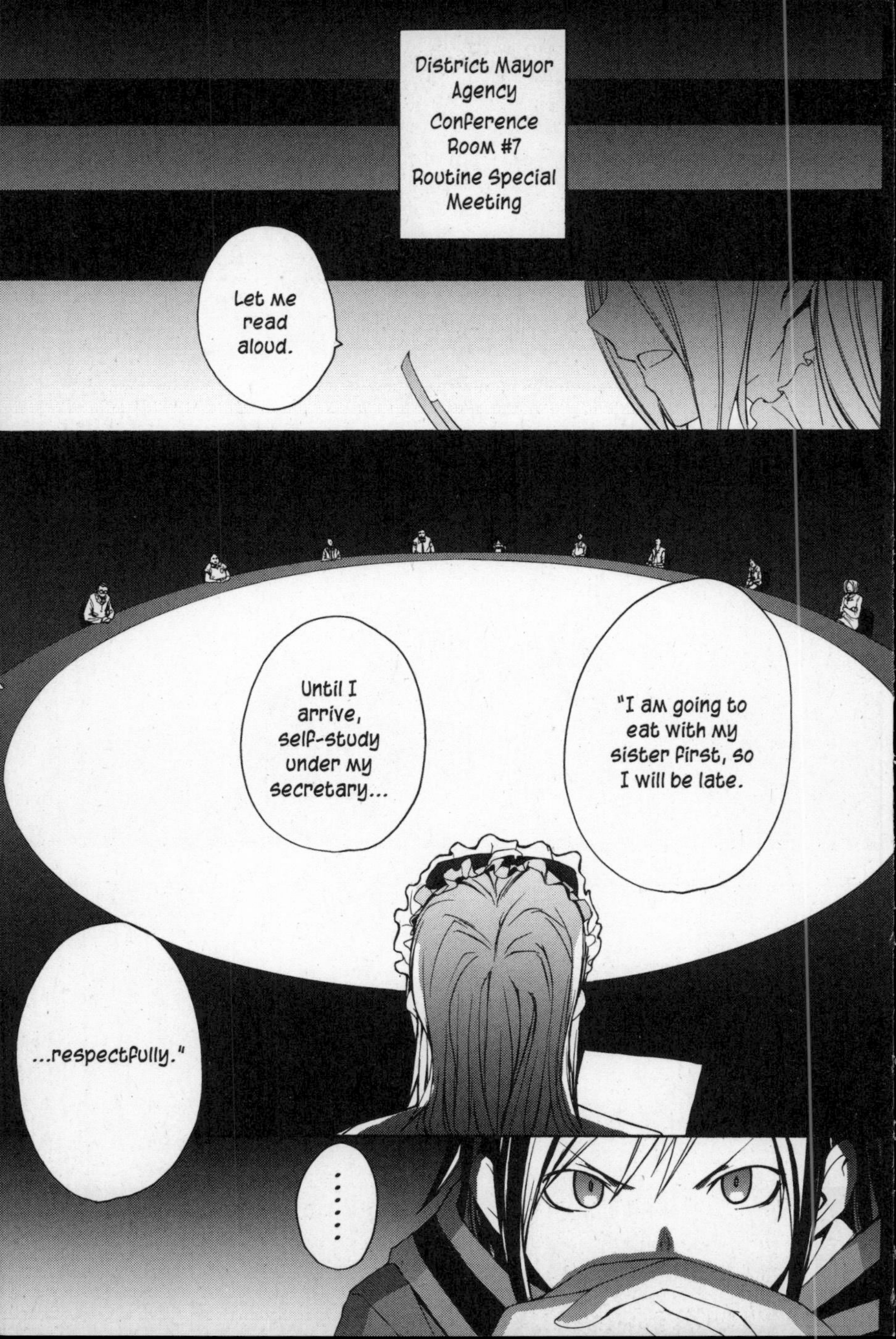
District Mayor Agency Conference Room #7 Routine Special Meeting
Let me read aloud.
"I am going to eat with my sister first, so I will be late.
Until I arrive, self-study under my secretary...
...respectfully."
......

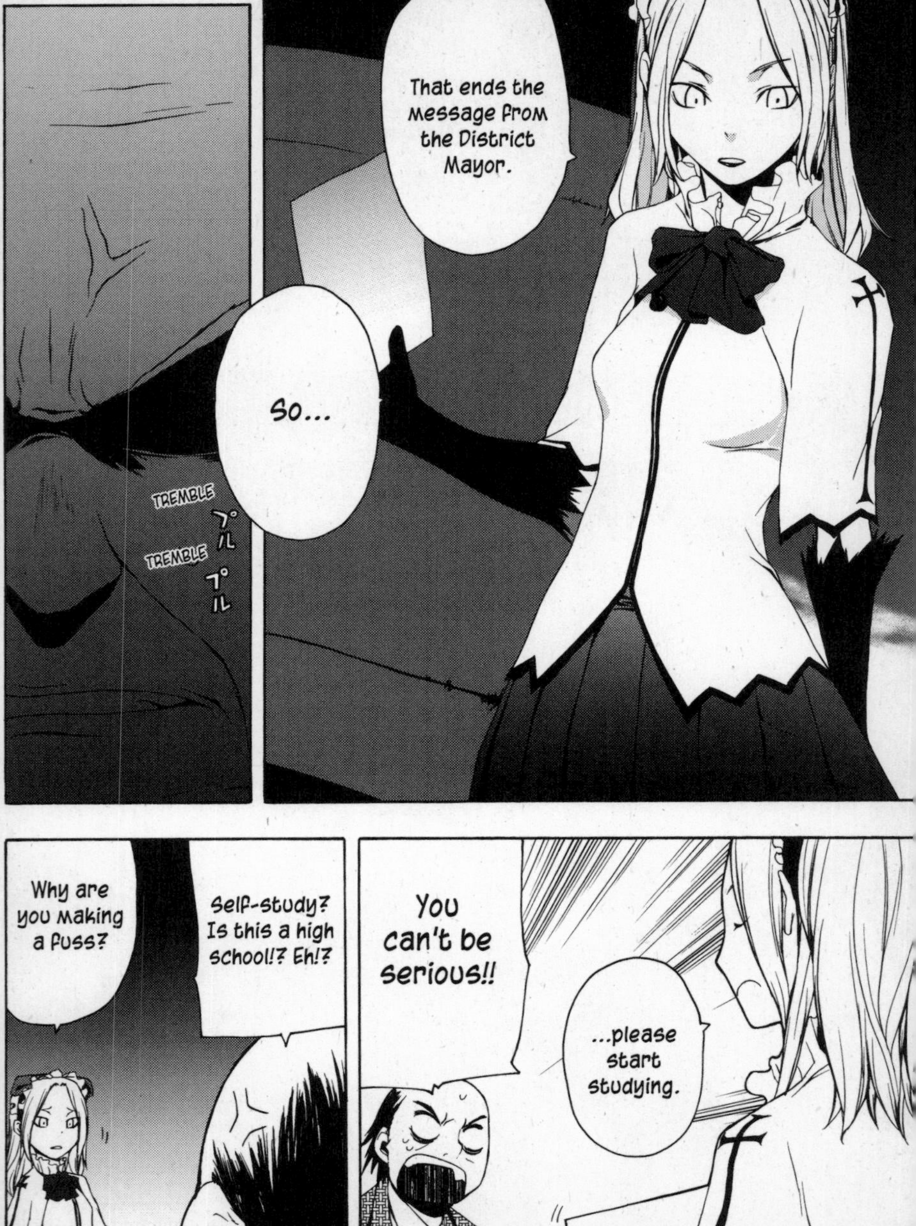
That ends the message from the District Mayor.
So...
TREMBLE プル
TREMBLE プル
...please start studying.
You can't be serious!!
Self-study? Is this a high school!? Eh!?
Why are you making a fuss?

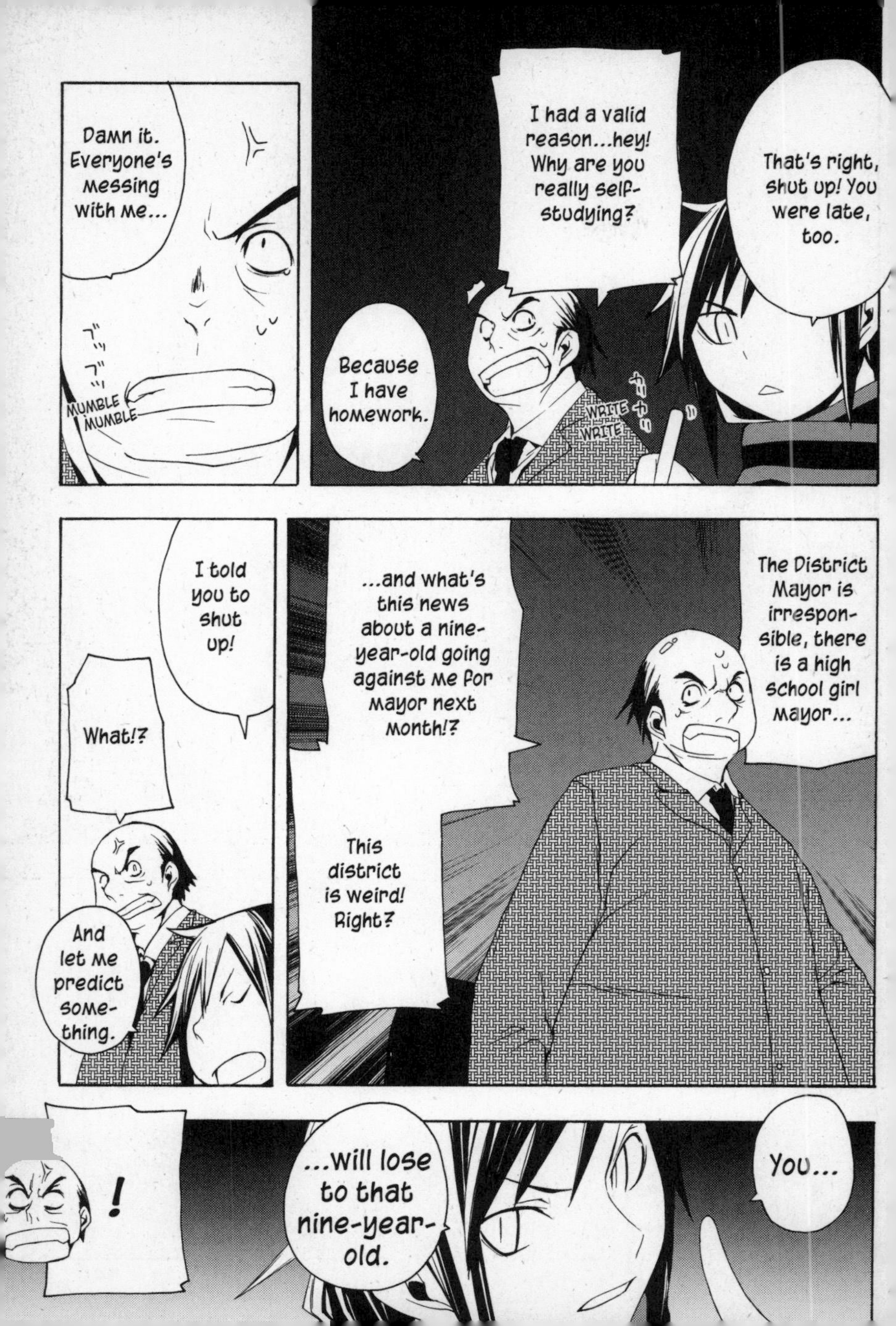

That's right, shut up! You were late, too.
I had a valid reason...hey! Why are you really self-studying?
Because I have homework.
WRITE WRITE
Damn it. Everyone's messing with me...
MUMBLE MUMBLE
The District Mayor is irresponsible, there is a high school girl mayor...
...and what's this news about a nine-year-old going against me for mayor next month!?
This district is weird! Right?
I told you to shut up!
What!?
And let me predict something.
You...
...will lose to that nine-year-old.
!

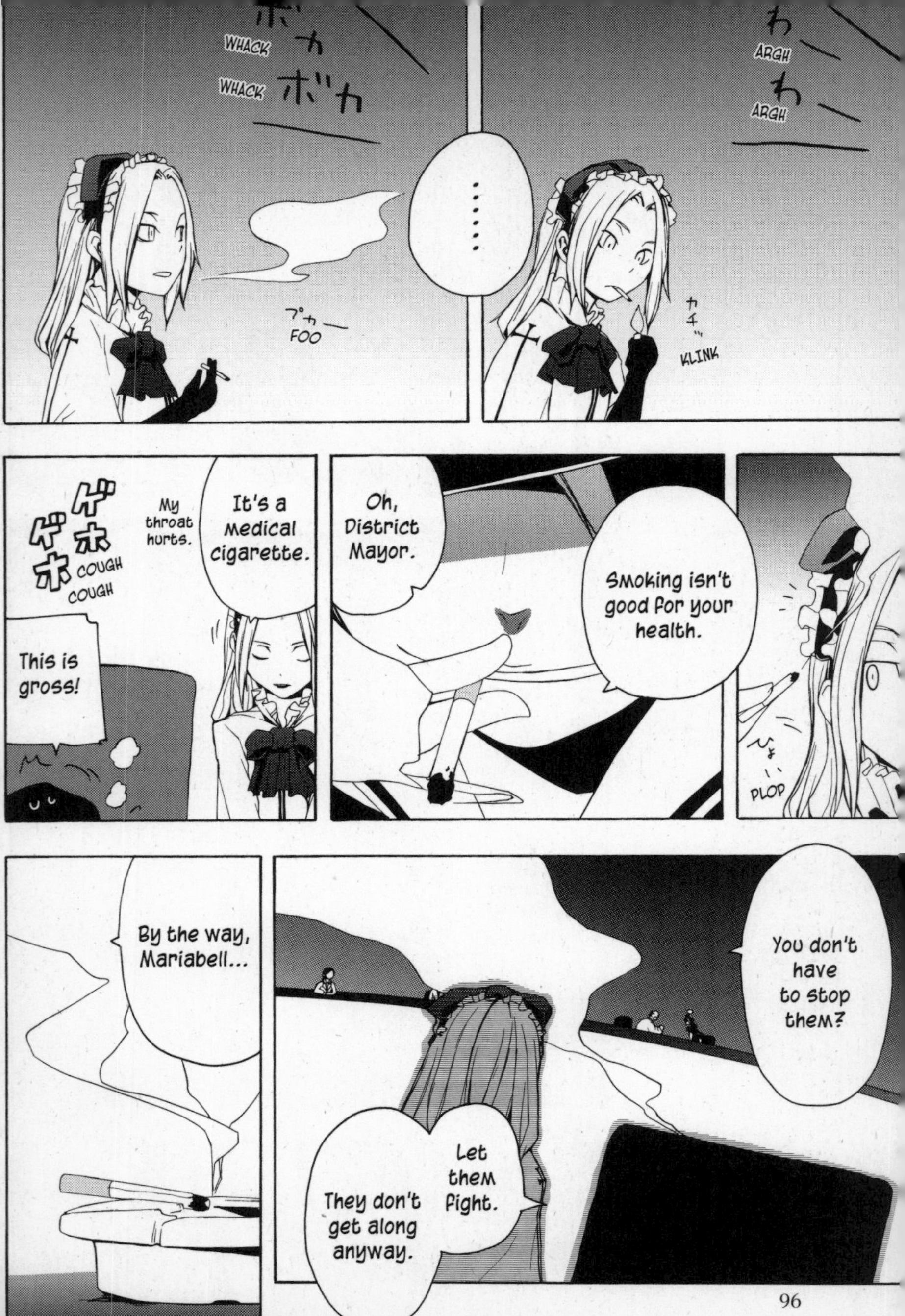
わ
ARGH
わ
ARGH
......
カチッ
KLINK
ボカ
WHACK
ボカ
WHACK
プカー
FOO
ぴょい
PLOP
Oh, District Mayor.
Smoking isn't good for your health.
It's a medical cigarette.
My throat hurts.
ゲホ
ゲホ
COUGH
COUGH
This is gross!
You don't have to stop them?
Let them fight.
They don't get along anyway.
By the way, Mariabell...

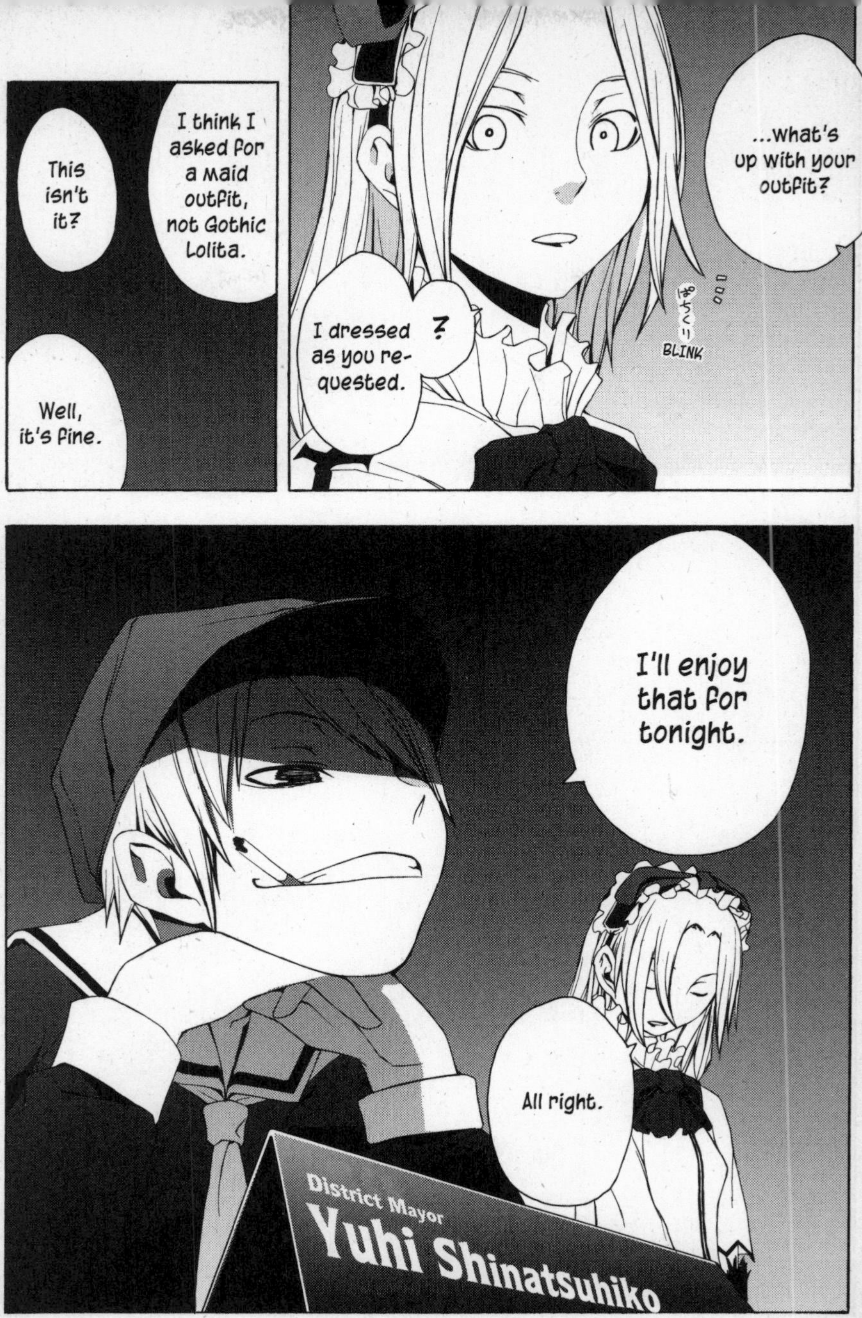
...what's up with your outfit?
ぱちくり
BLINK
?
I dressed as you requested.
I think I asked for a maid outfit, not Gothic Lolita.
This isn't it?
Well, it's fine.
I'll enjoy that for tonight.
All right.
District Mayor
Yuhi Shinatsuhiko

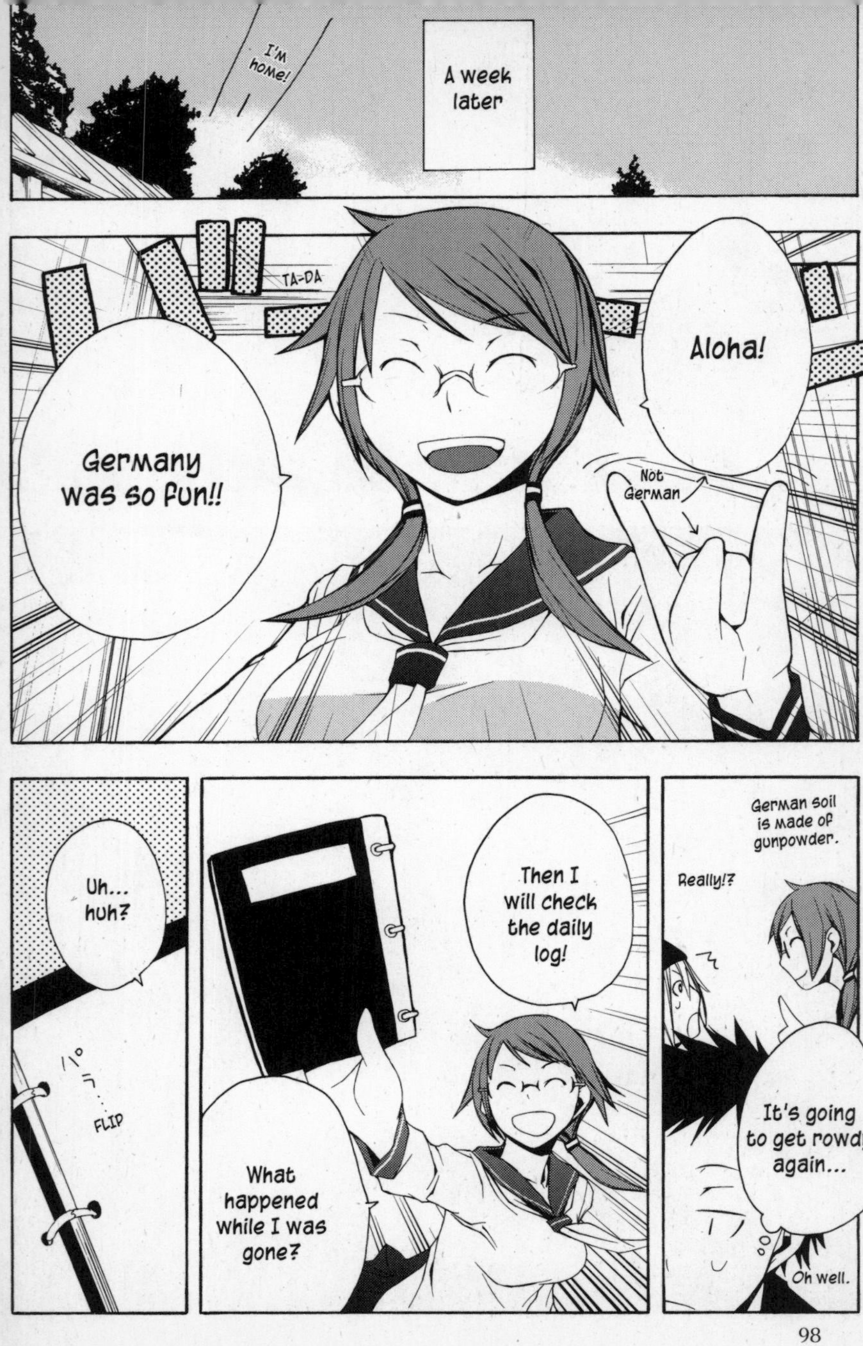
A week later
I'm home!
Aloha!
Not German
TA-DA
Germany was so fun!!
German soil is made of gunpowder.
Really!?
It's going to get rowdy again...
Oh well.
Then I will check the daily log!
What happened while I was gone?
Uh... huh?
パラ…
FLIP

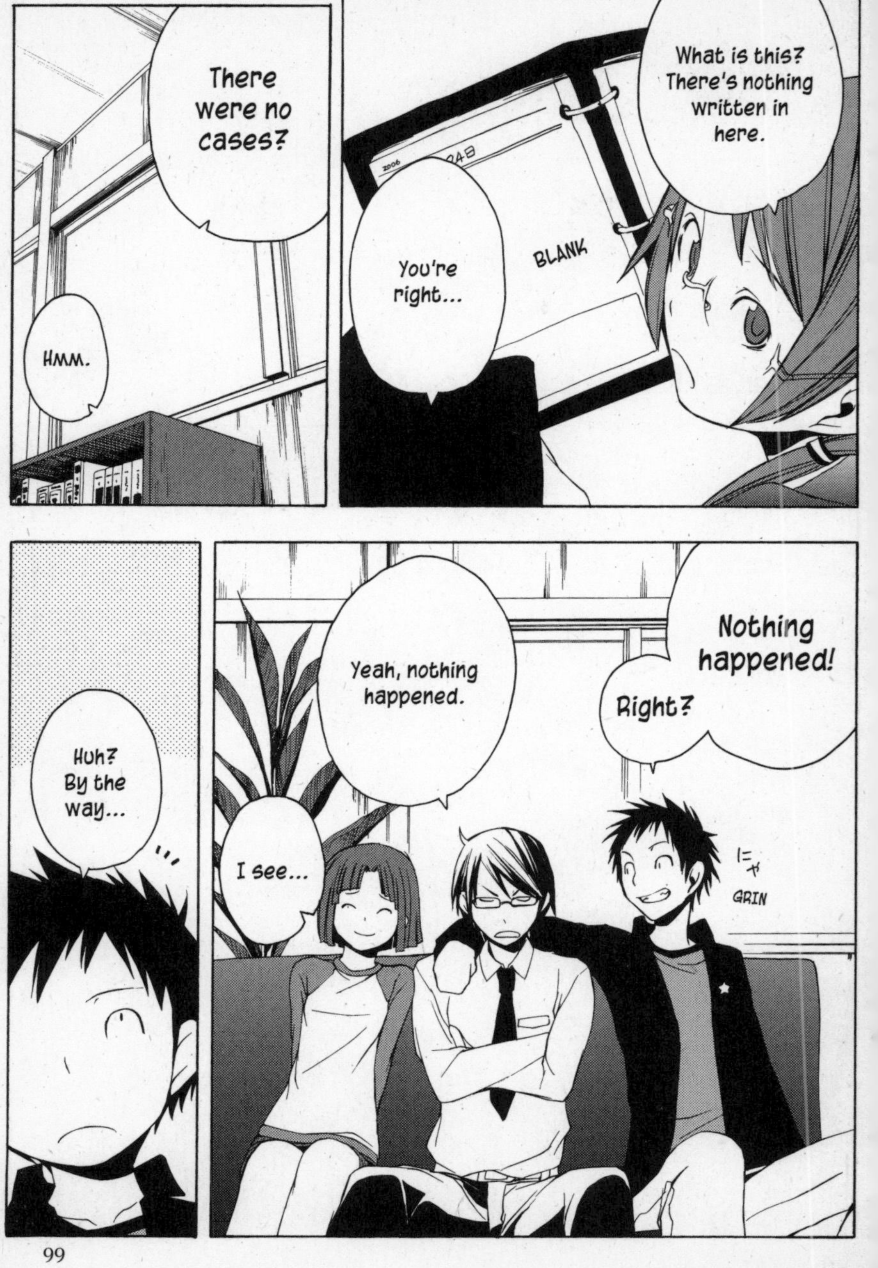
What is this? There's nothing written in here.
BLANK
You're right...
There were no cases?
Hmm.
Nothing happened!
Right?
Yeah, nothing happened.
にゃ
GRIN
I see...
Huh? By the way...

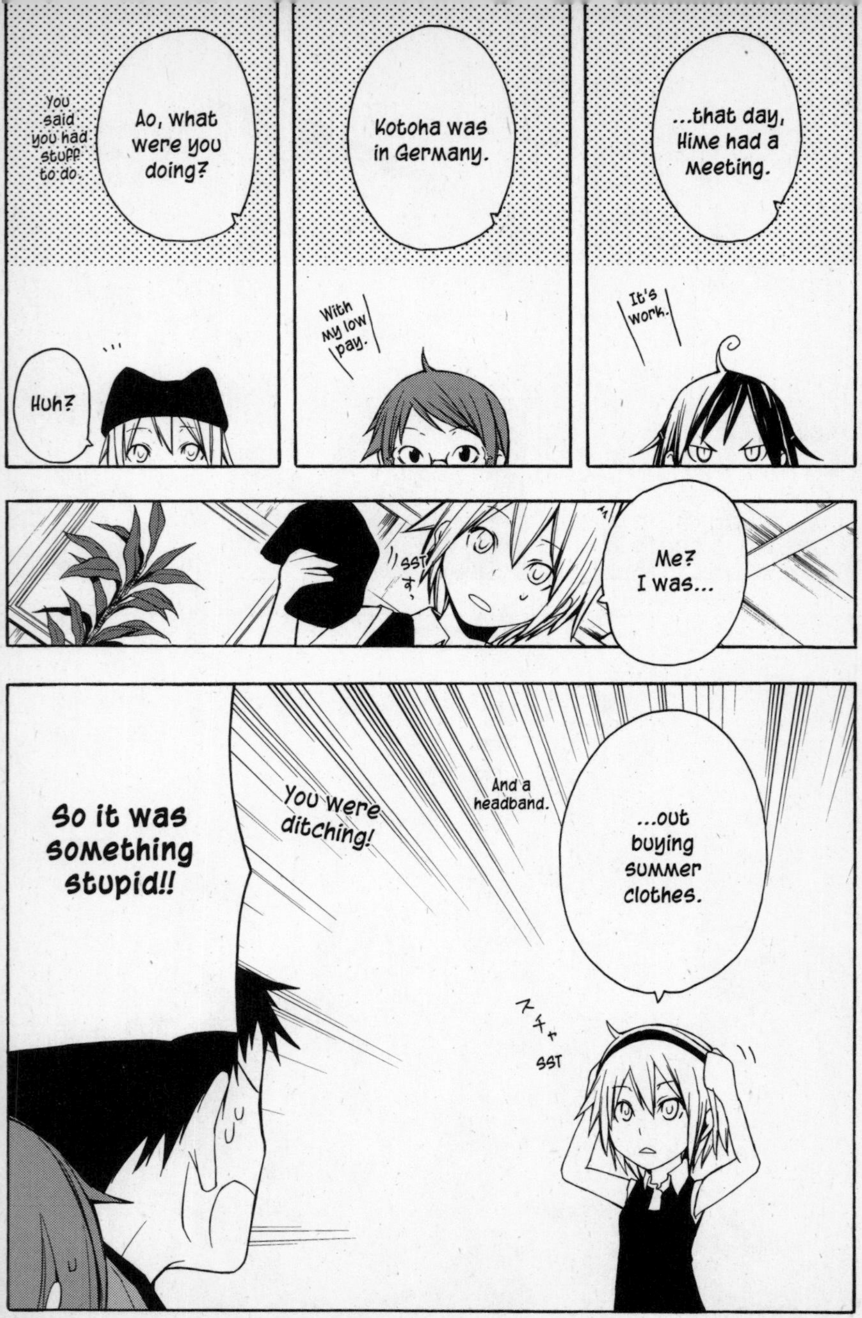
...that day, Hime had a meeting.
It's work.
Kotoha was in Germany.
With my low pay.
Ao, what were you doing?
You said you had stuff to do.
Huh?
Me? I was...
SST
す
...out buying summer clothes.
スチャ
SST
And a headband.
You were ditching!
So it was something stupid!!

8th Night: Moving Forward (Part 3) END

Yozakura Quartet 2

Primary Stages of Yozakura Quartet

 2

Akina

In "oyakume" mode

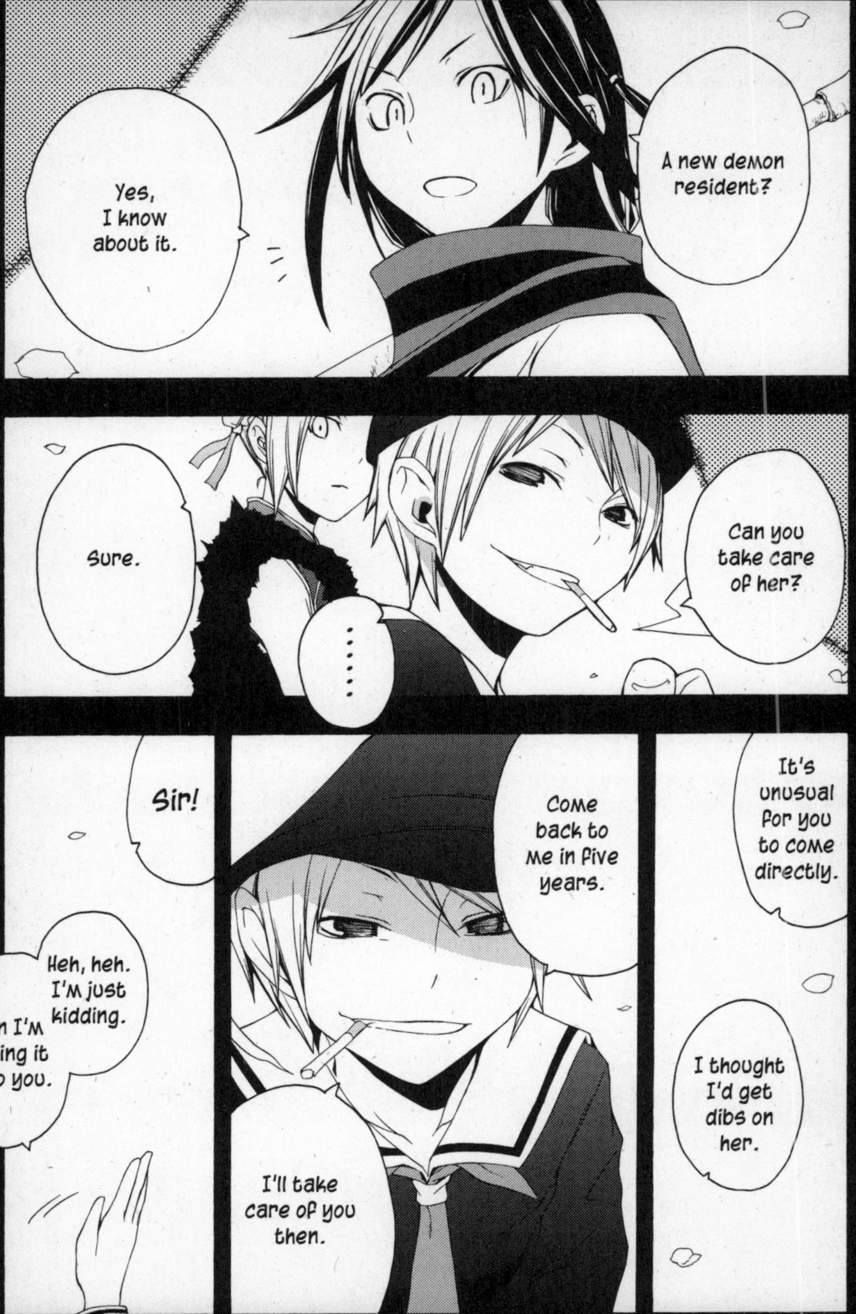
A new demon resident?
Yes, I know about it.
Can you take care of her?
......
Sure.
It's unusual for you to come directly.
I thought I'd get dibs on her.
Come back to me in five years.
I'll take care of you then.
Sir!
Heh, heh. I'm just kidding.
Then I'm leaving it up to you.

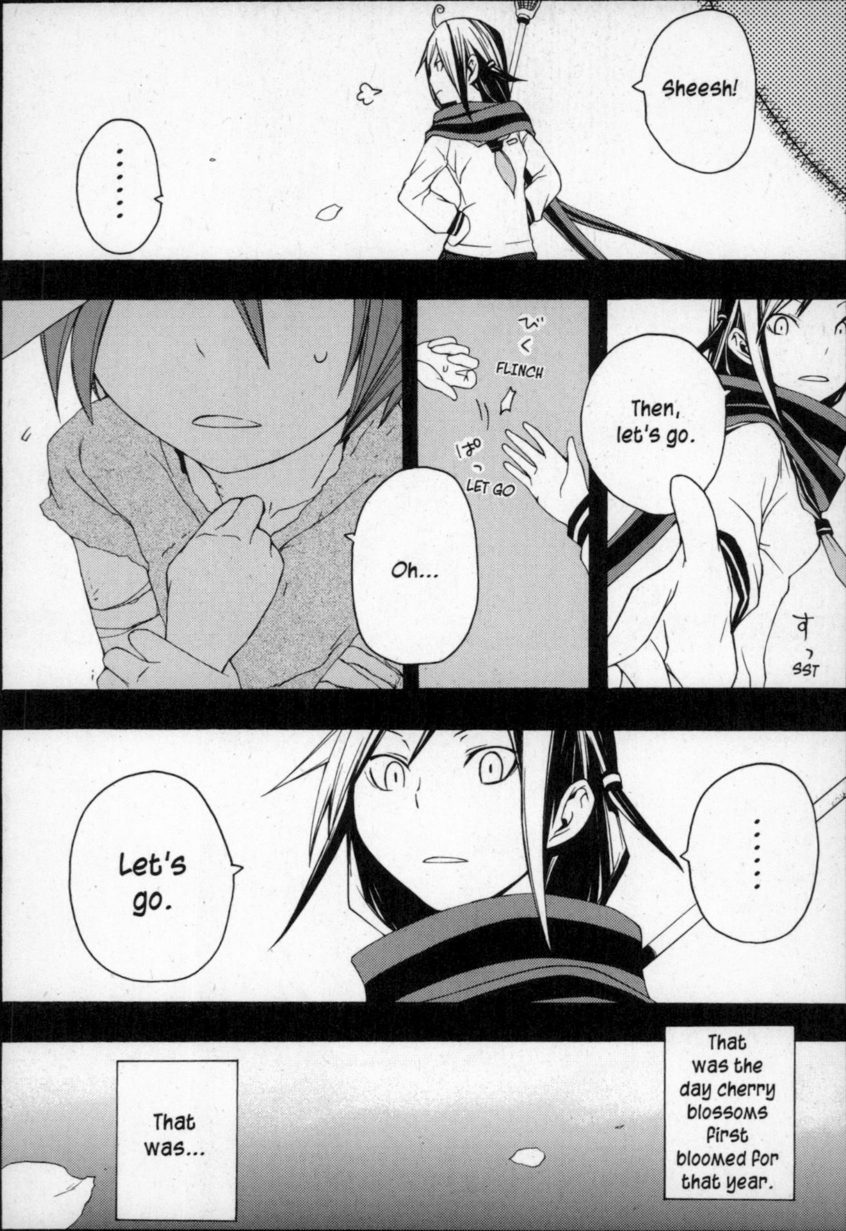
Sheesh!
......
Then, let's go.
すっ
SST
びく
FLINCH
ぱっ
LET GO
Oh...
......
Let's go.
That was the day cherry blossoms first bloomed for that year.
That was...

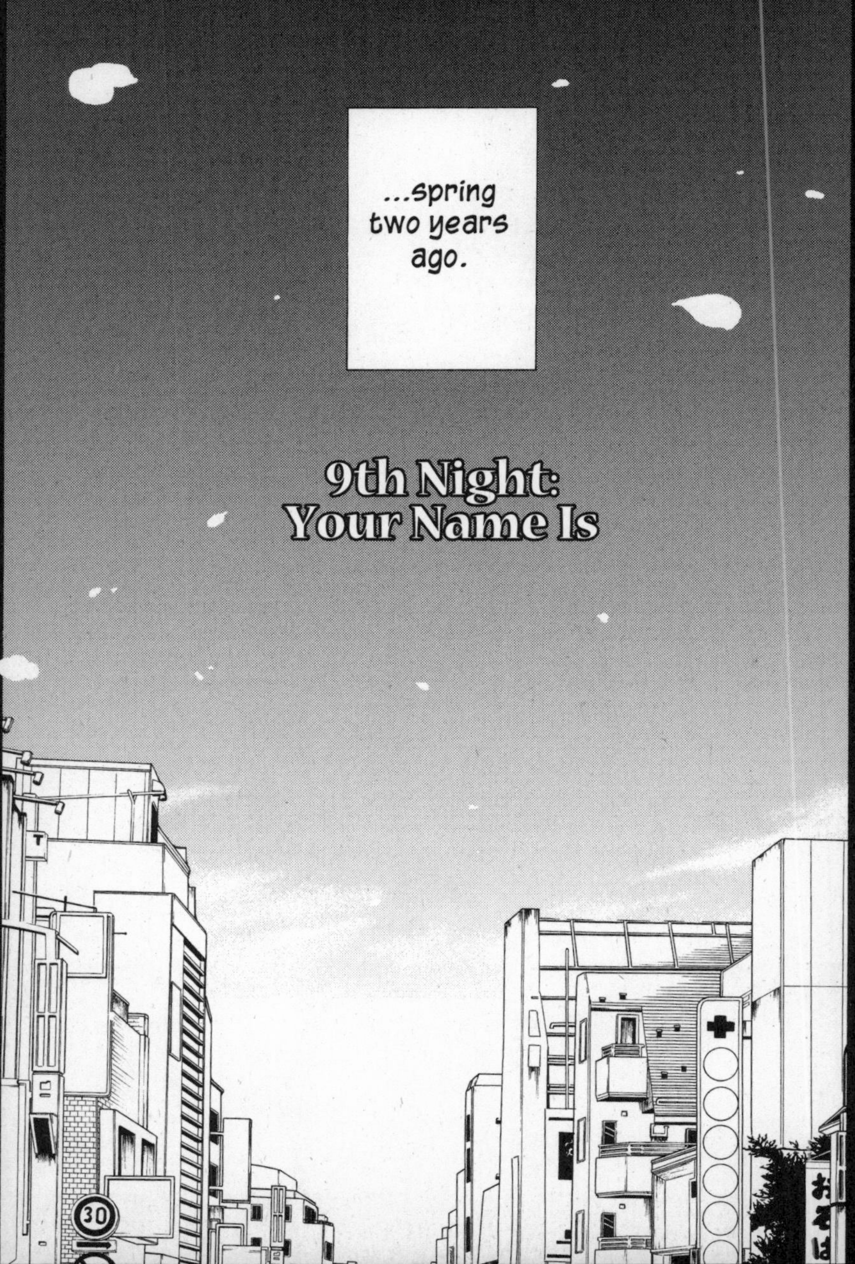
...spring two years ago.
9th Night: Your Name Is
30

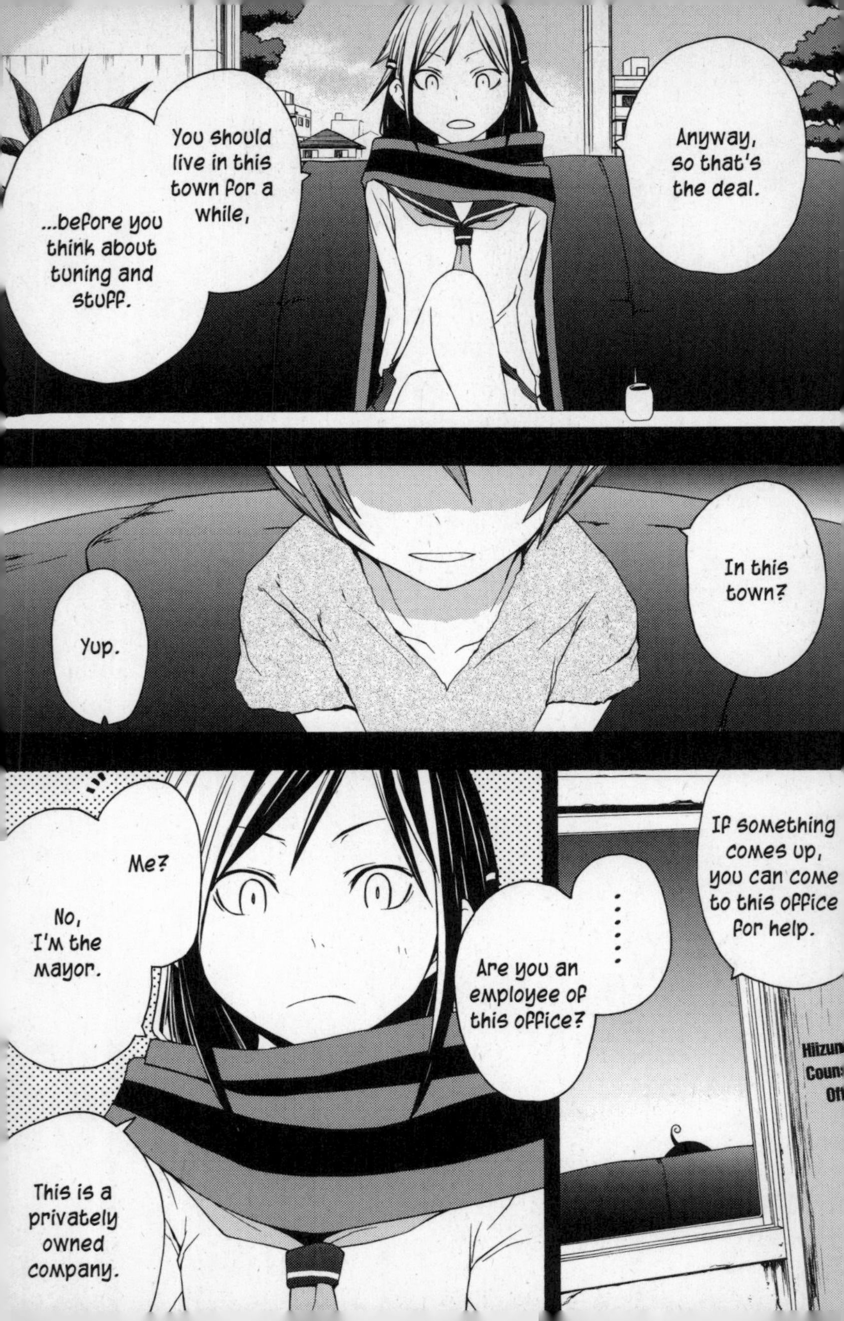
Anyway, so that's the deal.
You should live in this town for a while,
...before you think about tuning and stuff.
In this town?
Yup.
If something comes up, you can come to this office for help.
......
Are you an employee of this office?
Me?
No, I'm the mayor.
This is a privately owned company.

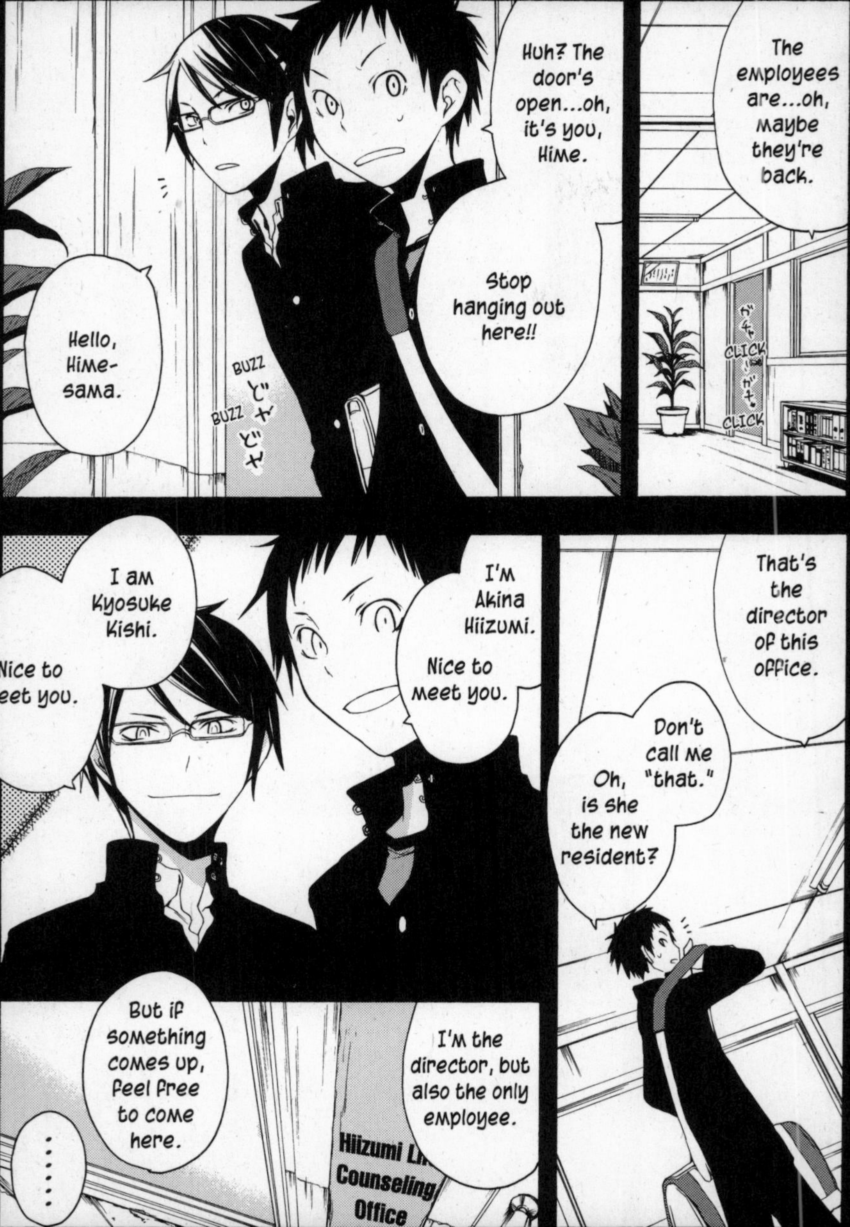
The employees are...oh, maybe they're back.
CLICK ガチャ
CLICK ガチャ
Huh? The door's open...oh, it's you, Hime.
Stop hanging out here!!
BUZZ どや
BUZZ どや
Hello, Hime-sama.
That's the director of this office.
Don't call me "that."
Oh, is she the new resident?
I'm Akina Hiizumi.
Nice to meet you.
I am Kyosuke Kishi.
Nice to meet you.
I'm the director, but also the only employee.
But if something comes up, feel free to come here.
......
Hiizumi Li
Counseling
Office

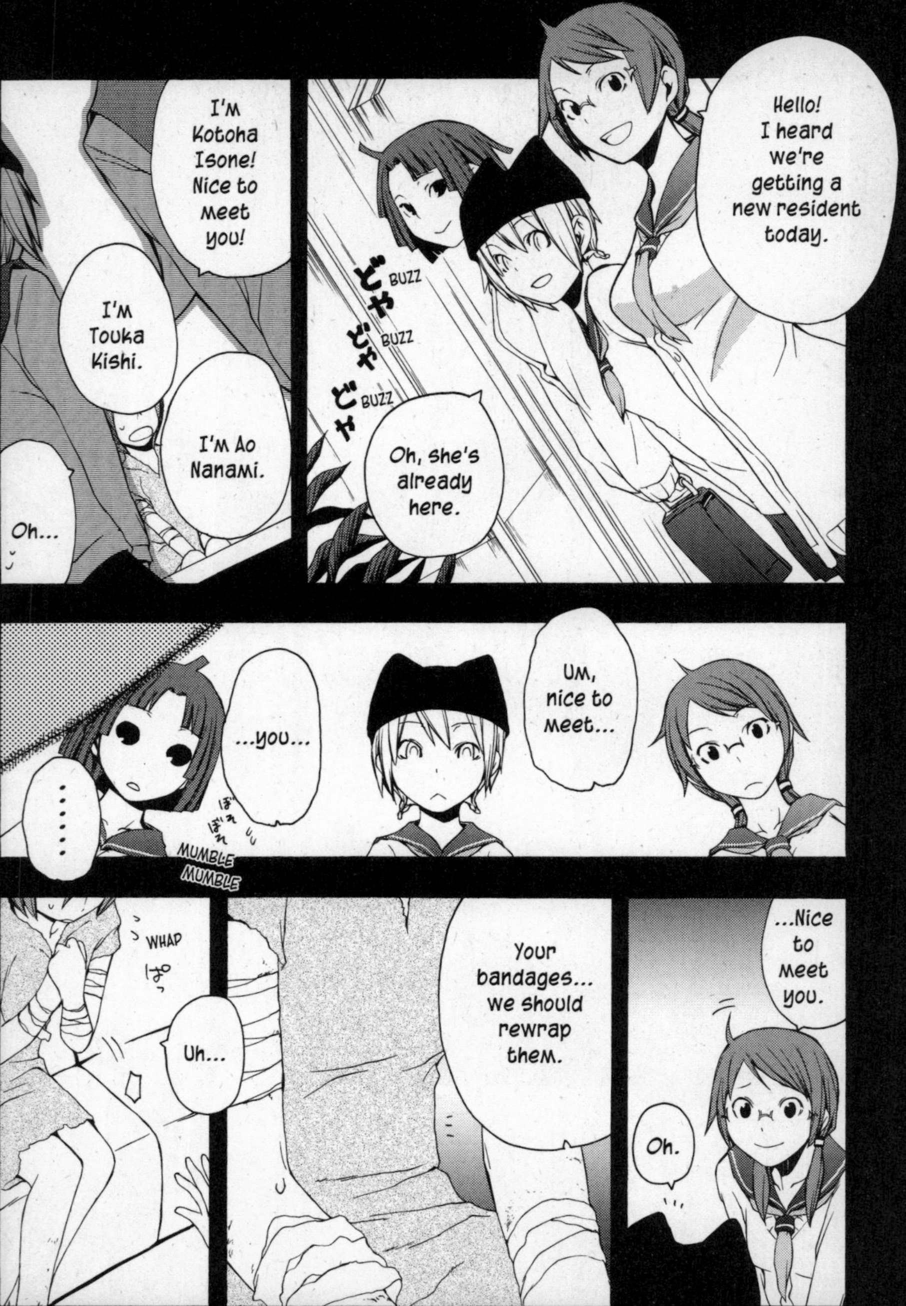
Hello! I heard we're getting a new resident today.
どや BUZZ
どや BUZZ
どや BUZZ
Oh, she's already here.
I'm Kotoha Isone! Nice to meet you!
I'm Touka Kishi.
I'm Ao Nanami.
Oh...
Um, nice to meet...
...you...
ぼそぼそ
MUMBLE MUMBLE
......
...Nice to meet you.
Oh.
Your bandages... we should rewrap them.
Uh...
WHAP
ぱっ

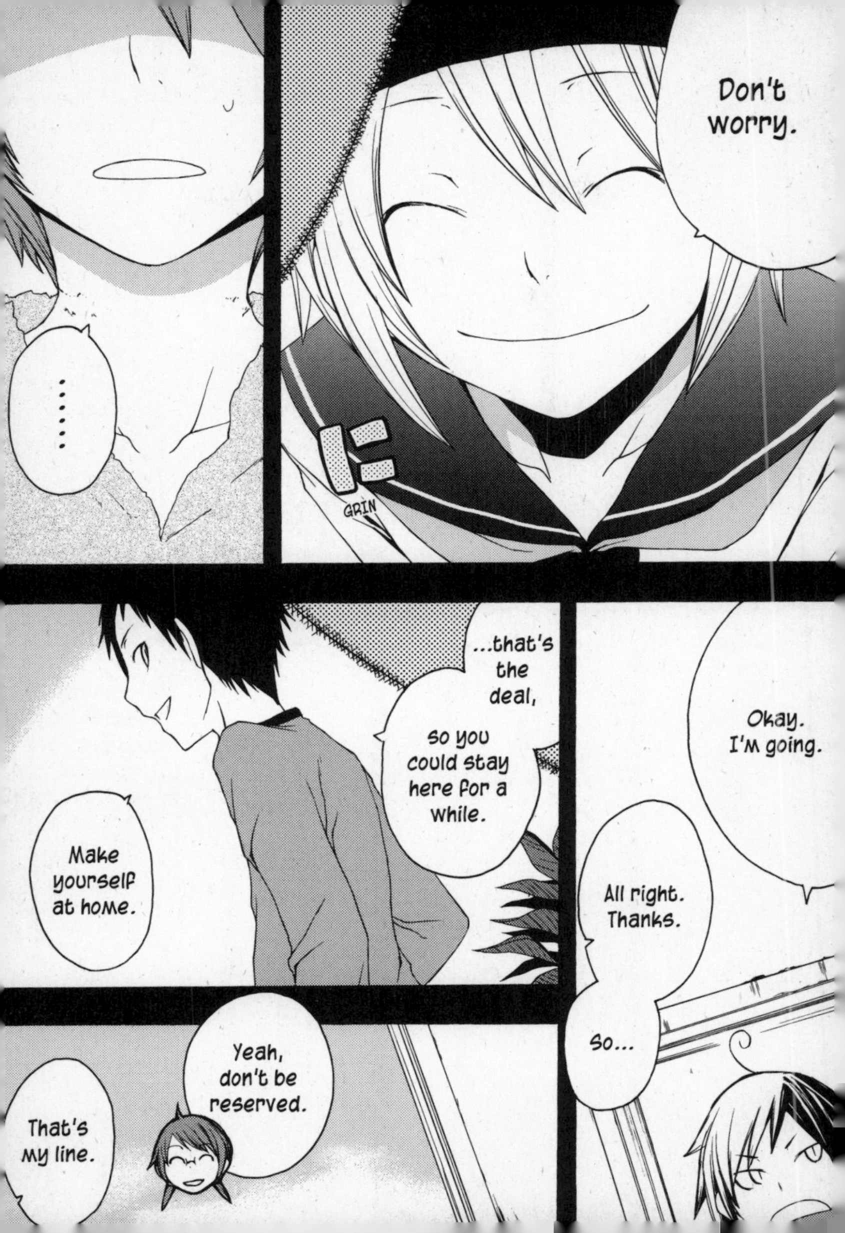
Don't worry.
GRIN
......
Okay. I'm going.
All right. Thanks.
So...
...that's the deal,
so you could stay here for a while.
Make yourself at home.
Yeah, don't be reserved.
That's my line.

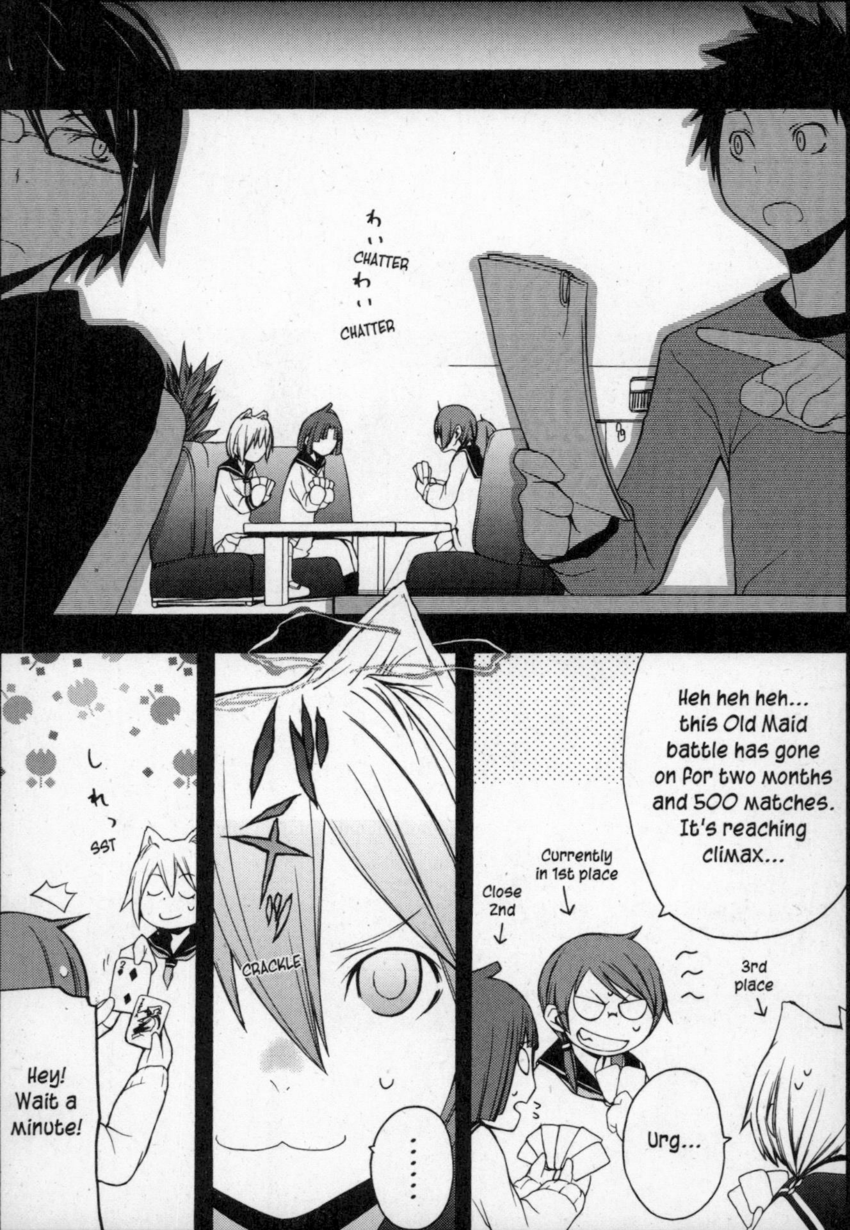
わい
CHATTER
わい
CHATTER
Heh heh heh... this Old Maid battle has gone on for two months and 500 matches. It's reaching climax...
3rd place
Currently in 1st place
Close 2nd
Urg...
CRACKLE
......
しれっ
SST
Hey! Wait a minute!

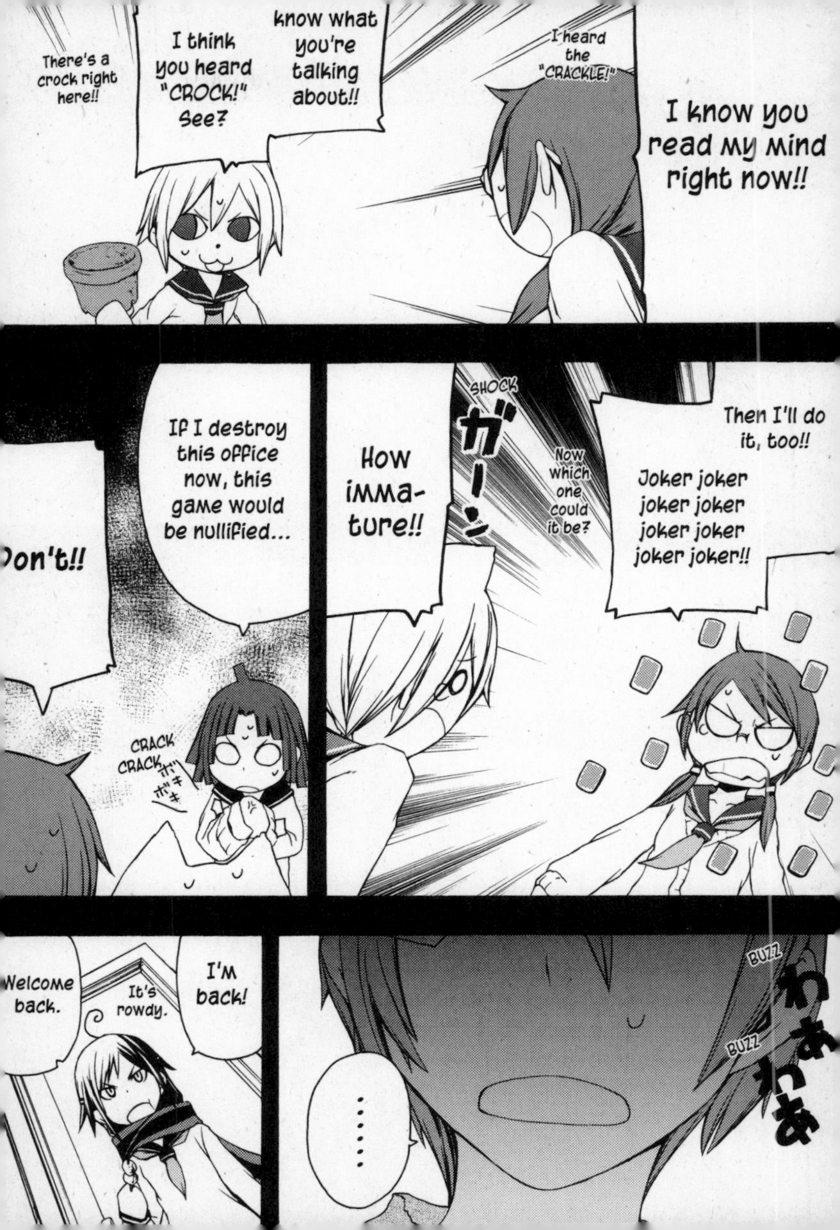
I know you read my mind right now!!
I heard the "CRACKLE!"
know what you're talking about!!
I think you heard "CROCK!" See?
There's a crock right here!!
Then I'll do it, too!!
Joker joker joker joker joker joker joker joker!!
Now which one could it be?
SHOCK
How imma-ture!!
If I destroy this office now, this game would be nullified...
Don't!!
CRACK CRACK
BUZZ
BUZZ
......
I'm back!
It's rowdy.
Welcome back.

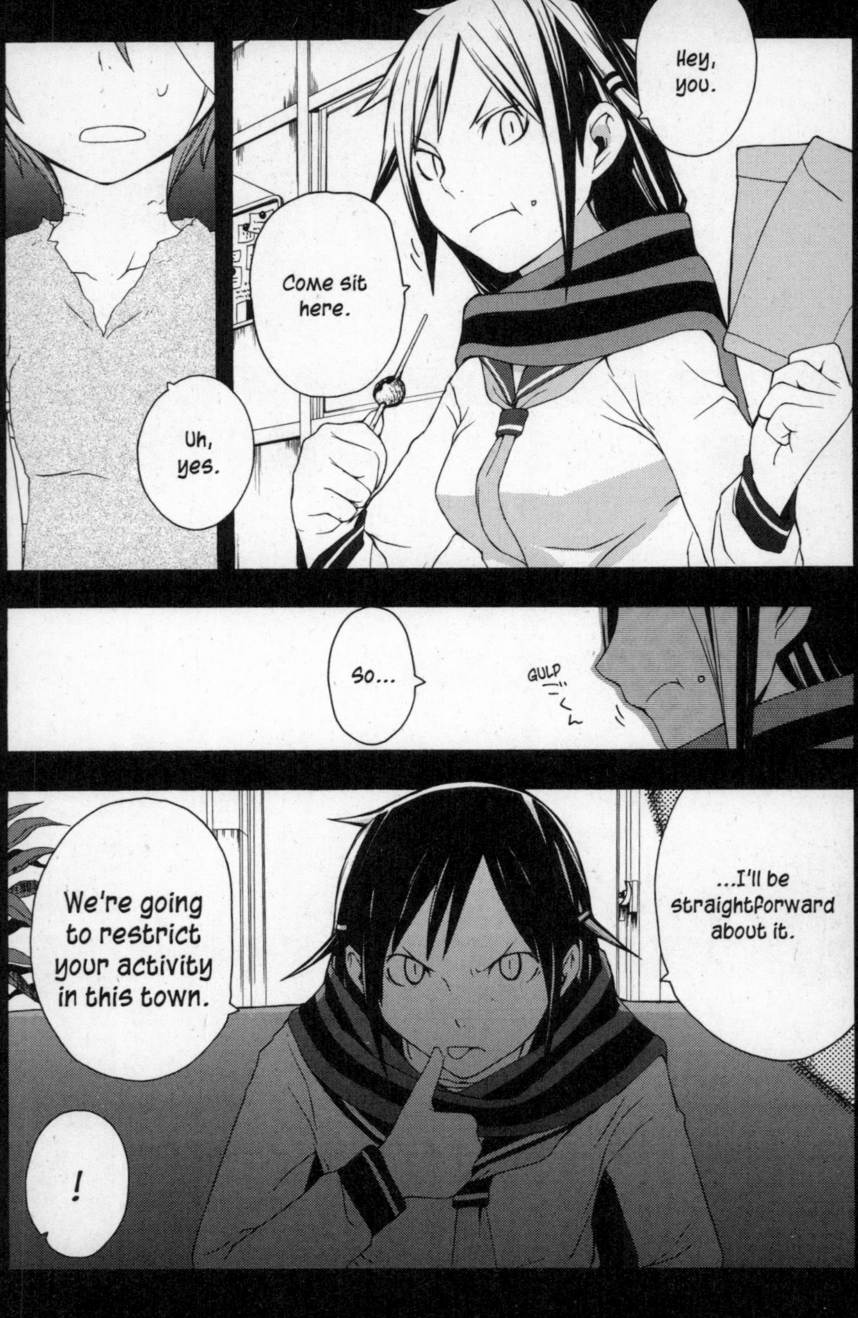
Hey, you.
Come sit here.
Uh, yes.
So...
GULP
ごくん
...I'll be straightforward about it.
We're going to restrict your activity in this town.
!

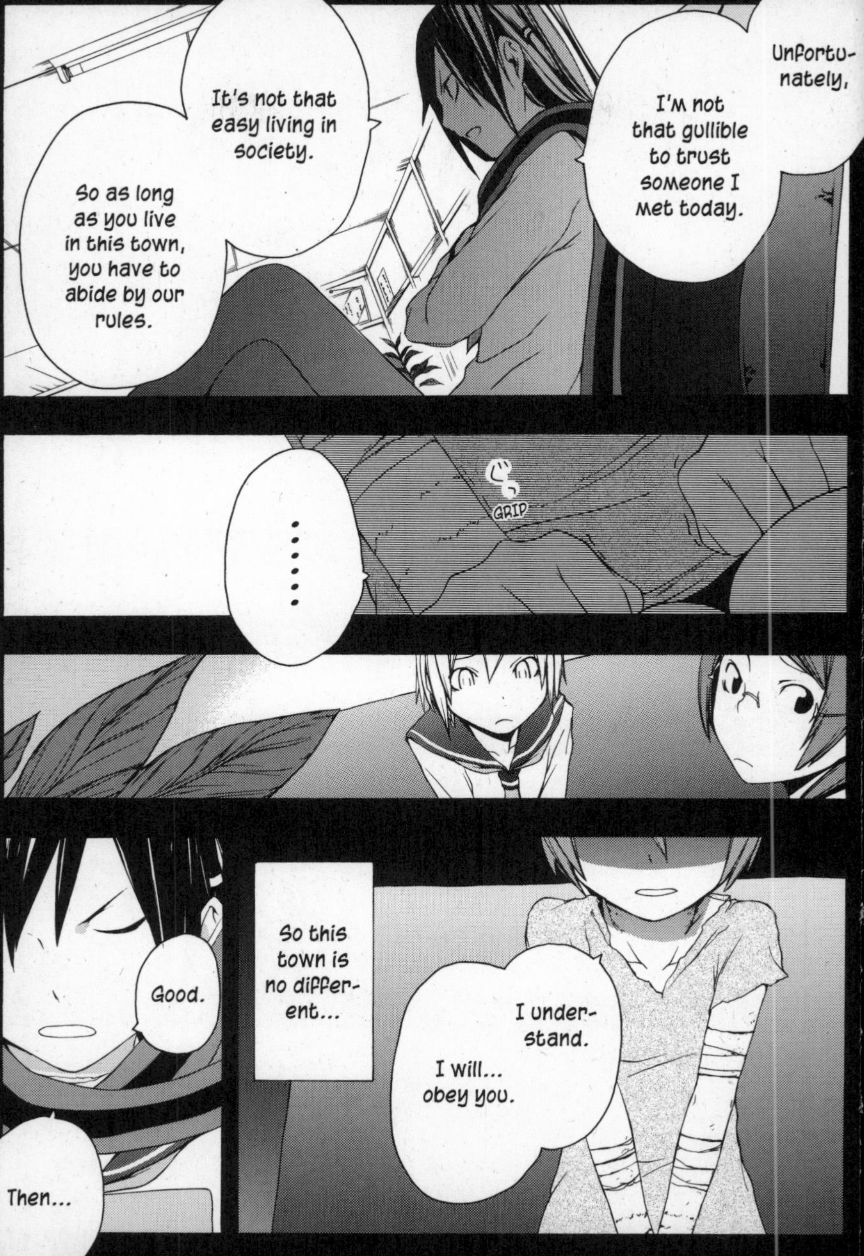

Unfortunately,
I'm not that gullible to trust someone I met today.
It's not that easy living in society.
So as long as you live in this town, you have to abide by our rules.
ぐっ
GRIP
......
I understand.
I will... obey you.
So this town is no different...
Good.
Then...

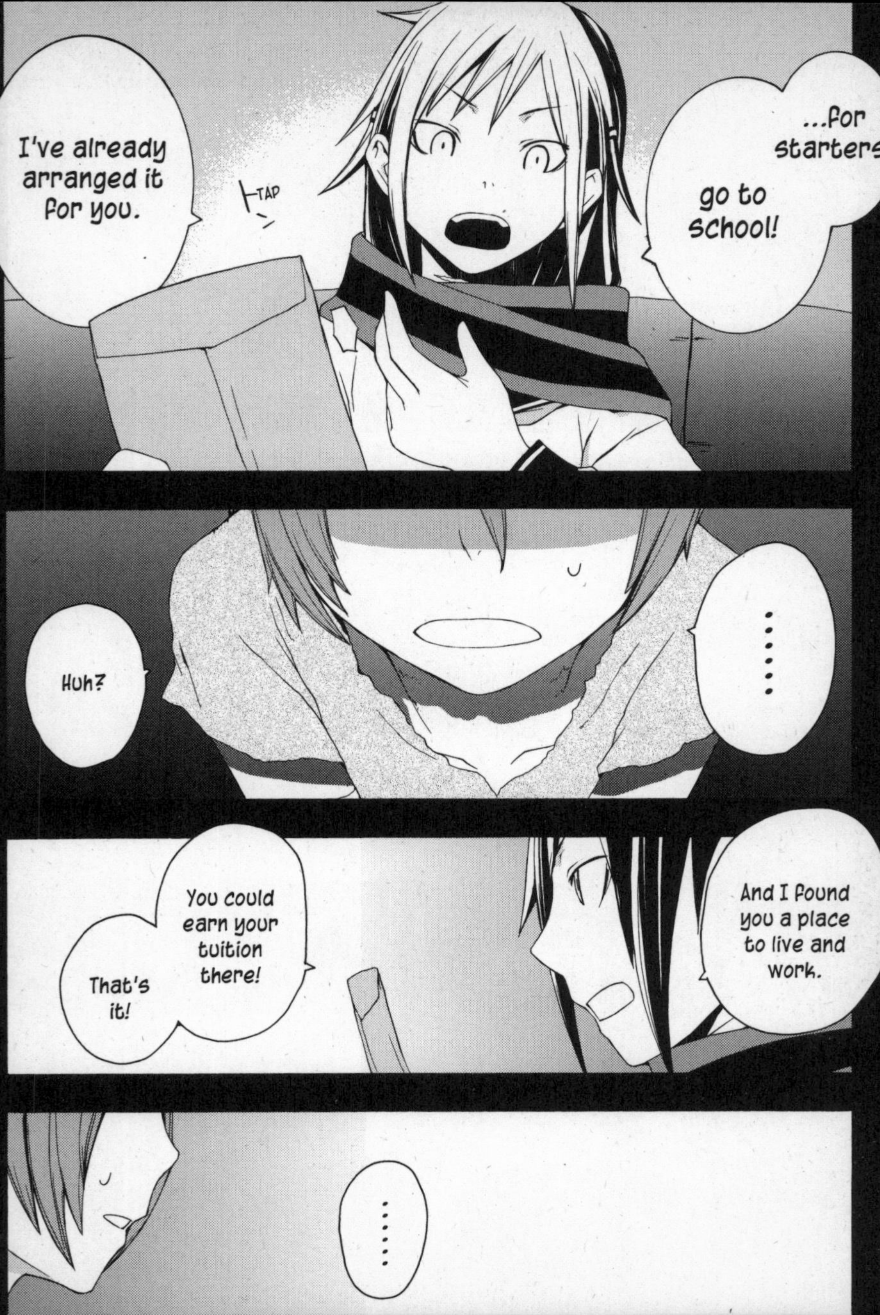
...for starters, go to school!
TAP
I've already arranged it for you.
......
Huh?
And I found you a place to live and work.
You could earn your tuition there!
That's it!
......

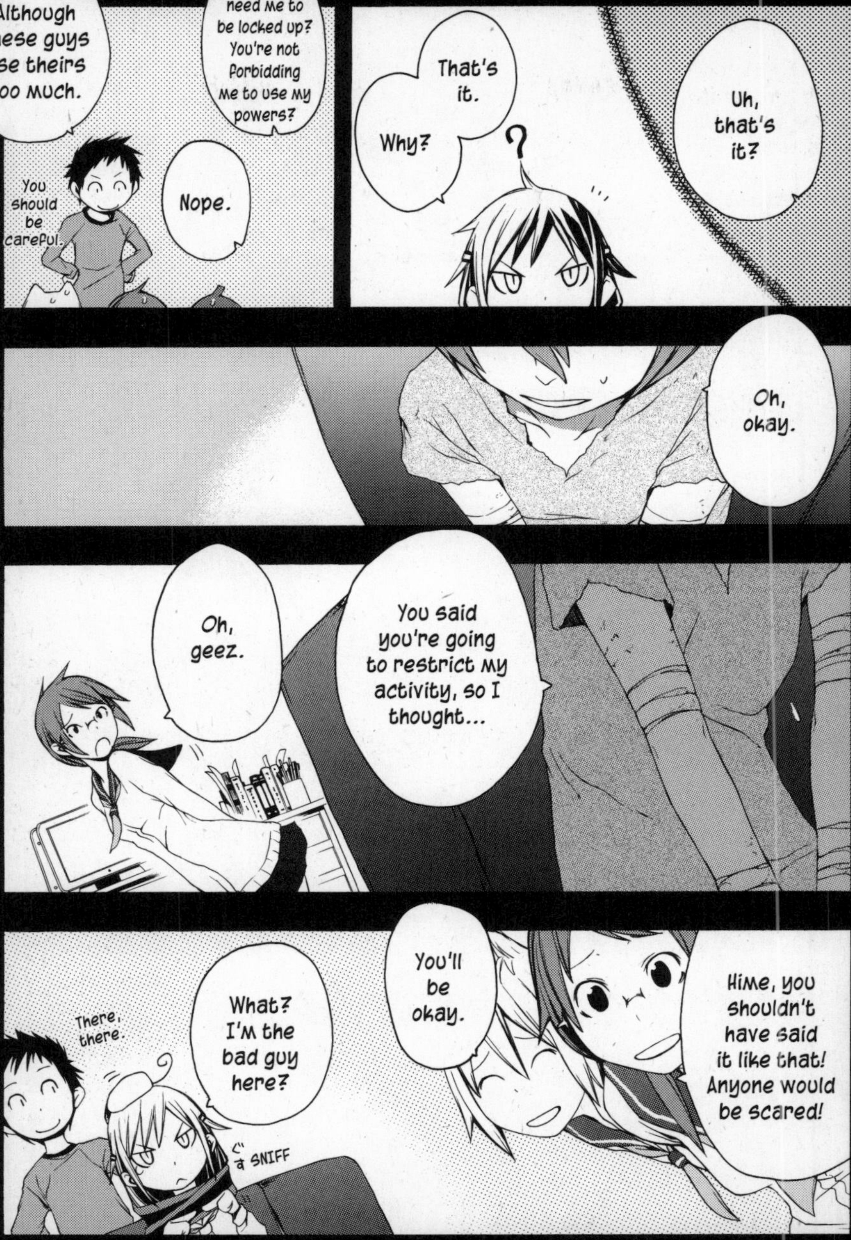
Uh, that's it?
That's it.
Why?
You don't need me to be locked up? You're not forbidding me to use my powers?
Although these guys use theirs too much.
Nope.
You should be careful.
Oh, okay.
You said you're going to restrict my activity, so I thought...
Oh, geez.
Hime, you shouldn't have said it like that! Anyone would be scared!
You'll be okay.
What? I'm the bad guy here?
SNIFF
There, there.

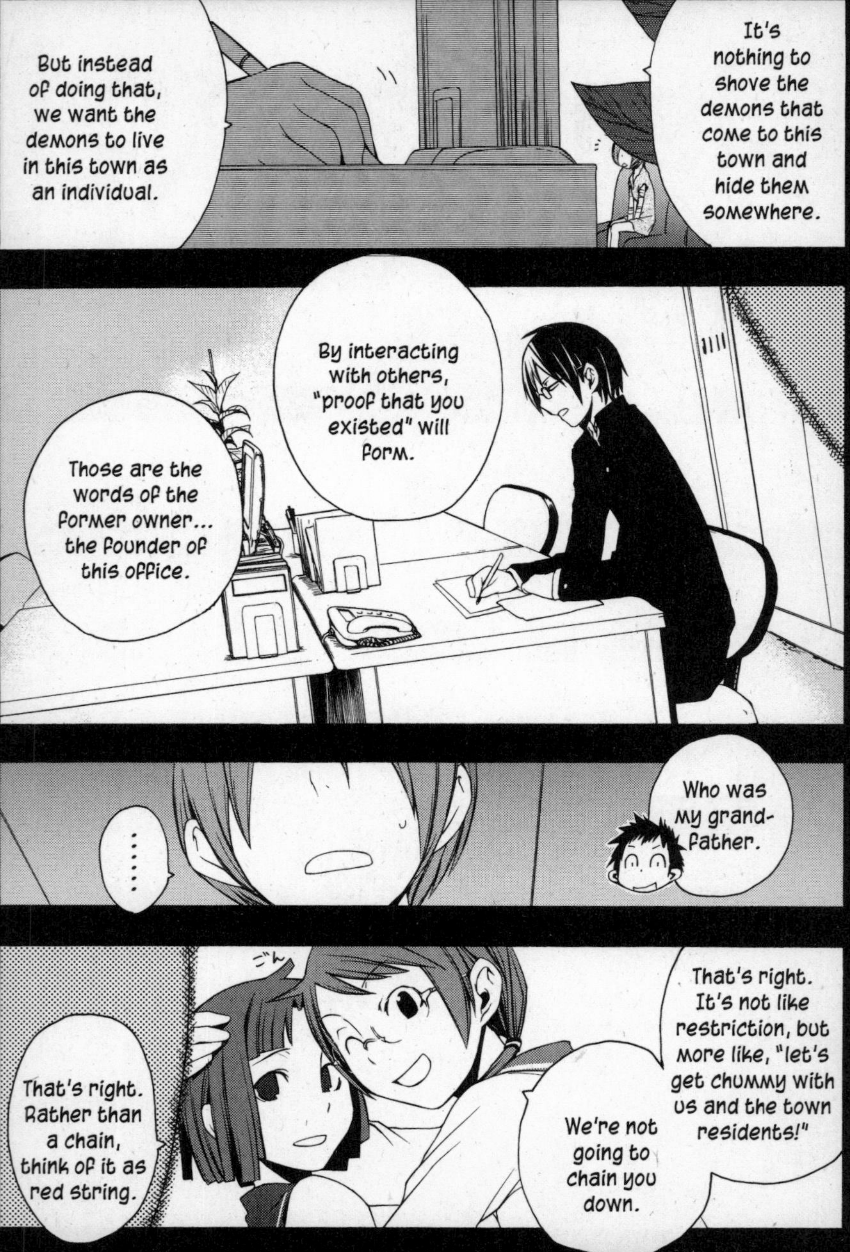
It's nothing to shove the demons that come to this town and hide them somewhere.
But instead of doing that, we want the demons to live in this town as an individual.
By interacting with others, "proof that you existed" will form.
Those are the words of the former owner... the founder of this office.
Who was my grand-father.
......
That's right. It's not like restriction, but more like, "let's get chummy with us and the town residents!"
We're not going to chain you down.
That's right. Rather than a chain, think of it as red string.

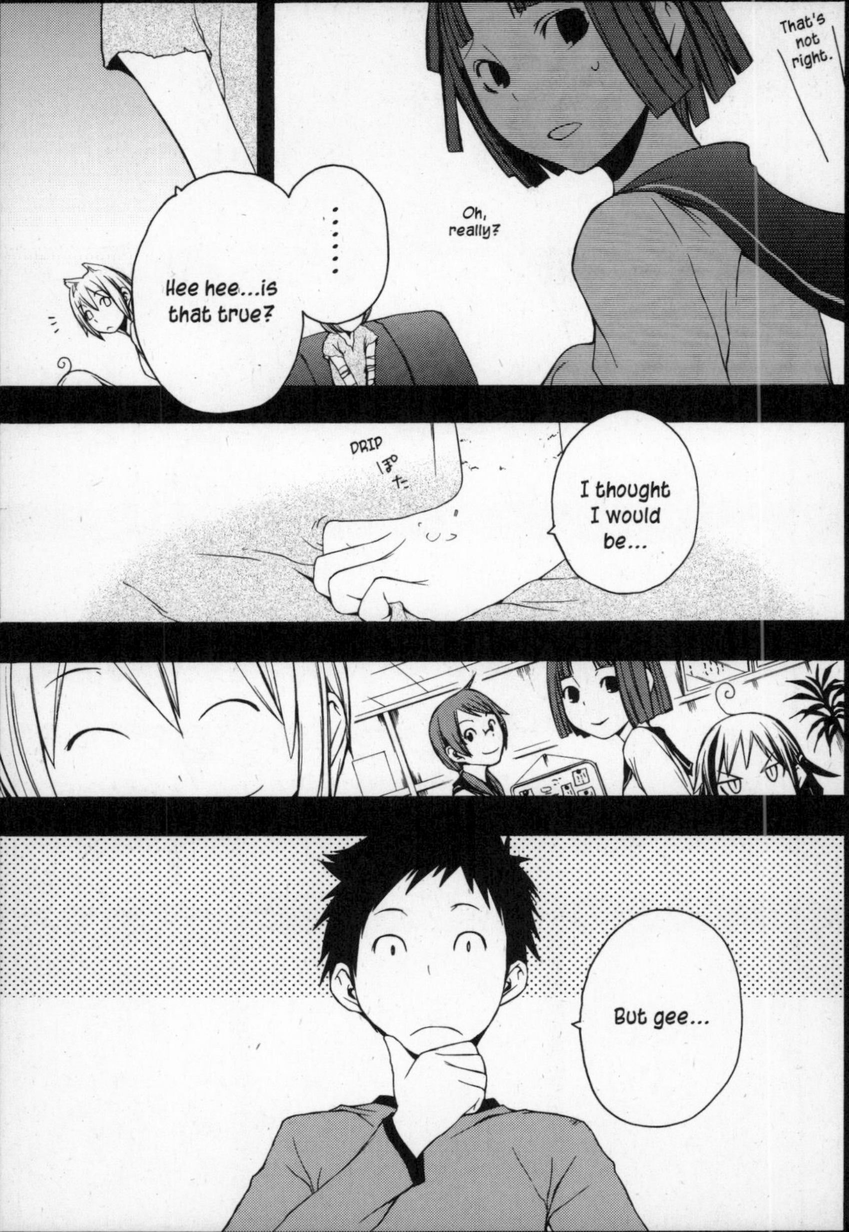
That's not right.
Oh, really?
......
Hee hee...is that true?
I thought I would be...
DRIP ぽた
But gee...

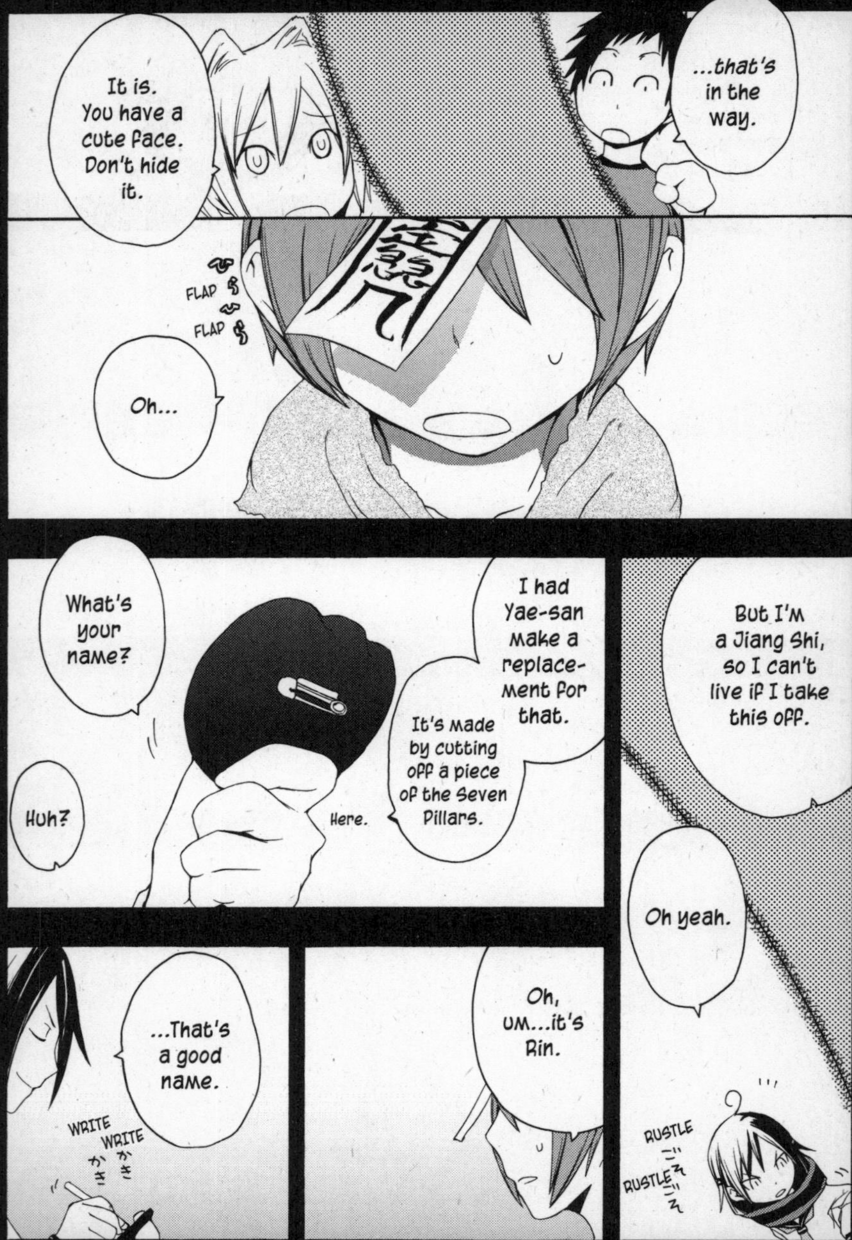
...that's in the way.
It is. You have a cute face. Don't hide it.
FLAP
FLAP
Oh...
But I'm a Jiang Shi, so I can't live if I take this off.
Oh yeah.
I had Yae-san make a replacement for that.
It's made by cutting off a piece of the Seven Pillars.
Here.
Huh?
What's your name?
RUSTLE
ごそ
RUSTLE
ごそ
Oh, um...it's Rin.
...That's a good name.
WRITE
WRITE
かき
かき

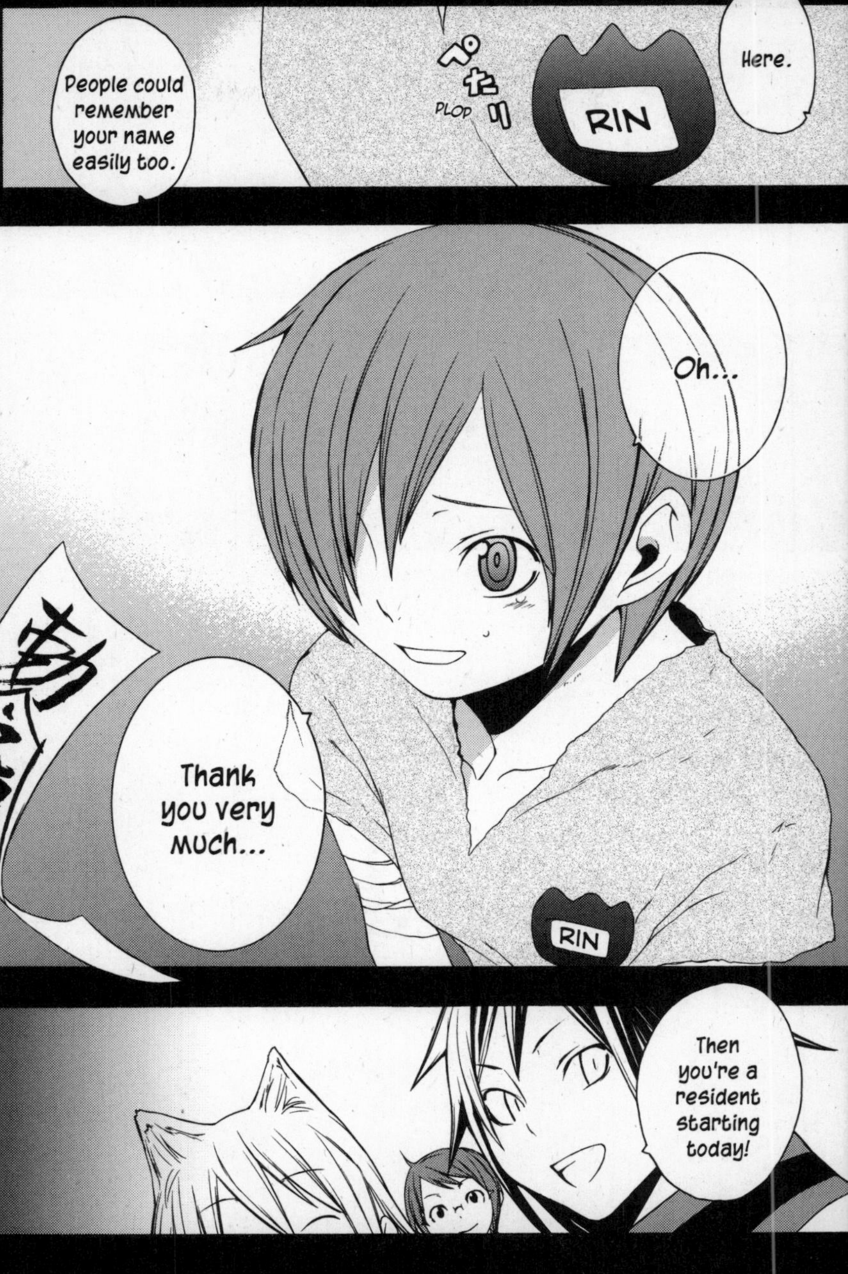
Here.
RIN
ぺたり
PLOP
People could remember your name easily too.
Oh...
Thank you very much...
RIN
Then you're a resident starting today!

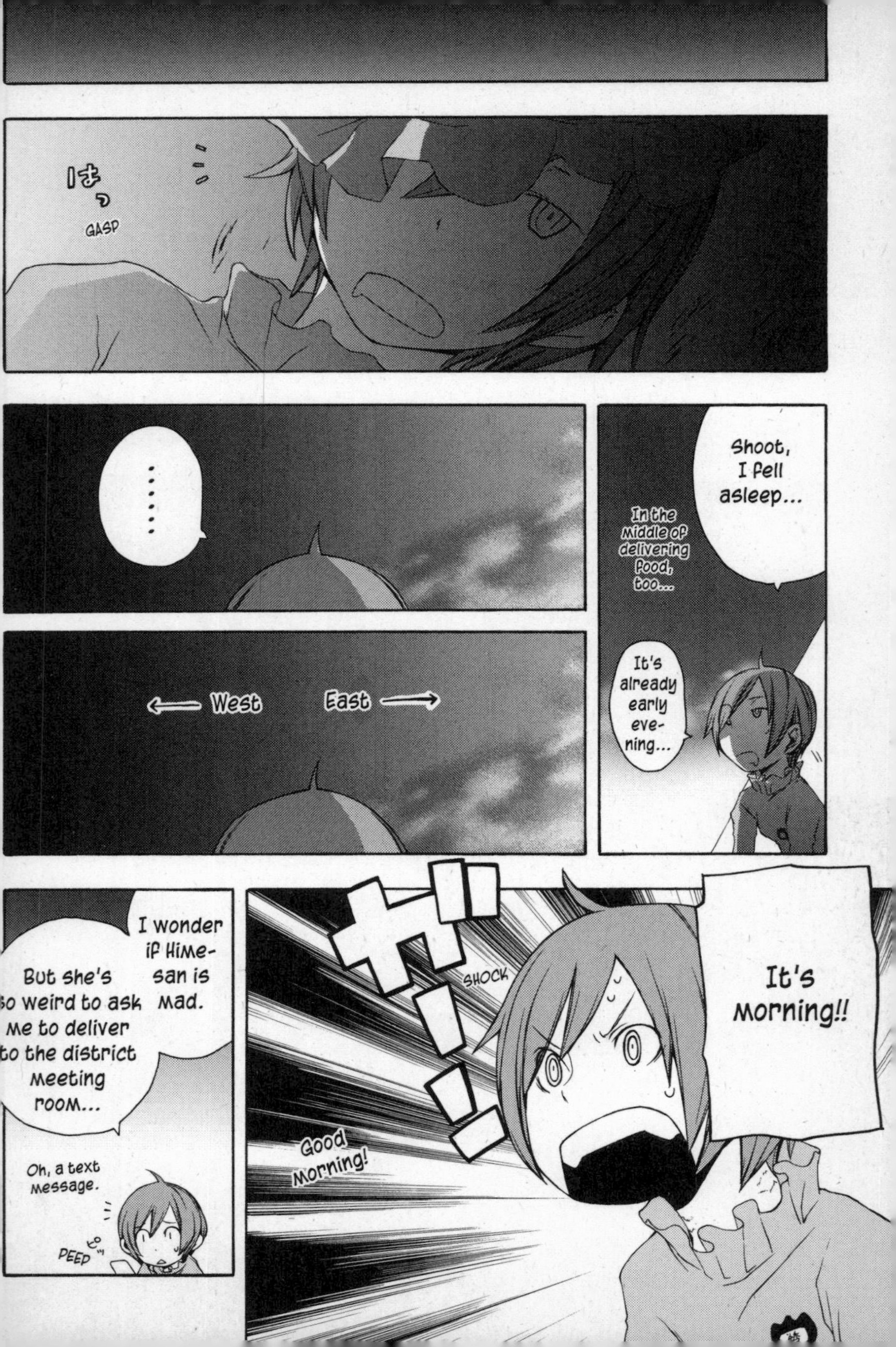

はっ
GASP
Shoot, I fell asleep...
In the middle of delivering food, too...
It's already early evening...
......
← West East →
It's morning!!
SHOCK
Good Morning!
I wonder if Hime-san is mad.
But she's so weird to ask me to deliver to the district meeting room...
Oh, a text message.
PEEP

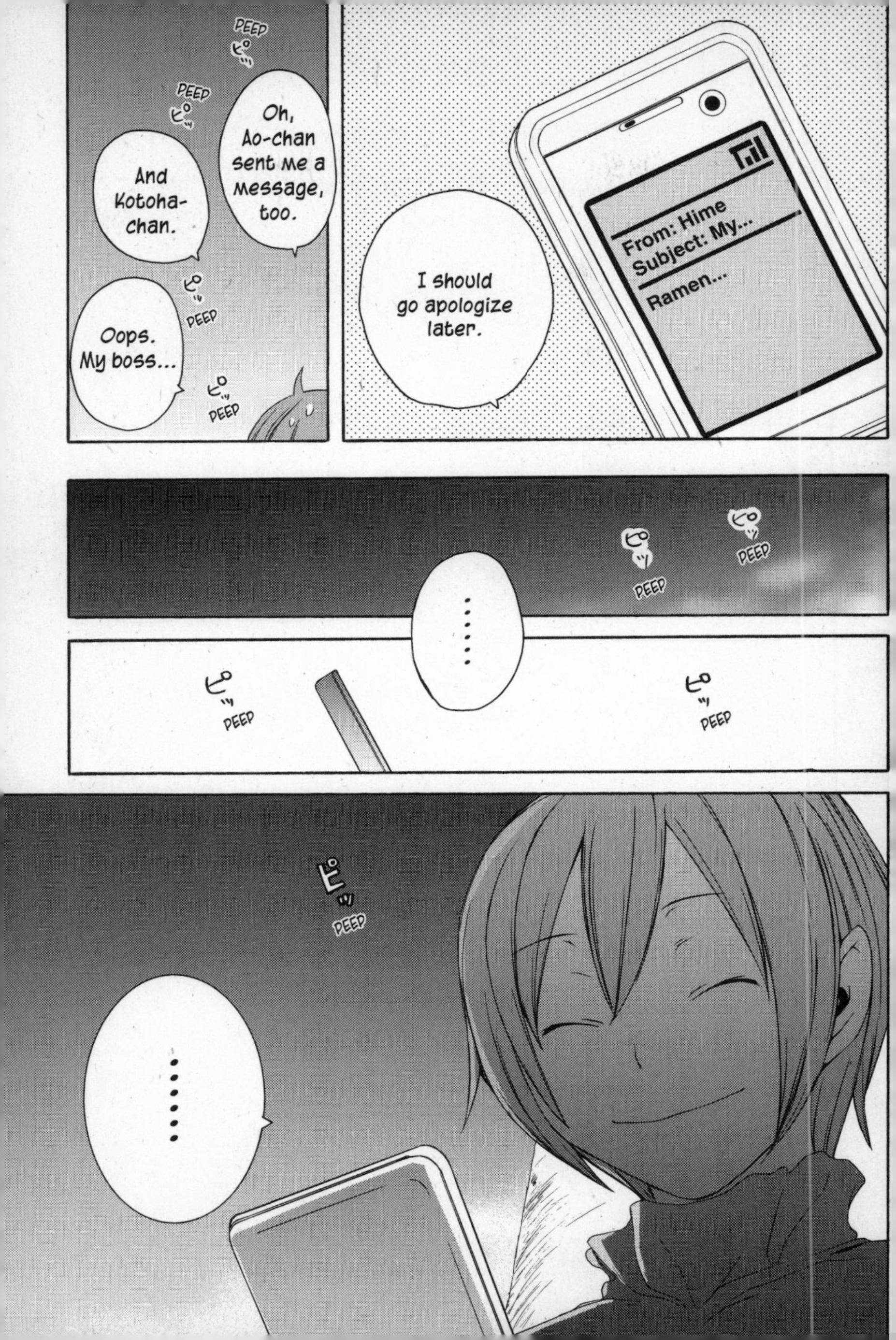
From: Hime
Subject: My...
Ramen...
I should go apologize later.
PEEP ピッ
Oh, Ao-chan sent me a message, too.
PEEP ピッ
And Kotoha-chan.
ピッ PEEP
Oops. My boss...
ピッ PEEP
ピッ PEEP
ピッ PEEP
......
ピッ PEEP
ピッ PEEP
ピッ PEEP
......

Then I'll work hard today, too!

Okay!

CLAMP

And maybe I'll give them a new dish as an apology, too.

And I end up making the food.

9th Night: Your Name Is END

Yozakura Quartet *2*

Primary Stages of Yozakura Quartet 2

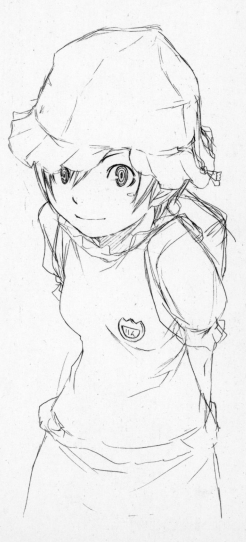

Age: 15

Hobbies:
eating at various places

Favorites

Food:
dumplings

Music:
cymbals

Comedian:
Kirin

Uchi-P Member:
Megu no Yasu

Little-Known Fact:
Although she is a Jiang Shi, she ages.

Rin
-san

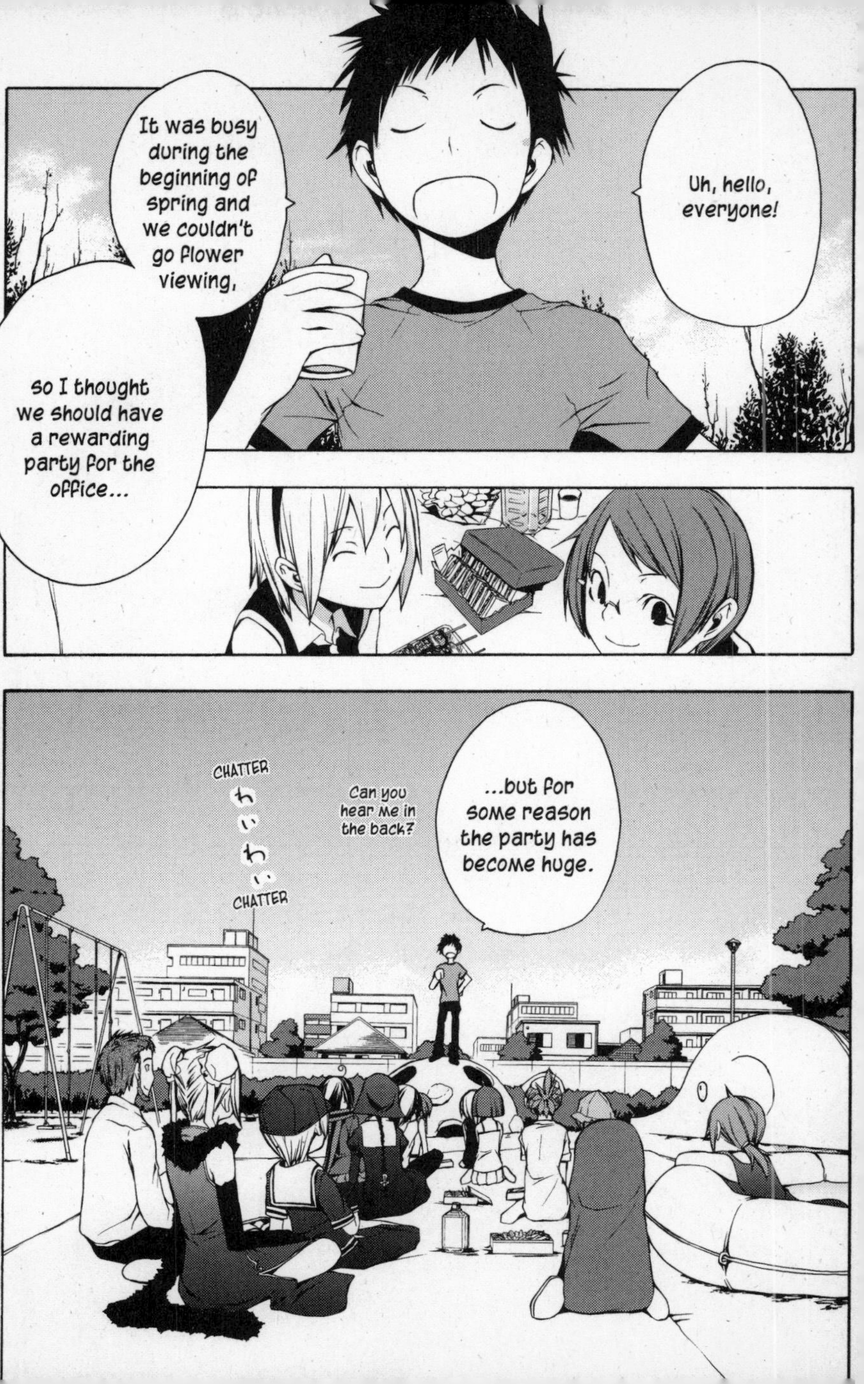
Uh, hello, everyone!
It was busy during the beginning of spring and we couldn't go flower viewing,
so I thought we should have a rewarding party for the office...
...but for some reason the party has become huge.
Can you hear me in the back?
CHATTER
わいわい
CHATTER

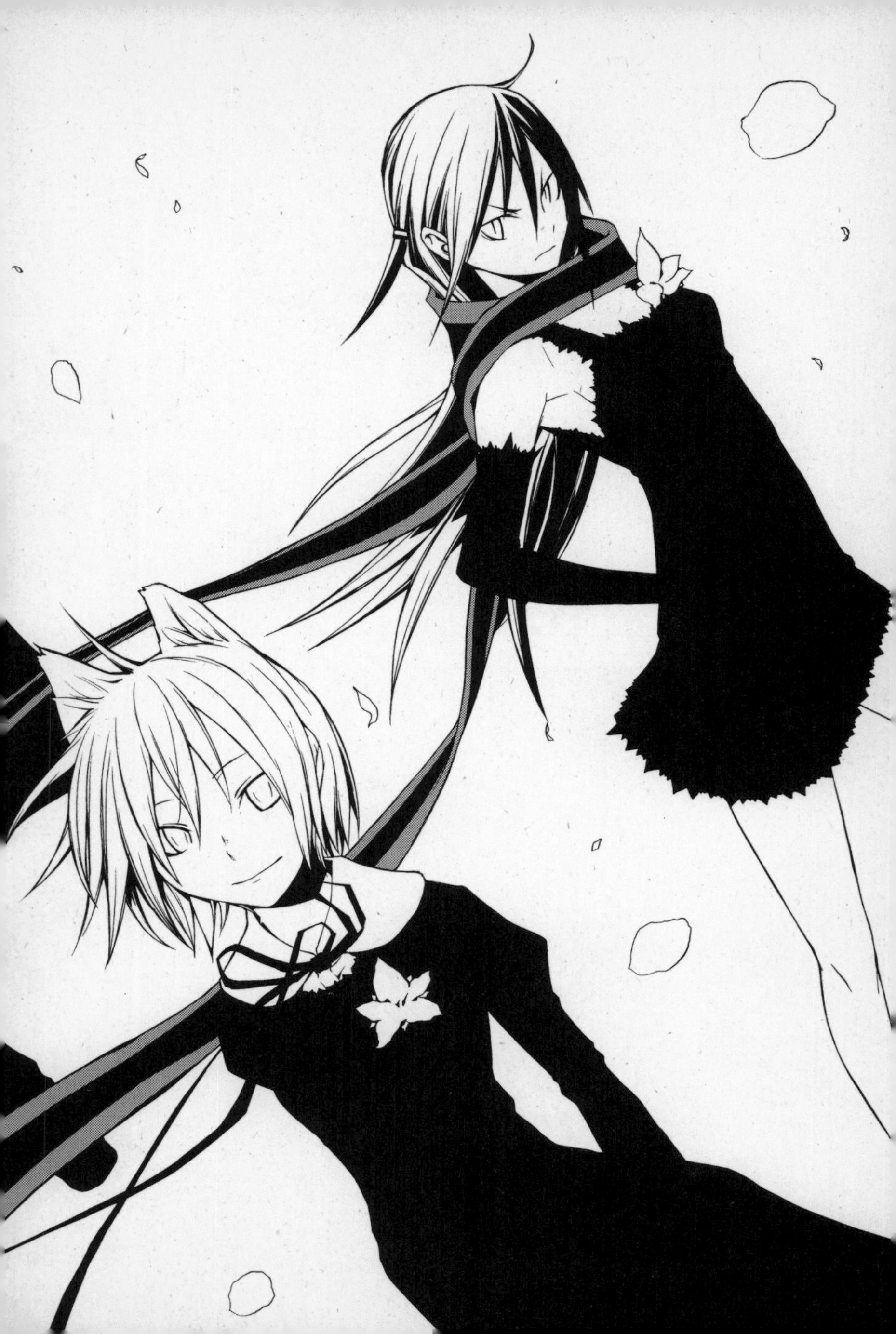

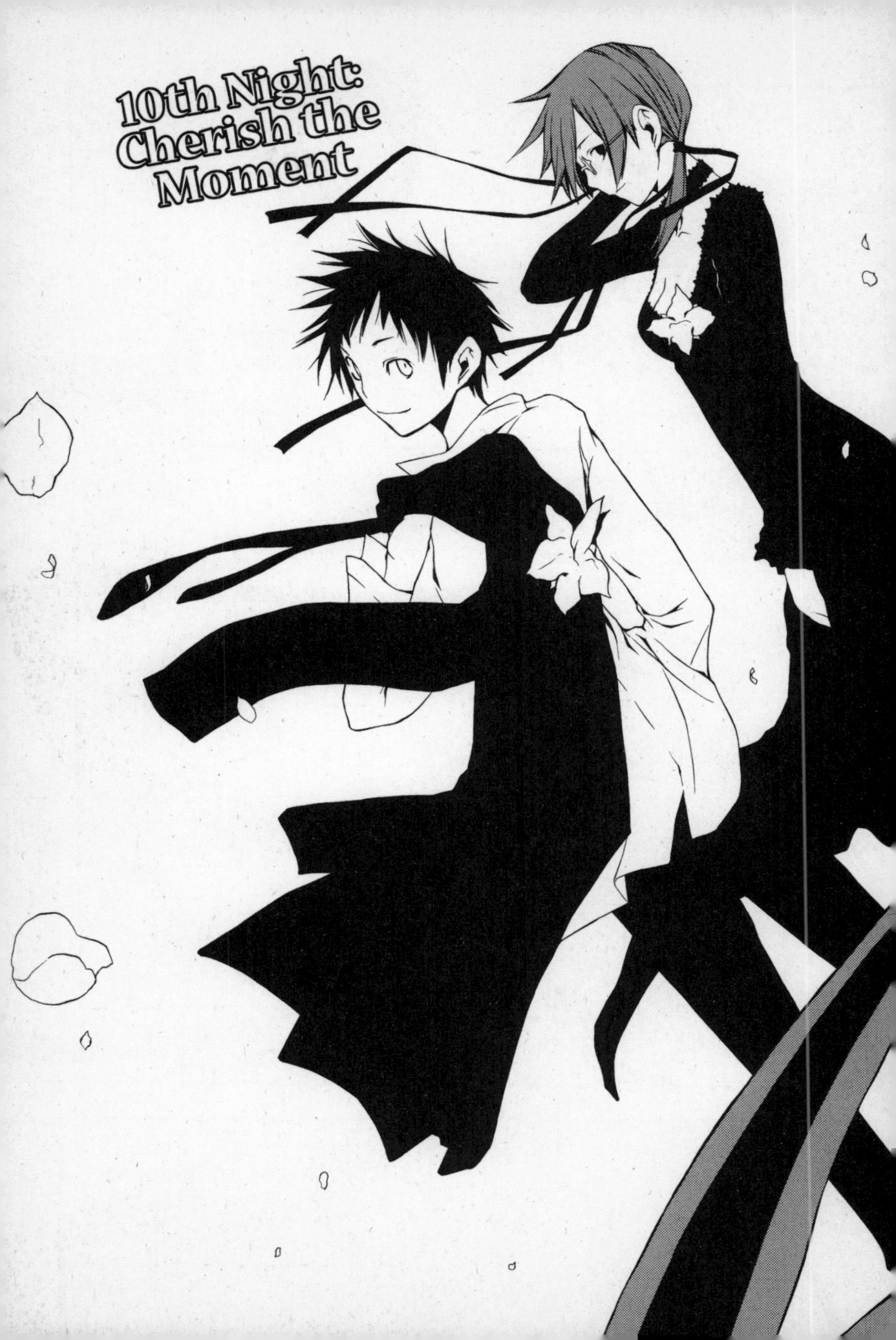
10th Night:
Cherish the
Moment

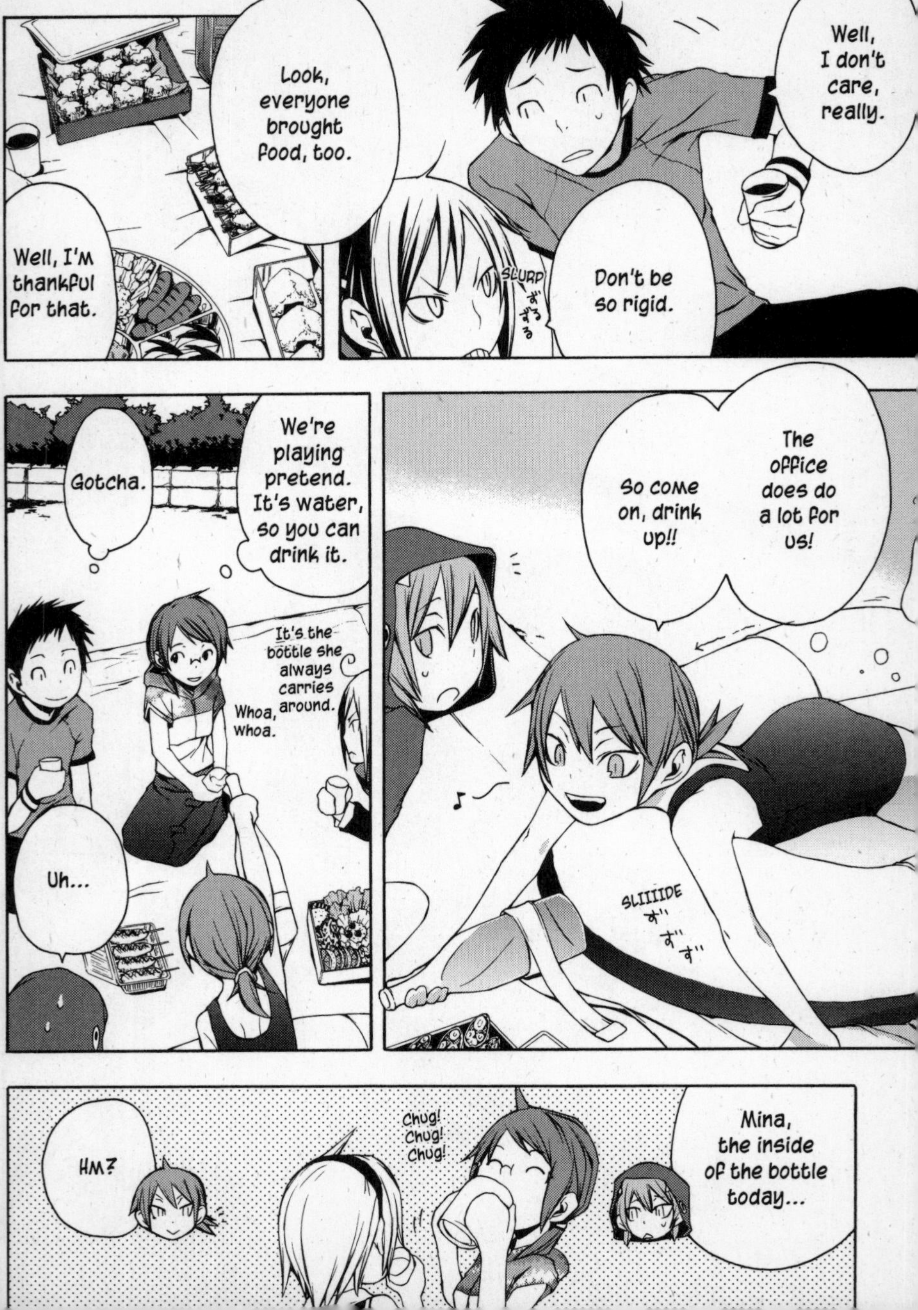
Phew
Well, I don't care, really.
Don't be so rigid.
SLURP
ずるずる
Look, everyone brought food, too.
Well, I'm thankful for that.
The office does do a lot for us!
So come on, drink up!!
SLIIIIDE
ずずず
We're playing pretend. It's water, so you can drink it.
Gotcha.
It's the bottle she always carries around.
Whoa, whoa.
Uh...
Mina, the inside of the bottle today...
Chug! Chug! Chug!
HM?

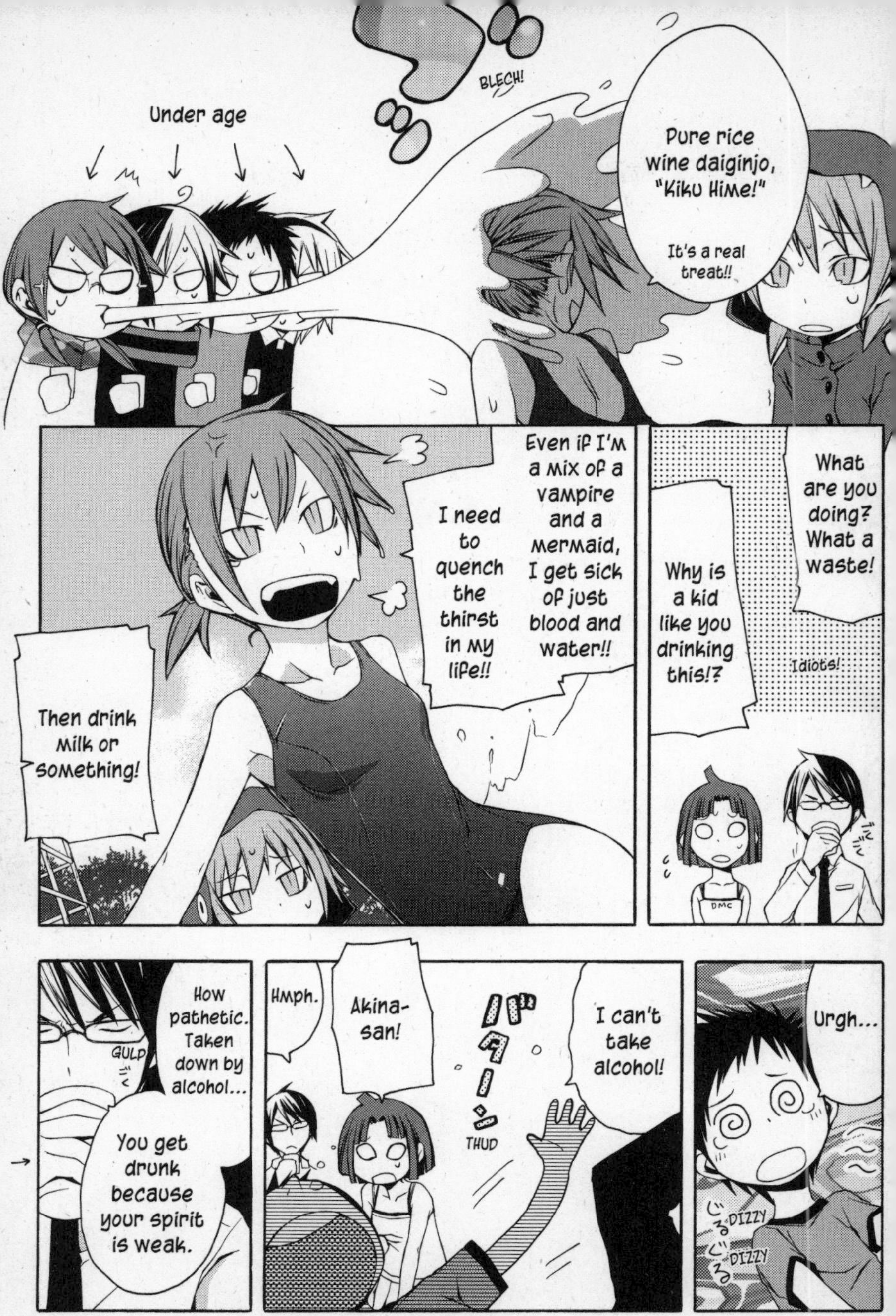
Pure rice wine daiginjo, "Kiku Hime!"
It's a real treat!!
BLECH!
Under age
What are you doing? What a waste!
Idiots!
Why is a kid like you drinking this!?
Even if I'm a mix of a vampire and a mermaid, I get sick of just blood and water!!
I need to quench the thirst in my life!!
Then drink milk or something!
Urgh...
DIZZY
DIZZY
I can't take alcohol!
THUD
Akina-san!
Hmph.
How pathetic. Taken down by alcohol...
GULP
You get drunk because your spirit is weak.

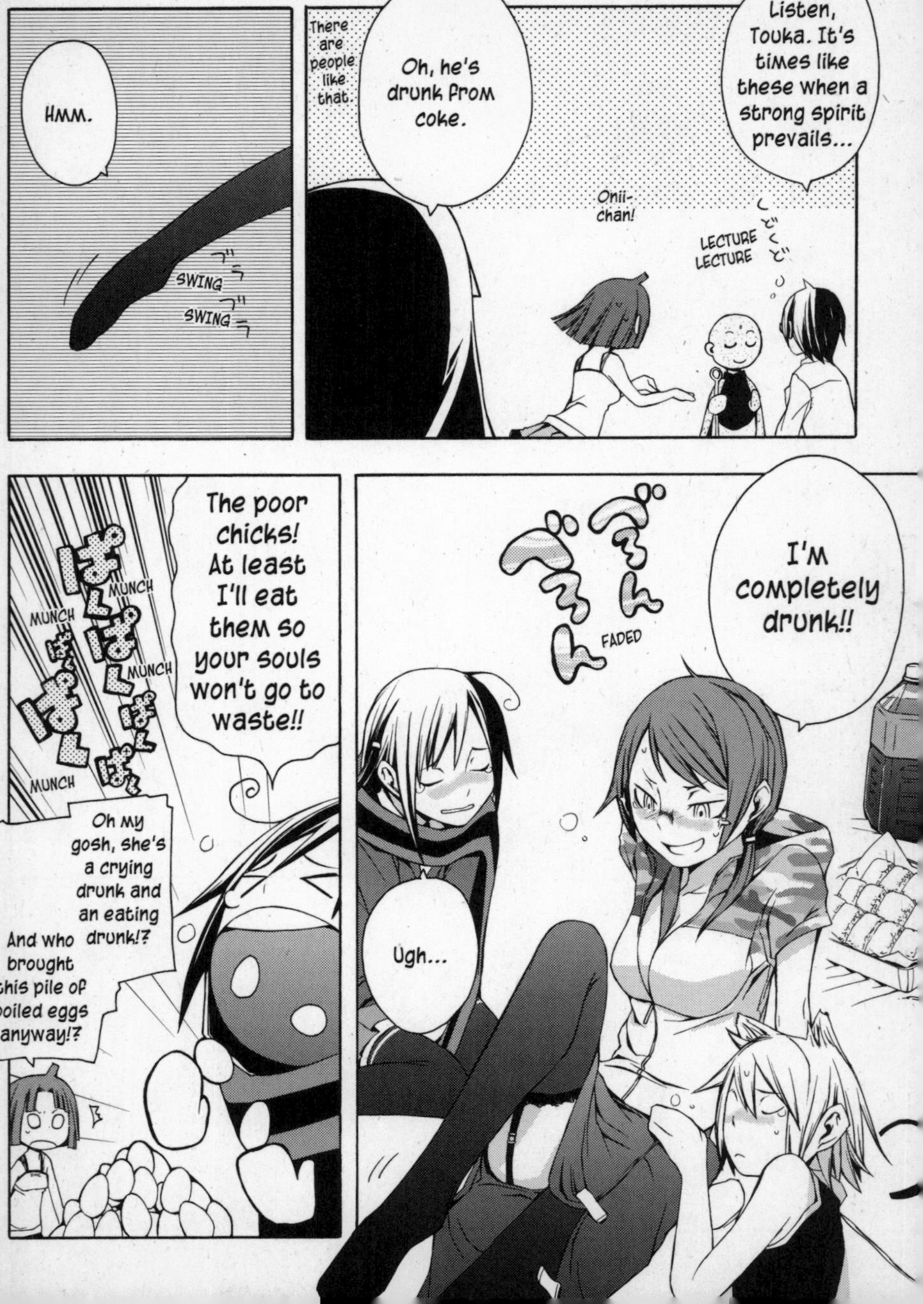
Listen, Touka. It's times like these when a strong spirit prevails...
Oh, he's drunk from coke.
There are people like that.
Onii-chan!
LECTURE LECTURE
HMM.
SWING
SWING
I'M completely drunk!!
FADED
Ugh...
The poor chicks! At least I'll eat them so your souls won't go to waste!!
MUNCH
MUNCH
MUNCH
MUNCH
Oh my gosh, she's a crying drunk and an eating drunk!?
And who brought this pile of boiled eggs anyway!?

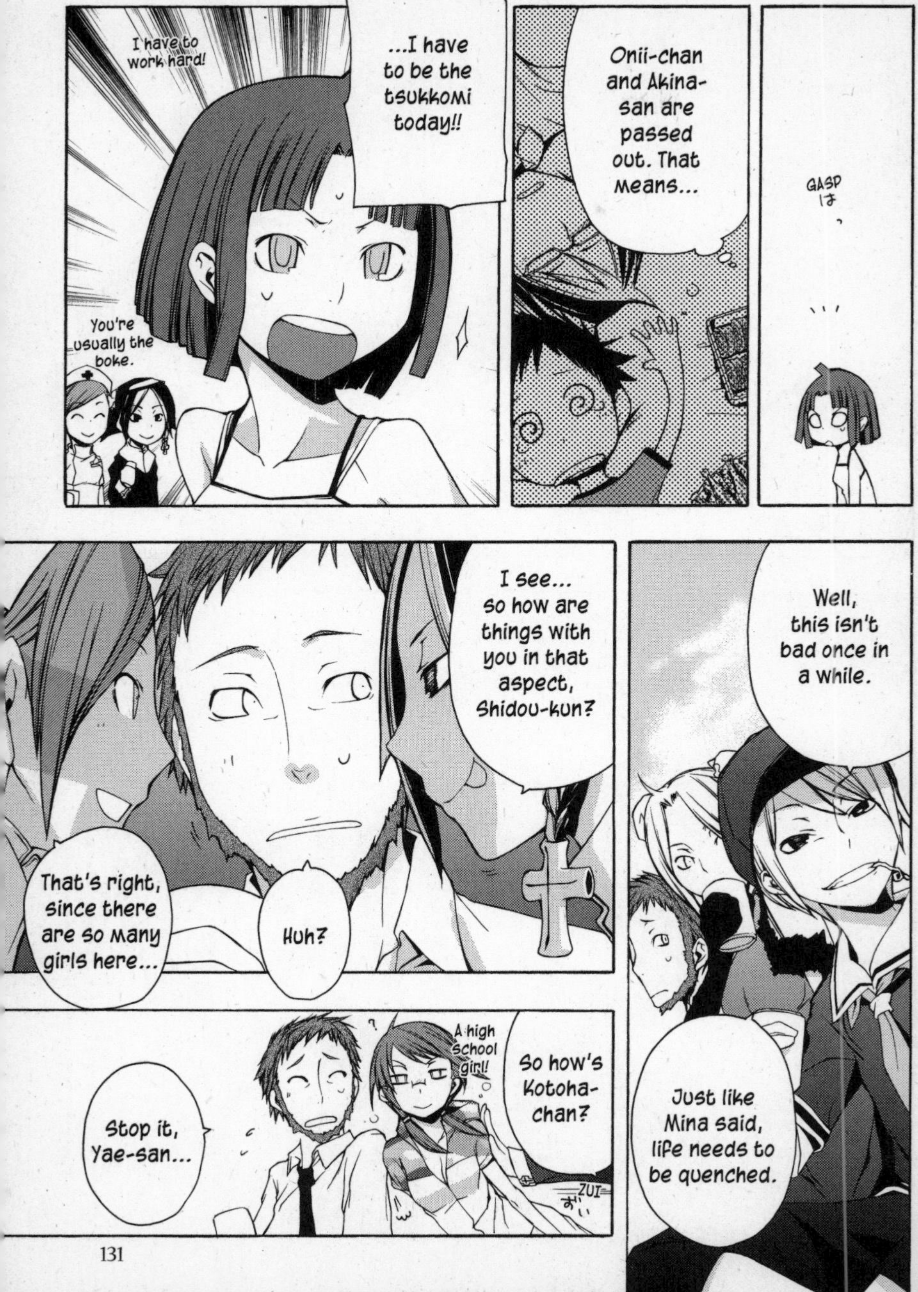
GASP
は
Onii-chan and Akina-san are passed out. That means...
...I have to be the tsukkomi today!!
I have to work hard!
You're usually the boke.
Well, this isn't bad once in a while.
Just like Mina said, life needs to be quenched.
I see... so how are things with you in that aspect, Shidou-kun?
Huh?
That's right, since there are so many girls here...
So how's Kotoha-chan?
A high school girl!
ZUI
ずい
Stop it, Yae-san...

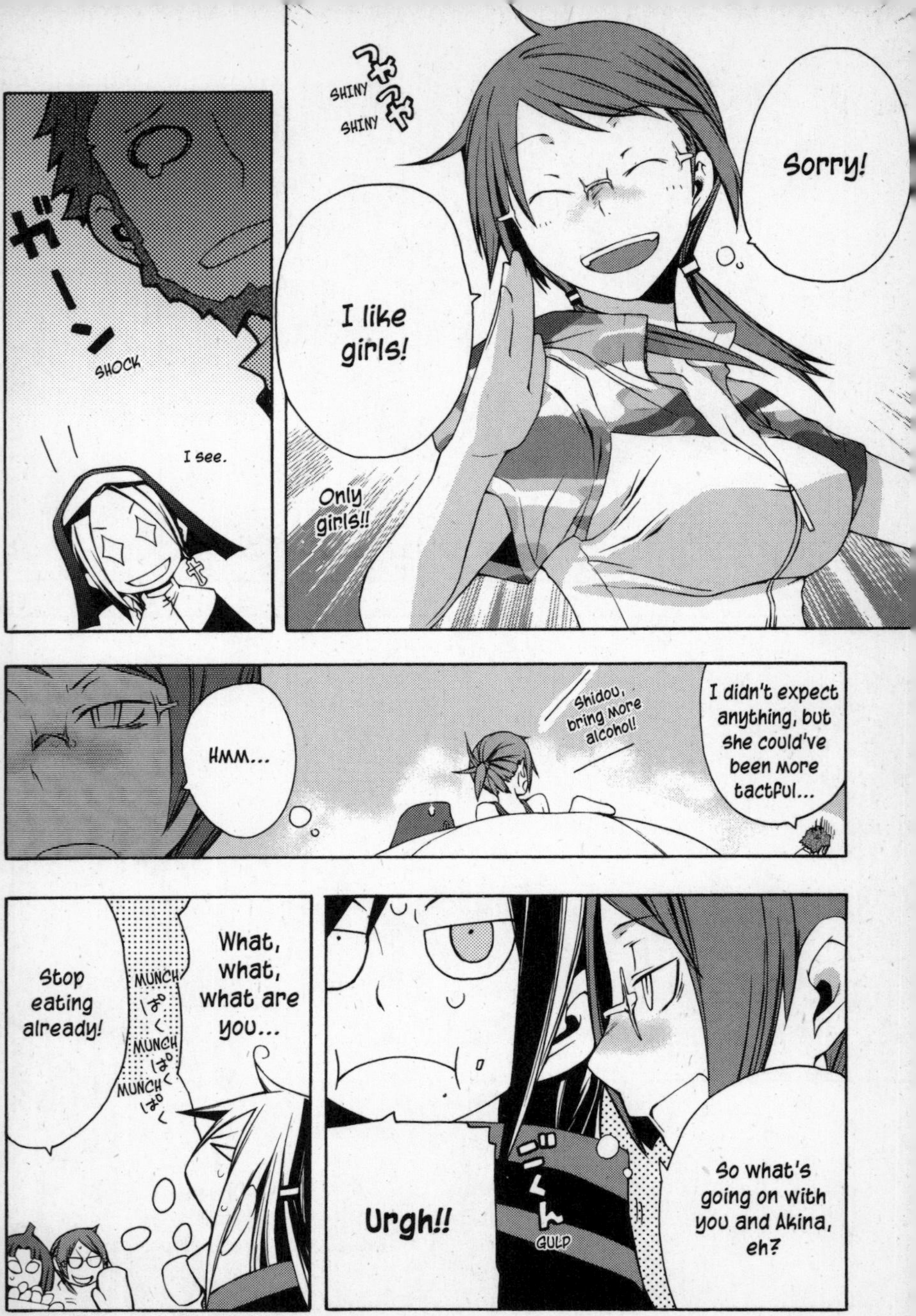
SHINY SHINY
Sorry!
I like girls!
Only girls!!
SHOCK
I see.
I didn't expect anything, but she could've been more tactful...
Shidou, bring more alcohol!
Hmm...
So what's going on with you and Akina, eh?
GULP
Urgh!!
What, what, what are you...
MUNCH MUNCH MUNCH
Stop eating already!

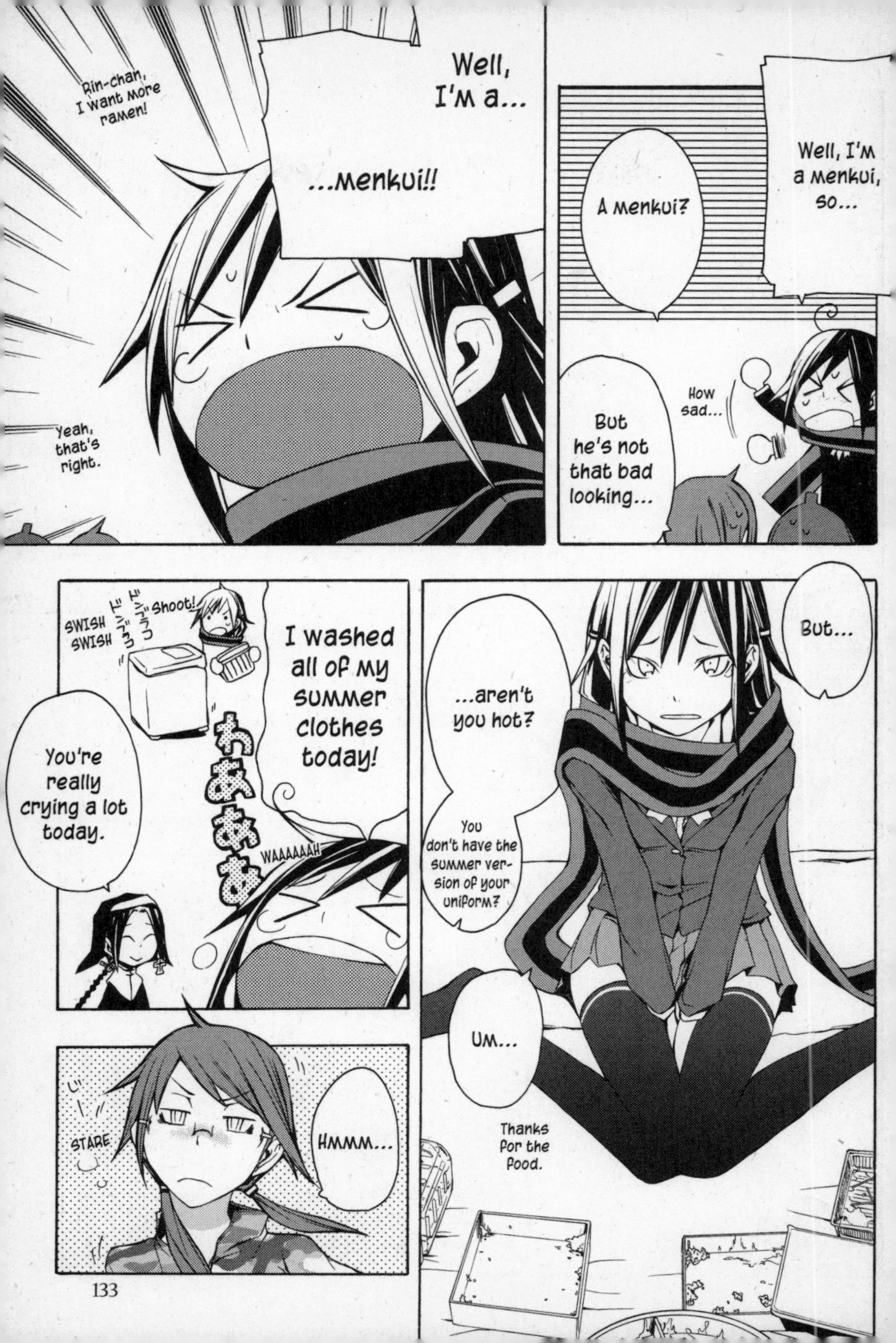
Well, I'm a menkui, so...
A menkui?
How sad...
But he's not that bad looking...
Well, I'm a...
...menkui!!
Rin-chan, I want more ramen!
Yeah, that's right.
But...
...aren't you hot?
You don't have the summer version of your uniform?
Um...
Thanks for the food.
I washed all of my summer clothes today!
WAAAAAAH
Shoot!
SWISH SWISH
You're really crying a lot today.
HMMM...
STARE

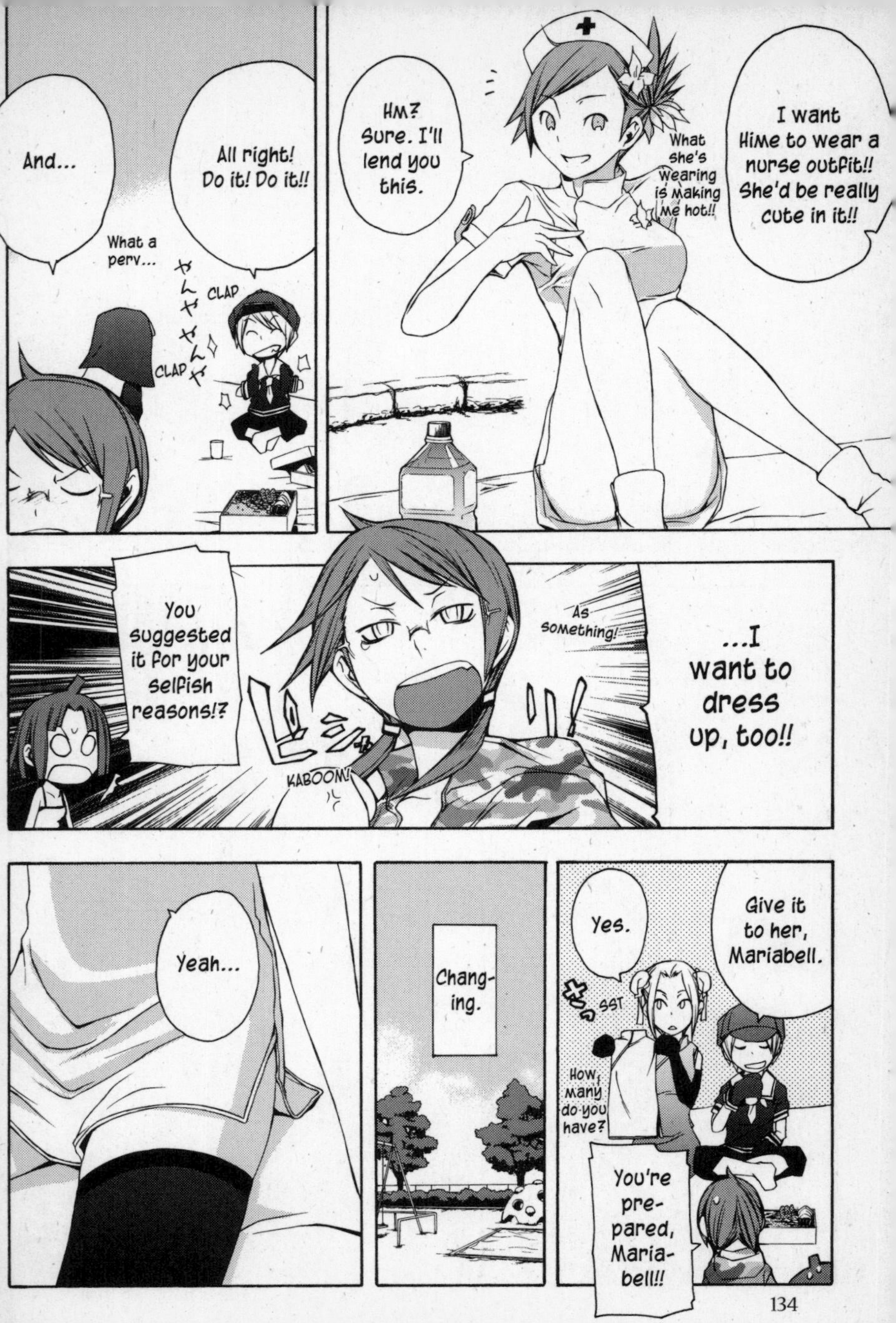

I want Hime to wear a nurse outfit!! She'd be really cute in it!!
What she's wearing is making me hot!!
Hm? Sure. I'll lend you this.
All right! Do it! Do it!!
CLAP
CLAP
And...
What a perv...
...I want to dress up, too!!
As something!
KABOOM!
You suggested it for your selfish reasons!?
Give it to her, Mariabell.
Yes.
SST
How many do you have?
You're pre-pared, Maria-bell!!
Chang-ing.
Yeah...

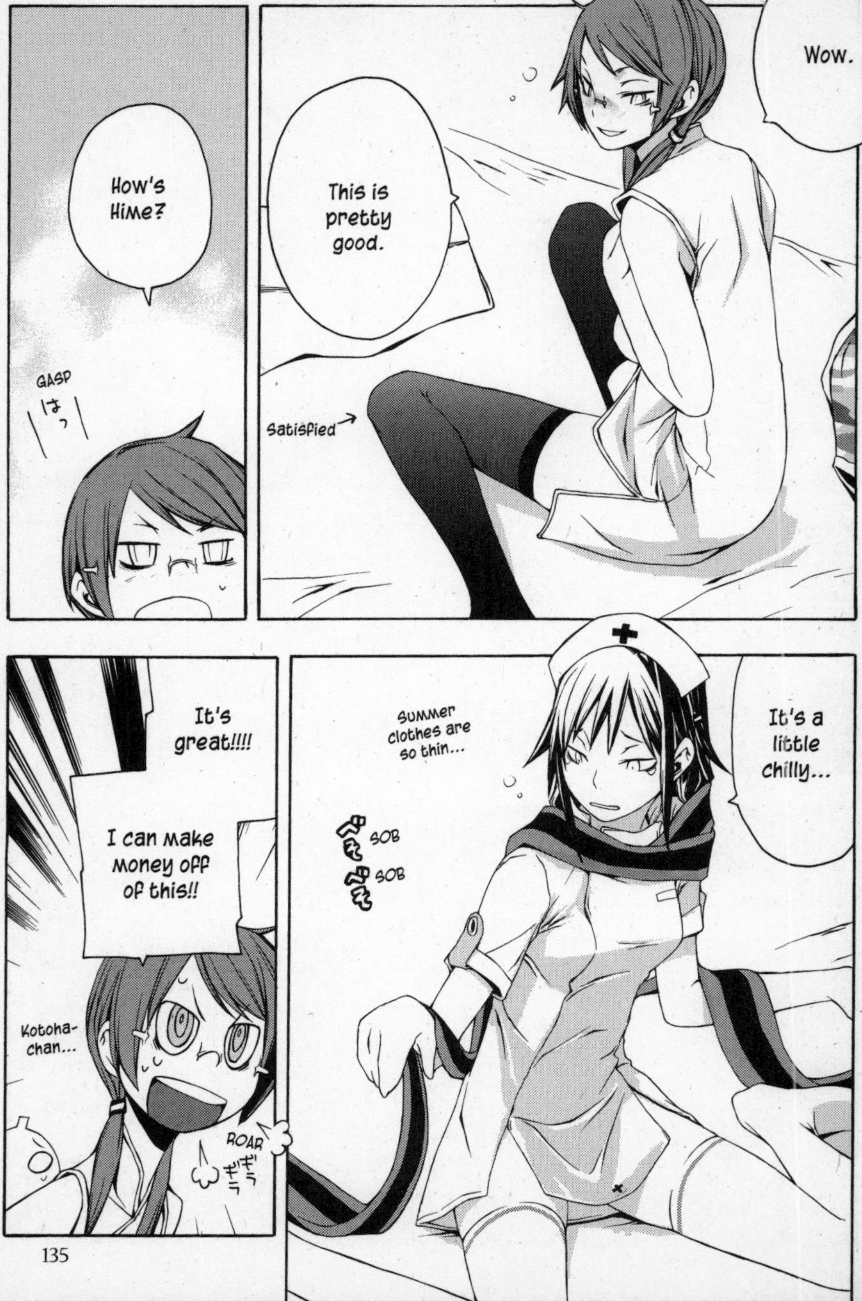
Wow.
This is pretty good.
Satisfied
How's Hime?
GASP
はっ
It's a little chilly...
Summer clothes are so thin...
SOB
SOB
It's great!!!!
I can make money off of this!!
Kotoha-chan...
ROAR

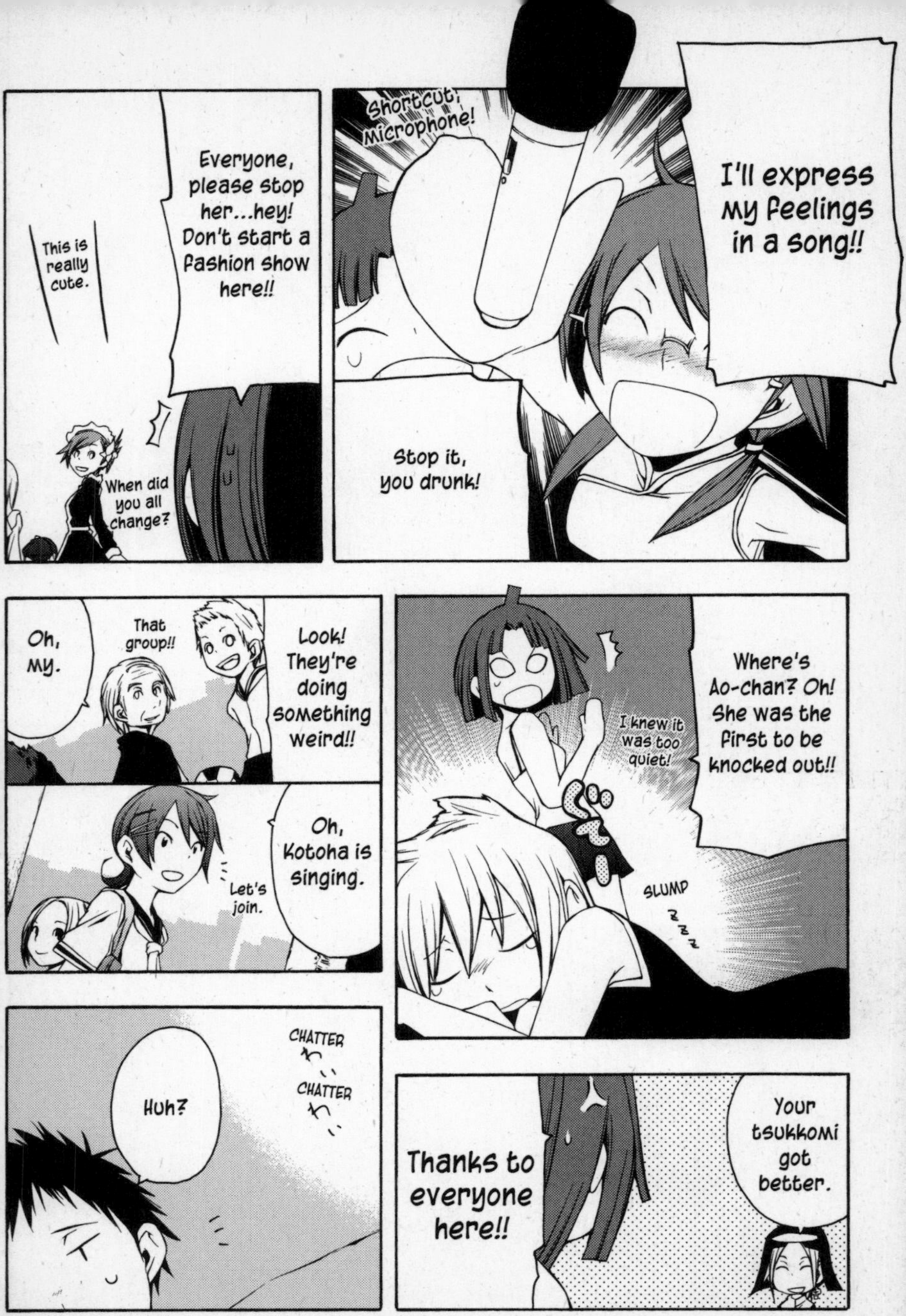
Shortcut, microphone!
I'll express my feelings in a song!!
Stop it, you drunk!
Everyone, please stop her...hey! Don't start a fashion show here!!
This is really cute.
When did you all change?
Where's Ao-chan? Oh! She was the first to be knocked out!!
I knew it was too quiet!
SLUMP
Look! They're doing something weird!!
That group!!
Oh, my.
Oh, Kotoha is singing.
Let's join.
Your tsukkomi got better.
Thanks to everyone here!!
CHATTER
CHATTER
Huh?

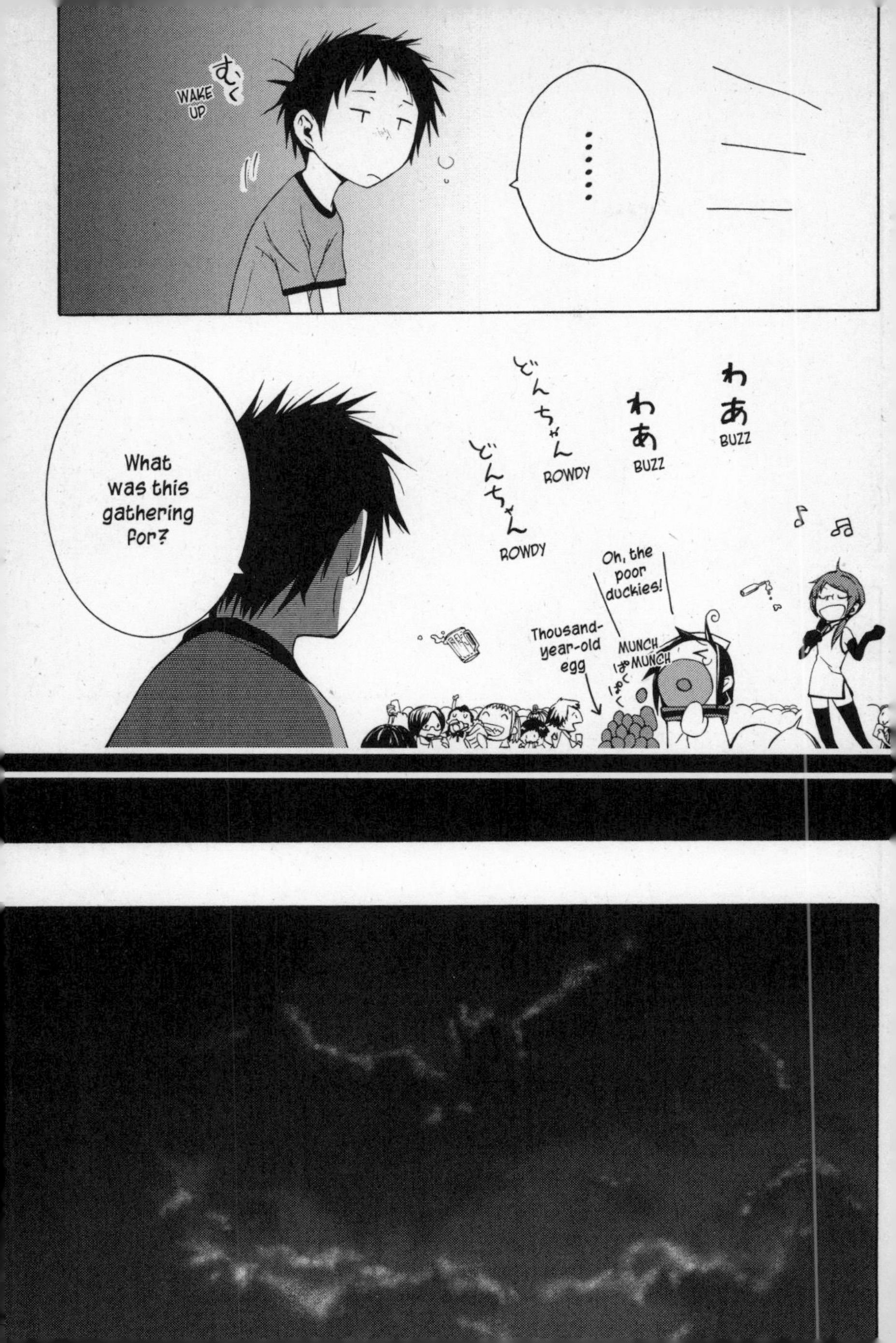
むく
WAKE UP
……
わあ
BUZZ
わあ
BUZZ
どんちゃん
ROWDY
どんちゃん
ROWDY
Oh, the poor duckies!
MUNCH MUNCH
ぱくぱく
Thousand-year-old egg
What was this gathering for?

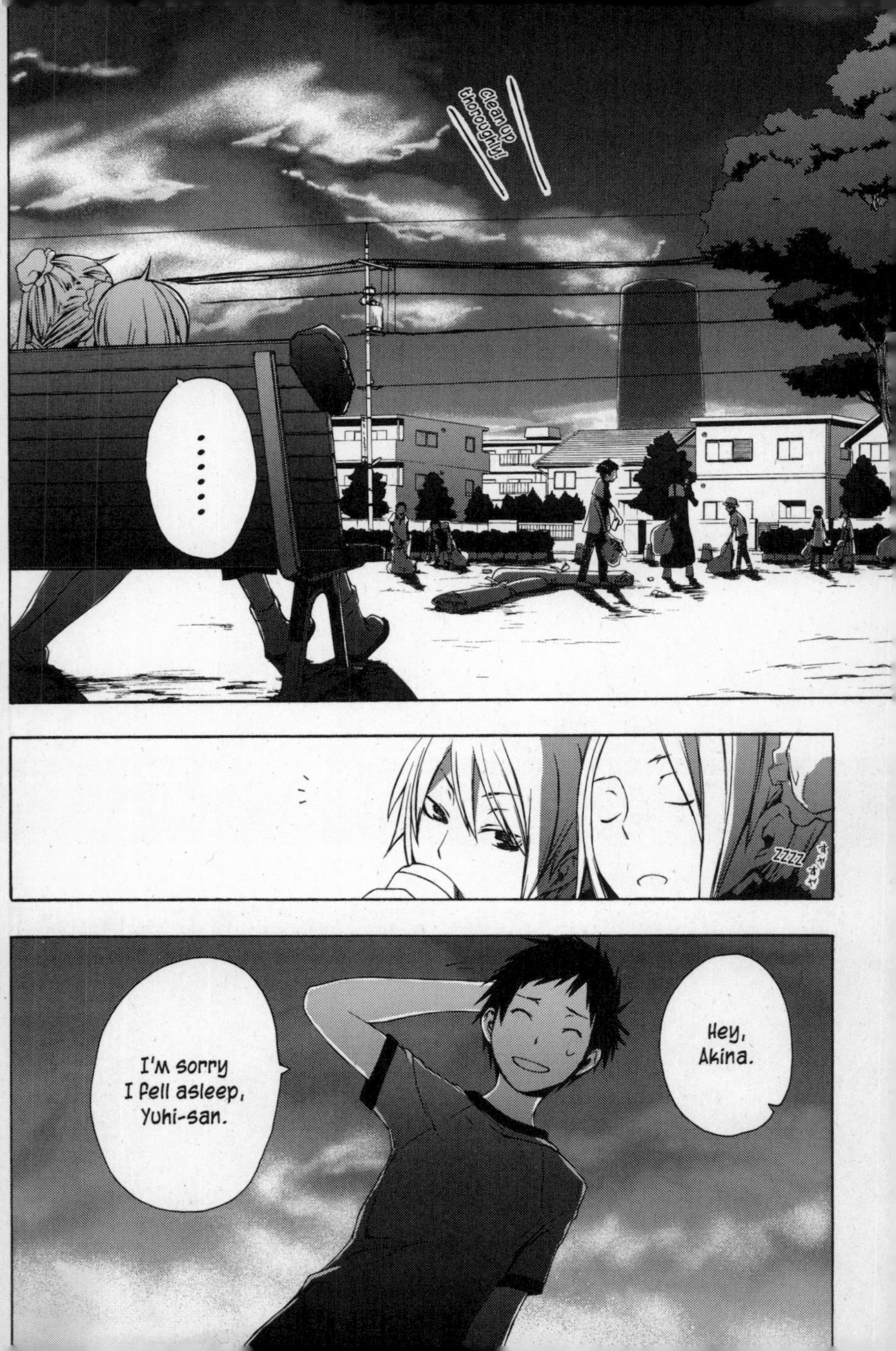
Clean up thoroughly!
......
すやすや
zzzz
Hey, Akina.
I'm sorry I fell asleep, Yuhi-san.

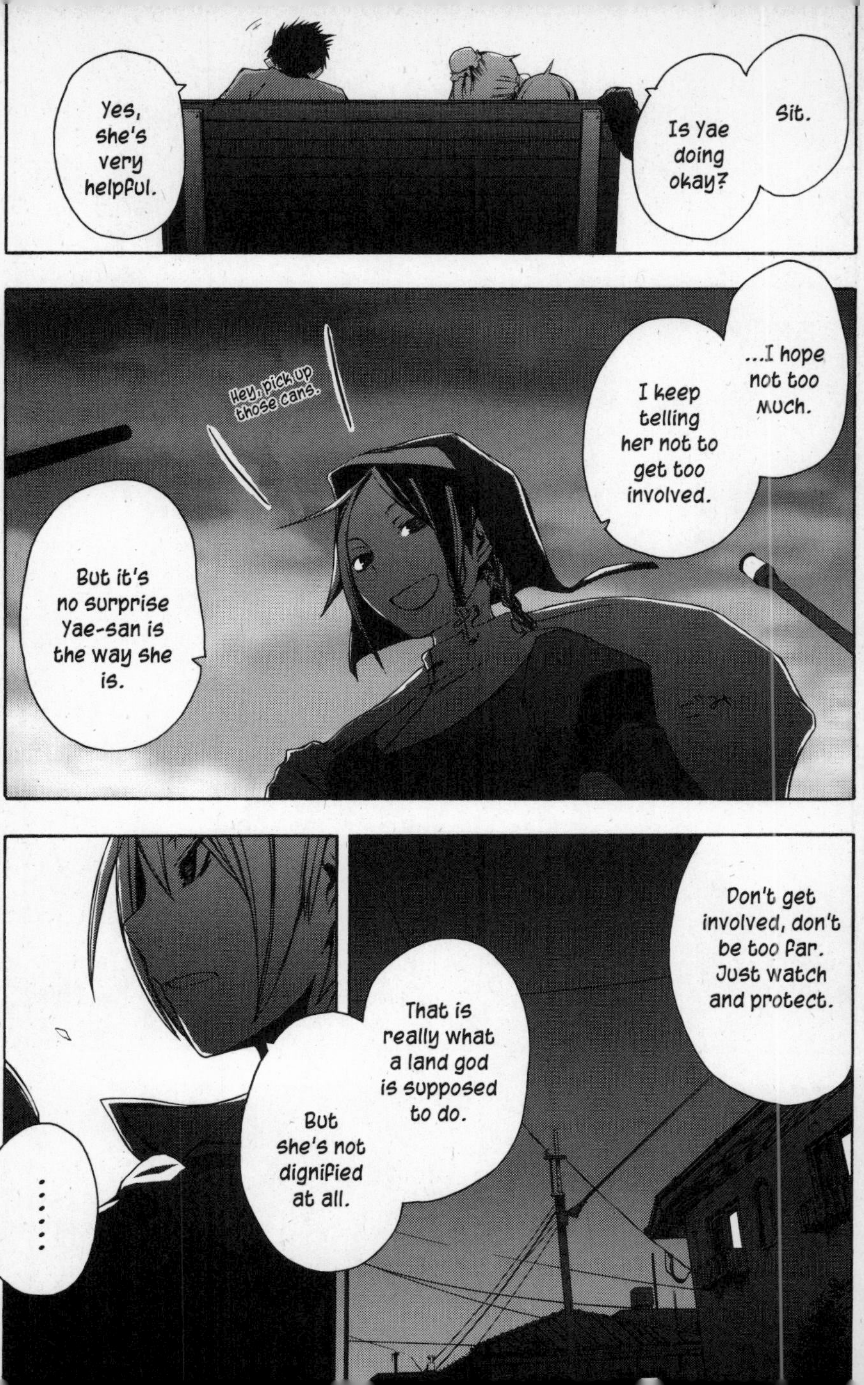
Sit.
Is Yae doing okay?
Yes, she's very helpful.
...I hope not too much.
I keep telling her not to get too involved.
Hey, pick up those cans.
But it's no surprise Yae-san is the way she is.
Don't get involved, don't be too far. Just watch and protect.
That is really what a land god is supposed to do.
But she's not dignified at all.
......

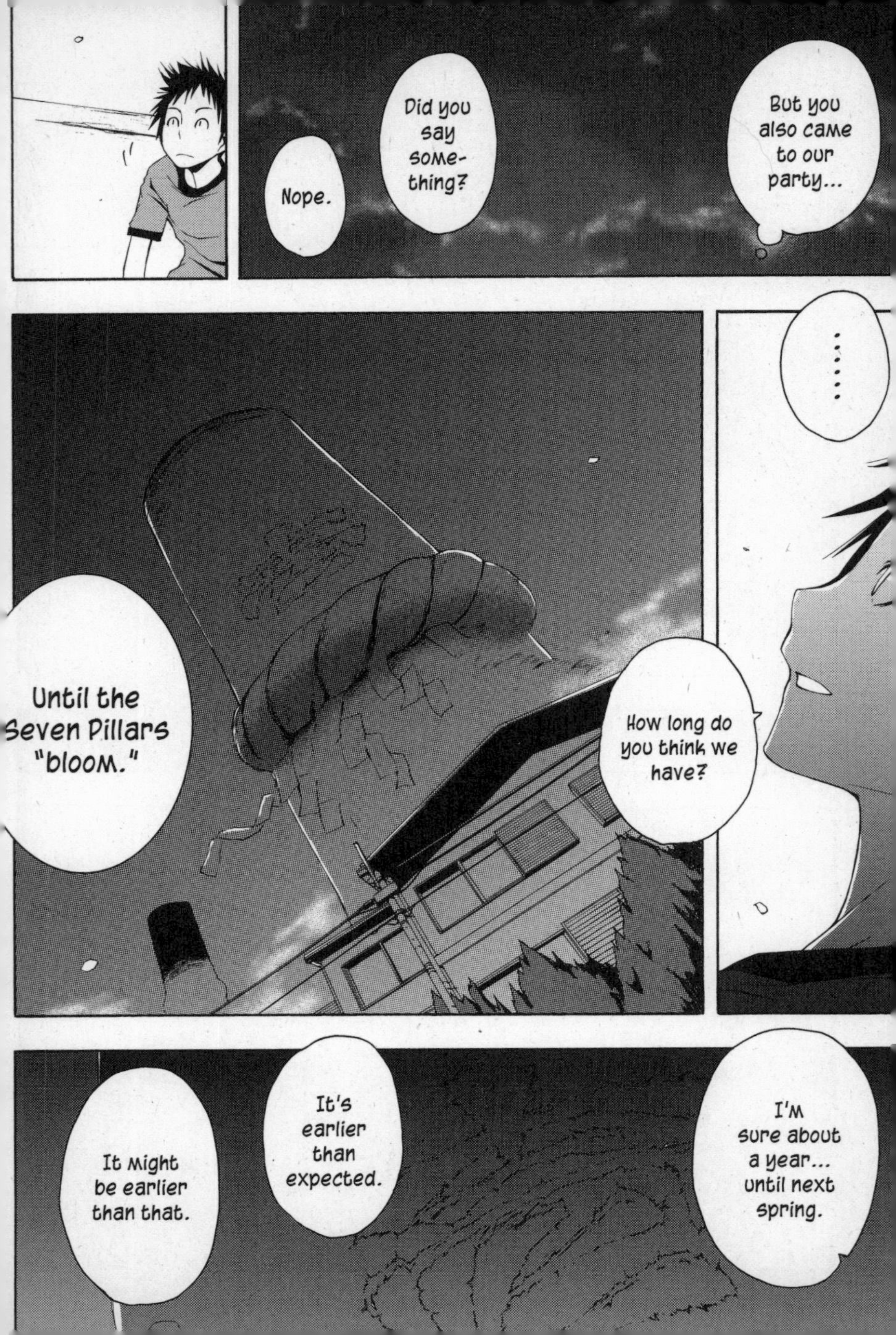
But you also came to our party...
Did you say something?
Nope.
......
How long do you think we have?
Until the Seven Pillars "bloom."
I'm sure about a year... until next spring.
It's earlier than expected.
It might be earlier than that.

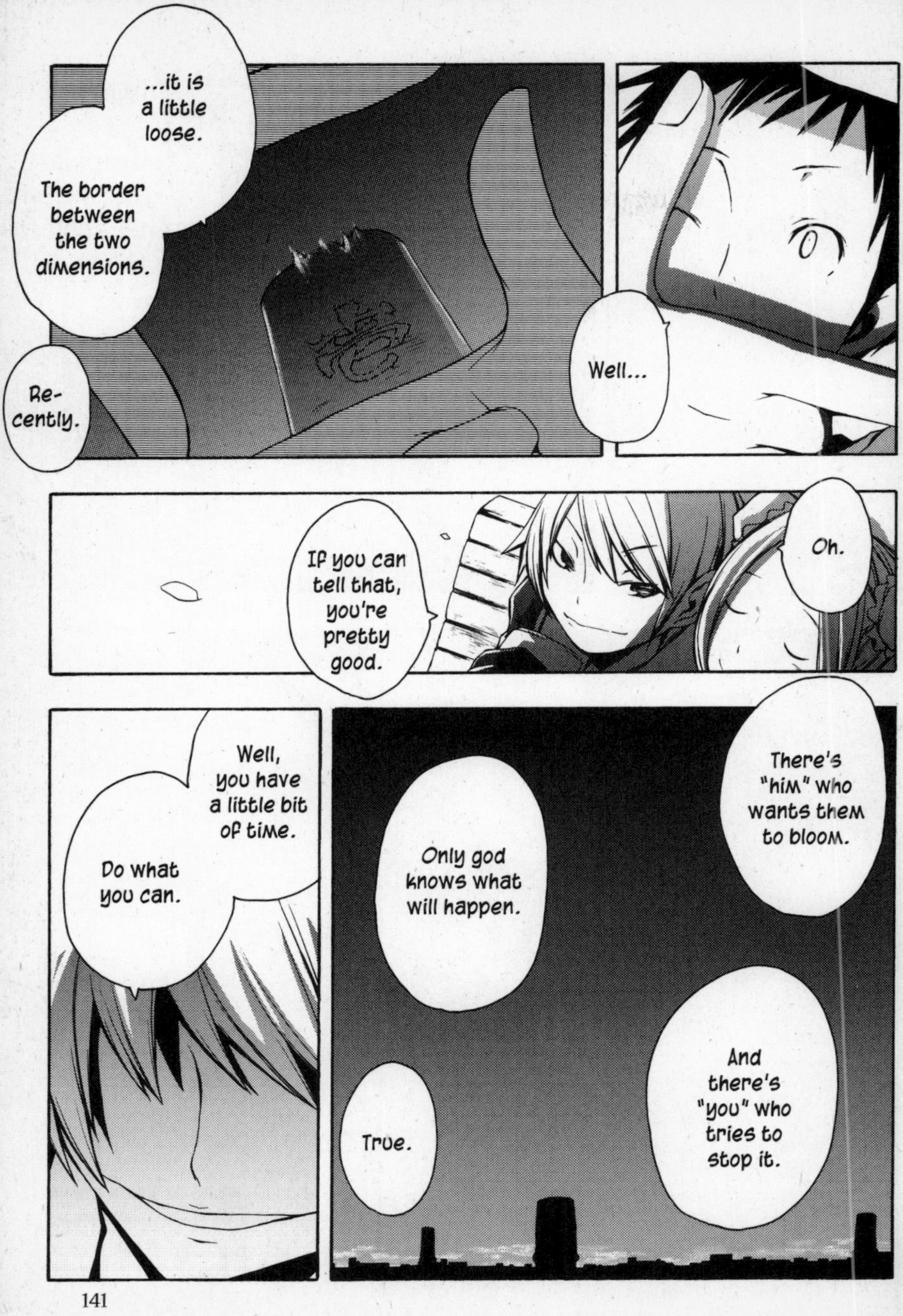
Well...
...it is a little loose.
The border between the two dimensions.
Re-cently.
Oh.
If you can tell that, you're pretty good.
There's "him" who wants them to bloom.
Only god knows what will happen.
And there's "you" who tries to stop it.
True.
Well, you have a little bit of time.
Do what you can.

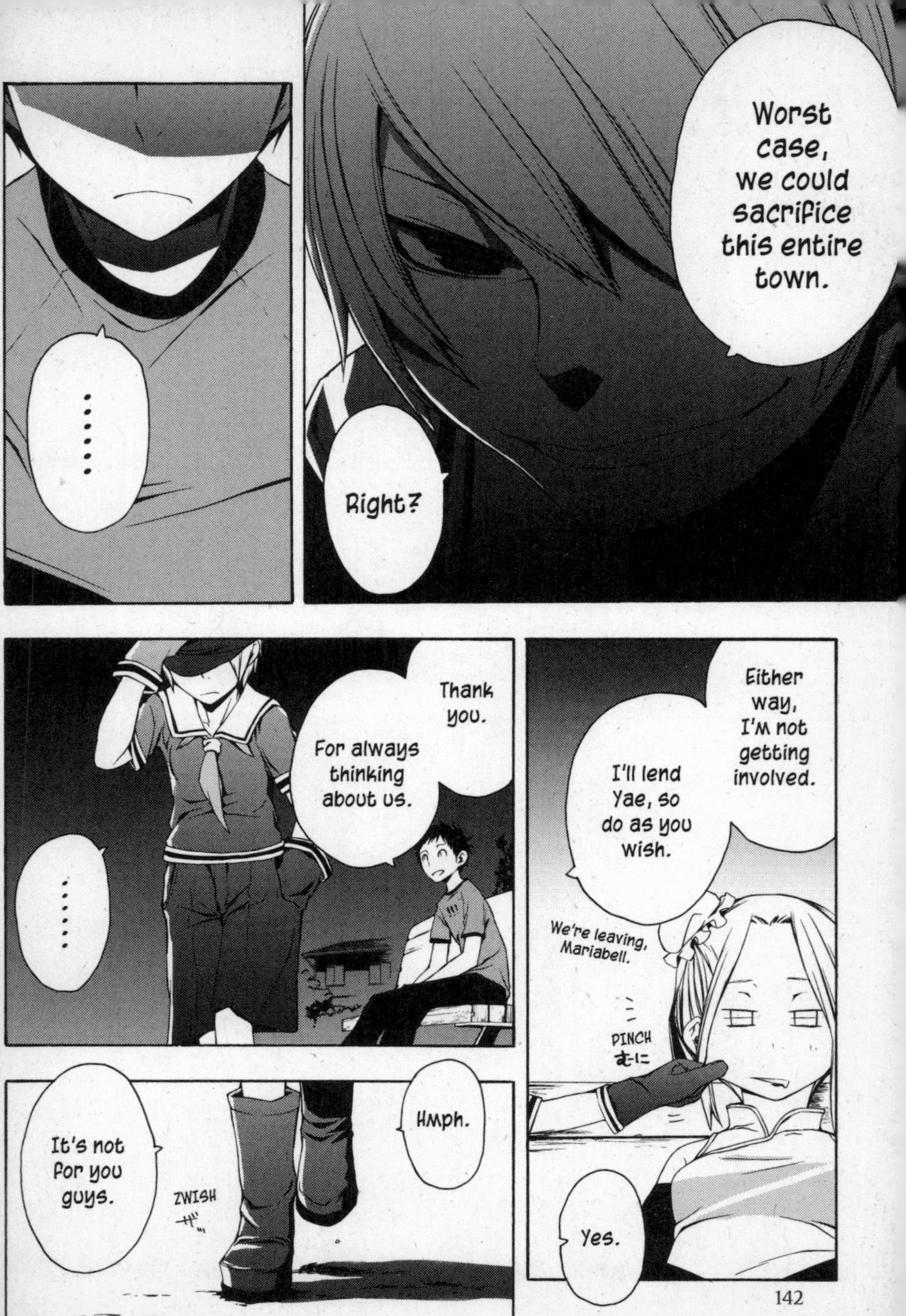
Worst case, we could sacrifice this entire town.
Right?
......
Either way, I'm not getting involved.
I'll lend Yae, so do as you wish.
We're leaving, Mariabell.
PINCH
むに
Yes.
Thank you.
For always thinking about us.
......
Hmph.
It's not for you guys.
ZWISH

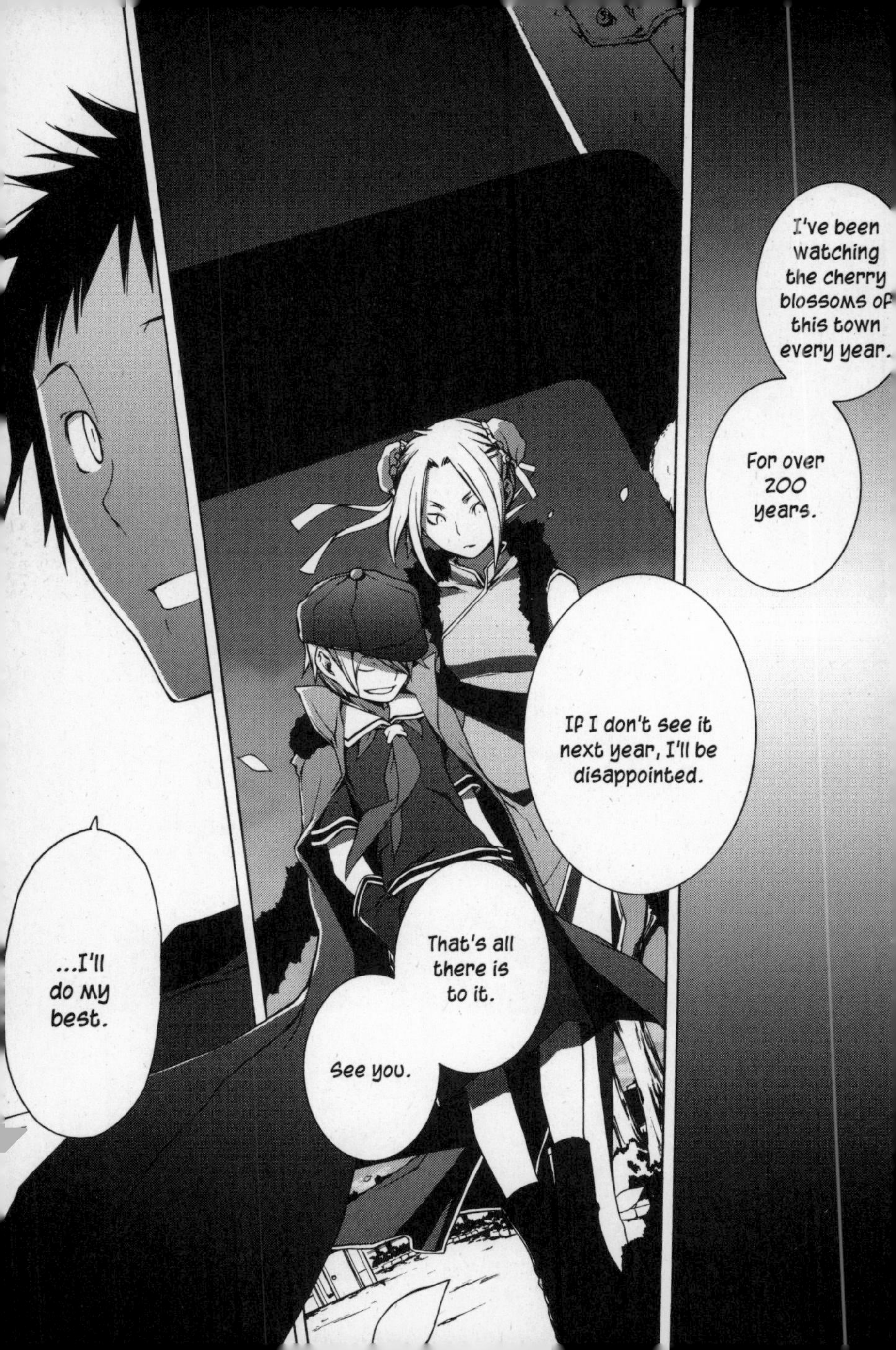
I've been watching the cherry blossoms of this town every year.
For over 200 years.
If I don't see it next year, I'll be disappointed.
That's all there is to it.
See you.
...I'll do my best.

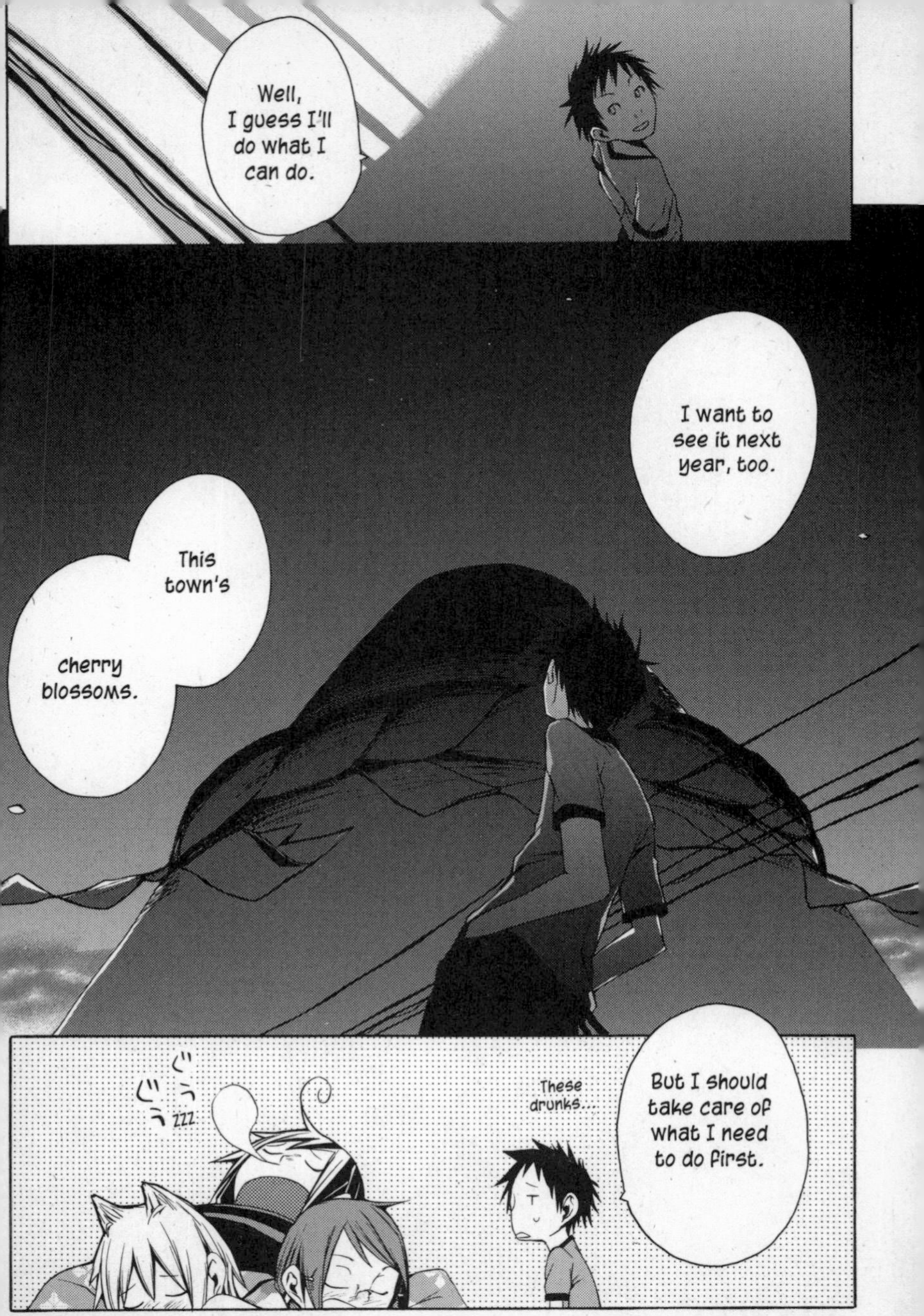
Well, I guess I'll do what I can do.
I want to see it next year, too.
This town's
cherry blossoms.
But I should take care of what I need to do first.
These drunks...
ぐぅ ぐぅ zzz

Yozakura Quartet 2

Primary Stages of Yozakura Quartet 2

Yae Shinatsuhiko
-san

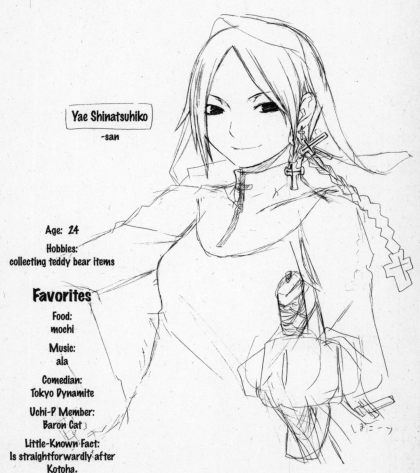

Age: 24

Hobbies:
collecting teddy bear items

Favorites

Food:
mochi

Music:
ala

Comedian:
Tokyo Dynamite

Uchi-P Member:
Baron Cat

Little-Known Fact:
Is straightforwardly after Kotoha.

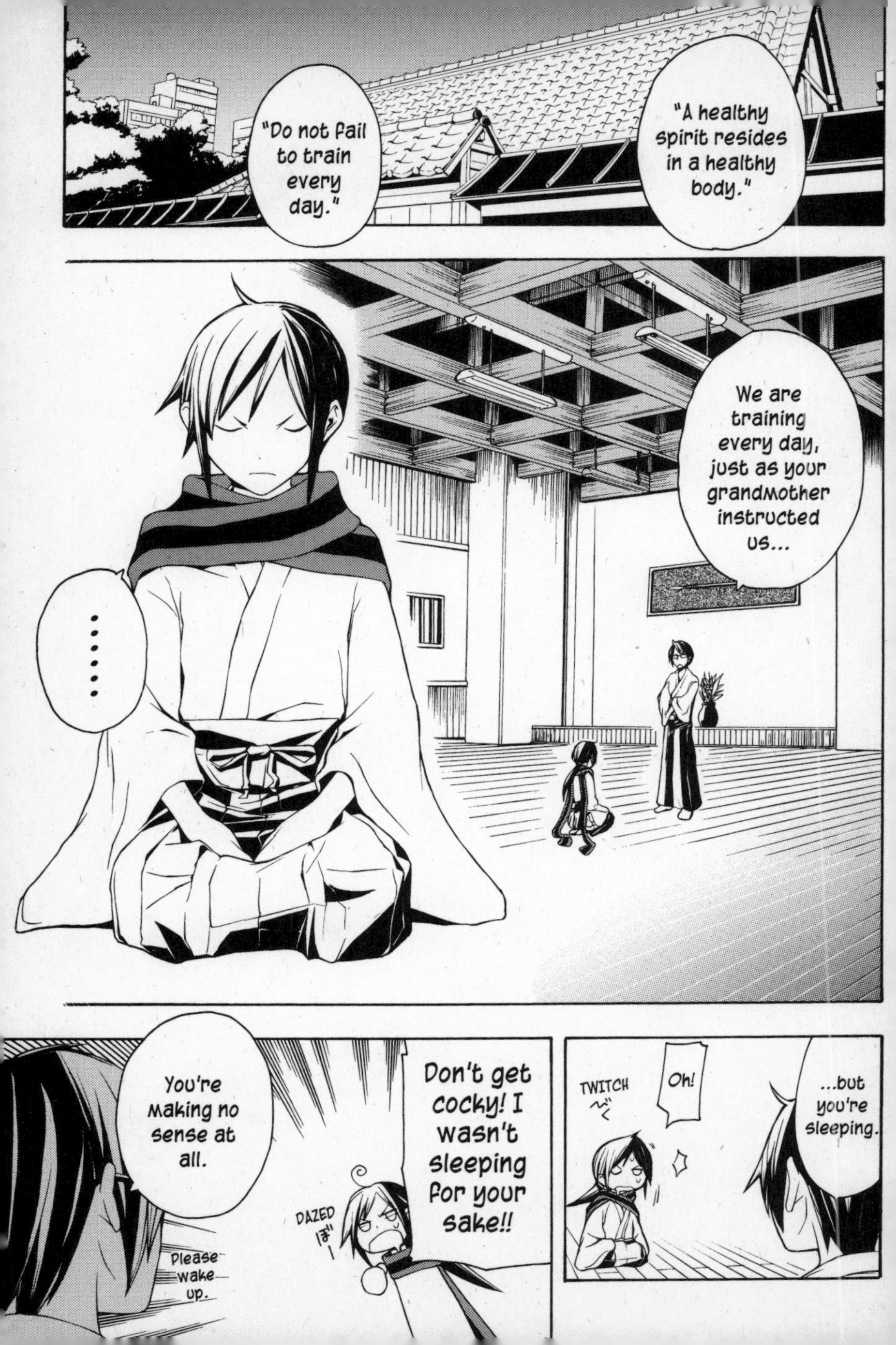
"A healthy spirit resides in a healthy body."
"Do not fail to train every day."
We are training every day, just as your grandmother instructed us...
......
...but you're sleeping.
Oh!
TWITCH
Don't get cocky! I wasn't sleeping for your sake!!
DAZED
You're making no sense at all.
Please wake up.

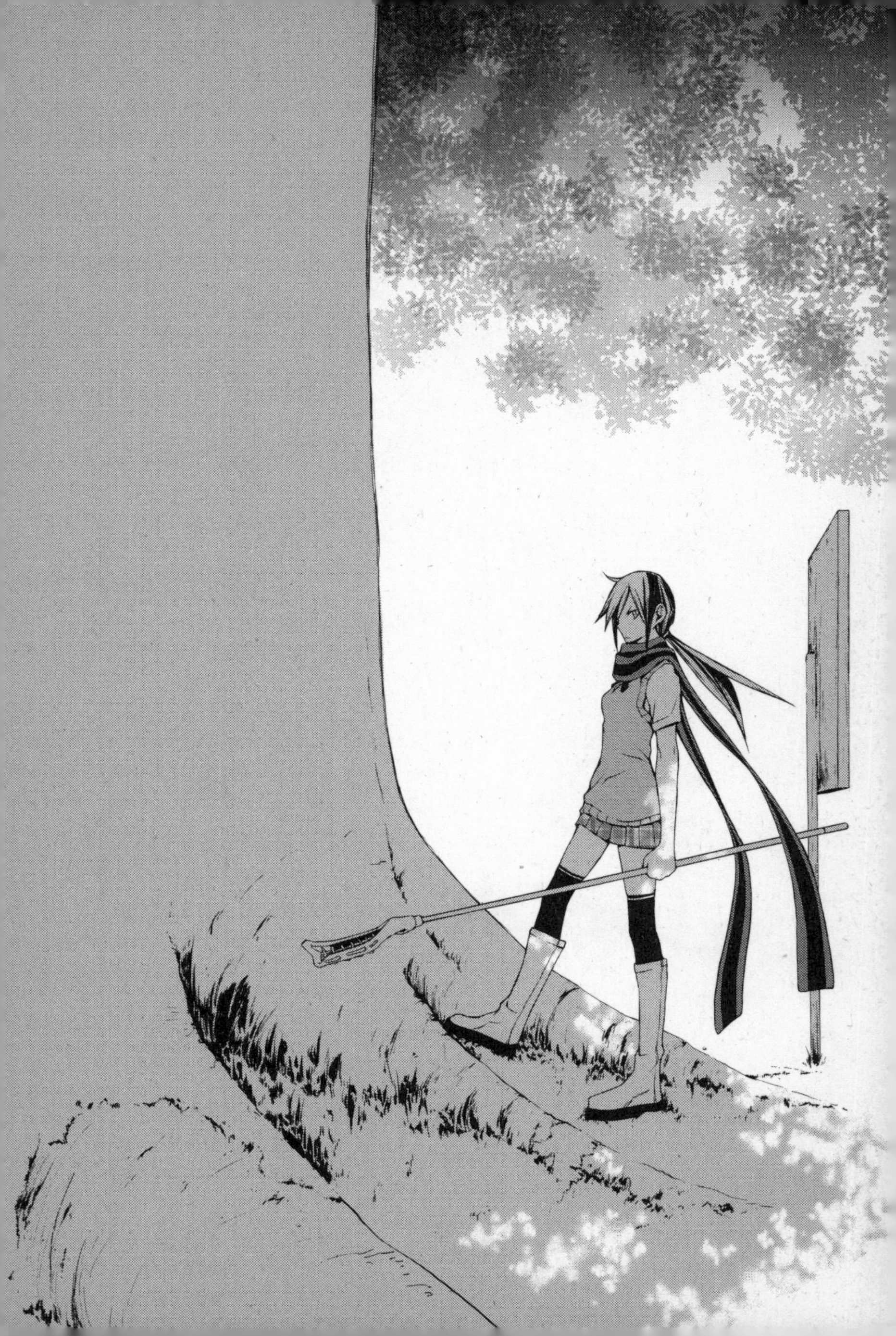

11th Night: Thorny Road (Part 1)

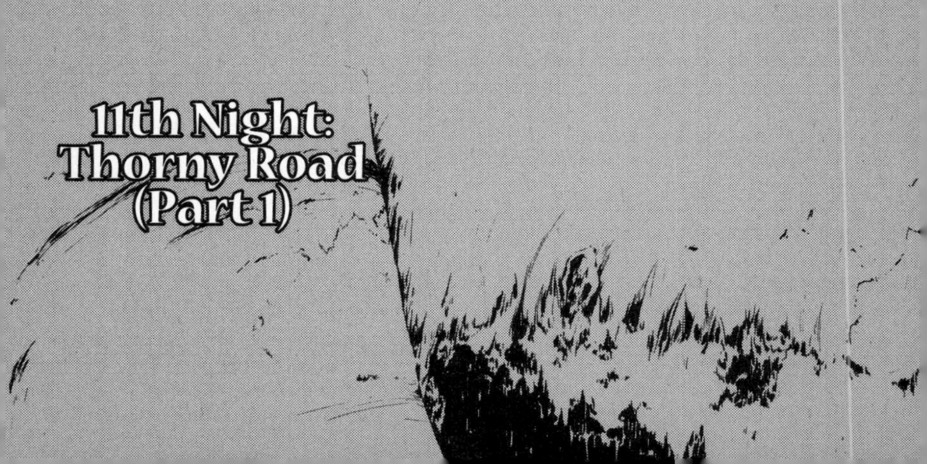

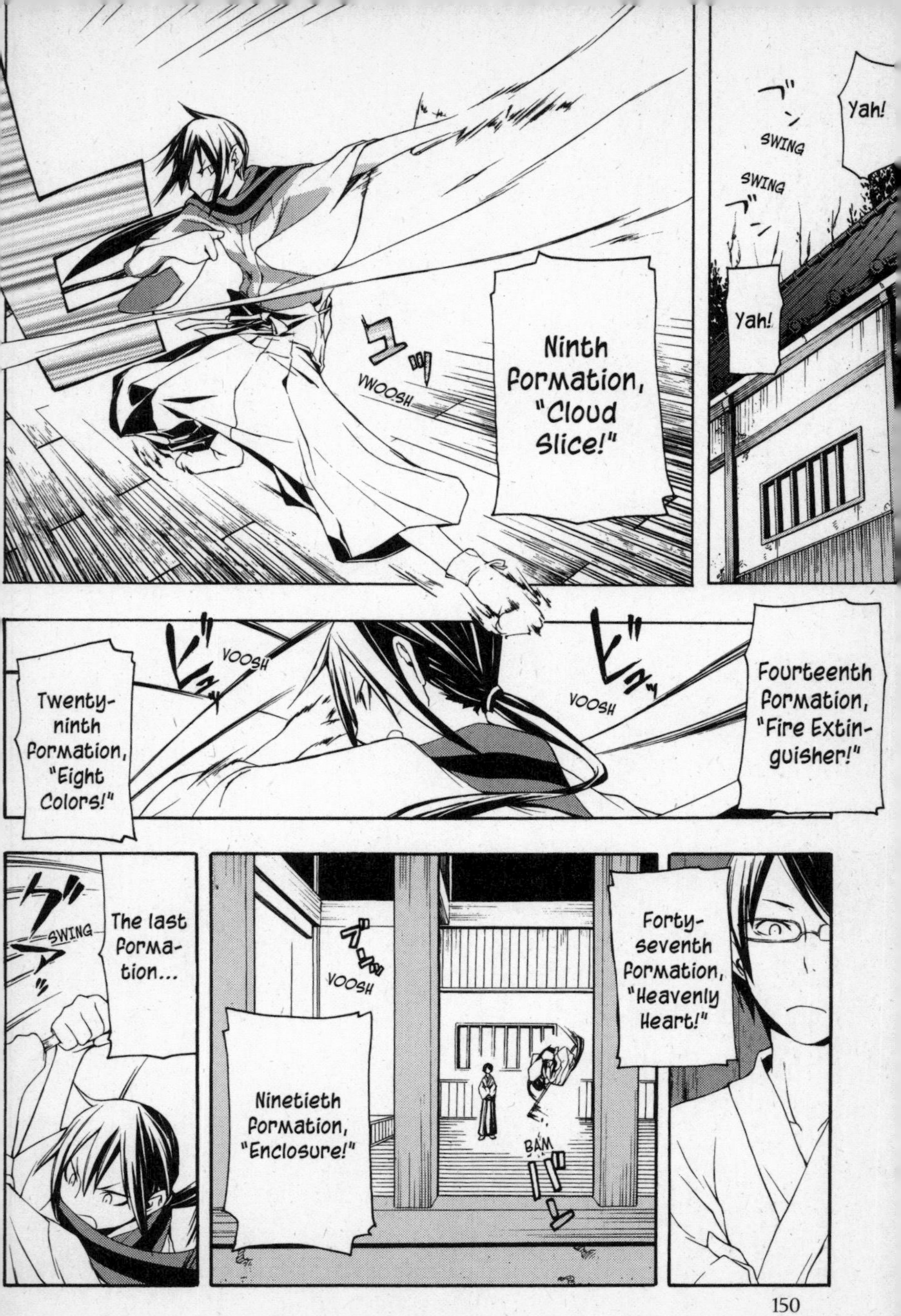
Yah!
SWING
SWING
Yah!
Ninth formation, "Cloud Slice!"
VWOOSH
Fourteenth formation, "Fire Extinguisher!"
VOOSH
VOOSH
Twenty-ninth formation, "Eight Colors!"
Forty-seventh formation, "Heavenly Heart!"
VOOSH
Ninetieth formation, "Enclosure!"
BAM
The last formation...
SWING

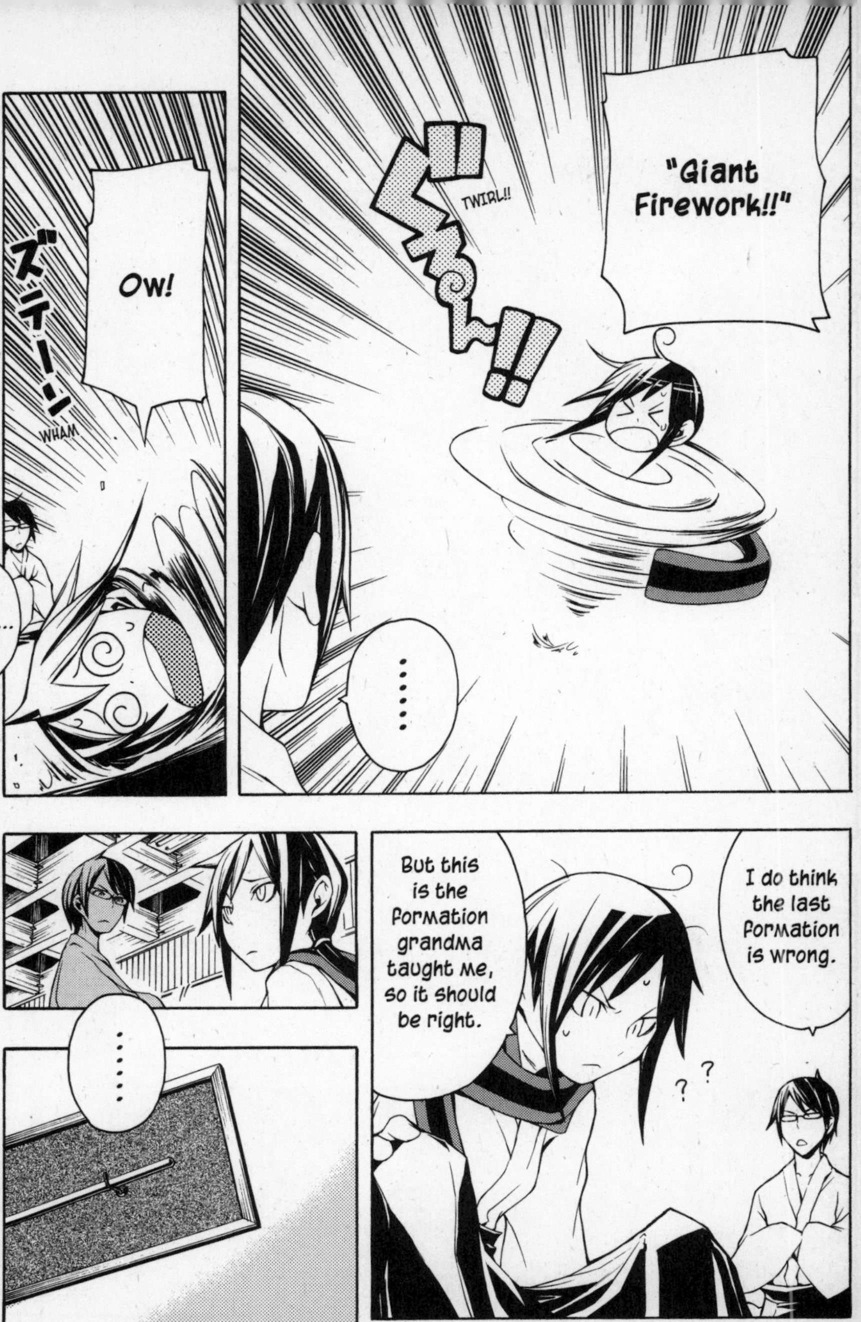
"Giant Firework!!"
TWIRL!!
......
Ow!
WHAM
Hmm...
I do think the last formation is wrong.
But this is the formation grandma taught me, so it should be right.
? ?
......

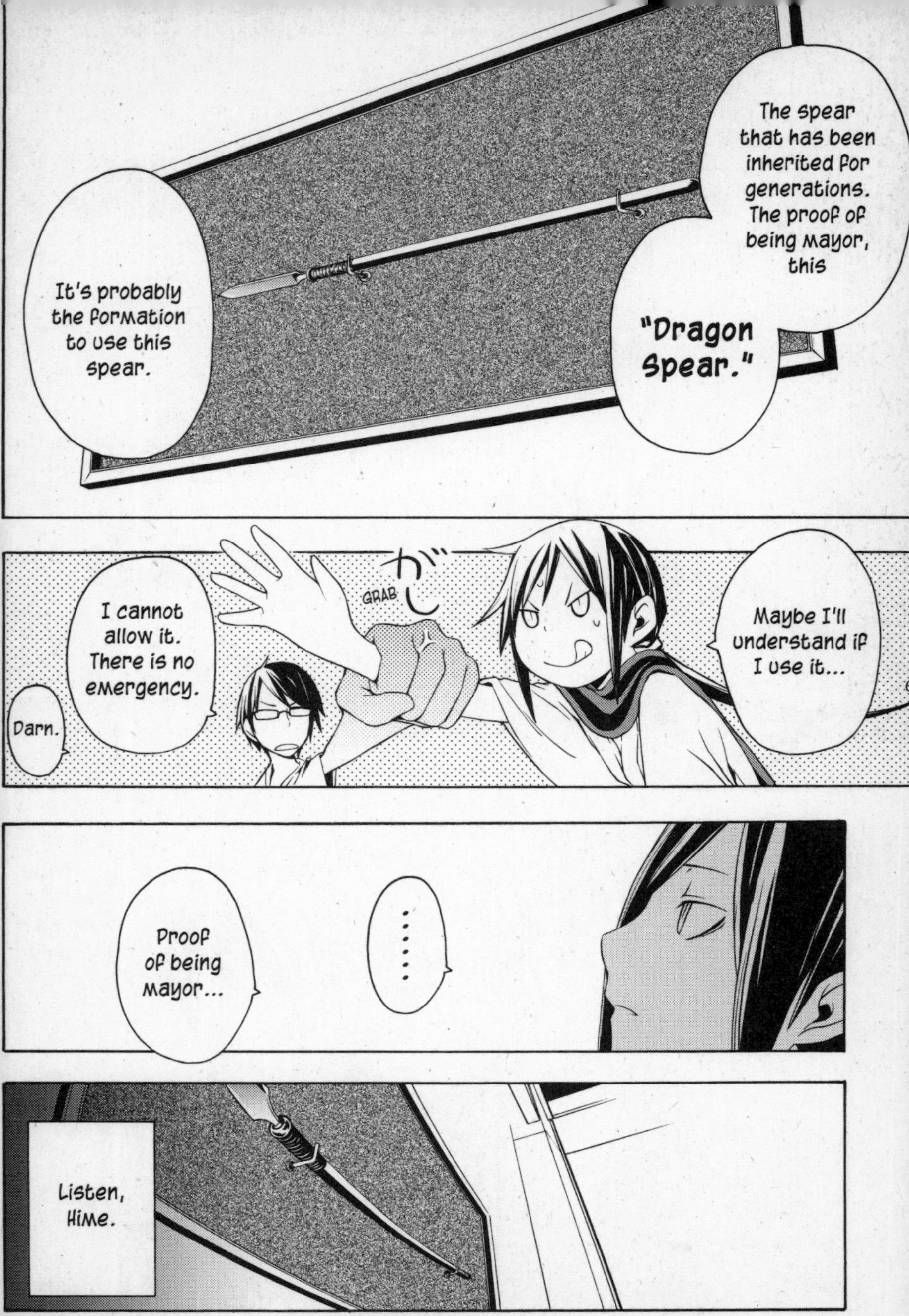
The spear that has been inherited for generations. The proof of being mayor, this
"Dragon Spear."
It's probably the formation to use this spear.
Maybe I'll understand if I use it...
がし
GRAB
I cannot allow it. There is no emergency.
Darn.
......
Proof of being mayor...
Listen, Hime.

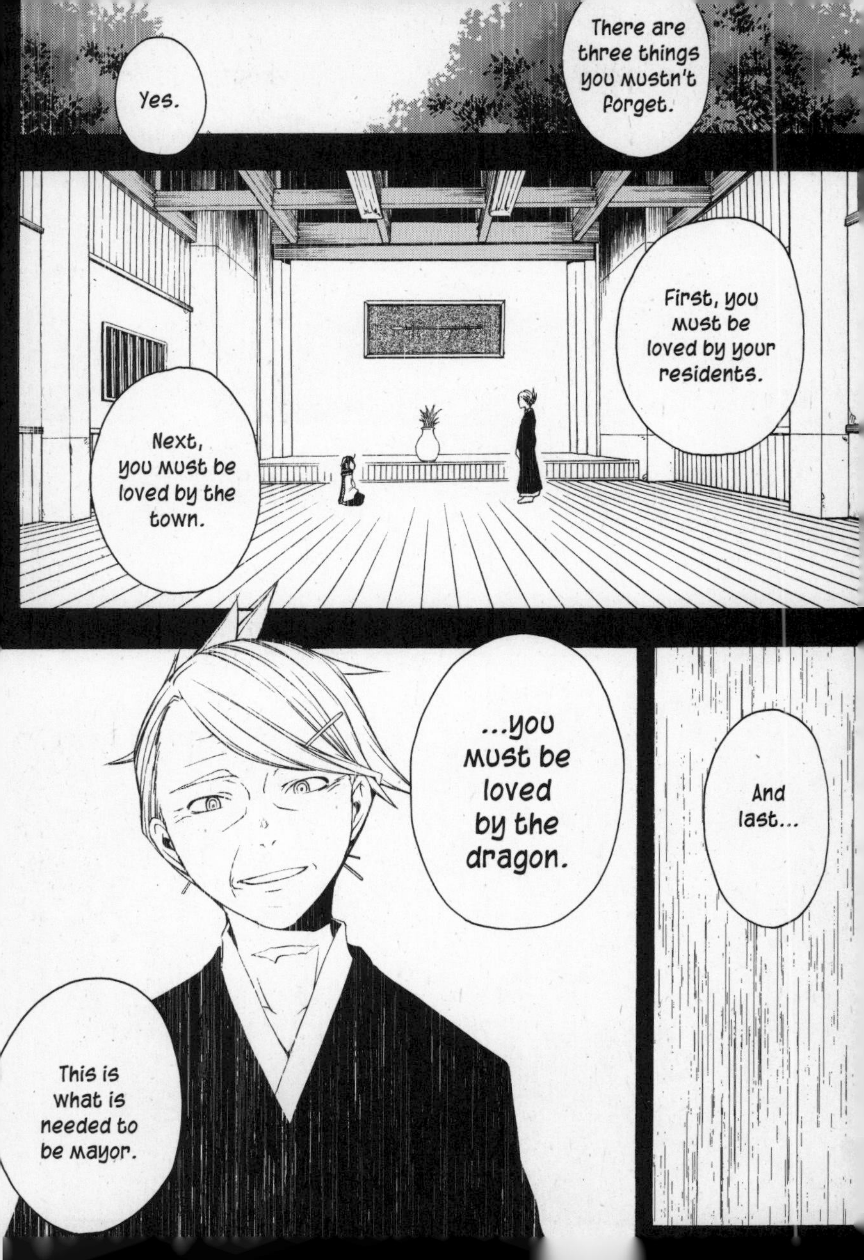
There are three things you mustn't forget.
Yes.
First, you must be loved by your residents.
Next, you must be loved by the town.
And last...
...you must be loved by the dragon.
This is what is needed to be mayor.

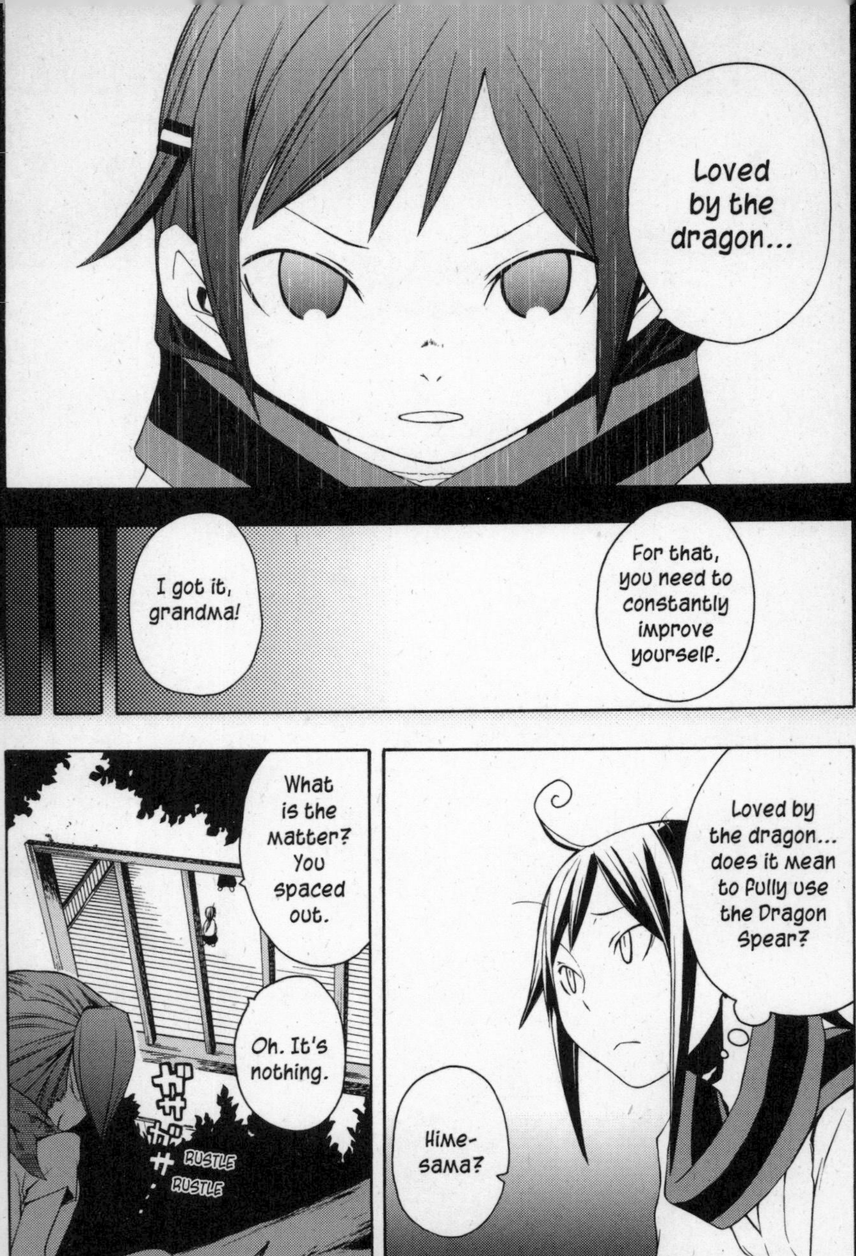
Loved by the dragon...
For that, you need to constantly improve yourself.
I got it, grandma!
Loved by the dragon... does it mean to fully use the Dragon Spear?
Hime-sama?
What is the matter? You spaced out.
Oh. It's nothing.
RUSTLE
RUSTLE

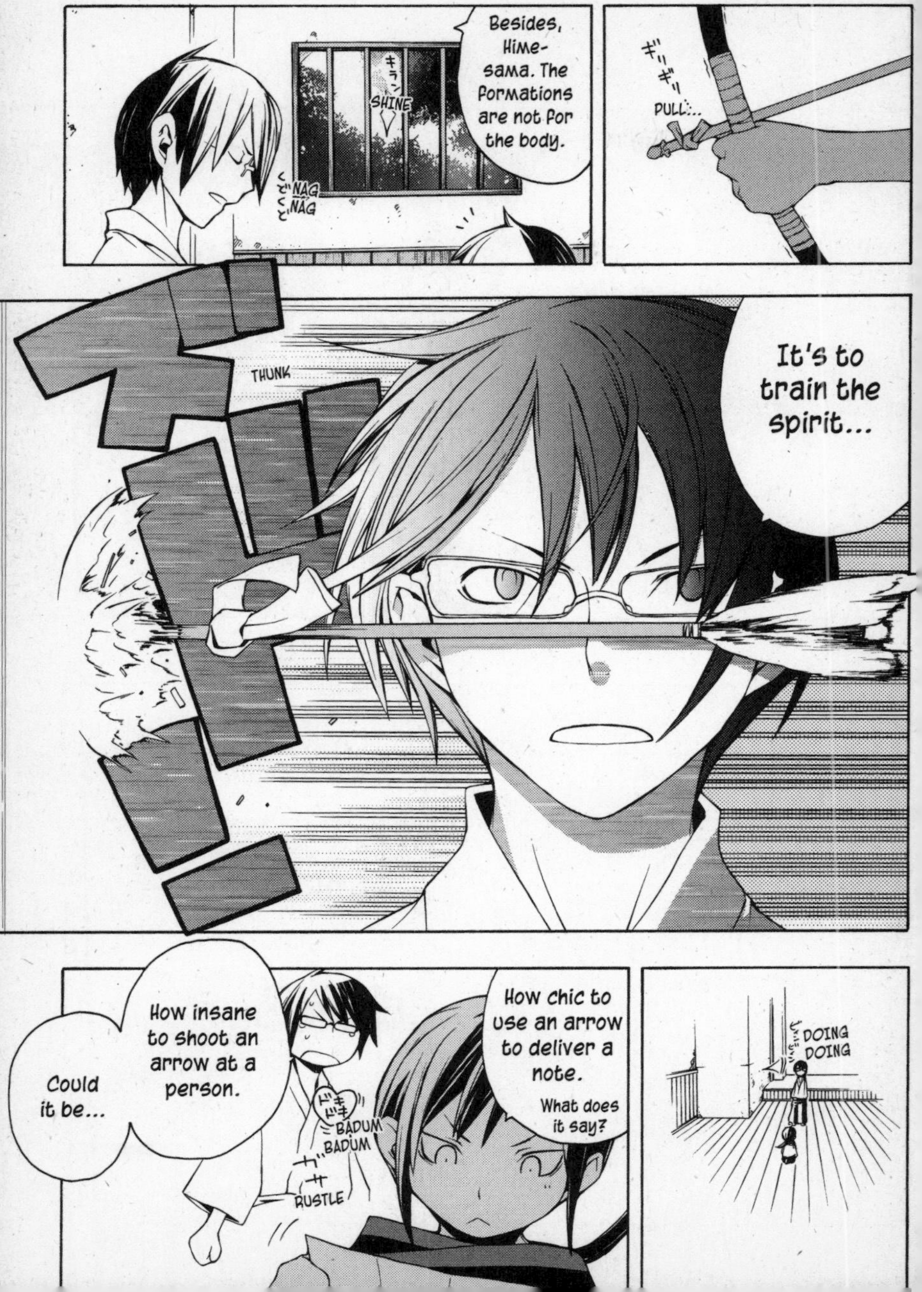
ギリギリ
PULL...
Besides, Hime-sama. The formations are not for the body.
キラン
SHINE
NAG NAG
It's to train the spirit...
THUNK
DOING DOING
How chic to use an arrow to deliver a note.
What does it say?
How insane to shoot an arrow at a person.
Could it be...
BADUM BADUM
RUSTLE

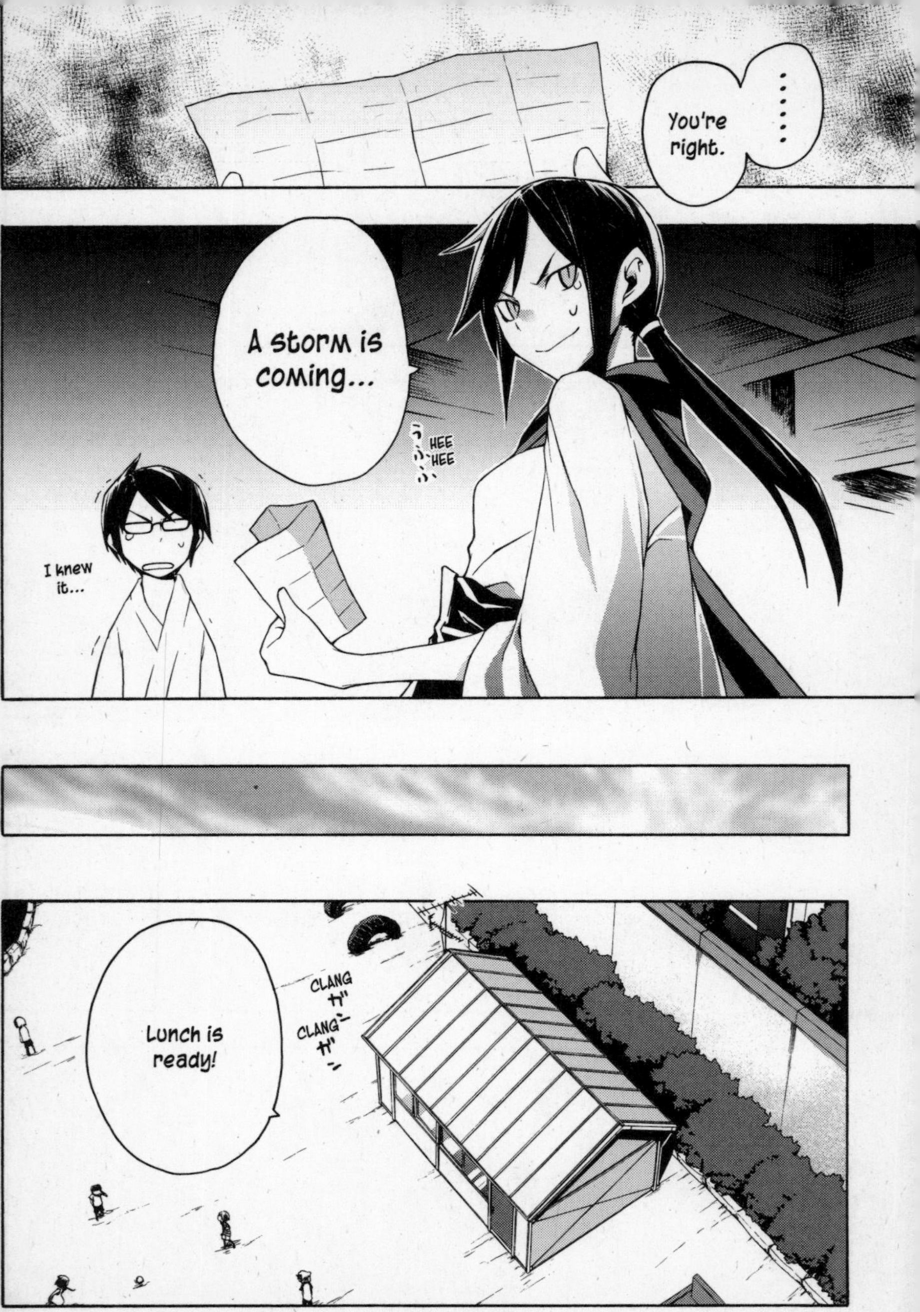

......
You're right.
A storm is coming...
HEE HEE
I knew it...
Lunch is ready!
CLANG
CLANG

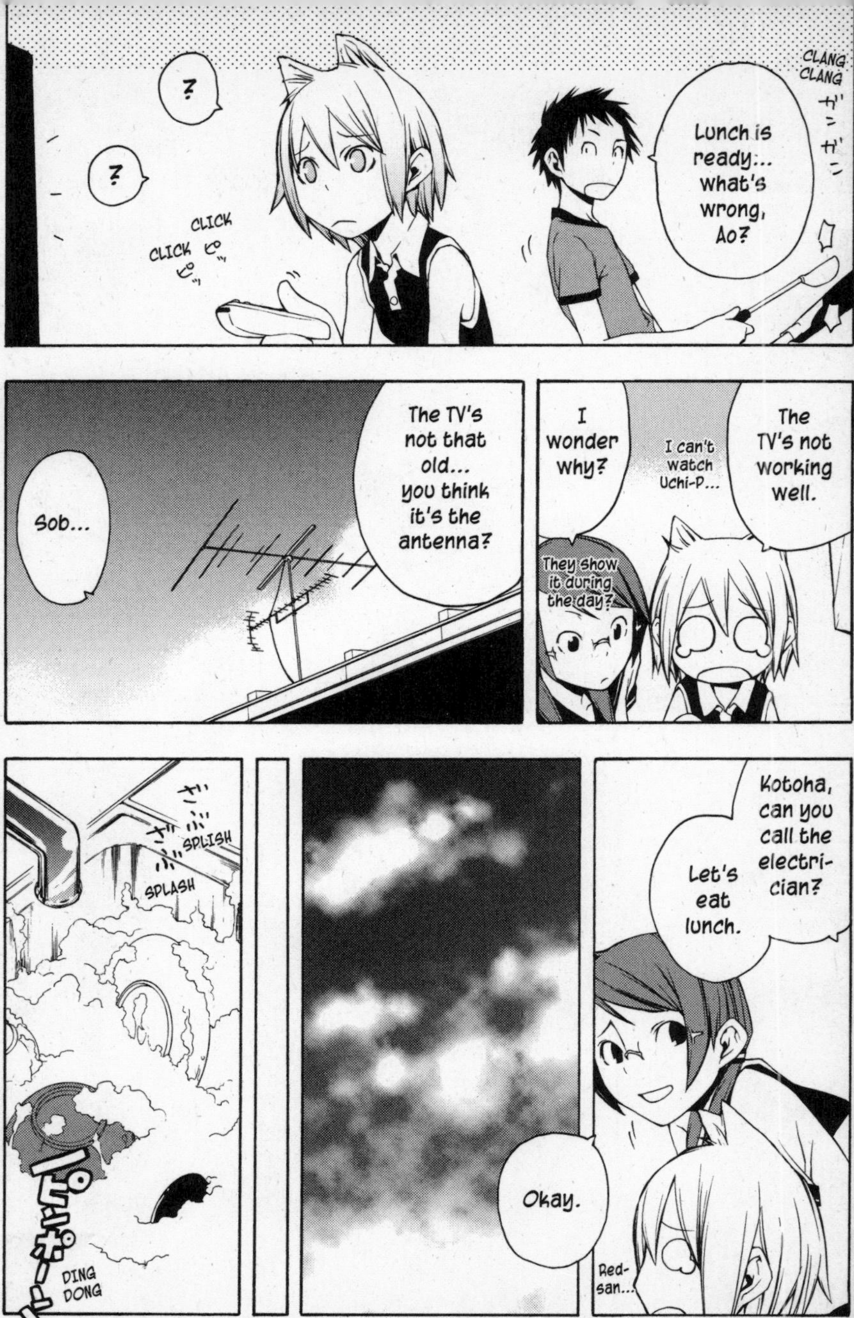
CLANG CLANG
Lunch is ready... what's wrong, Ao?
?
?
CLICK CLICK
The TV's not working well.
I can't watch Uchi-P...
I wonder why?
They show it during the day?
The TV's not that old... you think it's the antenna?
Sob...
Kotoha, can you call the electrician?
Let's eat lunch.
Okay.
Red-san...
SPLISH
SPLASH
DING DONG

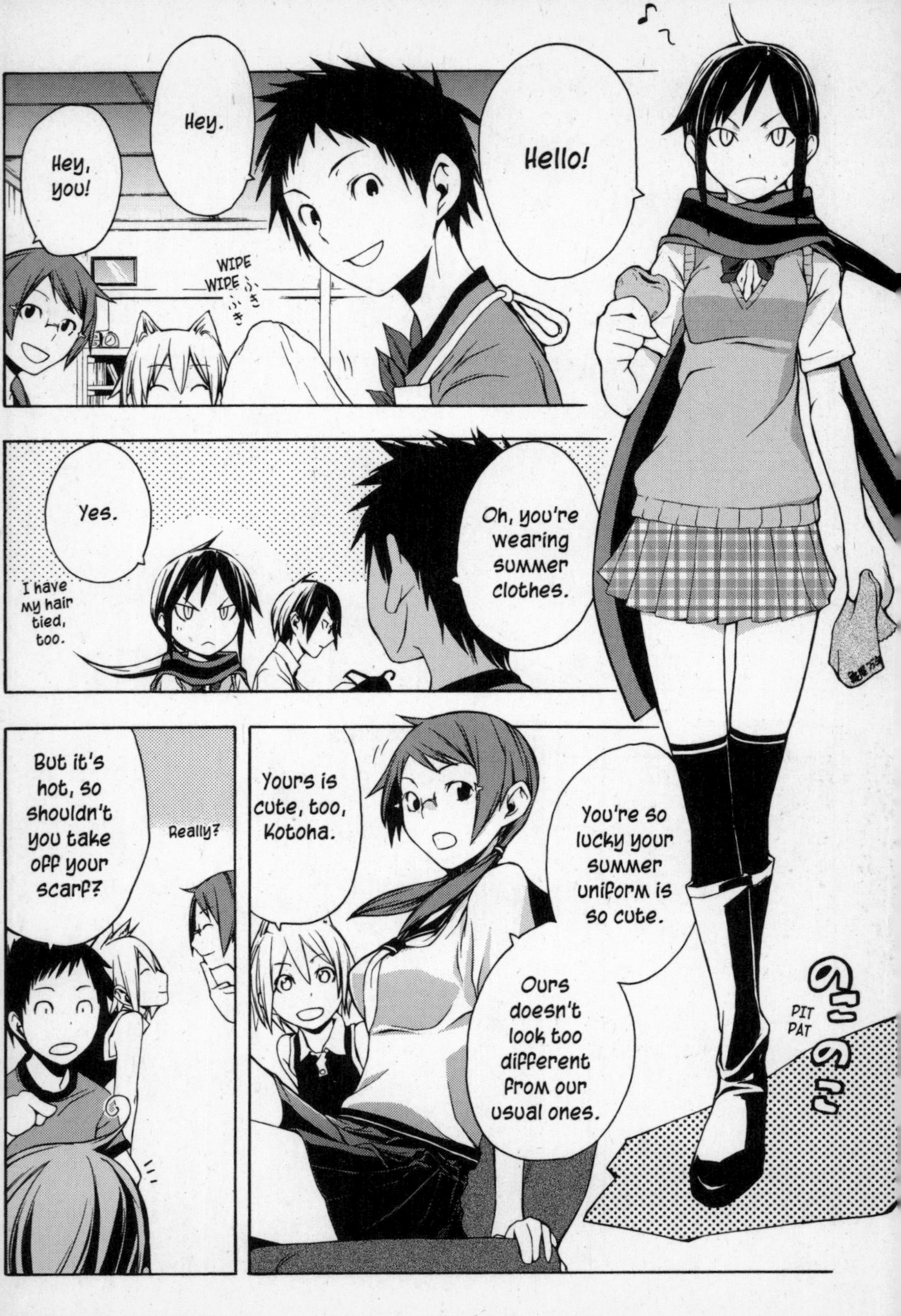
のこのこ
PIT PAT
Hello!
Hey.
Hey, you!
ふき ふき
WIPE WIPE
Oh, you're wearing summer clothes.
Yes.
I have my hair tied, too.
You're so lucky your summer uniform is so cute.
Yours is cute, too, Kotoha.
Ours doesn't look too different from our usual ones.
Really?
But it's hot, so shouldn't you take off your scarf?

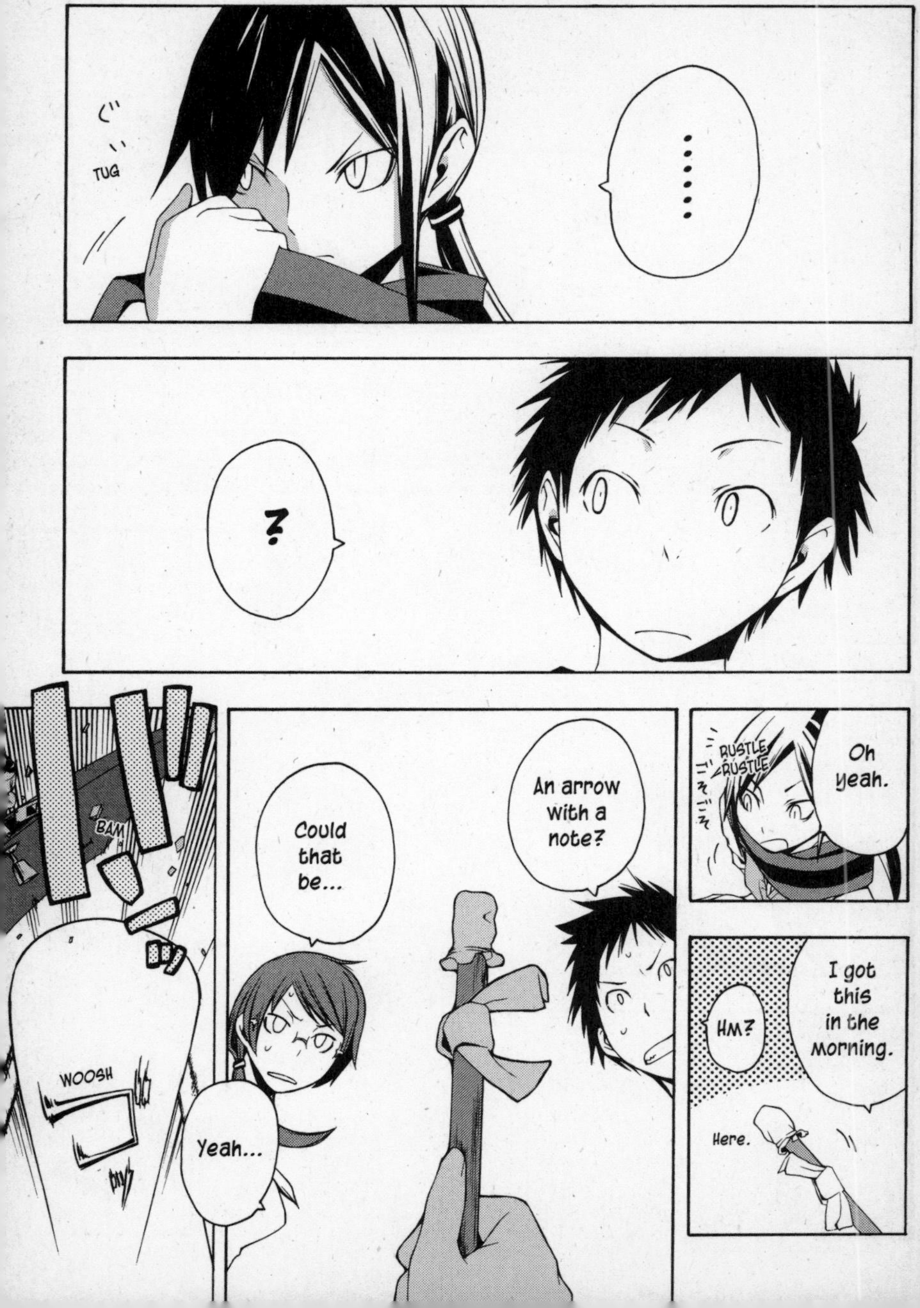

……
ぐい
TUG
?
Oh yeah.
RUSTLE RUSTLE
I got this in the morning.
HM?
Here.
An arrow with a note?
Could that be...
Yeah...
BAM
WOOSH

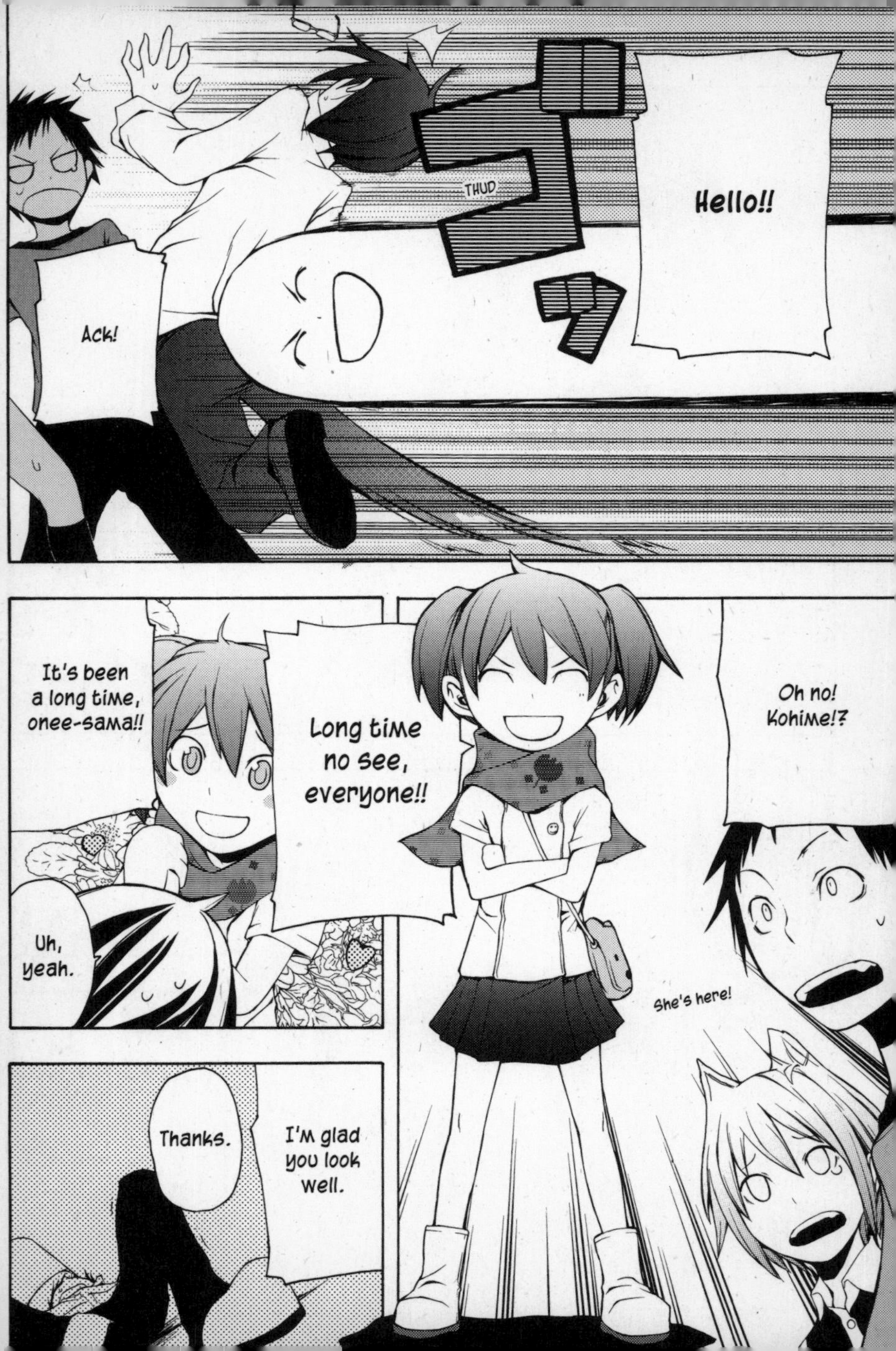
Hello!!
THUD
Ack!
Oh no! Kohime!?
Long time no see, everyone!!
She's here!
It's been a long time, onee-sama!!
Uh, yeah.
I'm glad you look well.
Thanks.

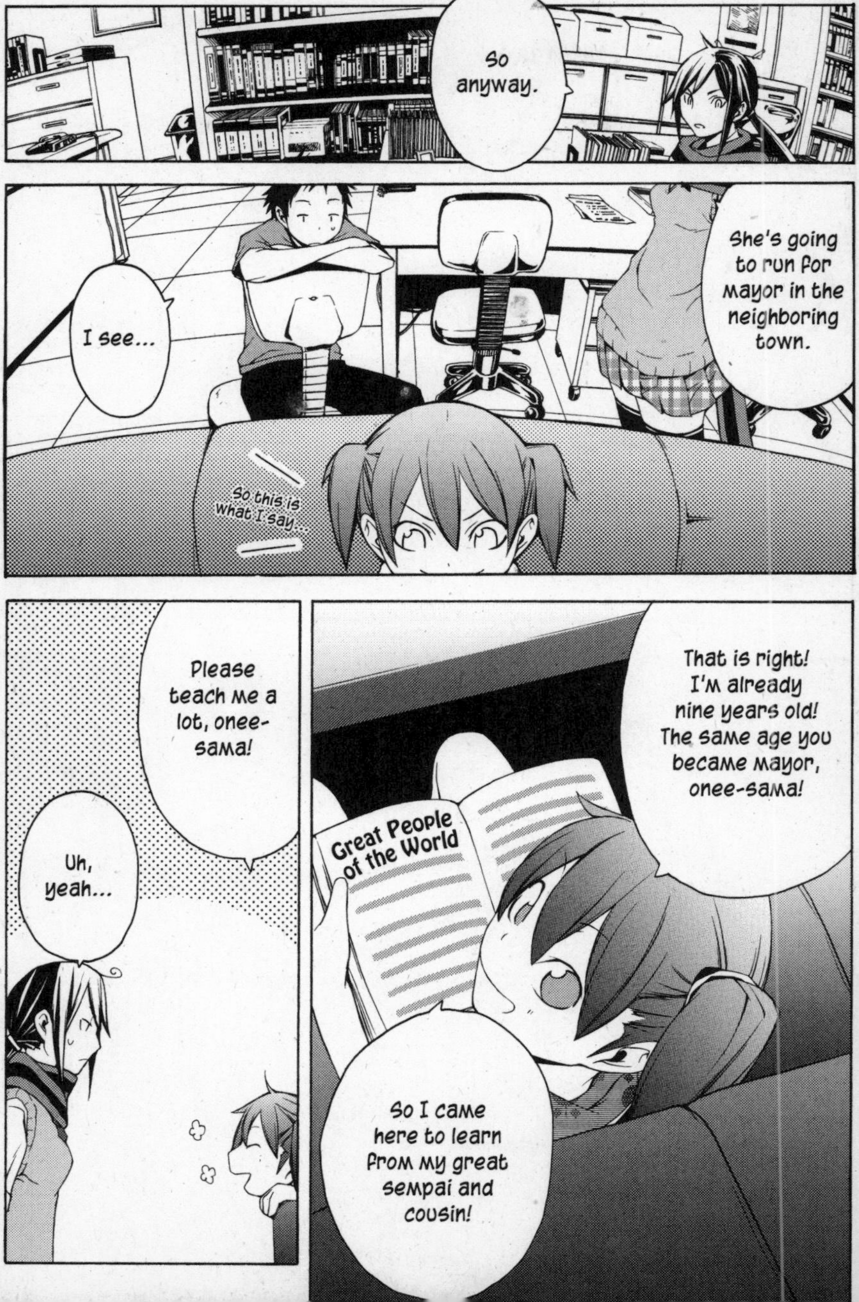
So anyway.
She's going to run for mayor in the neighboring town.
I see...
So this is what I say...
That is right! I'm already nine years old! The same age you became mayor, onee-sama!
Great People of the World
So I came here to learn from my great sempai and cousin!
Please teach me a lot, onee-sama!
Uh, yeah...

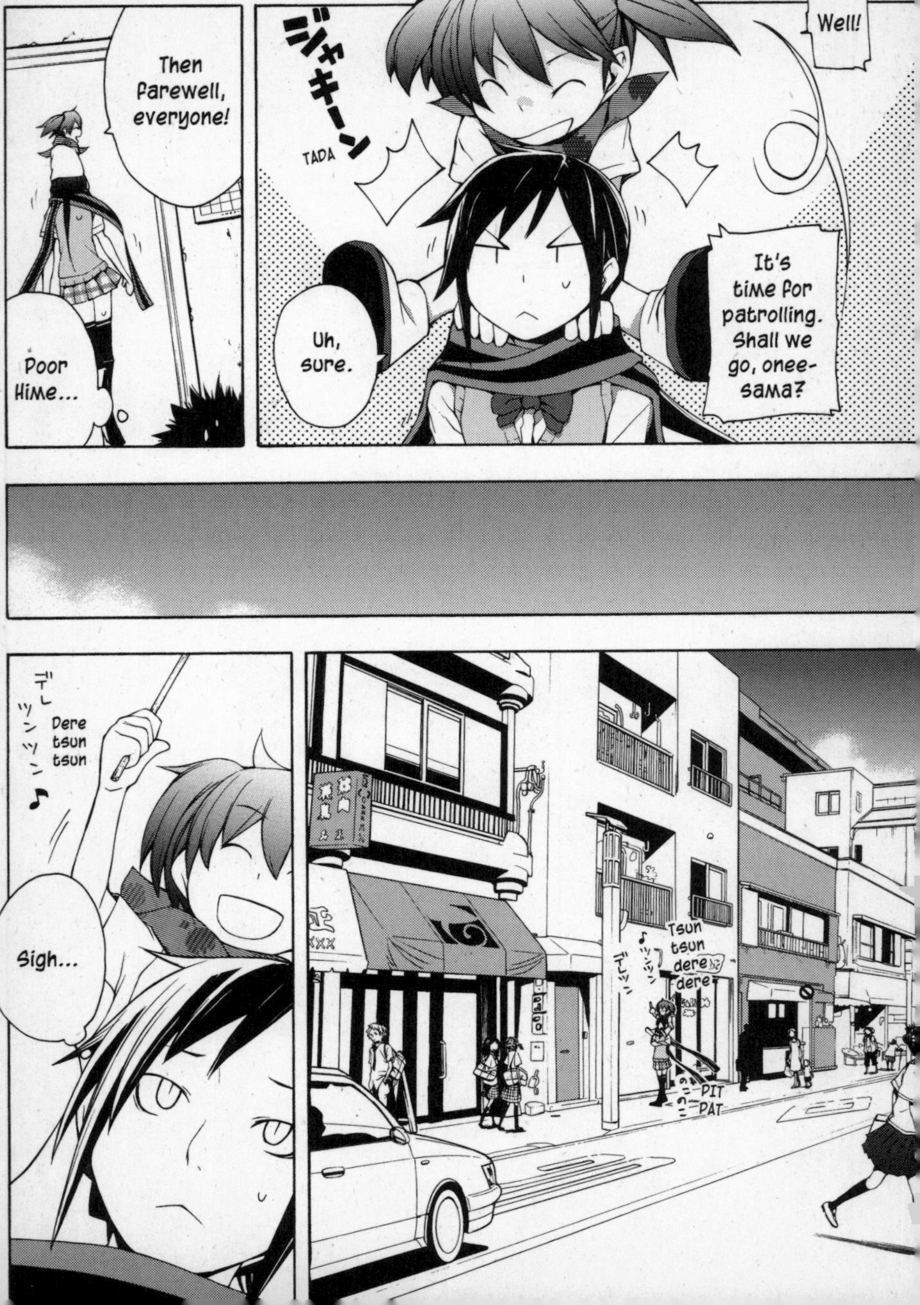
Well!
It's time for patrolling. Shall we go, onee-sama?
ジャキーン
TADA
Uh, sure.
Then farewell, everyone!
Poor Hime...
Tsun tsun dere dere
PIT PAT
デレツンツン
Dere tsun tsun
Sigh...

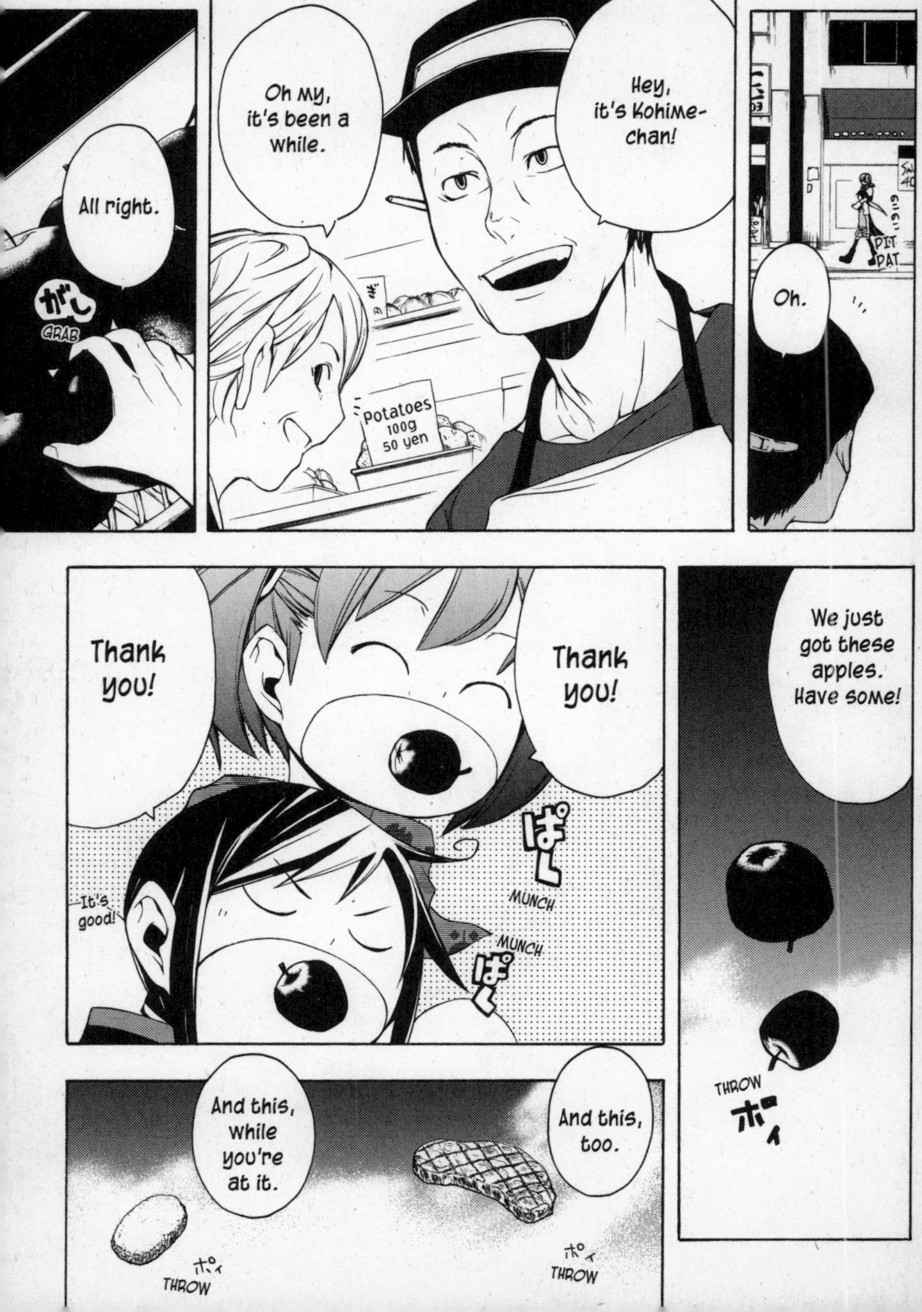
PIT
PAT
Oh.
Hey, it's Kohime-chan!
Oh my, it's been a while.
Potatoes 100g 50 yen
All right.
がし
GRAB
We just got these apples. Have some!
THROW
ポイ
Thank you!
Thank you!
ぱく
MUNCH
MUNCH
ぱく
It's good!
And this, too.
ポイ
THROW
And this, while you're at it.
ポイ
THROW

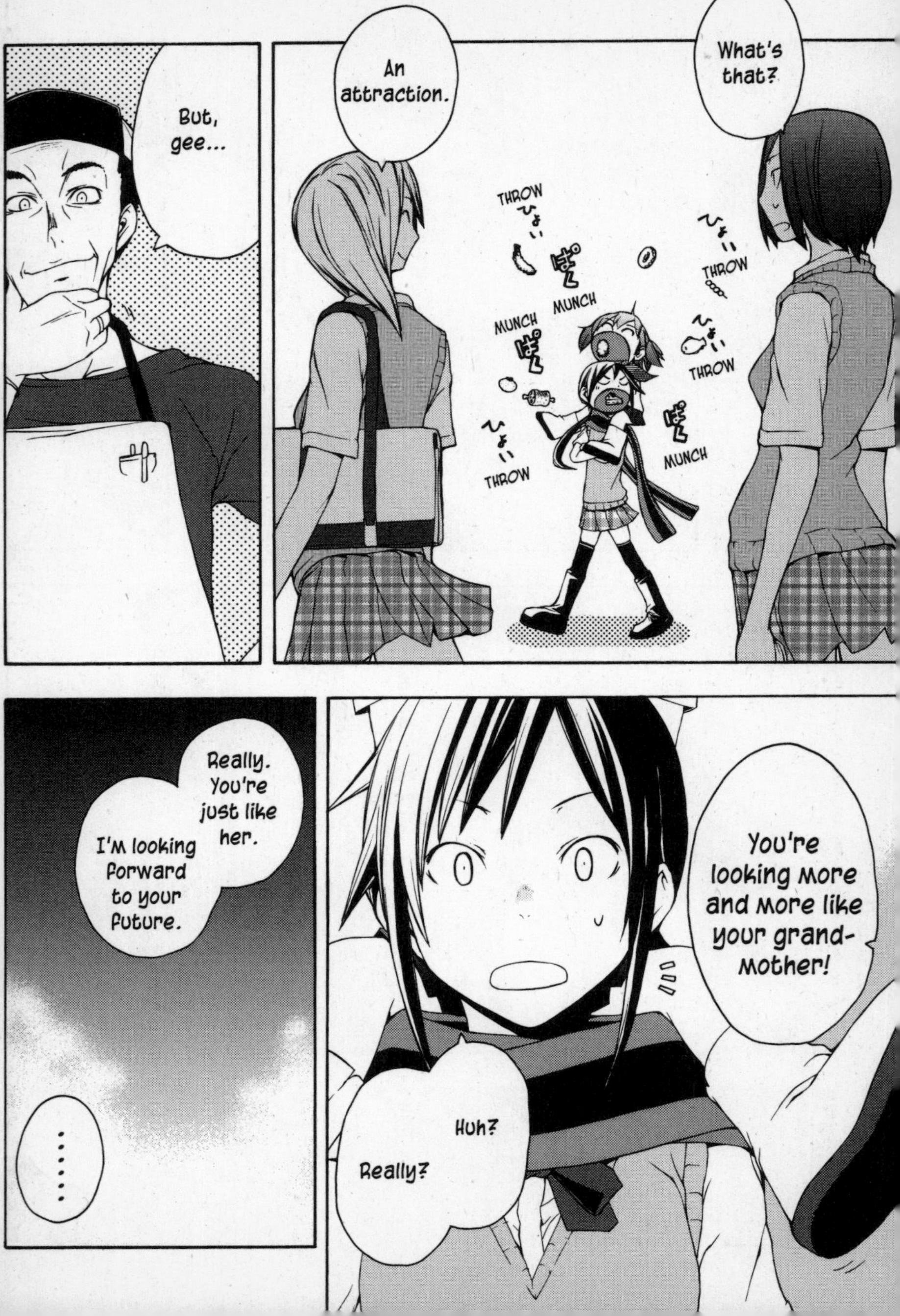
What's that?
An attraction.
THROW ひょい
ぱく MUNCH
ひょい THROW
MUNCH ぱく
ひょい THROW
ひょい THROW
ぱく MUNCH
But, gee...
You're looking more and more like your grand-mother!
Huh?
Really?
Really. You're just like her.
I'm looking forward to your future.
......

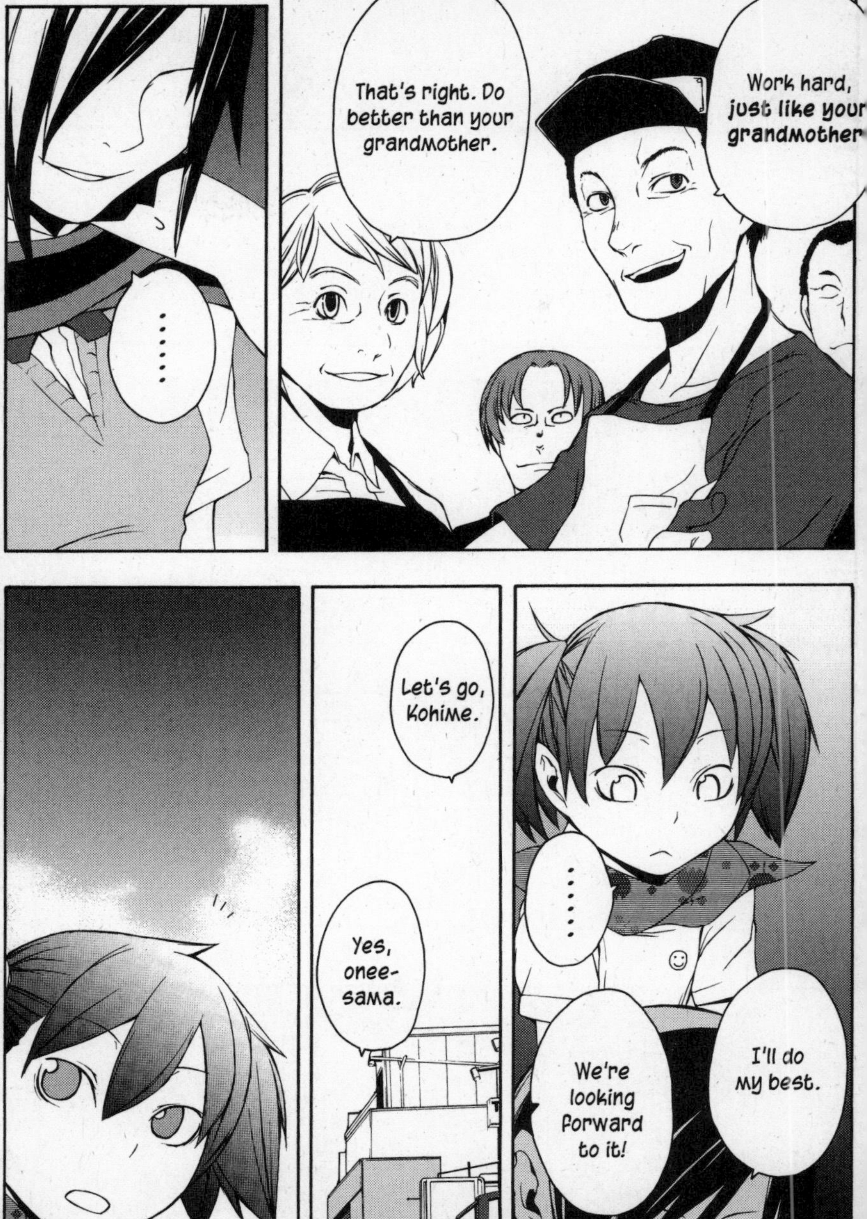
Work hard, just like your grandmother.
That's right. Do better than your grandmother.
......
......
I'll do my best.
We're looking forward to it!
Let's go, Kohime.
Yes, onee-sama.

Huh?

Onee-sama, look!

Kohime!

JUMP

Wow!

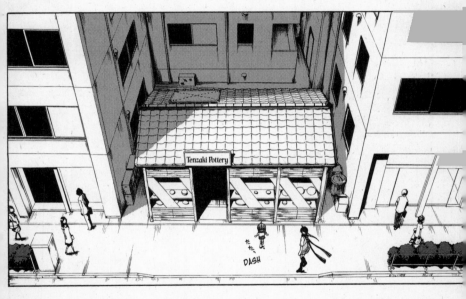

Tenzaki Pottery

DASH

Blue Clouds

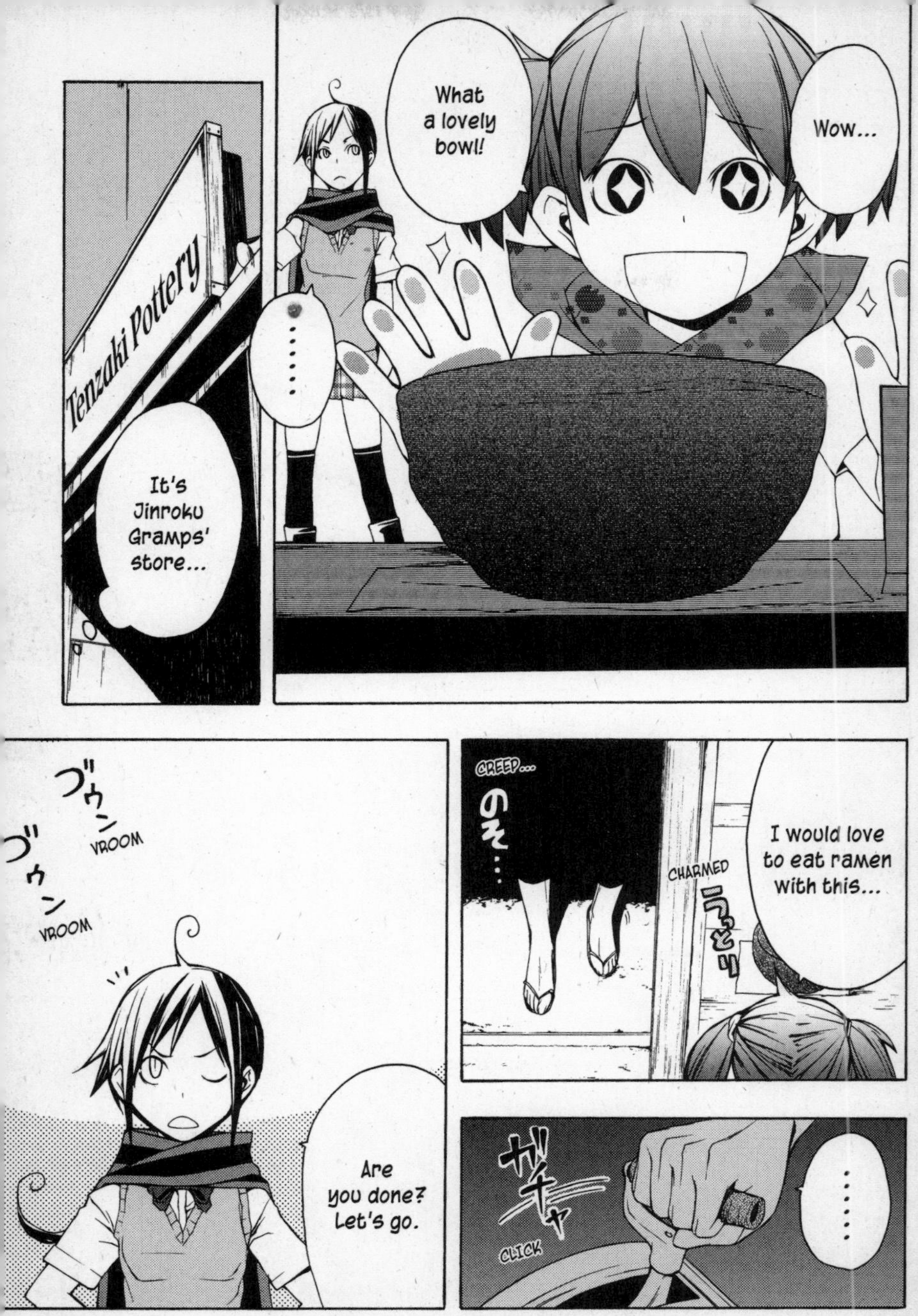
Wow...
What a lovely bowl!
......
Tenzaki Pottery
It's Jinroku Gramps' store...
I would love to eat ramen with this...
うっとり
CHARMED
のぞ…
CREEP...
......
ガチャ
CLICK
ヴゥン
VROOM
ヴゥン
VROOM
Are you done? Let's go.

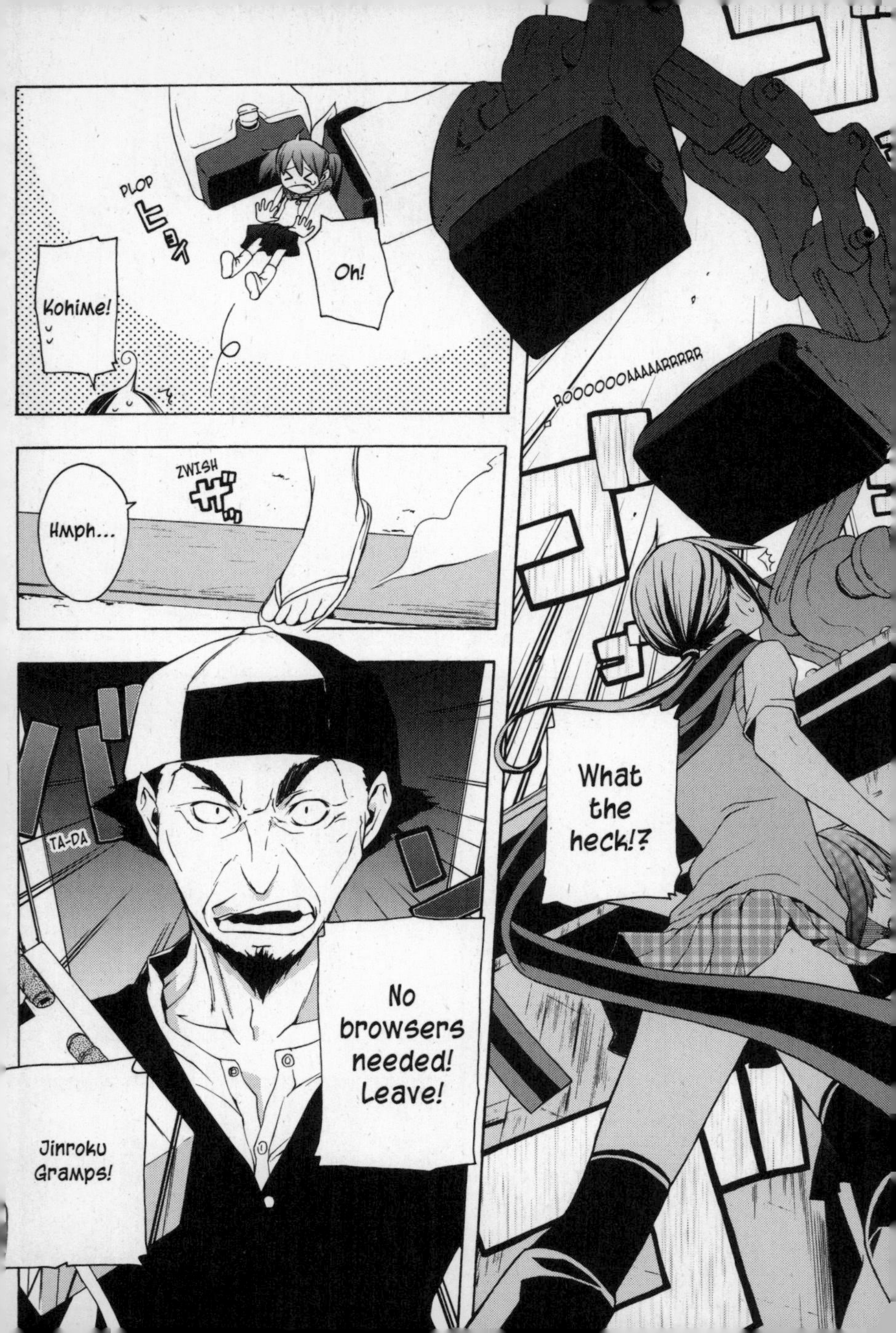
ROOOOOOAAAAARRRRR
What the heck!?
Oh!
PLOP
Kohime!
ZWISH
Hmph...
No browsers needed! Leave!
TA-DA
Jinroku Gramps!

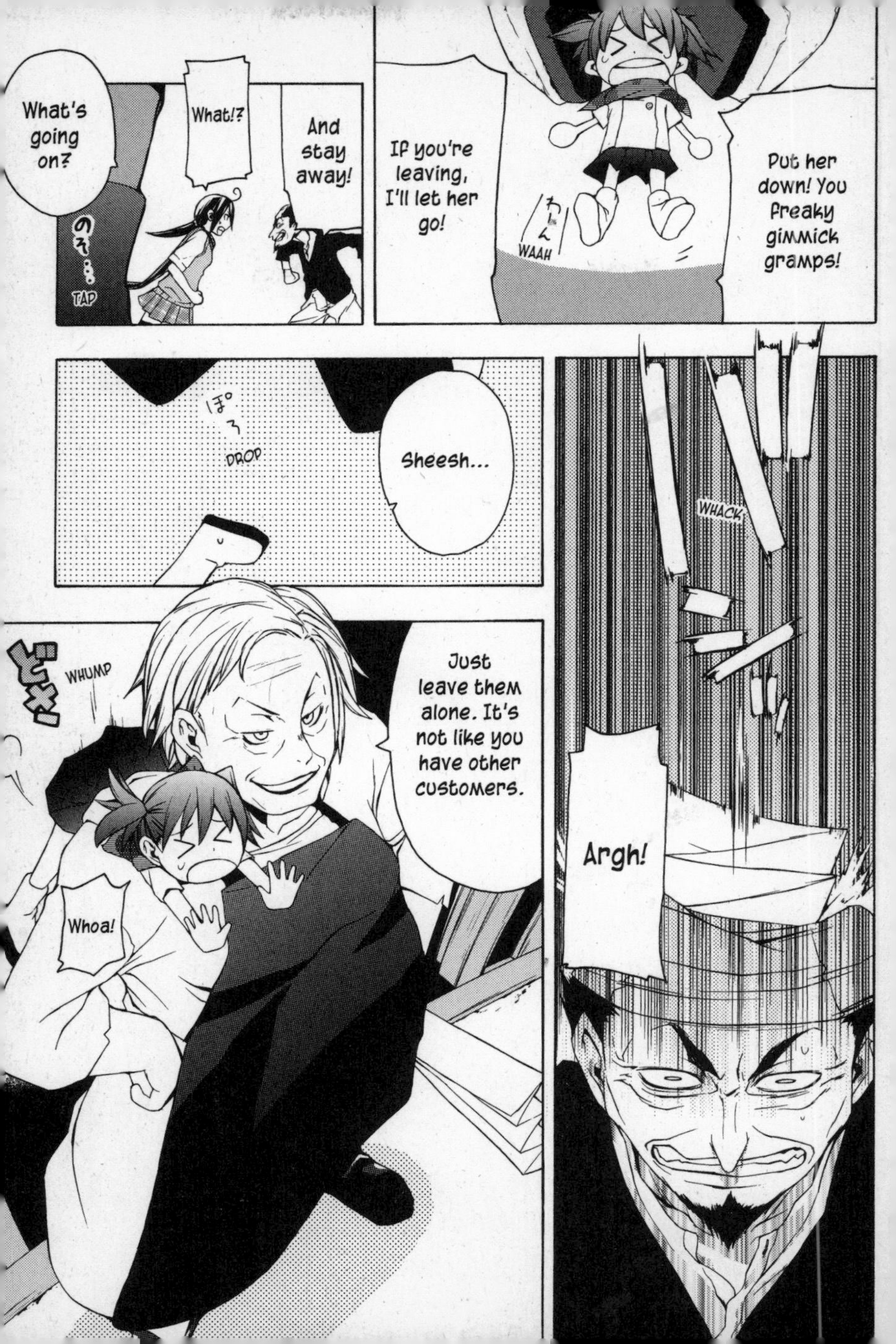

Put her down! You freaky gimmick gramps!
わーん
WAAH
If you're leaving, I'll let her go!
And stay away!
What!?
What's going on?
のそ…
TAP
WHACK
Argh!
ぽろ
DROP
Sheesh...
Just leave them alone. It's not like you have other customers.
WHUMP
Whoa!

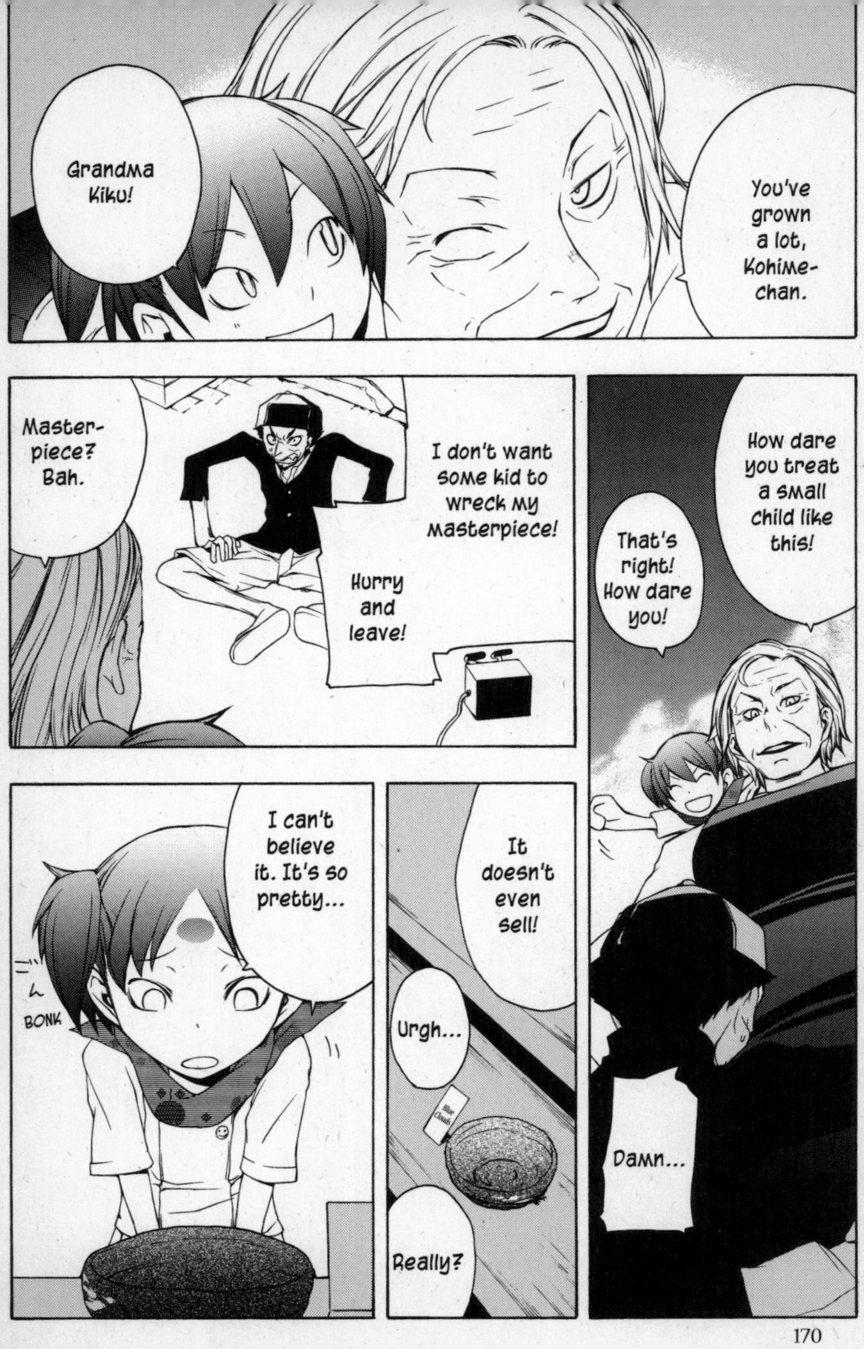
You've grown a lot, Kohime-chan.
Grandma Kiku!
How dare you treat a small child like this!
That's right! How dare you!
Damn...
I don't want some kid to wreck my masterpiece!
Hurry and leave!
Masterpiece? Bah.
It doesn't even sell!
Urgh...
Blue Clouds
Really?
I can't believe it. It's so pretty...
BONK

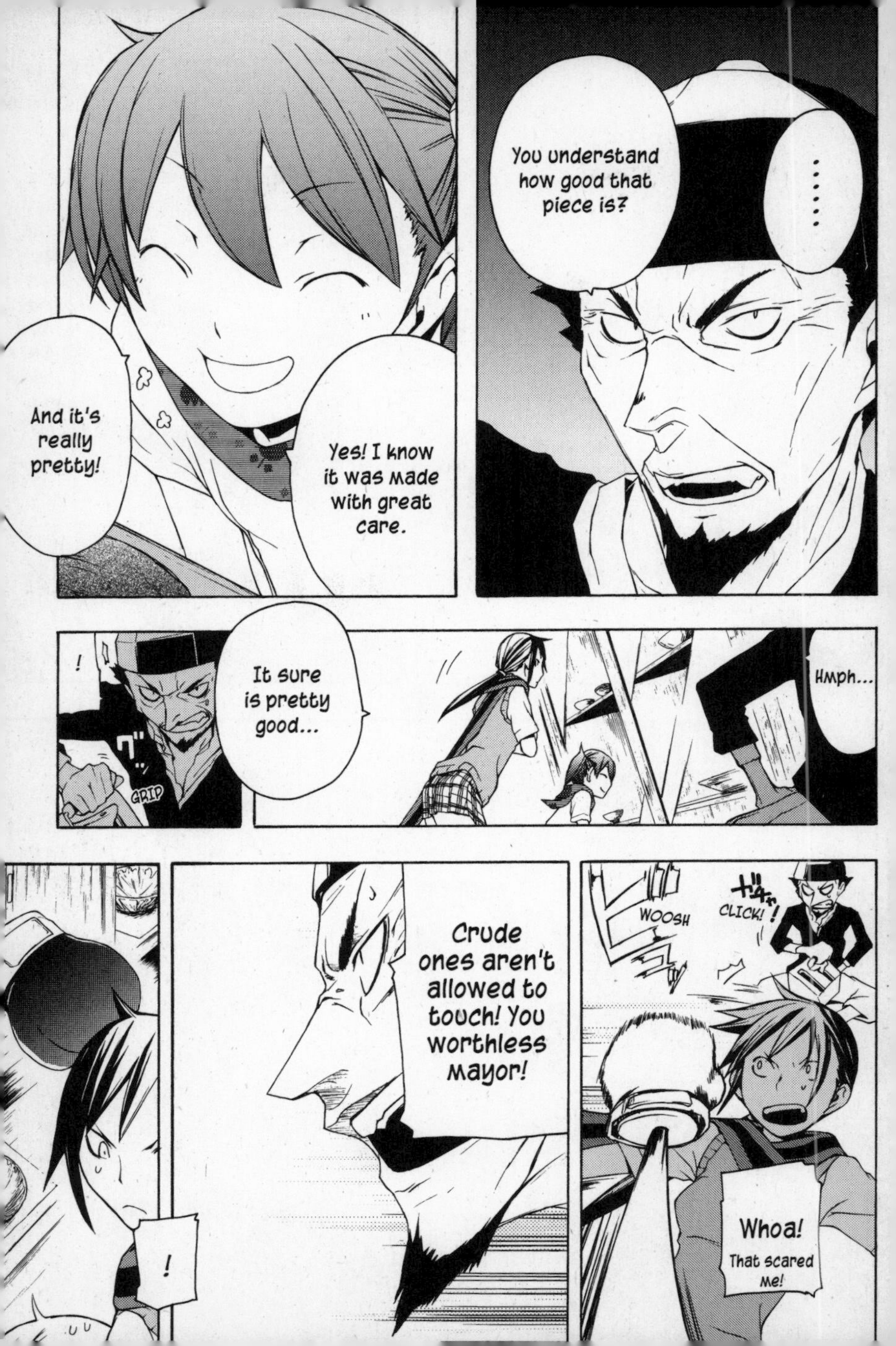
......
You understand how good that piece is?
Yes! I know it was made with great care.
And it's really pretty!
Hmph...
It sure is pretty good...
!
GRIP
CLICK!
WOOSH
Whoa! That scared me!
Crude ones aren't allowed to touch! You worthless mayor!
!

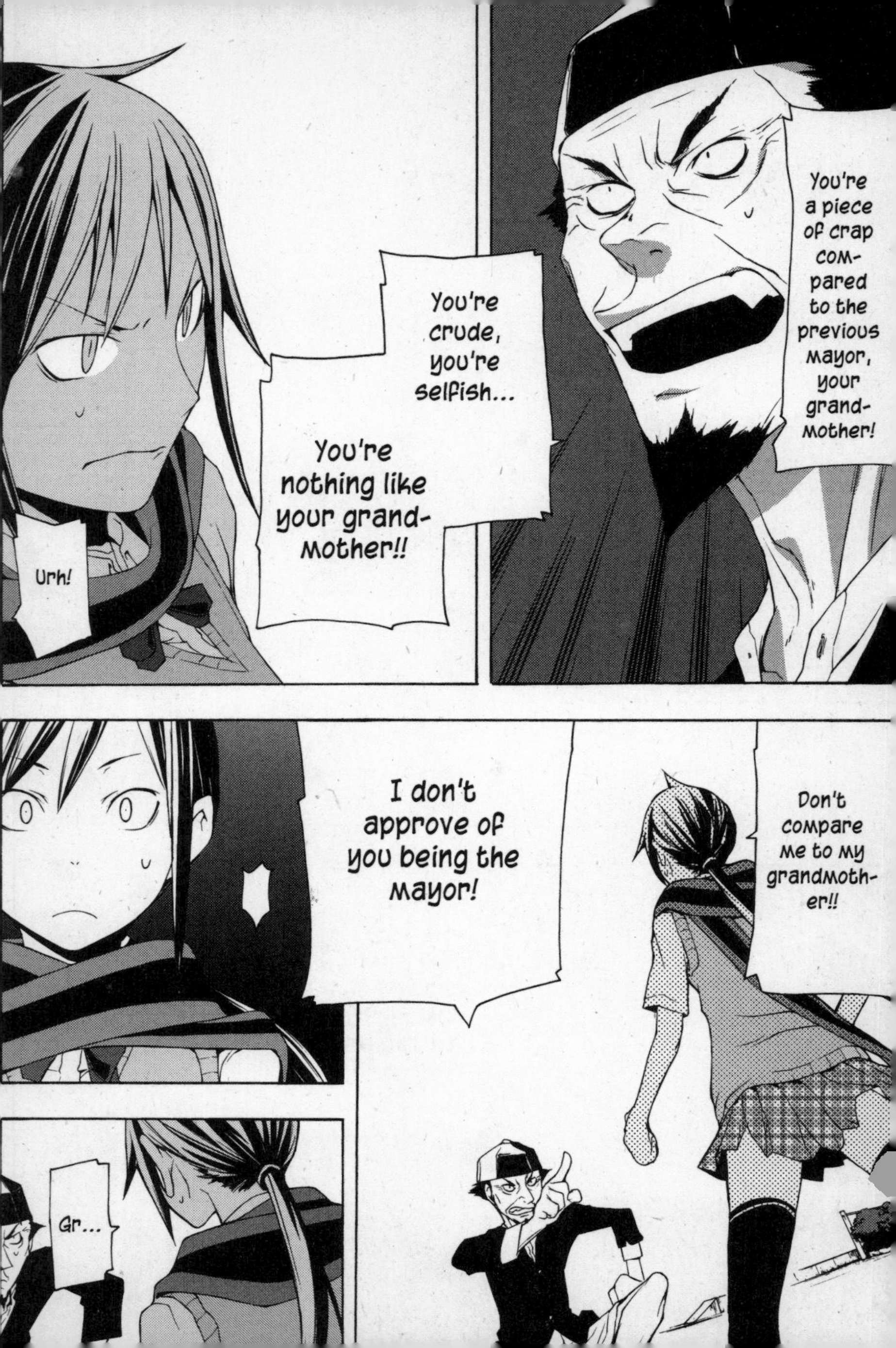
You're a piece of crap compared to the previous mayor, your grandmother!
You're crude, you're selfish...
You're nothing like your grandmother!!
Urh!
Don't compare me to my grandmother!!
I don't approve of you being the mayor!
Gr...

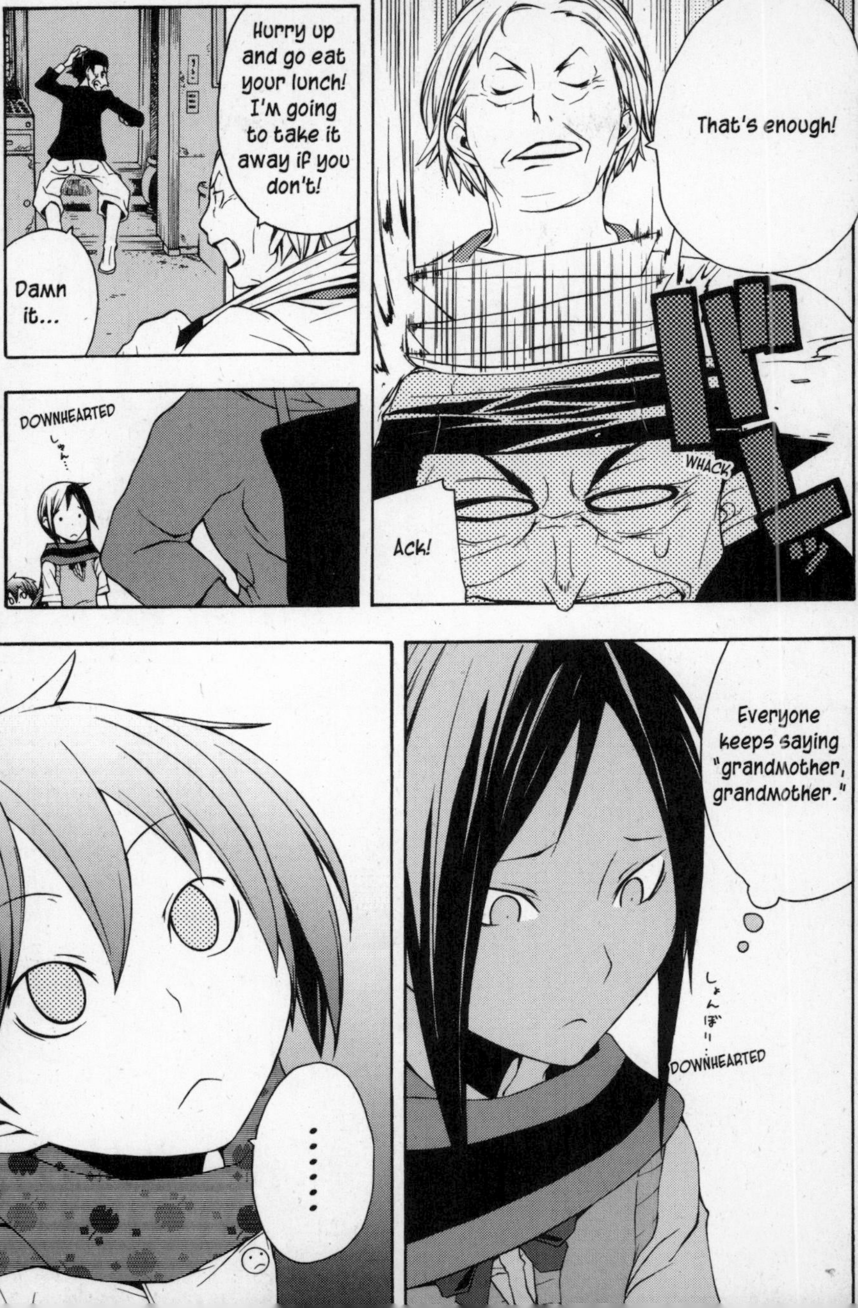
That's enough!
WHACK
Ack!
Hurry up and go eat your lunch! I'm going to take it away if you don't!
Damn it...
DOWNHEARTED
しゅん…
Everyone keeps saying "grandmother, grandmother."
しょんぼり
DOWNHEARTED
......

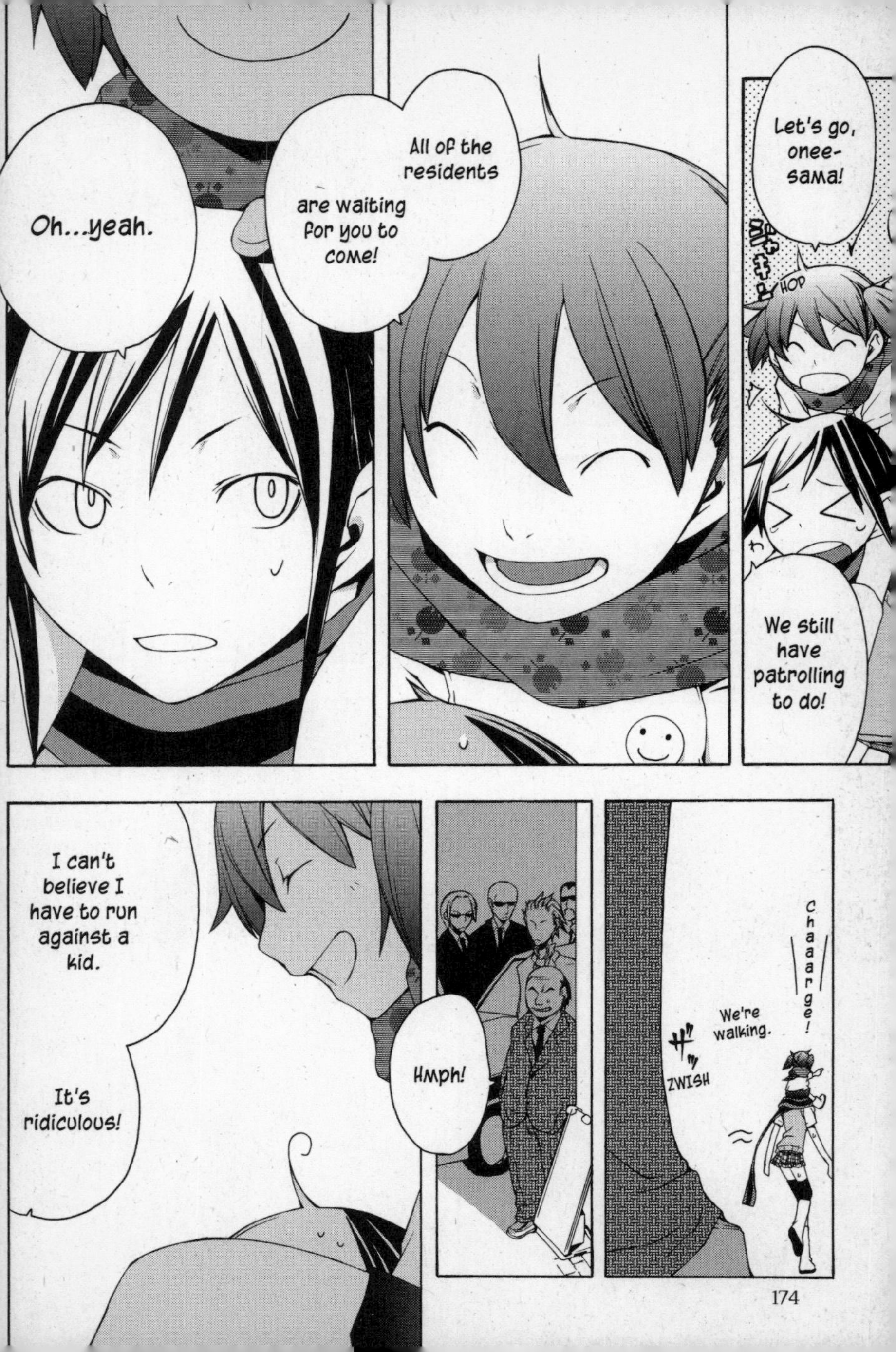

Let's go, onee-sama!
HOP
We still have patrolling to do!
All of the residents are waiting for you to come!
Oh...yeah.
Chaaarge!
We're walking.
ZWISH
Hmph!
I can't believe I have to run against a kid.
It's ridiculous!

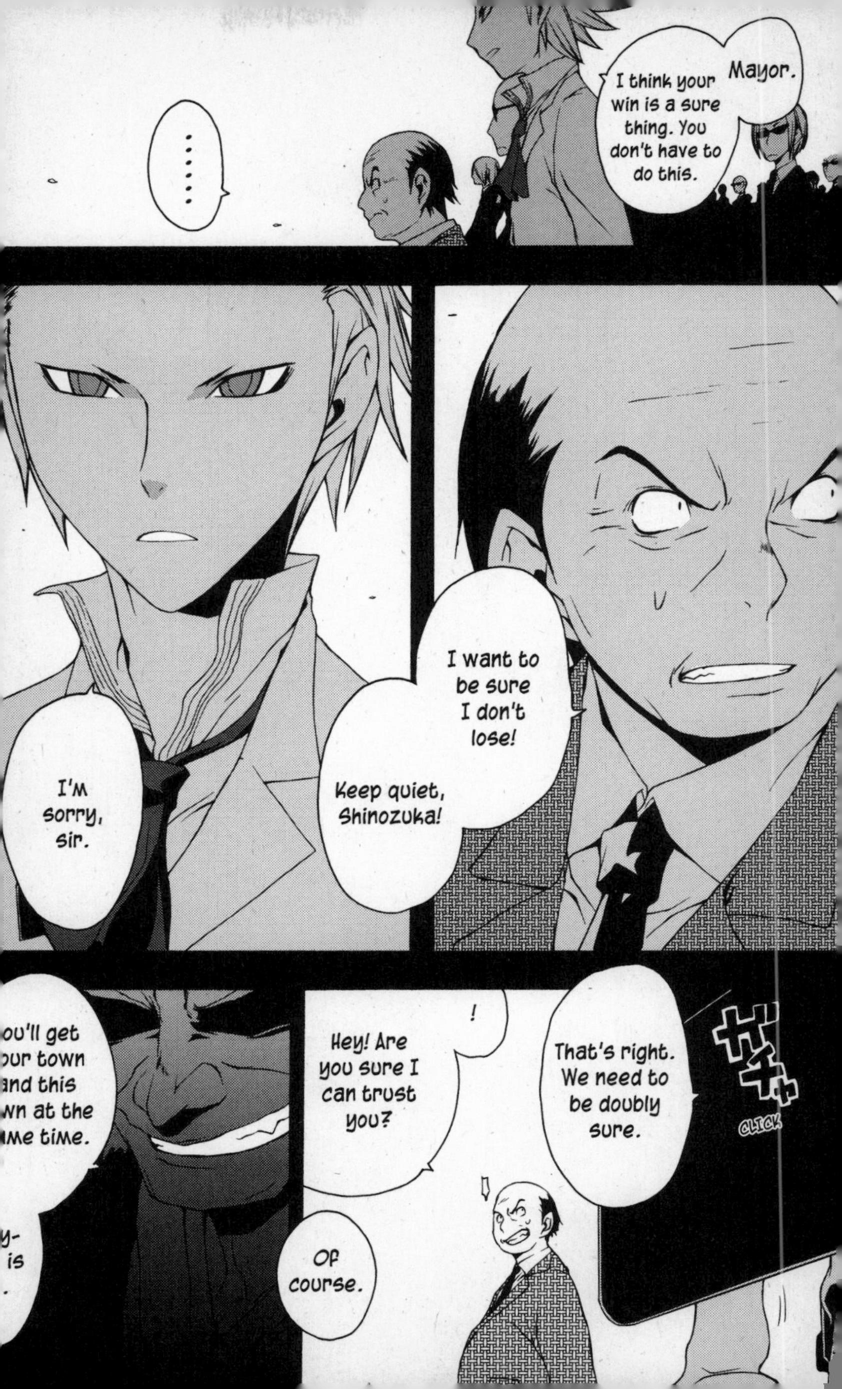
Mayor.
I think your win is a sure thing. You don't have to do this.
......
I want to be sure I don't lose!
Keep quiet, Shinozuka!
I'm sorry, sir.
That's right. We need to be doubly sure.
CLICK
!
Hey! Are you sure I can trust you?
Of course.
ou'll get our town and this wn at the me time.
y- is

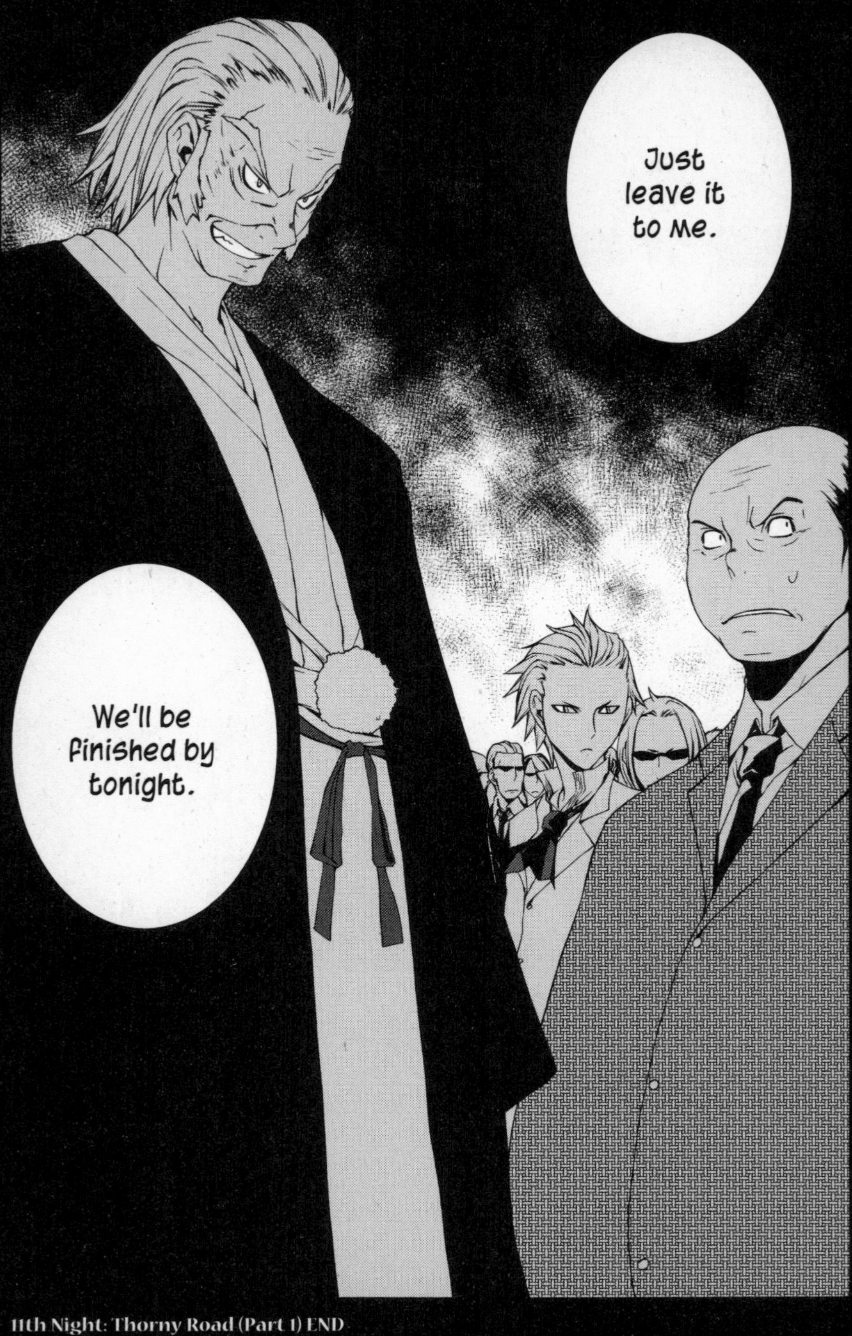
Just leave it to me.
We'll be finished by tonight.

11th Night: Thorny Road (Part 1) END

Yozakura Quartet **2**

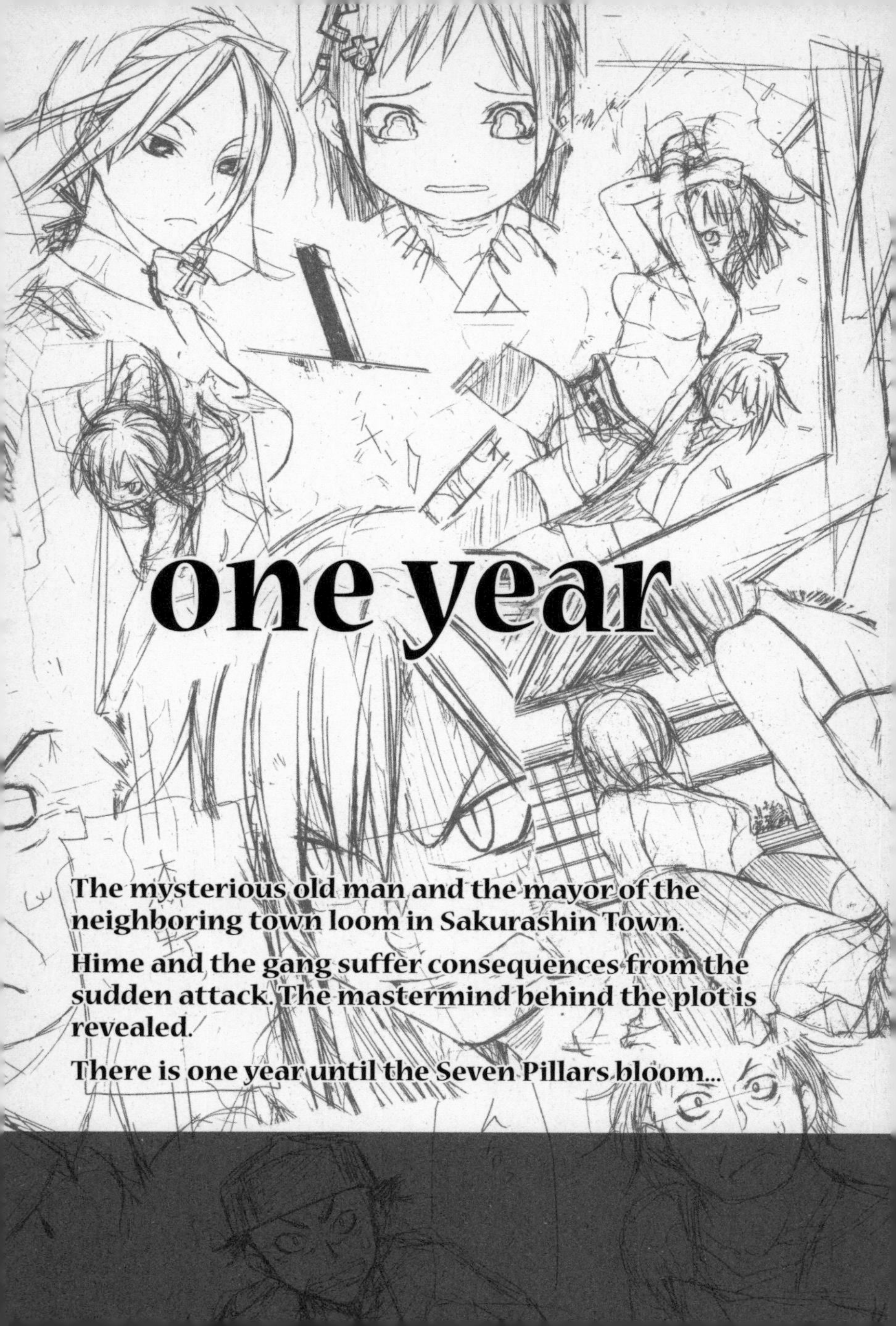

one year

The mysterious old man and the mayor of the neighboring town loom in Sakurashin Town.

Hime and the gang suffer consequences from the sudden attack. The mastermind behind the plot is revealed.

There is one year until the Seven Pillars bloom...

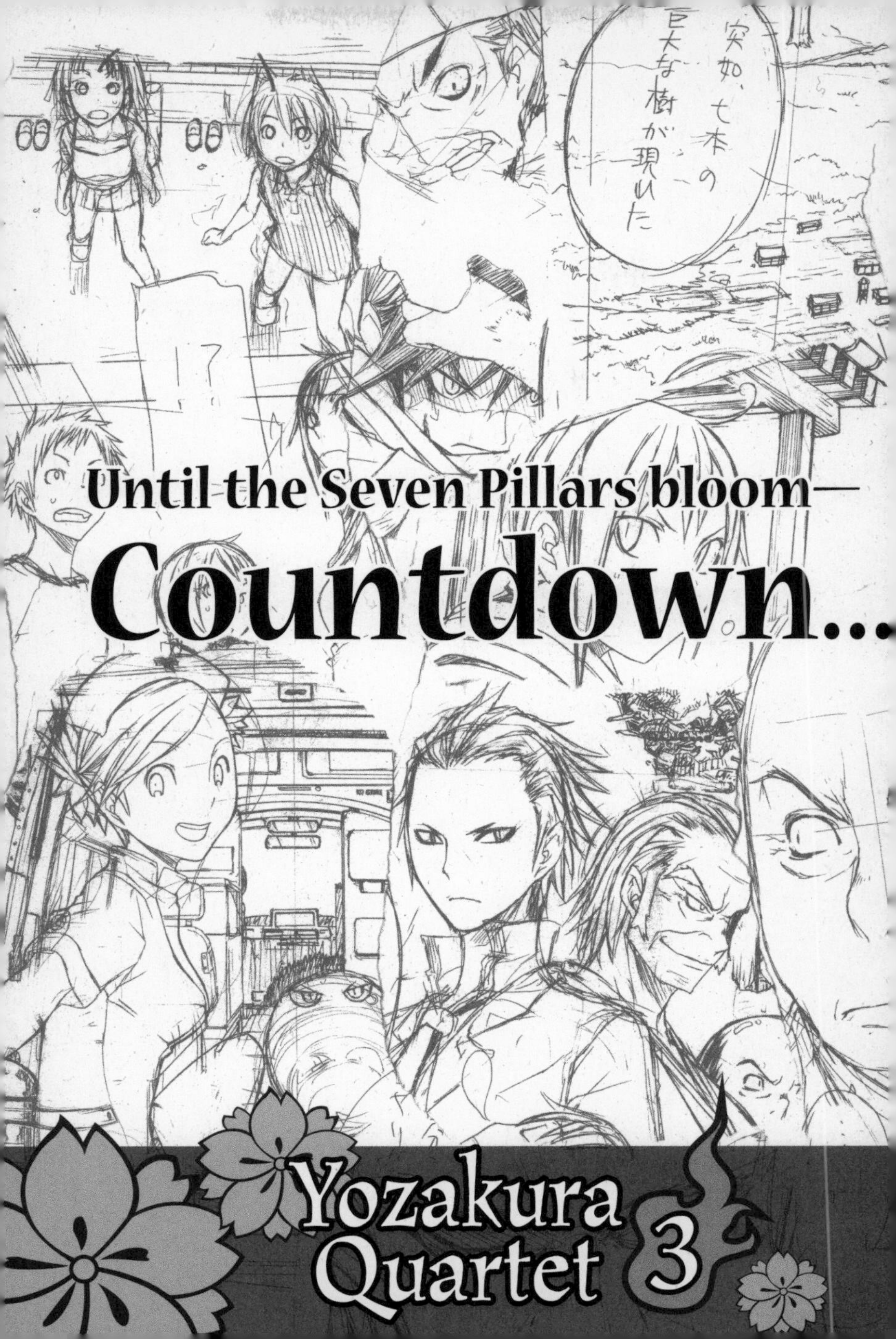
突如、七本の巨大な樹が現れた
Until the Seven Pillars bloom—
Countdown...
Yozakura Quartet 3

Liaozhai Zhiyi

A collection of supernatural stories with ghosts, demons, and vixen spirits. Originally these tales were passed on orally, but they were compiled by Pu Sung-ling during the Qing dynasty. There are over 431 stories in the collection.

"The Beauty in the Book"

Once there was a man who loved to read. One day, he was reading in his library with a bookmark depicting a beautiful lady. As he stared at the picture, the lady stood up and smiled at him. In order to make the man take a break from reading, the lady taught the man how to play the Japanese harp and cards.

(Featured in *Monthly Shonen Sirius* February 2007 Special issue on "Ghost Stories in the Winter")

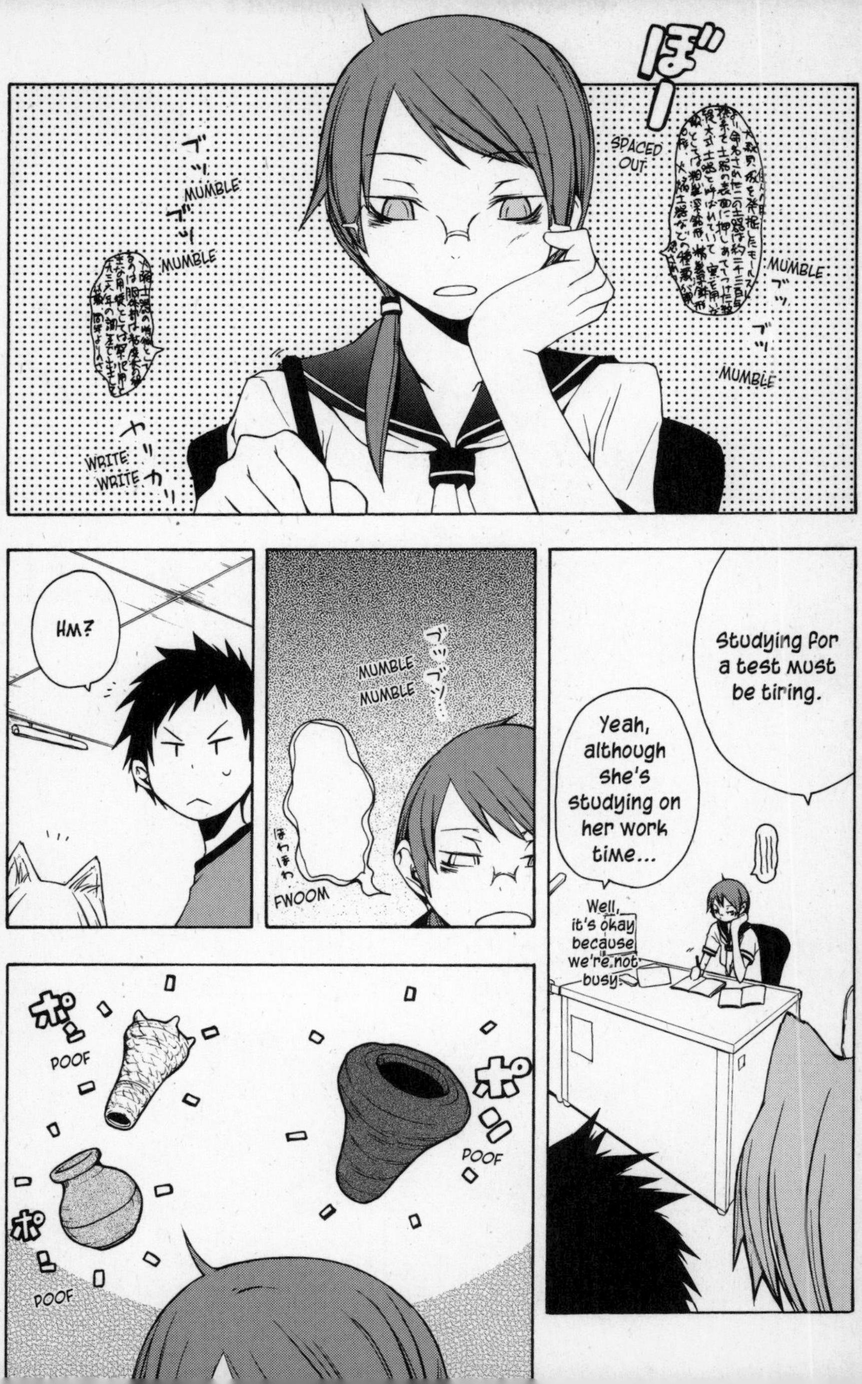
ぼー
SPACED OUT
ブツ
MUMBLE
ブツ
MUMBLE
ブツ
MUMBLE
ブツ
MUMBLE
カリ
WRITE
カリ
WRITE
Studying for a test must be tiring.
Yeah, although she's studying on her work time...
Well, it's okay because we're not busy.
ブツブツ…
MUMBLE
MUMBLE
ほわほわ
FWOOM
HM?
ポン
POOF
ポン
POOF
ポン
POOF

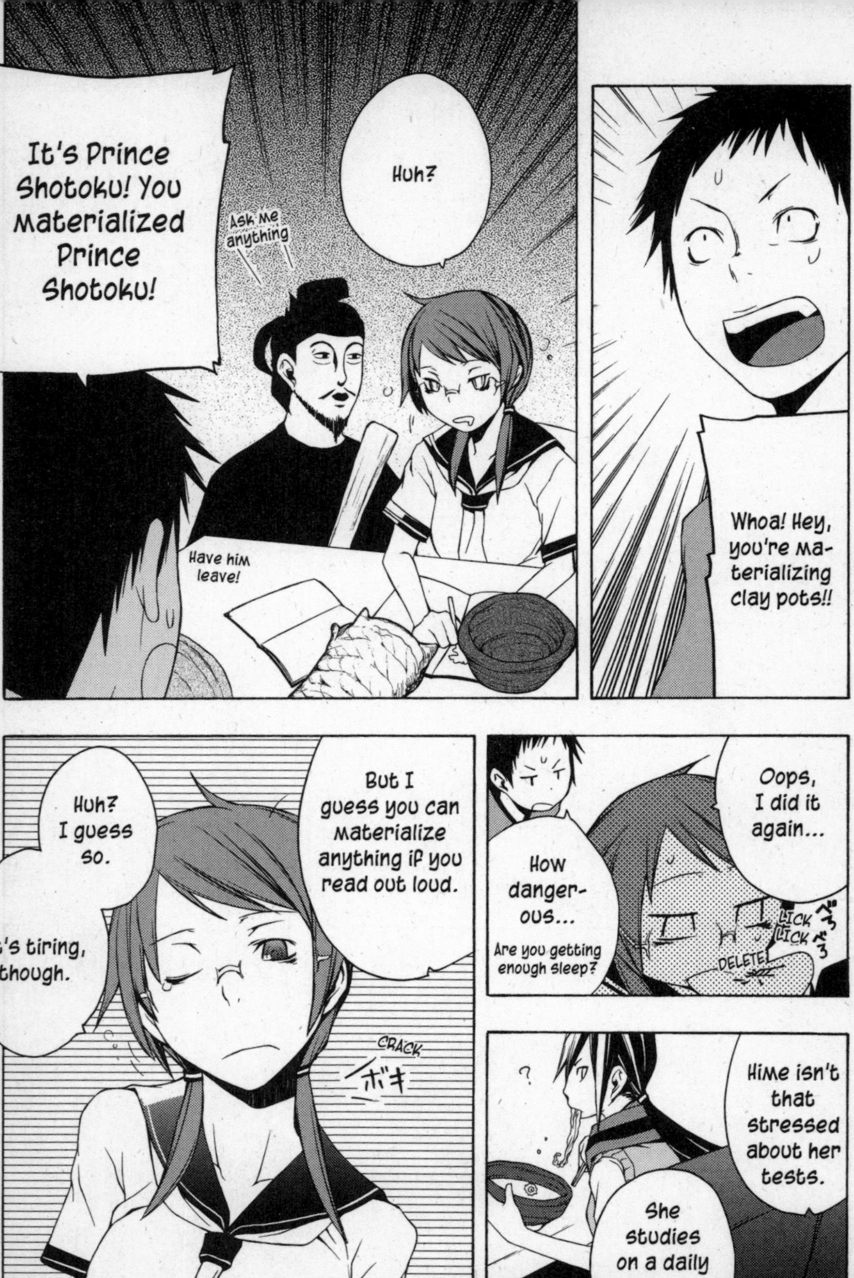
Whoa! Hey, you're ma-terializing clay pots!!
Huh?
It's Prince Shotoku! You Materialized Prince Shotoku!
Ask Me anything
Have him leave!
Oops, I did it again...
How danger-ous...
Are you getting enough sleep?
LICK LICK
べろべろ
DELETE
Hime isn't that stressed about her tests.
She studies on a daily basis.
Even though she's busy...
But I guess you can materialize anything if you read out loud.
Huh? I guess so.
t's tiring, though.
CRACK
ボキ

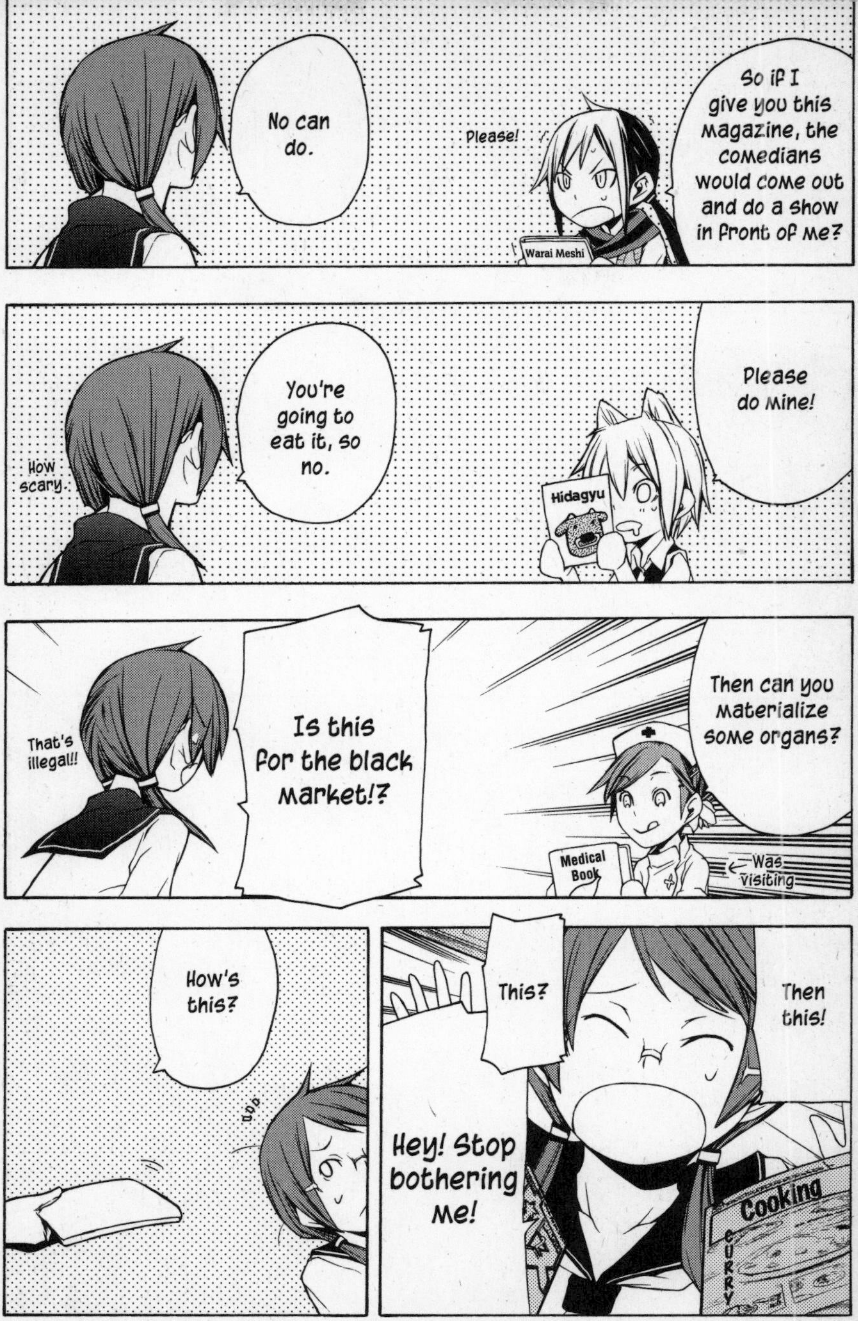
So if I give you this magazine, the comedians would come out and do a show in front of me?
Warai Meshi
Please!
No can do.
Please do mine!
Hidagyu
You're going to eat it, so no.
How scary.
Then can you materialize some organs?
Was visiting
Medical Book
Is this for the black market!?
That's illegal!!
Then this!
This?
Hey! Stop bothering me!
Cooking
CURRY
How's this?

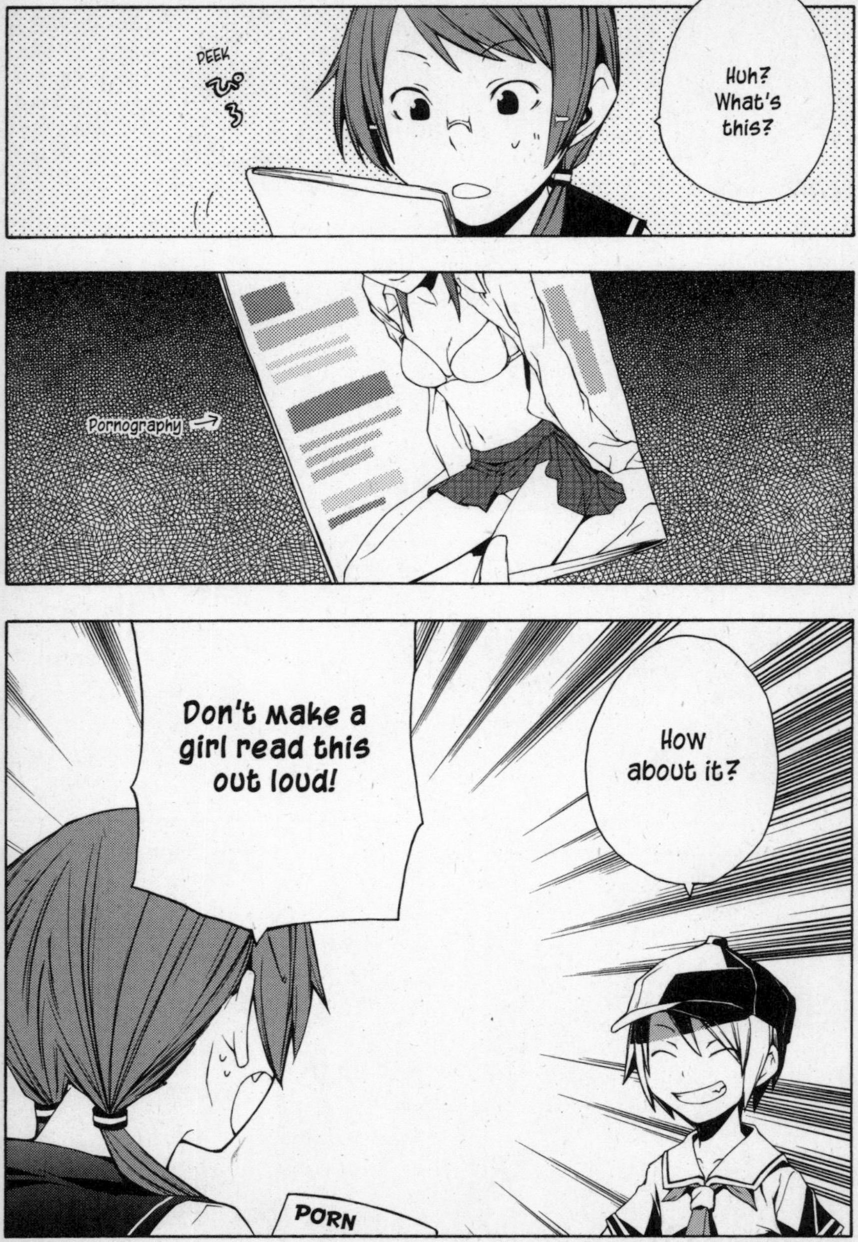
Huh? What's this?
PEEK
Pornography
How about it?
Don't make a girl read this out loud!
PORN

This isn't Hime!
• Rides a bicycle to get around
That's weird!
Whoa!

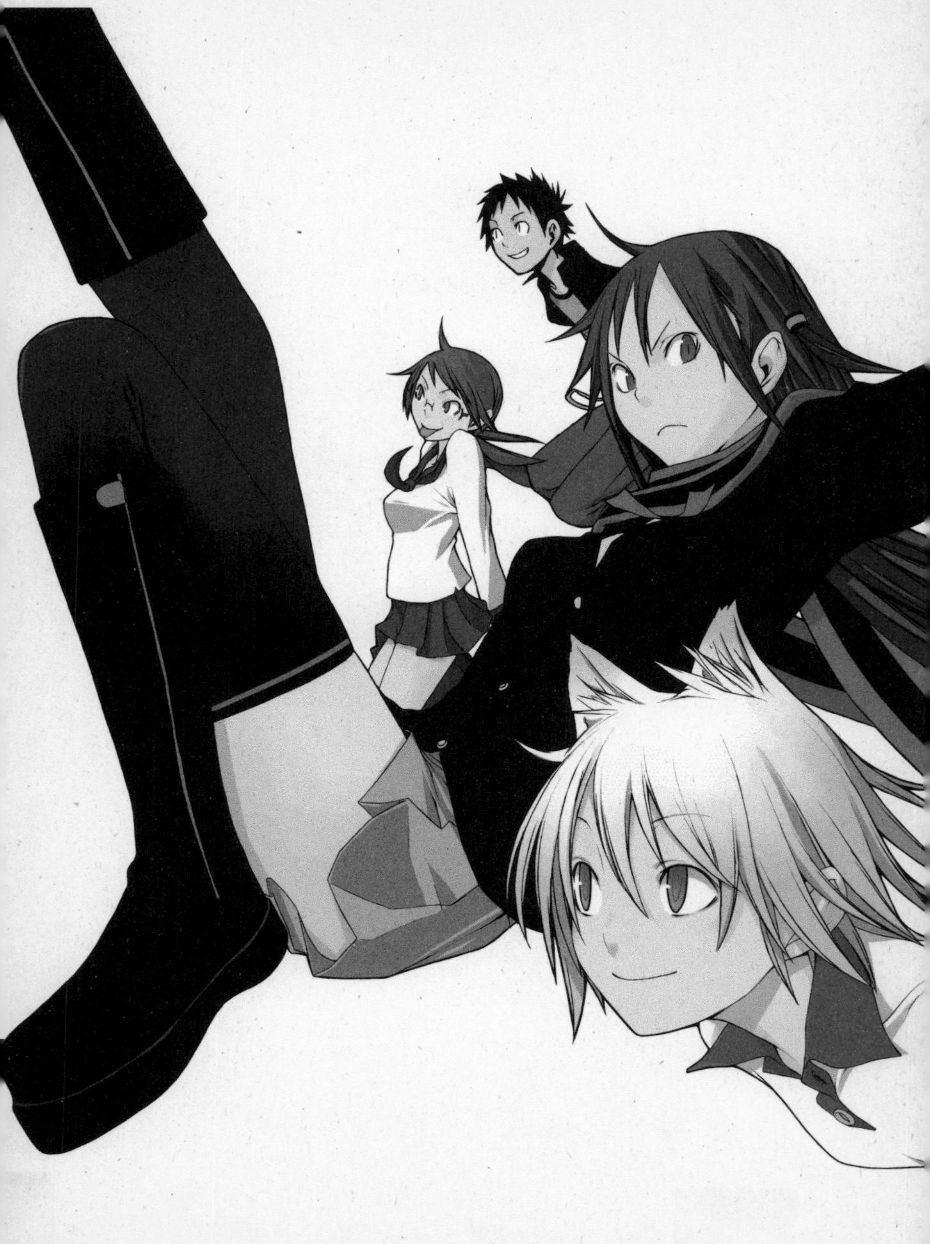

Illustration for the cover of *Monthly Shonen Sirius* November 2006 issue

Illustration for 1st anniversary of magazine (Monthly Shonen Sirius July 2006 issue)

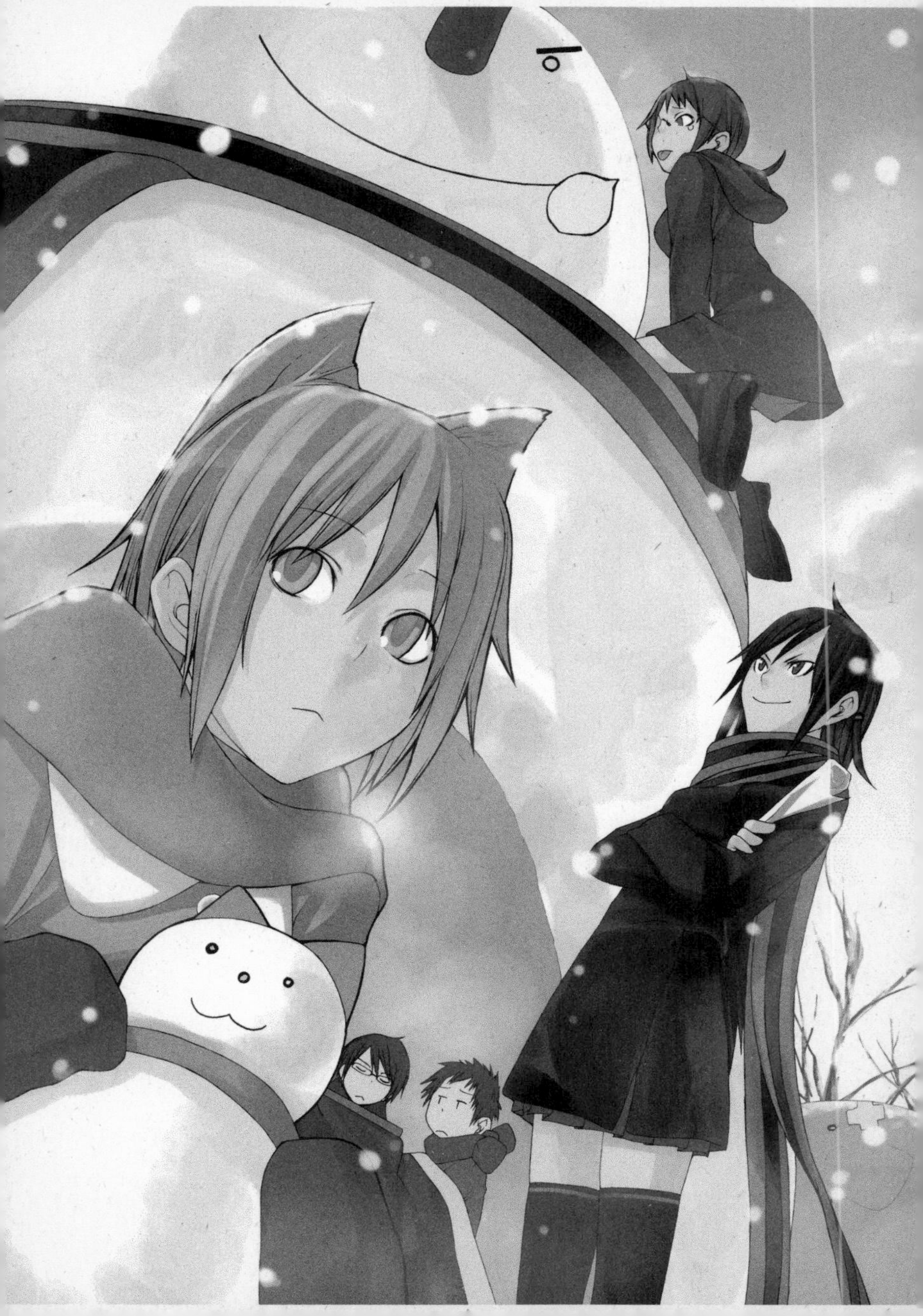

This isn't Hime!

· Normal black socks

You're like a high school girl!

She is.

Whoa!

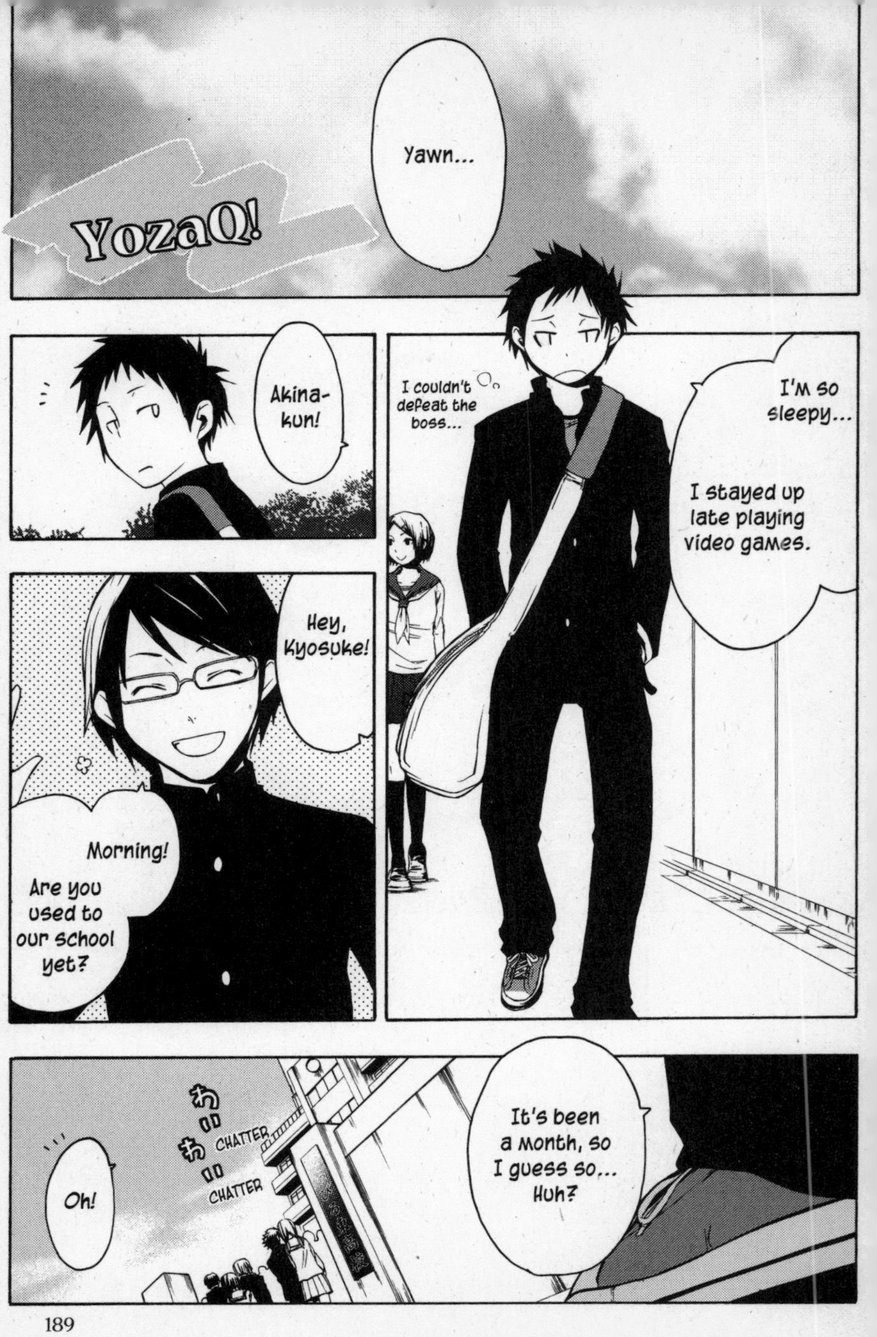
Yawn...
YozaQ!
I'm so sleepy...
I stayed up late playing video games.
I couldn't defeat the boss...
Akina-kun!
Hey, Kyosuke!
Morning!
Are you used to our school yet?
It's been a month, so I guess so... Huh?
CHATTER
CHATTER
Oh!

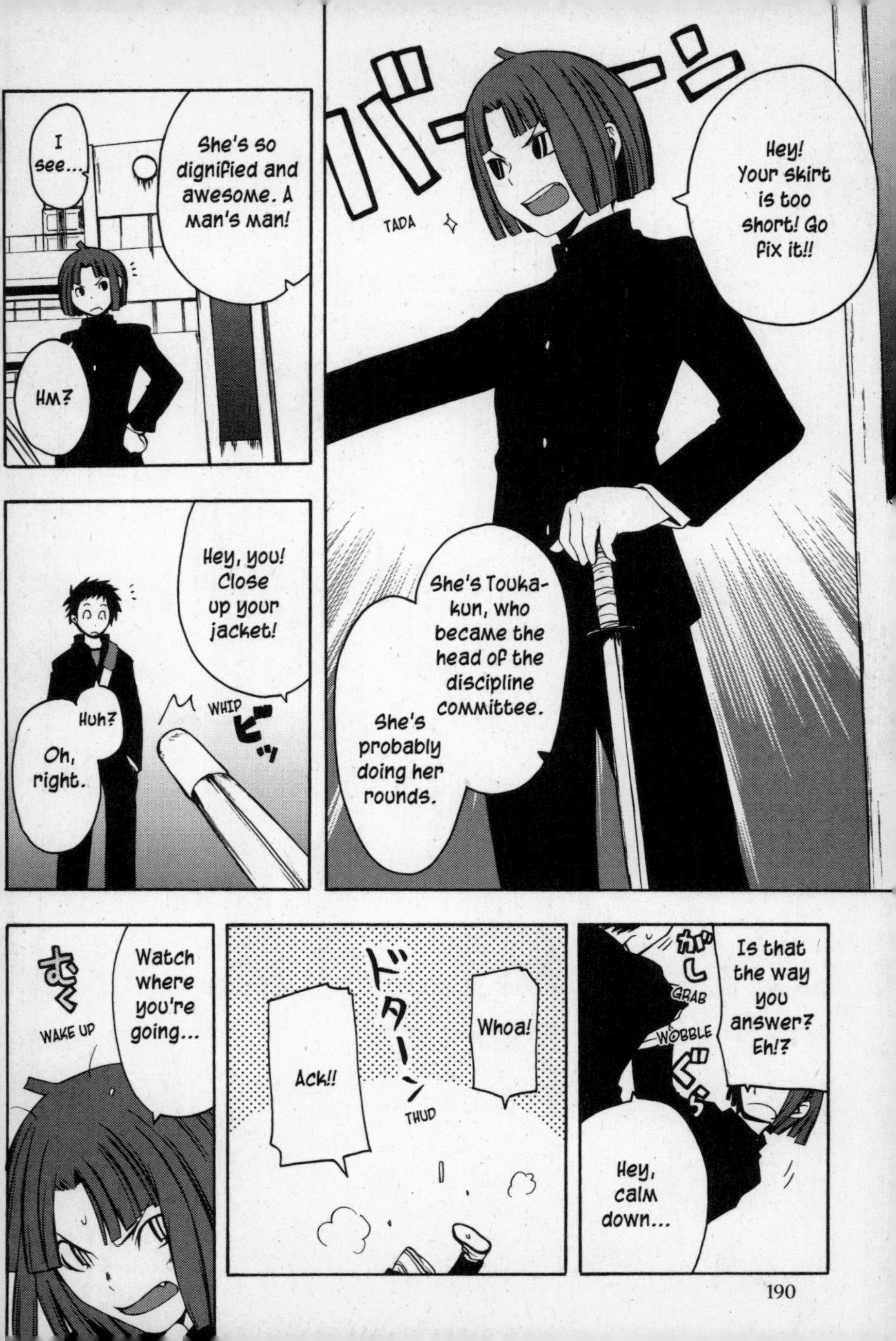

TADA
Hey! Your skirt is too short! Go fix it!!
She's Touka-kun, who became the head of the discipline committee.
She's probably doing her rounds.
She's so dignified and awesome. A man's man!
I see...
HM?
Hey, you! Close up your jacket!
WHIP
Huh?
Oh, right.
Is that the way you answer? Eh!?
GRAB
WOBBLE
Hey, calm down...
Whoa!
THUD
Ack!!
Watch where you're going...
WAKE UP

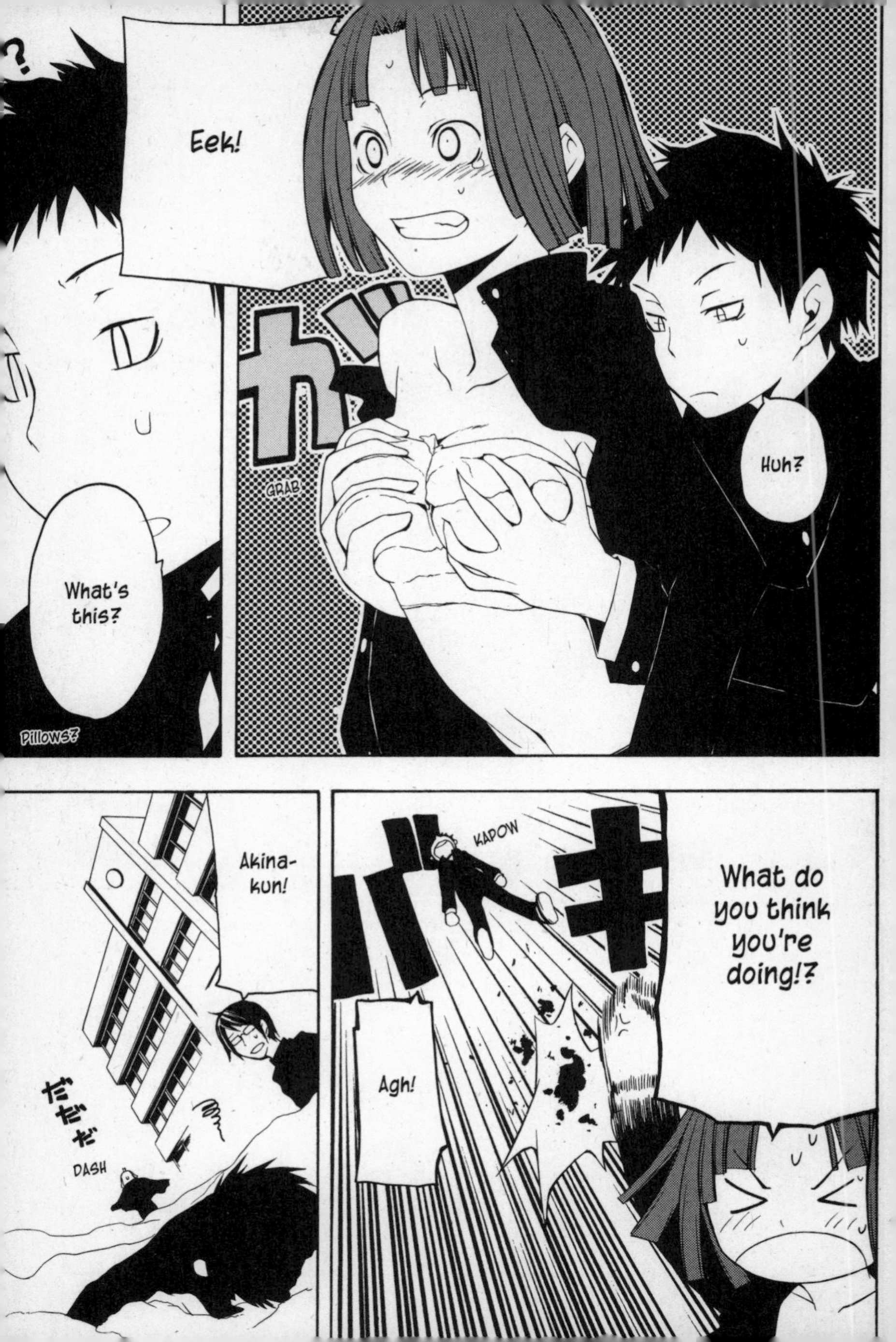
Eek!
Huh?
GRAB
?
What's this?
Pillows?
What do you think you're doing!?
KAPOW
Agh!
Akina-kun!
だだだ
DASH

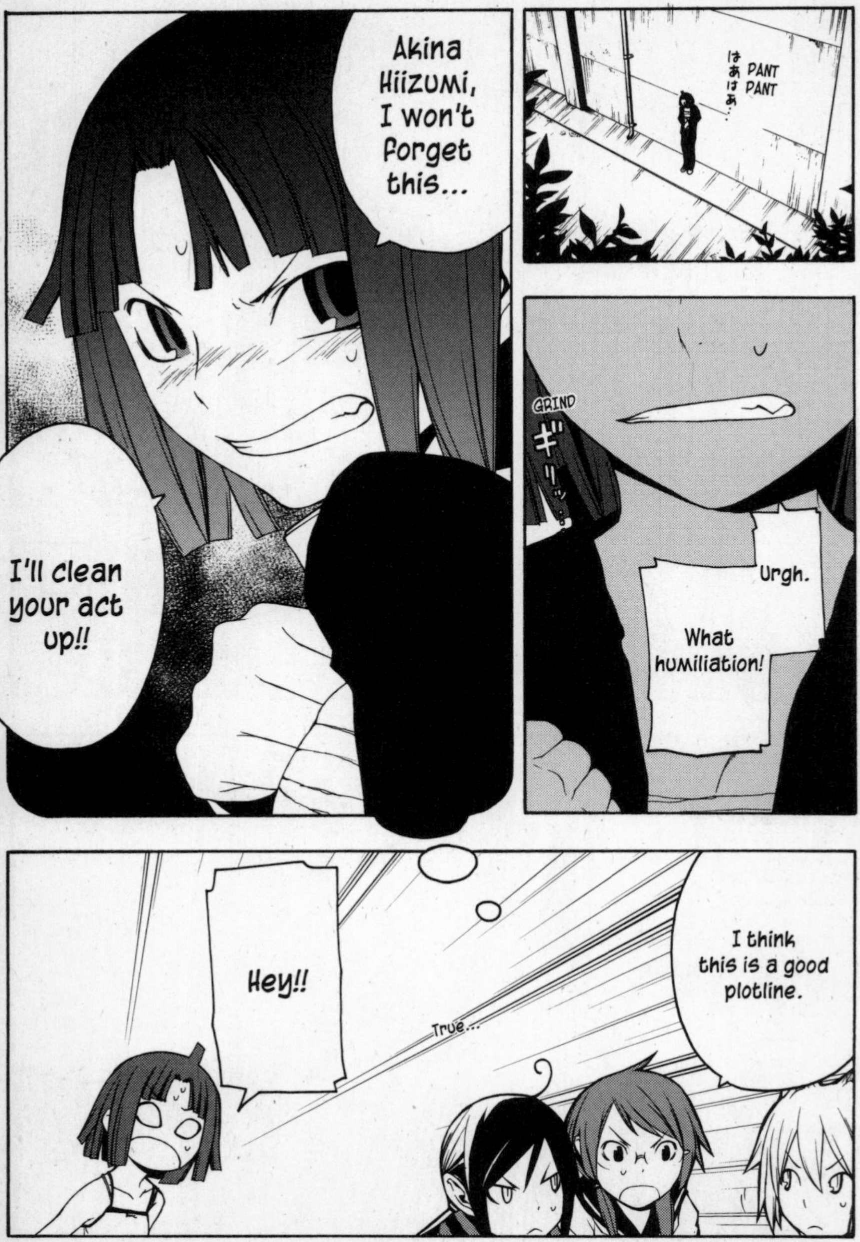
PANT PANT
はあはあ…
GRIND
ギリッ…
Urgh.
What humiliation!
Akina Hiizumi, I won't forget this...
I'll clean your act up!!
I think this is a good plotline.
True...
Hey!!

Bonus Manga

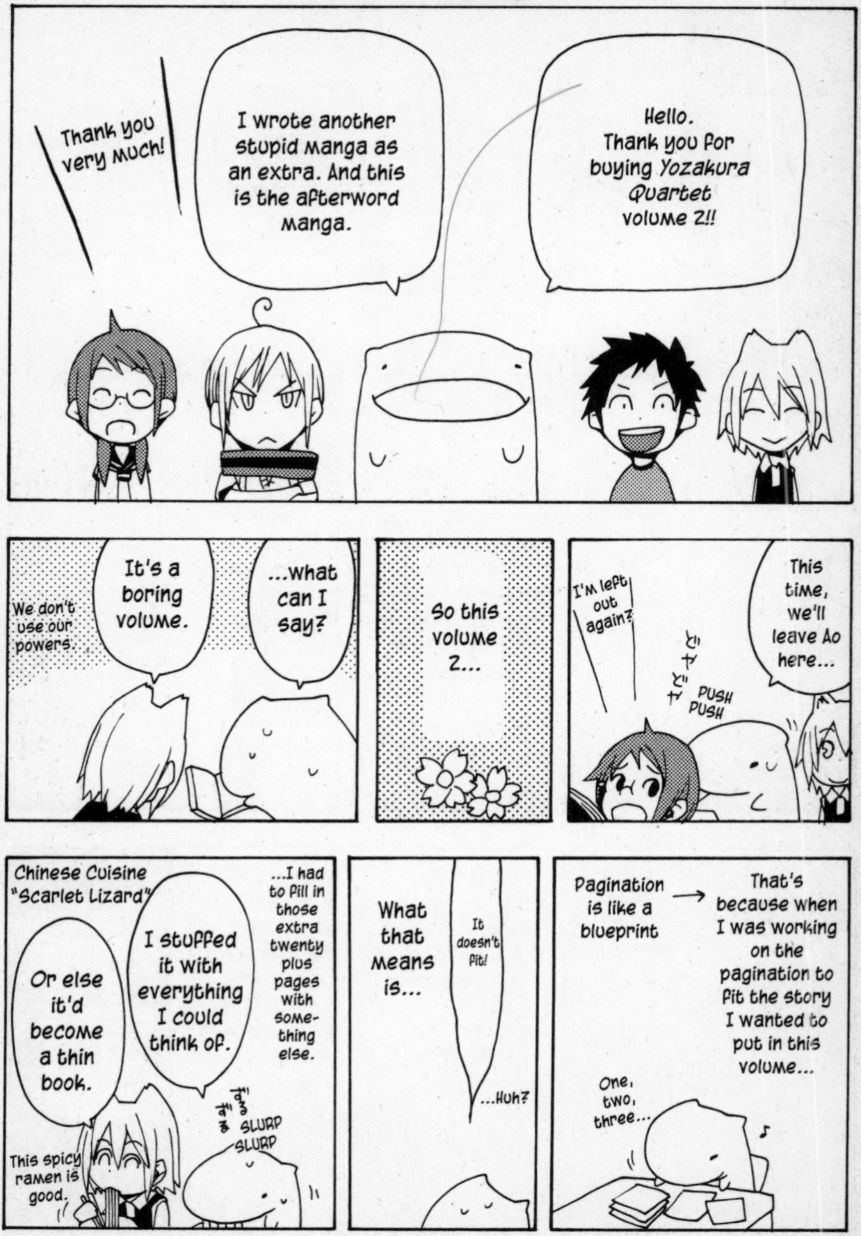
Hello. Thank you for buying *Yozakura Quartet* volume 2!!
I wrote another stupid manga as an extra. And this is the afterword manga.
Thank you very much!
This time, we'll leave Ao here...
どやどや PUSH PUSH
I'm left out again?
So this volume 2...
...what can I say?
It's a boring volume.
We don't use our powers.
That's because when I was working on the pagination to fit the story I wanted to put in this volume...
Pagination is like a blueprint →
One, two, three...
What that means is...
It doesn't fit!
...Huh?
...I had to fill in those extra twenty plus pages with some-thing else.
I stuffed it with everything I could think of.
Chinese Cuisine "Scarlet Lizard"
Or else it'd become a thin book.
ずるずる SLURP SLURP
This spicy ramen is good.

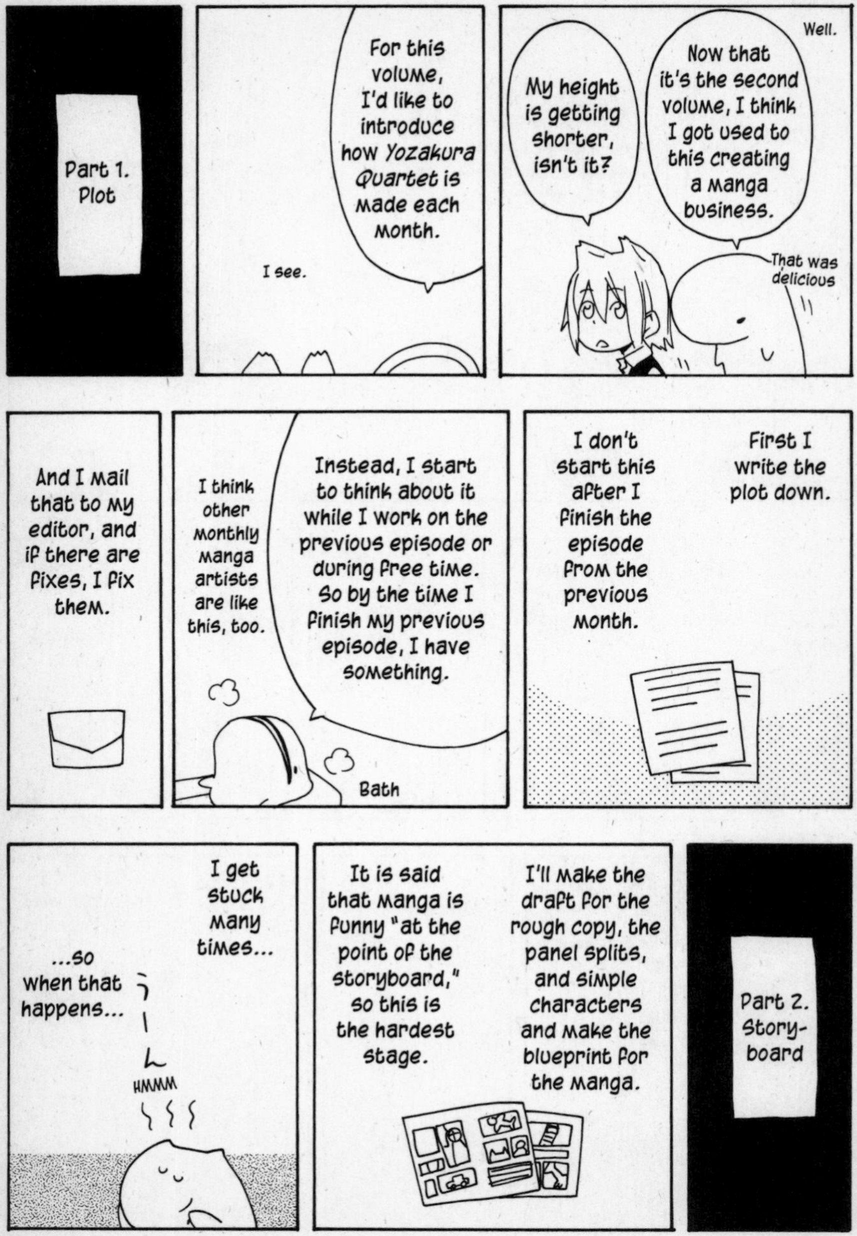
Well.
Now that it's the second volume, I think I got used to this creating a manga business.
My height is getting shorter, isn't it?
That was delicious
For this volume, I'd like to introduce how *Yozakura Quartet* is made each month.
I see.
Part 1. Plot
First I write the plot down.
I don't start this after I finish the episode from the previous month.
Instead, I start to think about it while I work on the previous episode or during free time. So by the time I finish my previous episode, I have something.
I think other monthly manga artists are like this, too.
Bath
And I mail that to my editor, and if there are fixes, I fix them.
Part 2. Storyboard
I'll make the draft for the rough copy, the panel splits, and simple characters and make the blueprint for the manga.
It is said that manga is funny "at the point of the storyboard," so this is the hardest stage.
I get stuck many times...
...so when that happens...
HMMM

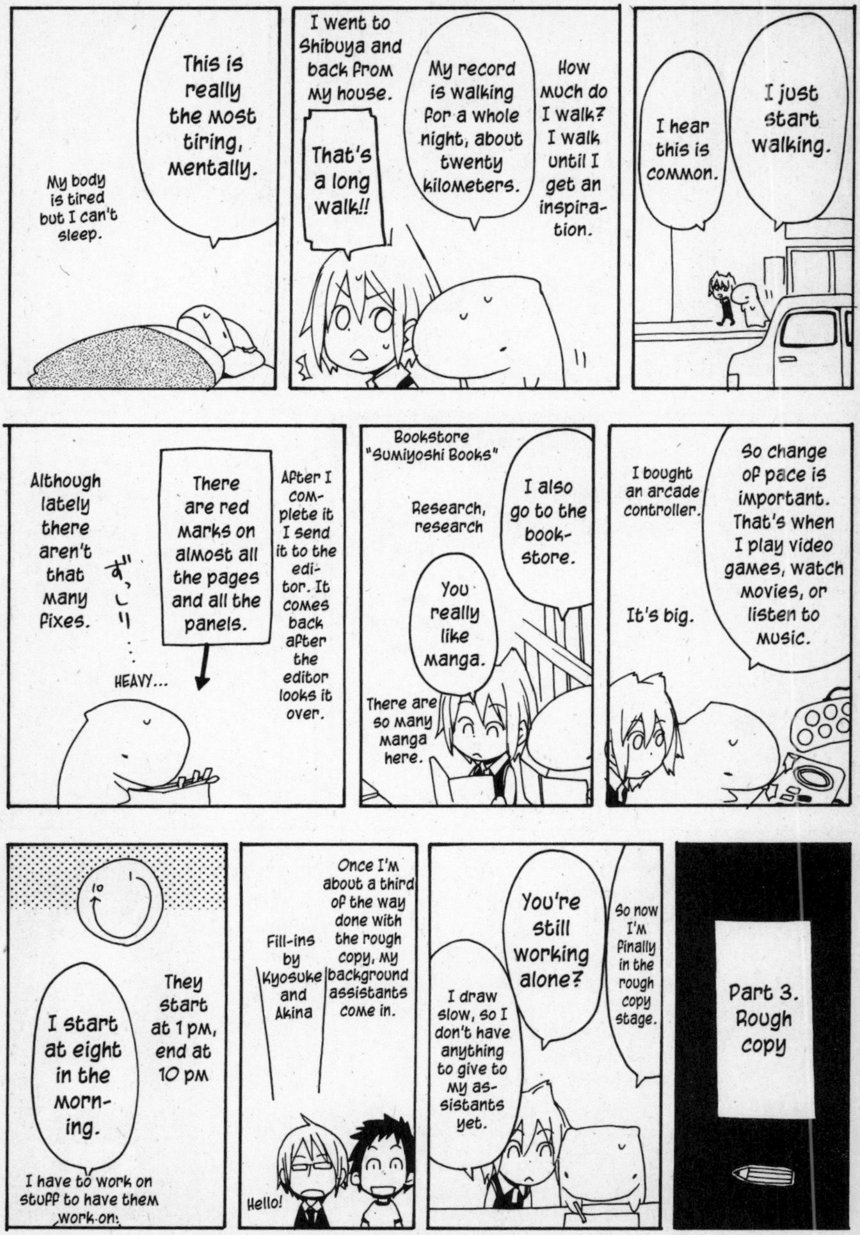
I just start walking.
I hear this is common.
How much do I walk? I walk until I get an inspiration.
My record is walking for a whole night, about twenty kilometers.
I went to Shibuya and back from my house.
That's a long walk!!
This is really the most tiring, mentally.
My body is tired but I can't sleep.
So change of pace is important. That's when I play video games, watch movies, or listen to music.
I bought an arcade controller.
It's big.
Bookstore "Sumiyoshi Books"
I also go to the bookstore.
Research, research
You really like manga.
There are so many manga here.
After I complete it I send it to the editor. It comes back after the editor looks it over.
There are red marks on almost all the pages and all the panels.
Although lately there aren't that many fixes.
ずしり…
HEAVY...
Part 3. Rough copy
So now I'm finally in the rough copy stage.
You're still working alone?
I draw slow, so I don't have anything to give to my assistants yet.
Once I'm about a third of the way done with the rough copy, my background assistants come in.
Fill-ins by Kyosuke and Akina
Hello!
They start at 1 pm, end at 10 pm
I start at eight in the morning.
I have to work on stuff to have them work on.

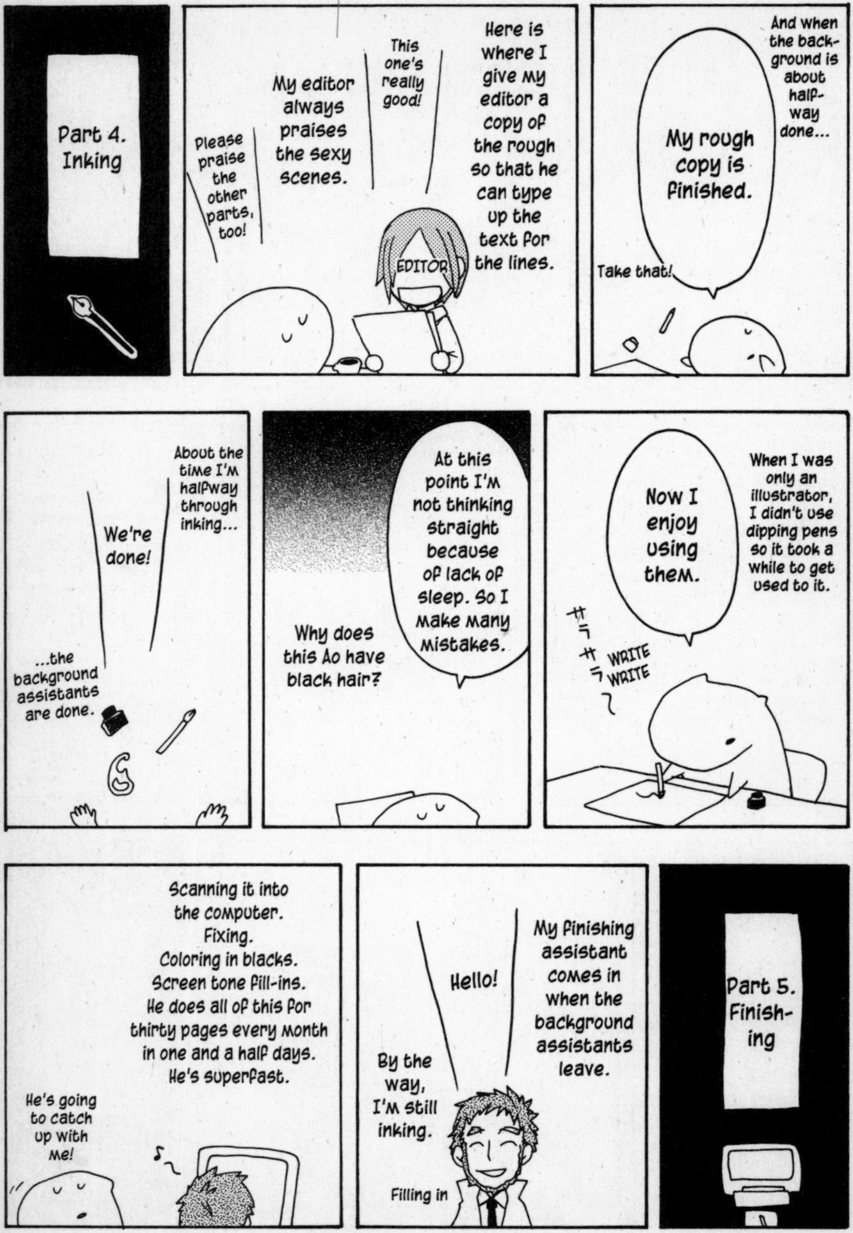
And when the back-ground is about half-way done...
My rough copy is finished.
Take that!
Here is where I give my editor a copy of the rough so that he can type up the text for the lines.
This one's really good!
My editor always praises the sexy scenes.
Please praise the other parts, too!
EDITOR
Part 4. Inking
When I was only an illustrator, I didn't use dipping pens so it took a while to get used to it.
Now I enjoy using them.
WRITE WRITE
At this point I'm not thinking straight because of lack of sleep. So I make many mistakes.
Why does this Ao have black hair?
About the time I'm halfway through inking...
We're done!
...the background assistants are done.
Part 5. Finish-ing
My finishing assistant comes in when the background assistants leave.
Hello!
By the way, I'm still inking.
Filling in
Scanning it into the computer. Fixing. Coloring in blacks. Screen tone fill-ins. He does all of this for thirty pages every month in one and a half days. He's superfast.
He's going to catch up with me!

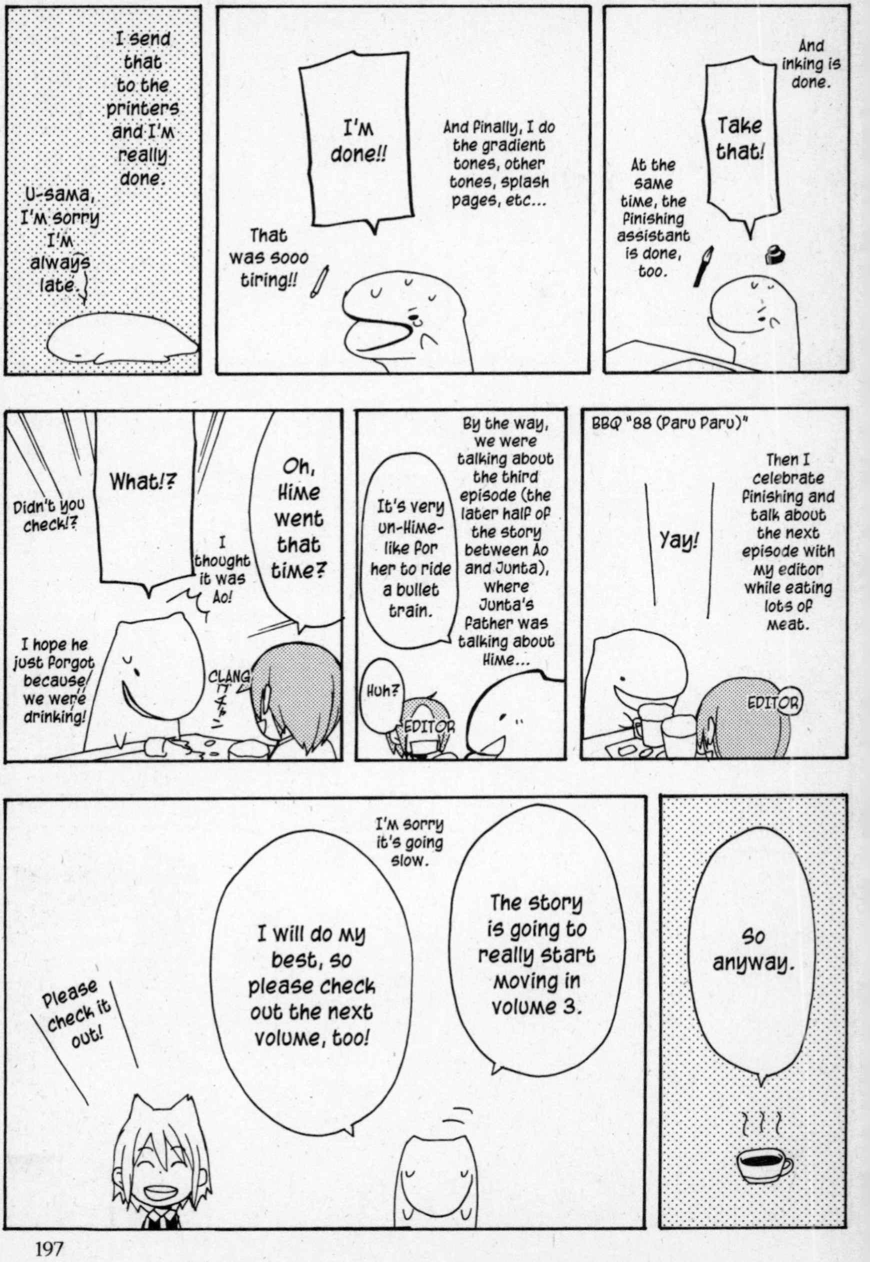
And inking is done.
Take that!
At the same time, the finishing assistant is done, too.
And finally, I do the gradient tones, other tones, splash pages, etc...
I'm done!!
That was sooo tiring!!
I send that to the printers and I'm really done.
U-sama, I'm sorry I'm always late.
BBQ "88 (Paru Paru)"
Then I celebrate finishing and talk about the next episode with my editor while eating lots of meat.
Yay!
EDITOR
By the way, we were talking about the third episode (the later half of the story between Ao and Junta), where Junta's father was talking about Hime...
It's very un-Hime-like for her to ride a bullet train.
Huh?
EDITOR
Oh, Hime went that time?
I thought it was Ao!
What!?
Didn't you check!?
CLANG
I hope he just forgot because we were drinking!
So anyway.
I'm sorry it's going slow.
The story is going to really start moving in volume 3.
I will do my best, so please check out the next volume, too!
Please check it out!

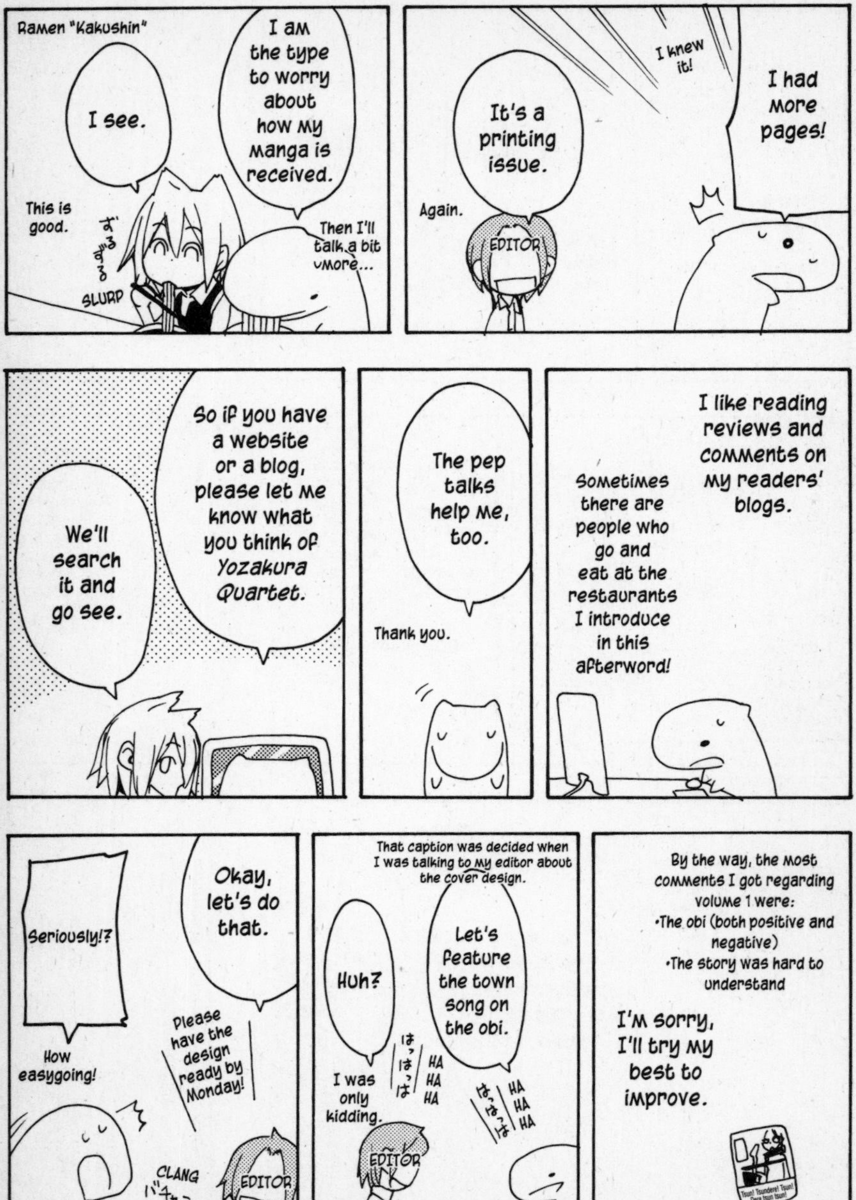
I had more pages!
I knew it!
It's a printing issue.
Again.
EDITOR
I am the type to worry about how my manga is received.
Ramen "Kakushin"
I see.
Then I'll talk a bit more...
This is good.
ずるずる
SLURP
I like reading reviews and comments on my readers' blogs.
Sometimes there are people who go and eat at the restaurants I introduce in this afterword!
The pep talks help me, too.
Thank you.
So if you have a website or a blog, please let me know what you think of *Yozakura Quartet*.
We'll search it and go see.
By the way, the most comments I got regarding volume 1 were:
•The obi (both positive and negative)
•The story was hard to understand
I'm sorry, I'll try my best to improve.
That caption was decided when I was talking to my editor about the cover design.
Let's feature the town song on the obi.
はっはっは HA HA HA
Huh?
はっはっは HA HA HA
I was only kidding.
EDITOR
Okay, let's do that.
Seriously!?
Please have the design ready by Monday!
How easygoing!
CLANG
バチャン
EDITOR

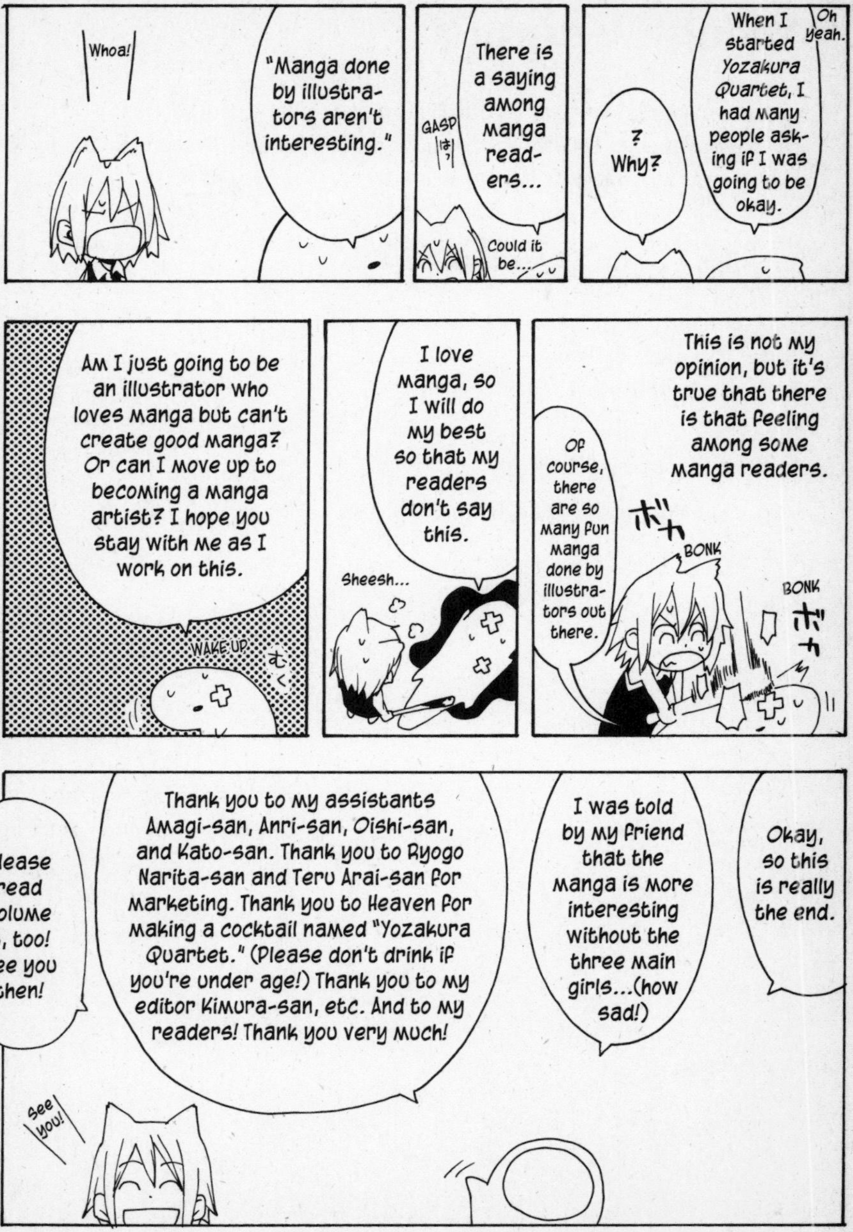
Oh yeah.
When I started Yozakura Quartet, I had many people asking if I was going to be okay.
? Why?
There is a saying among manga readers...
GASP
はっ
Could it be...
"Manga done by illustrators aren't interesting."
Whoa!
This is not my opinion, but it's true that there is that feeling among some manga readers.
Of course, there are so many fun manga done by illustrators out there.
ボカ
BONK
BONK
ボカ
I love manga, so I will do my best so that my readers don't say this.
Sheesh...
Am I just going to be an illustrator who loves manga but can't create good manga? Or can I move up to becoming a manga artist? I hope you stay with me as I work on this.
WAKE UP
むく
Okay, so this is really the end.
I was told by my friend that the manga is more interesting without the three main girls...(how sad!)
Thank you to my assistants Amagi-san, Anri-san, Oishi-san, and Kato-san. Thank you to Ryogo Narita-san and Teru Arai-san for marketing. Thank you to Heaven for making a cocktail named "Yozakura Quartet." (Please don't drink if you're under age!) Thank you to my editor Kimura-san, etc. And to my readers! Thank you very much!
Please read volume 3, too! See you then!
See you!

About the Author

Suzuhito Yasuda's cute and colorful character designs, sharp linework, and unique design talents have made him a popular artist in the fields of both manga and novel illustration. He has illustrated such Japanese novels as *Kamisama Kazoku*, *Scarlet Sword*, and *Maid Machinegun*. He has also worked on the manga series *Pinky:Comic* and *Ebony & Ivory*; *Yozakura Quartet* is his latest work.

His Preferred Tools:
PowerMAC G4 933Mhz
Apple studio display 17 TFT

PowerMAC G4 Cube
Apple Studio Display 17 CRT

Sony VAIO Notebook PCG542B

Translation Notes

Japanese is a tricky language for most Westerners, and translation is often more an art than a science. For your edification and reading pleasure, here are notes on some of the places where we could have gone in a different direction, or where a Japanese cultural reference is used.

Sakura, page 3

Sakura is the Japanese term for cherry blossoms. "Yozakura" in the title refers to *sakura* at night or viewing *sakura* at night.

FamiTsu, page 5

FamiTsu is the biggest Japanese video game magazine. It introduces and reviews various video games. It covers DVDs, TV shows, and books, too.

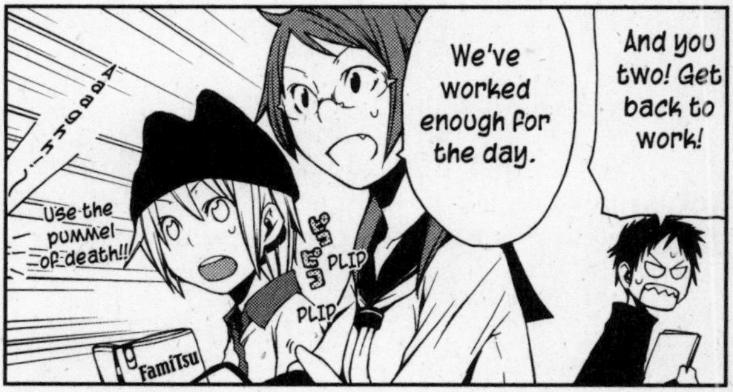

And you two! Get back to work!
We've worked enough for the day.
Use the pummel of death!!
PLIP
PLIP
FamiTsu

Onii-chan, page 32

Onii-chan is an honorific for an "older brother."

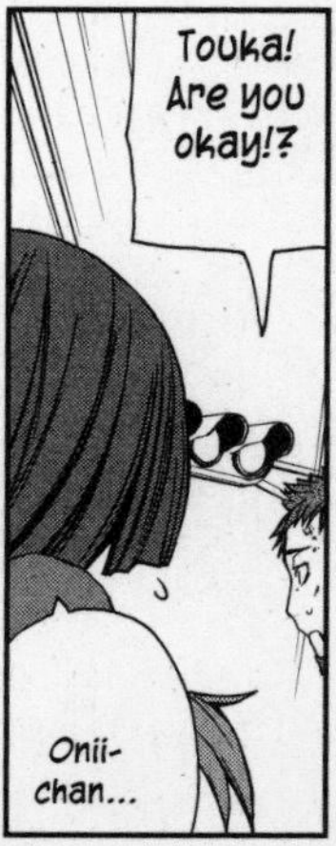

Touka! Are you okay!?
Onii-chan...

Chidori, page 36

Chidori is a comedy duo made of Daigo and Nobu. They are from the Okayama Prefecture. Their name comes from the high school nickname of their neighborhood school. They are known for their street-punk style.

Uchi-P, page 36

Uchi-P is an abbreviated term for *Uchimura Produce*, a TV show featuring comedians doing comedy sketches.

Fukawa, page 36

Ryo Fukawa is a Japanese comedian, DJ, and musician. He is known for his logic jokes.

Okayama, page 36

Okayama is a prefecture located in the Chugoku region, which is the westernmost region of Honshu, the largest island of Japan. It borders the prefectures of Hiroshima, Tottori, and Hyogo.

***Piko Piko* hammer, page 37**

Mina is using a *piko piko* hammer to hit Touka and Shidou. This is a toy hammer made out of plastic that makes a squeaky sound when it hits something.

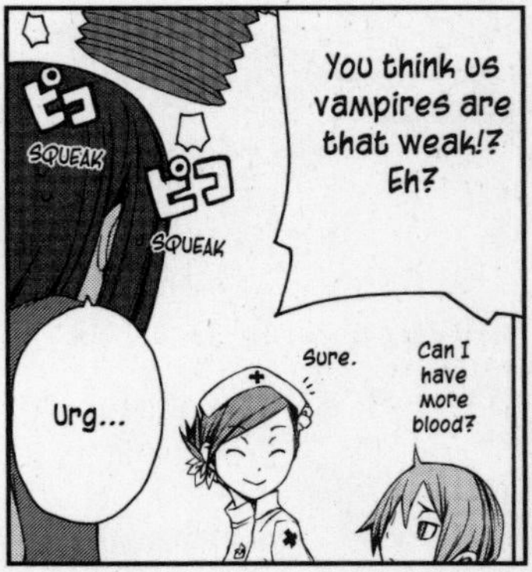
You think us vampires are that weak!? Eh?
SQUEAK
SQUEAK
Can I have more blood?
Sure.
Urg...

ROCO, page 64

ROCO is a singer and songwriter. Her first album was promoted through small retail shops and then spread throughout Japan by word of mouth.

Golgo, page 64

Golgo is part of the comedy duo TIM. He is known for his short gags and using his body to make letters or kanji characters.

District mayor, page 93

In Japan, the head of any city, town, village, or ward/district is referred to as mayor. City mayors are known as *shichou*, town mayors as *chouchou*, village mayors as *sonchou*, and ward/district mayors as *kuchou*. In the Japanese text, Hime is *chouchou* of Sakurashin Town, and Yuhi is referred to as *kuchou*. It is not clear in the story which ward/district Yuhi is mayor of.

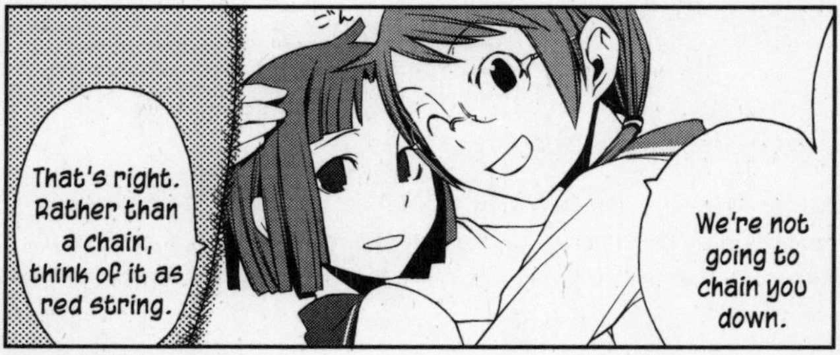
We're not going to chain you down.
That's right. Rather than a chain, think of it as red string.

Red string, Page 116

Touka makes a reference to a red string, which refers to the Japanese belief that destined lovers are connected by a red string of fate. This red string is usually attatched to the left little fingers.

Jiang Shi, Page 118

A *Jiang Shi* is a Chinese demon. These zombies hop around and prey on living creatures to absorb their chi (living energy).

Kirin, page 124

Kirin is a comedy duo composed of Akira Kawashima and Hiroshi Tamura. Although their first impressions of each other were not good, they eventually became good friends and formed their group.

Megu no Yasu, page 124

Megu no Yasu is a nickname for Megumi Yasu, which she only uses when she's with Uchi-P. She is a swimsuit model and an actress.

Daiginjo Kiku Hime, page 129

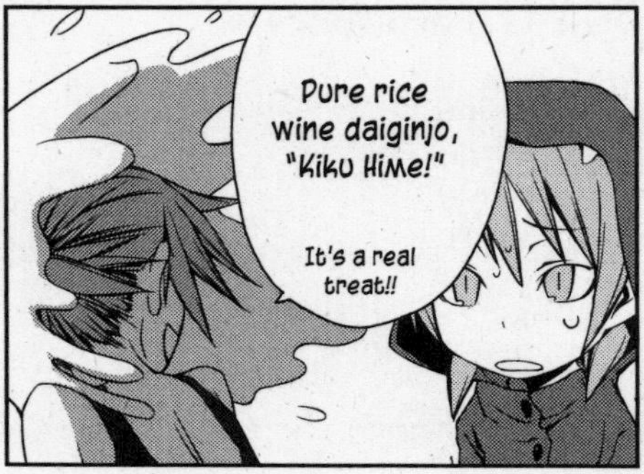
Pure rice wine daiginjo, "Kiku Hime!"
It's a real treat!!

Kiku Hime is a type of sake (Japanese rice wine) made in the Ishikawa Prefecture. It is one of the better known labels. *Daiginjo* means that the rice weight is polished to 40 percent or less. It has a milder aroma than other sake.

Tsukkomi and *boke*, page 131

In Japanese comedy, the comedians are separated into a *tsukkomi* and a *boke*. A *boke* is a person who says something stupid or nonsensical, and the *tsukkomi* is the one who reacts. The *tsukkomi* is the straight man.

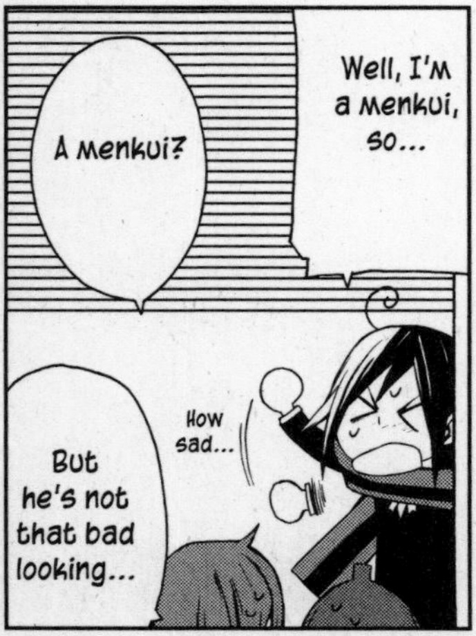
Well, I'm a menkui, so...
A menkui?
How sad...
But he's not that bad looking...

Menkui, page 133

Menkui means two different things depending on which characters are used. It typically describes someone who is a sucker for good-looking people. The "men" means "face" in this case. Kotoha mistook Hime's words for this meaning. In the next panel, Hime says it again with different characters. In this case, she is saying that she's a noodle eater. The "men" in this example means "noodles."

Thousand-year-old egg, page 137

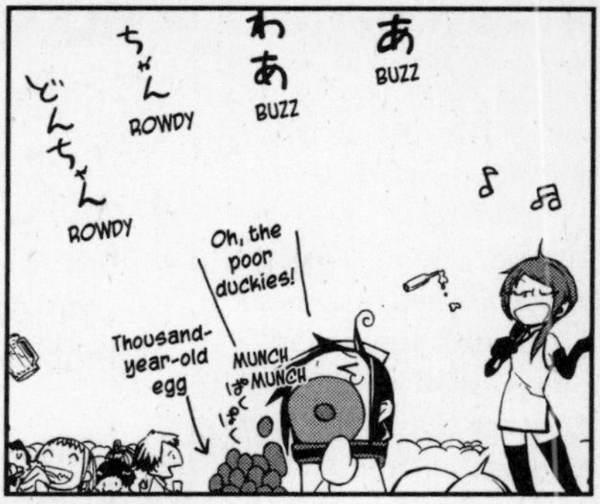
あ
BUZZ
わあ
BUZZ
ちゃん
ROWDY
どんちゃん
ROWDY
Oh, the poor duckies!
MUNCH
MUNCH
Thousand-year-old egg

The thousand-year-old egg is an ingredient in Chinese cuisine. It is made by preserving duck eggs in a mixture of lime and wood ash and placing them in jars or baskets. When the lime and wood ash mixture dries, the eggs are edible. The eggs are dark green in color and the texture is similar to gelatin.

ala, page 146

ala is a Japanese rock band. It's made up of six men and one woman. They belong to their own label, FREEKOUT RECORDS.

Tokyo Dynamite, page 146

Tokyo Dynamite is a comedy duo composed of Daisuke Matsuda and Jiro Hachimitsu. Matsuda is known for his surreal jokes, and Hachimitsu tends to react coldly to him.

Baron Cat, page 146

The Baron Cat is Hiroiki Ariyoshi's character on Uchi-P. He is naked and wears catlike makeup.

Red-san, page 157

Ao is referring to Red Yoshida, a Japanese comedian. He belongs to the duo TIM with his partner, Golgo Matsumoto. He is Ao's favorite comedian in the show Uchi-P.

***Tsundere*, page 162**

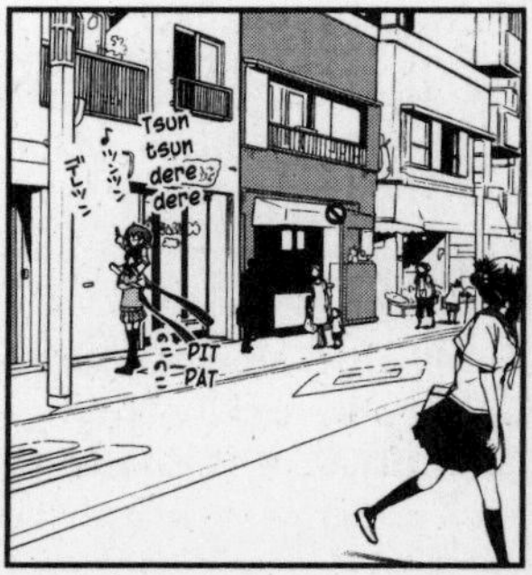
Tsun tsun dere dere
PIT
PAT

Kohime is singing the town song, "Tsundere." Hime was teaching it to kids in volume 1. *Tsundere* is a term for a specific character trait. It describes a person who is standoffish or aloof but can become loveable and adorable in different situations. This term first started in Japanese dating simulation games, then moved on to anime and manga, but is now widely used in mass media.

Prince Shotoku, page 182

Prince Shotoku was a politician during the Asuka period (588–710) in Japan. He is one of the most famous figures in Japan, although he is surrounded with enough mystery that some say he never existed. He was depicted on the old 10,000 yen bill that was in circulation until 1984.

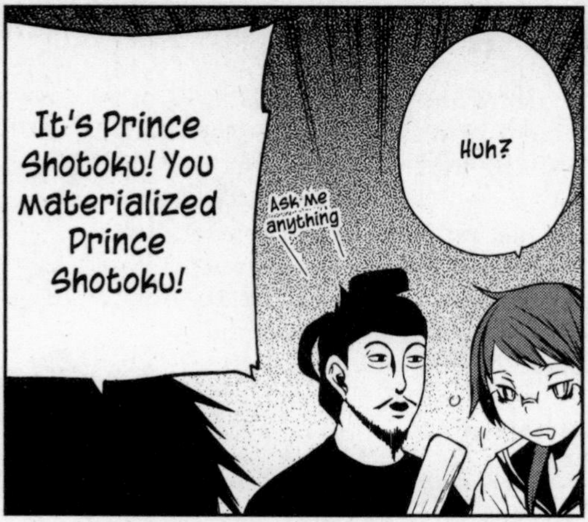
Huh?
It's Prince Shotoku! You materialized Prince Shotoku!
Ask me anything

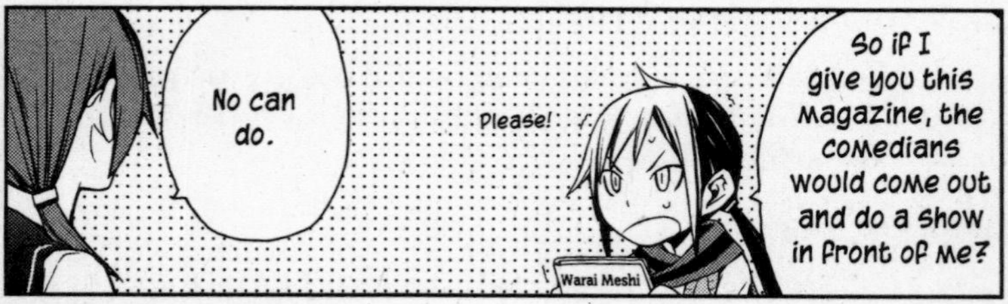
So if I give you this magazine, the comedians would come out and do a show in front of me?
Please!
Warai Meshi
No can do.

Warai Meshi, page 183

Warai Meshi is a Japanese comedy duo composed of Koji Nishida and Tetsuo. Both were separately part of different duos, but their partners couldn't keep up with their strong personalities and disbanded. Their name means "making a living with comedy."

Hidagyu, page 183

Hidagyu is a Japanese beef from cattle raised in Hida, a city in Gifu Prefecture. It's fatty and known to be expensive.

Obi, page 198

An *obi* is the loop of folded paper found on books that advertises the book. For manga, it is about 6 cm high and placed on the bottom of the book. In Japan, the *obi* on volume 1 said: "*Tsun! Tsundere! Tsun! Dere tsun tsun*!" which was the town song Hime was singing in that volume.

Preview of Volume 3

We're pleased to present you with a preview of volume 3. Please check
our website (www.delreymanga.com) to see when this volume will be
available in English. For now you'll have to make do with Japanese!

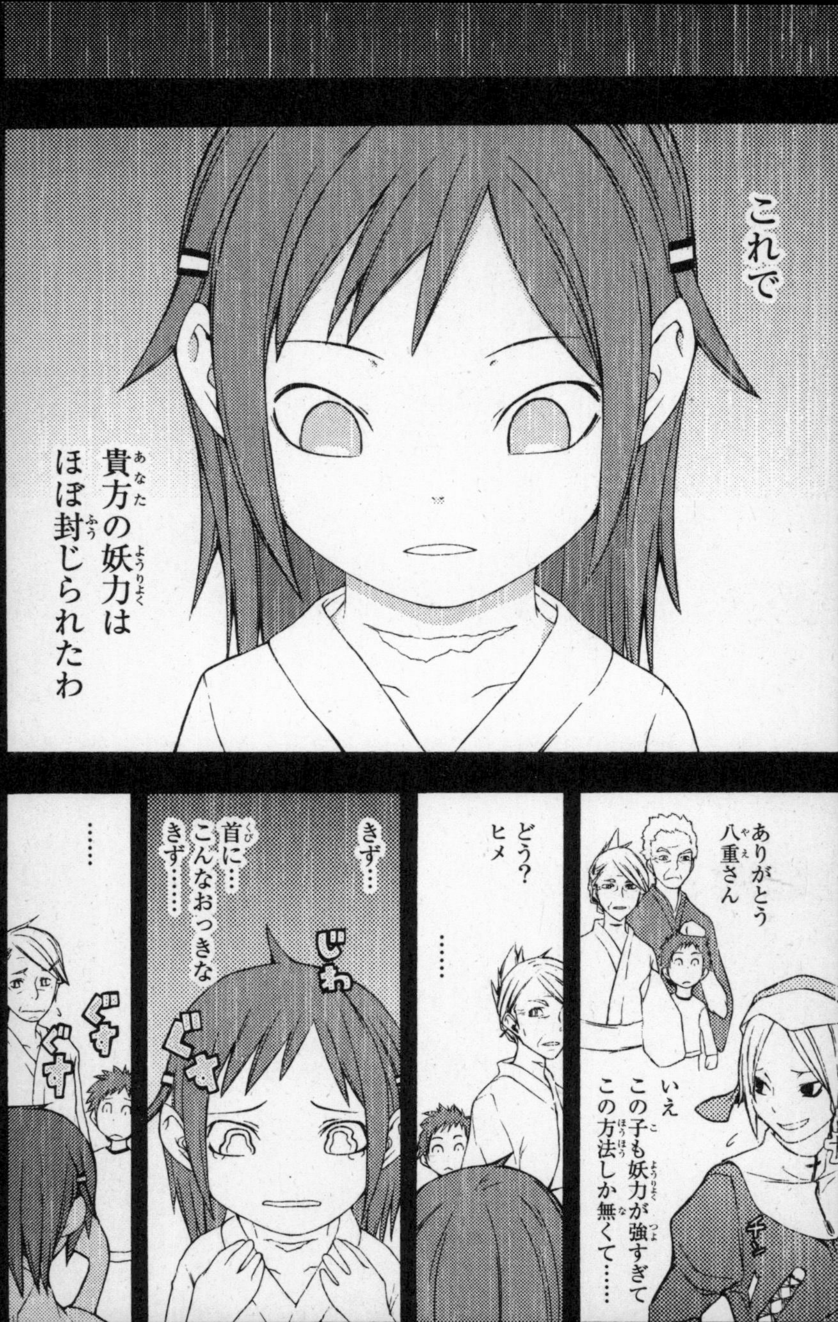

これで
貴方の妖力は
ほぼ封じられたわ
ありがとう
八重さん
いえ
この子も妖力が強すぎて
この方法しか無くて……
チャ
どう？
ヒメ
……
きず…
首に…
こんなおっきな
きず……
じわ
ぐす
……
ぐす
ぐす

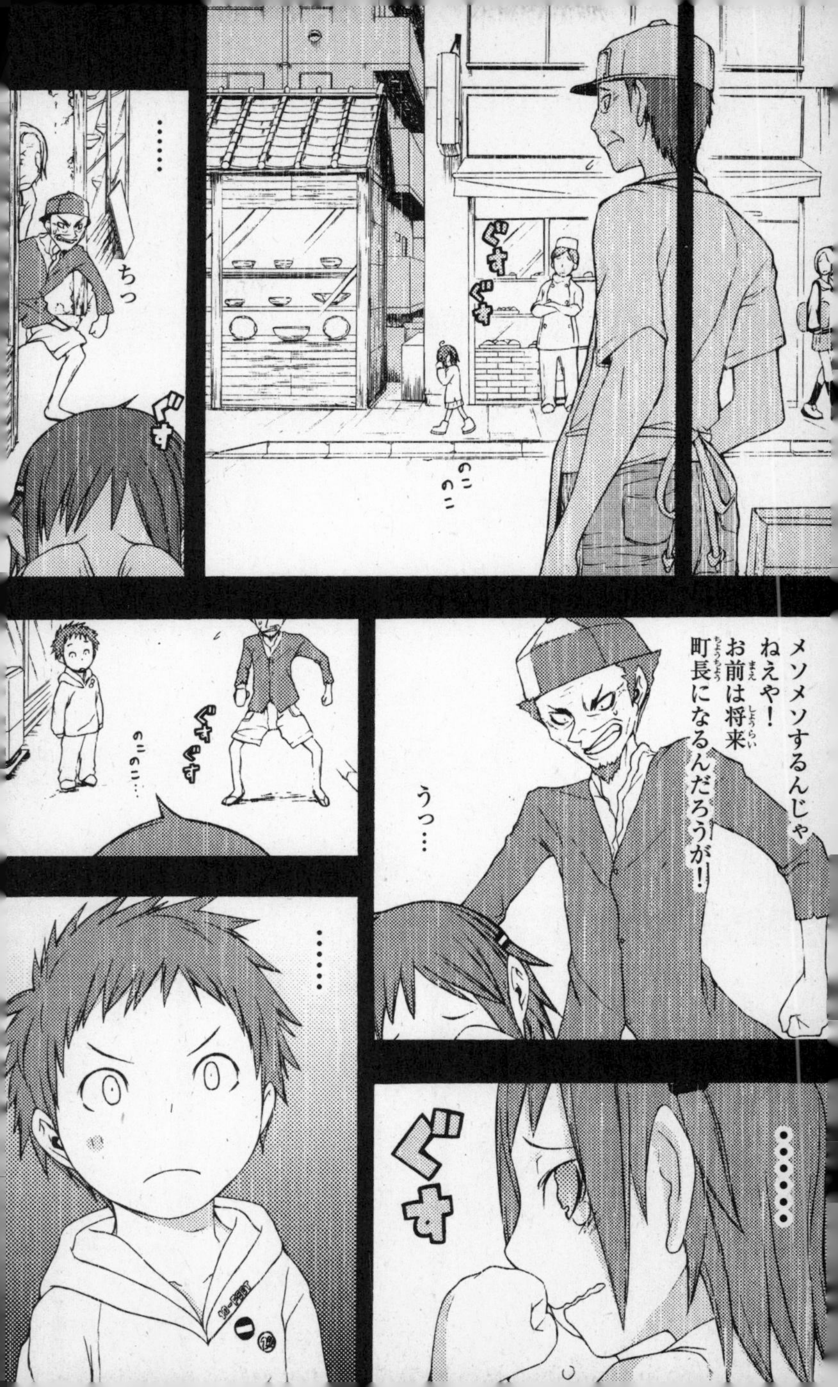
ぐすぐす
のこのこ
……
ちっ
ぐす
メソメソするんじゃねえや！
お前は将来町長になるんだろうが！
うっ…
ぐす
……
ぐすぐす
のこのこ…
……

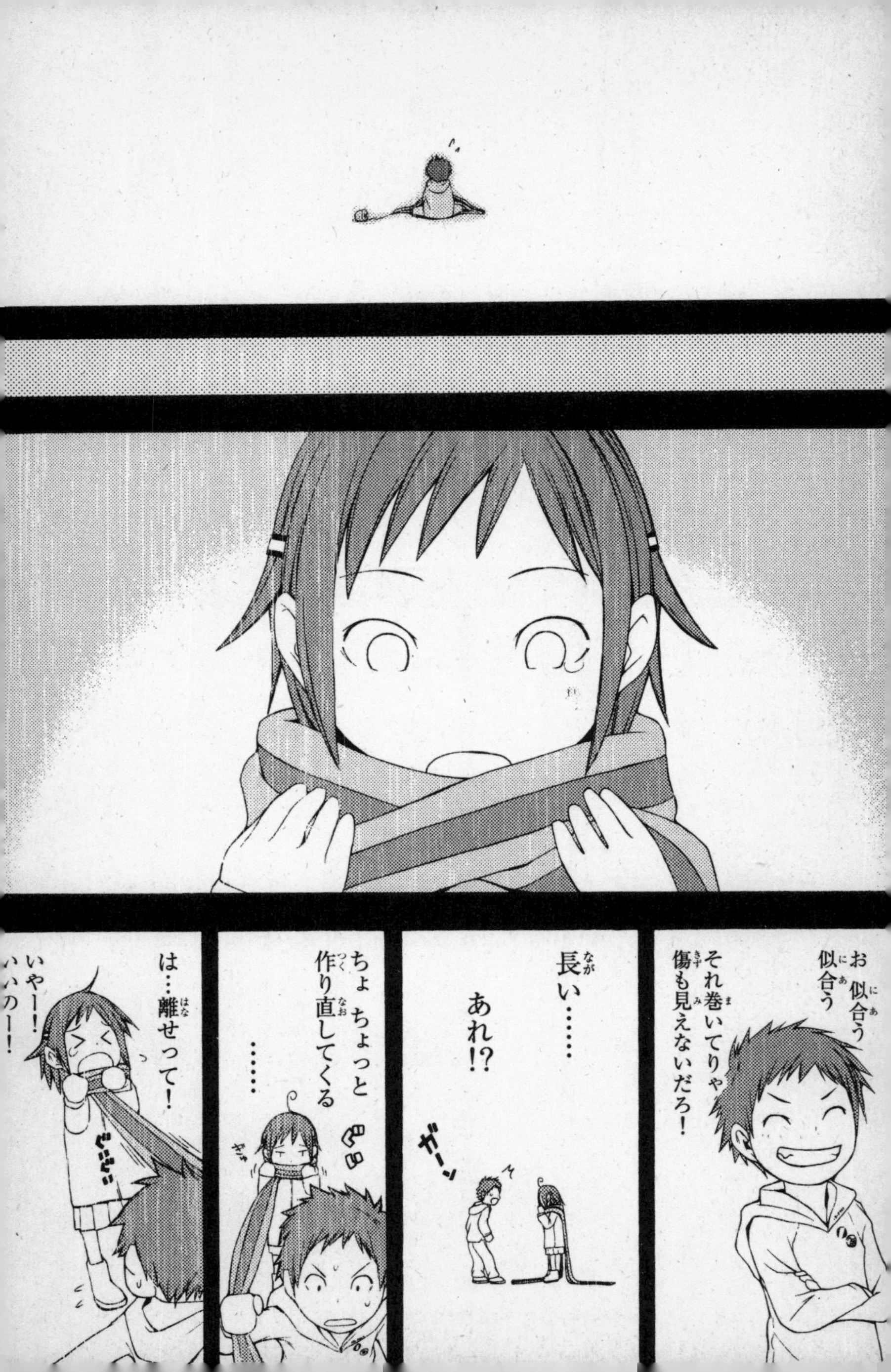
お似合う 似合う
それ巻いてりゃ傷も見えないだろ！
長い……
あれ!?
ガーッ
ちょ ちょっと作り直してくる
……
ぐい
は…離せって！
いやー！いいのー！
ぐいぐい

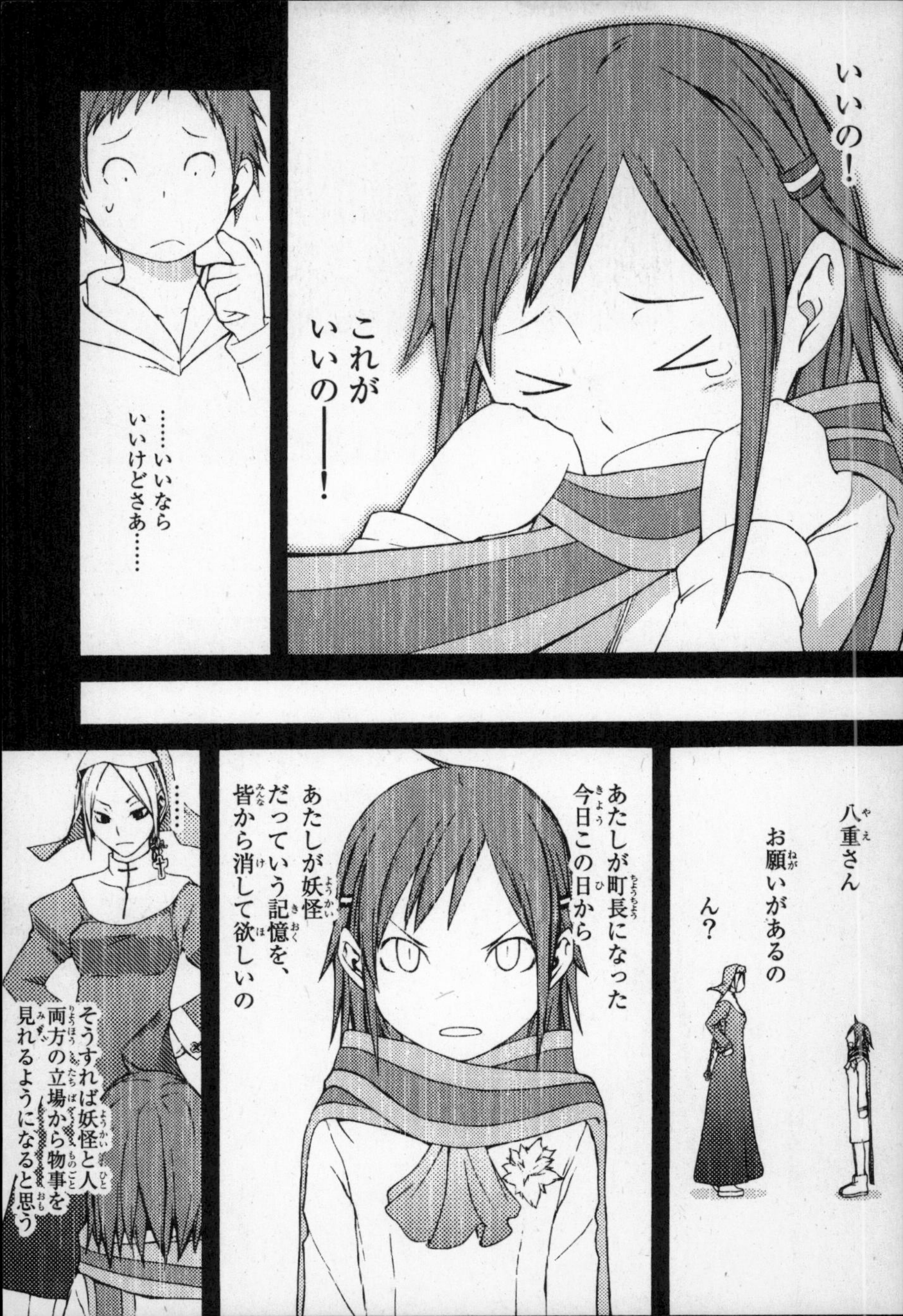
いいの！
これがいいのーー！
……いいならいいけどさあ……
八重さん
お願いがあるの
ん？
あたしが町長になった今日この日から
あたしが妖怪だっていう記憶を、皆から消して欲しいの
……
そうすれば妖怪と人両方の立場から物事を見れるようになると思う

構わないけど…

あなたが妖怪だってことに起因する 全ての記憶も一緒に封印されるわ

マフラーの事とかね

・・・・・
・・・・・

例えば
その・・・・・

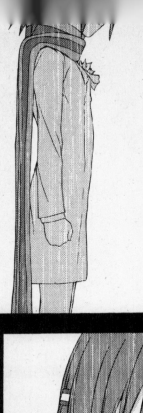

これが

あたしの覚悟です

…構いません
お願いします

…全部一人で
抱えちゃう気？

・・・・・

DRAGON EYE

BY KAIRI FUJIYAMA

HUMANITY'S SECRET WEAPON

Dracules—bloodthirsty, infectious monsters—have hunted human beings to the brink of extinction. Only the elite warriors of the VIUS squad stand as humanity's last best hope.

Young Leila Mikami is one of the squad's most promising recruits, but she's not only training to battle the Dracules, she's determined to find the magical Dragon Eye, a weapon that will make her the most powerful warrior in the world.

Special extras in each volume! Read them all!

SHIKI TSUKAI

STORY BY TO-RU ZEKUU
ART BY YUNA TAKANAGI

DEFENDING THE NATURAL ORDER OF THE UNIVERSE!

The *shiki tsukai* are "Keepers of the Seasons"—magical warriors pledged to defend the planet's natural order against those who would threaten it.

When 14-year-old Akira Kizuki joins the *shiki tsukai,* he knows that it'll be a difficult life. But with his new friends and mentors, he's up to the challenge!

TO-RU ZEKUU
YUNA TAKANAGI
1
SHIKI TSUKAI

Special extras in each volume! Read them all!

VISIT WWW.DELREYMANGA.COM TO:

- Read sample pages
- View release date calendars for upcoming volumes
- Sign up for Del Rey's free manga e-newsletter
- Find out the latest about new Del Rey Manga series

RATING T AGES 13+

DEL REY MANGA
The Otaku's Choice™

Psycho Busters

MANGA BY AKINARI NAO
STORY BY YUYA AOKI

PSYCHIC TEENS ON THE RUN!

Out of the blue, a beautiful girl asks Kakeru to run away with her. This could be any boy's dream come true, but there's something strange afoot.

It turns out that this girl is on the run from a shadowy government organization intent on using her psychic abilities for its own nefarious ends. But why does she need Kakeru's help? Could it be that he has secret powers, too?

• Story by Yuya Aoki, creator of *Get Backers*

Special extras in each volume! Read them all!

VISIT WWW.DELREYMANGA.COM TO:
• Read sample pages
• View release date calendars for upcoming volumes
• Sign up for Del Rey's free manga e-newsletter
• Find out the latest about new Del Rey Manga series

RATING OT AGES 16+

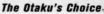

The Otaku's Choice™

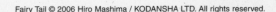

TOMARE!

止まれ

[STOP!]

You're going the wrong way!

Manga is a completely different type of reading experience.

To start at the *beginning*, go to the *end*!

That's right! Authentic manga is read the traditional Japanese way— from right to left, exactly the *opposite* of how American books are read. It's easy to follow: Just go to the other end of the book, and read each page—and each panel—from right side to left side, starting at the top right. Now you're experiencing manga as it was meant to be!